ZAGAT®

Philadelphia
Restaurants
2009

LOCAL EDITOR
Michael Klein
LOCAL COORDINATOR
Marilyn Kleinberg
STAFF EDITOR
Sharon Gintzler

Published and distributed by
Zagat Survey, LLC
4 Columbus Circle
New York, NY 10019
T: 212.977.6000
E: philadelphia@zagat.com
www.zagat.com

ACKNOWLEDGMENTS

We thank Fran and Joe Alberstadt; Charlotte Ann, Dick and Ann-Michelle Albertson; Carol Bedics and Ben Preston; Cindy and Richard Blum; Suzanne and Norman Cohn; HughE Dillon; Jennifer Dorazio; Jack and Mia Dorazio; Pete and Gregg Dorazio; G. Fogelman; Marcia Gelbart; Larry Gershon; Ellen and Steve Goldman; Lisa and Tom Haflett; Loretta and Tom Jordan; Jodi and Alan Klein; Diane Klein; Rachel and Lindsay Klein; Maria McLaughlin; Sybil Rothstein; Alan Scott; Doris and Joe Segel; Rob Seixas; Kelly Stewart; Jennifer Thompson and Adam Welsh; and the *Philadelphia Inquirer*'s food crew: Maureen Fitzgerald, Craig LaBan and Rick Nichols, as well as the following members of our staff: Amy Cao (editorial assistant), Sean Beachell, Maryanne Bertollo, Sandy Cheng, Reni Chin, Larry Cohn, Deirdre Donovan, Alison Flick, Jeff Freier, Justin Hartung, Roy Jacob, Natalie Lebert, Mike Liao, Dave Makulec, Andre Pilette, Kimberly Rosado, Becky Ruthenburg, Liz Borod Wright, Yoji Yamaguchi, Sharon Yates, Anna Zappia and Kyle Zolner.

Contents

Ratings & Symbols

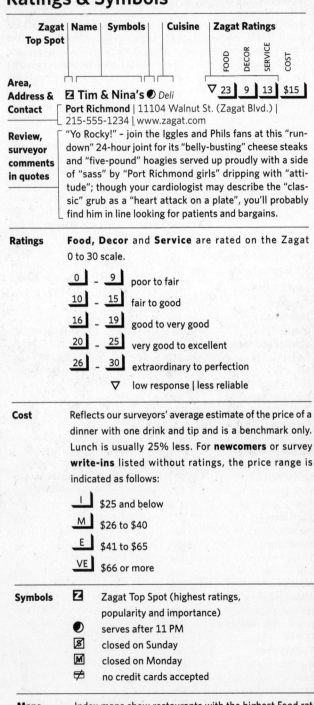

	Name	Symbols	Cuisine	Zagat Ratings			
Zagat Top Spot				FOOD	DECOR	SERVICE	COST

Area, Address & Contact

Z Tim & Nina's ◗ *Deli*   ▽ 23 | 9 | 13 | $15

Port Richmond | 11104 Walnut St. (Zagat Blvd.) | 215-555-1234 | www.zagat.com

Review, surveyor comments in quotes

"Yo Rocky!" – join the Iggles and Phils fans at this "run-down" 24-hour joint for its "belly-busting" cheese steaks and "five-pound" hoagies served up proudly with a side of "sass" by "Port Richmond girls" dripping with "attitude"; though your cardiologist may describe the "classic" grub as a "heart attack on a plate", you'll probably find him in line looking for patients and bargains.

Ratings

Food, Decor and **Service** are rated on the Zagat 0 to 30 scale.

0	–	9	poor to fair
10	–	15	fair to good
16	–	19	good to very good
20	–	25	very good to excellent
26	–	30	extraordinary to perfection
	▽		low response	less reliable

Cost

Reflects our surveyors' average estimate of the price of a dinner with one drink and tip and is a benchmark only. Lunch is usually 25% less. For **newcomers** or survey **write-ins** listed without ratings, the price range is indicated as follows:

I	$25 and below
M	$26 to $40
E	$41 to $65
VE	$66 or more

Symbols

Z	Zagat Top Spot (highest ratings, popularity and importance)
◗	serves after 11 PM
🅢	closed on Sunday
🅜	closed on Monday
⇎	no credit cards accepted

Maps

Index maps show restaurants with the highest Food ratings in those areas.

subscribe to ZAGAT.com

About This Survey

Here are the results of our **2009 Philadelphia Restaurants Survey,** covering 1,038 eateries in the Philadelphia area and in nearby New Jersey and Delaware. Like all of our guides, this one is based on the collective opinions of thousands of local consumers. Ratings have been updated throughout. We have retained a prior year's review for some places that have had no significant factual or ratings changes.

WHO PARTICIPATED: Input from 5,507 frequent diners forms the basis for the ratings and reviews in this guide (their comments are shown in quotation marks within the reviews). Of these surveyors, 54% are women, 46% men; the breakdown by age is 15% in their 20s; 23%, 30s; 21%, 40s; 23%, 50s; and 18%, 60s or above. Collectively they bring roughly 736,000 annual meals worth of experience to this Survey. We sincerely thank each of these participants – this book is really "theirs."

HELPFUL LISTS: Our top lists and indexes should help you find exactly the right place for any occasion. See Most Popular (page 7), Key Newcomers (page 9), Top Ratings (pages 10–16) and Best Buys (page 17). We've also provided 49 handy indexes.

OUR LOCAL TEAM: Special thanks go to our local editor, Michael Klein, a features columnist at the *Philadelphia Inquirer,* who has written its restaurant-news column, "Table Talk," since 1993 – his first year as Zagat's Philadelphia editor, and to our coordinator, Marilyn Kleinberg, president of MTK Enterprises, Inc. and local franchise operator of CruiseOne in Cherry Hill, NJ.

ABOUT ZAGAT: This marks our 29th year reporting on the shared experiences of consumers like you. What started in 1979 as a hobby involving 200 of our friends has come a long way. Today we have over 325,000 surveyors and now cover airlines, bars, clubs, dining, entertaining, golf, hotels, lounges, movies, music, resorts, shopping, spas, theater and tourist attractions worldwide.

VOTE AND COMMENT: We invite you to join any of our upcoming surveys at **ZAGAT.com.** There you can rate and review establishments year-round without charge. In fact, in exchange for participating you will receive a free copy of the resulting guide when published.

AVAILABILITY: Zagat guides are available in all major bookstores as well as on **ZAGAT.com, ZAGAT.mobi** (for web-enabled mobile phones) and **ZAGAT TO GO** (for smartphones). All of these products allow you to reserve at thousands of places with just one click.

FEEDBACK: There is always room for improvement, thus we invite your comments and suggestions about any aspect of our performance. Just contact us at **philadelphia@zagat.com.**

New York, NY
August 20, 2008

Nina and Tim Zagat

What's New

Despite the unsettled economy, Philadelphians' fervor for restaurants remains undaunted. In fact, 84% of our surveyors report eating out as much as or even more than they did two years ago. Restaurateurs are responding in kind with dining options to suit every taste and budget.

 SEEING STARS: High-profile names have hot new spots. Prolific Stephen Starr (**Buddakan, Continental, Morimoto**) goes the French brasserie route with **Parc** on Rittenhouse Square, his first Philly opening since 2004's **Continental Mid-town,** while Eric Ripert (of NYC's **Le Bernardin** fame) offers **10 Arts,** a majestic New American in the grand lobby of Center City's Ritz-Carlton. At press time, Jose Garces (**Amada, Tinto**) is launching **Distrito** in University City, featuring creative Mexican street food.

BEEF BONANZA: Steakhouses are surging. Georges Perrier (**Brasserie Perrier, Georges', Le Bec-Fin**) and Chris Scarduzio (**Brasserie Perrier**) steer toward steer with the posh **Table 31** in the new Comcast Center (Center City's splashiest and tallest office building). In nearby Logan Square, the high-end **Chima Brazilian Steakhouse** provides beef galore with churrascaria. West Chester offers **Pietro's Prime** and Cherry Hillers have **William Douglas.**

HEALTH WATCH: Philadelphians may love their steakhouses (and cheese steaks) but health-conscious eating is also a priority. Sixty percent say they will pay more for food that is sustainably raised, while 55% will dig deeper into their pockets for organics. Another 60% also think trans fats should be banned in restaurants – a good thing given the city council's ban on frying in trans fat in 2007 and its more recent decision that by late 2008 the city's eating places must be totally free of partially hydrogenated oil. Pennsylvania has also recently joined New Jersey, Delaware and the city of Philadelphia in banning most indoor smoking. The law goes into effect in mid-September 2008, affecting all restaurants and bars that draw 20% or more of annual revenue in food sales.

RESTAURANT REDUX: Established operators are eager to expand their presence on the dining scene. Media's **Azie** (from the **Mikado, Teikoku** and **Thai Pepper** crew), Center City's **Field House** (from the folks behind **Mission Grill** and **Public House**), Villanova's **Maia** (**Nectar**), Feasterville's **Toscana 52** (**Italian Bistro**), West Philly's **Vietnam Café** (**Vietnam**) and Society Hill's **Zahav** (**Marigold Kitchen, Xochitl**) are the latest yearlings on the scene.

CHECK IT OUT: The average cost of a meal has risen about 1.3% annually to $33.69 since our last Survey, putting Philly almost smack at the national average of $33.90. Interestingly, although 75% of surveyors report that service is their main gripe when dining out, Philadelphians are the nation's highest tippers, leaving 19.6% on average.

Philadelphia, PA
August 20, 2008

Michael Klein

Most Popular

These places are plotted on the map at the back of the book.

1. Buddakan | *Pan-Asian*
2. Amada | *Spanish*
3. Le Bec-Fin | *French*
4. Alma de Cuba | *Nuevo Latino*
5. Capital Grille | *Steak*
6. Lacroix | *French*
7. Brasserie Perrier | *French*
8. Fountain | *Continental/French*
9. Vetri | *Italian*
10. Morimoto | *Japanese*
11. Osteria | *Italian*
12. Matyson | *American*
13. Fork | *American*
14. Barclay Prime | *Steak*
15. Susanna Foo | *Chinese/French*
16. Dmitri's | *Greek*
17. Yangming | *Chinese*
18. Continental Mid-town | *Eclectic*
19. Cheesecake Factory | *American*
20. Tinto | *Spanish*
21. Tangerine | *Mediterranean*
22. Mercato | *American/Italian*
23. Cuba Libre | *Cuban*
24. El Vez | *Mexican*
25. Maggiano's | *Italian*
26. Lolita | *Mexican*
27. Alison/Blue Bell | *American*
28. Birchrunville | *French/Italian*
29. Blackfish | *Seafood*
30. Nectar* | *Pan-Asian*
31. Continental, The | *Eclectic*
32. White Dog | *Eclectic*
33. Reading Term. Mkt. | *Eclectic*
34. P.F. Chang's | *Chinese*
35. Chickie's & Pete's | *Pub Food*
36. Vietnam | *Vietnamese*
37. Fogo de Chão | *Brazilian*
38. Morton's Steak | *Steak*
39. Gilmore's | *French*
40. Estia | *Greek*

It's obvious that many of the above restaurants are among the Philadelphia area's most expensive, but if popularity were calibrated to price, we suspect that a number of other restaurants would join their ranks. Thus, we have added a list of 80 Best Buys on page 17.

---

* Indicates a tie with restaurant above

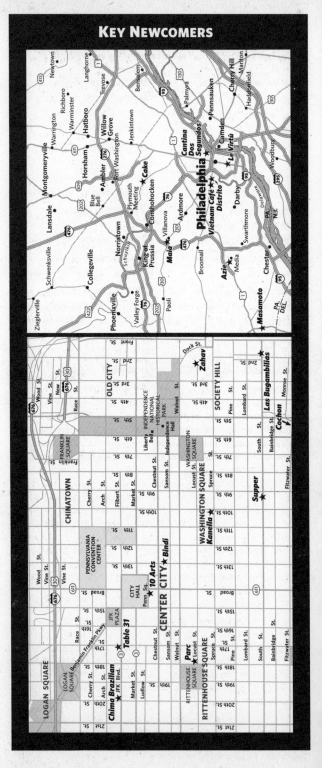

Key Newcomers

Our editors' take on the year's top arrivals. See page 230 for a full list.

Azie	*Asian Fusion*	Le Virtù	*Italian*
Bindi	*Indian*	Maia	*European*
Cake	*Bakery*	Masamoto	*Pan-Asian*
Cantina Dos Segundos	*Mex.*	Parc	*French*
Chima	*Brazilian/Steak*	Supper	*American*
Cochon	*French*	Table 31	*Steak*
Distrito	*Mexican*	10 Arts	*American*
Kanella	*Greek*	Vietnam Café	*Vietnamese*
Las Bugambilias	*Mex.*	Zahav	*Israeli*

In the year to come, Philadelphians will witness a continuation of the steakhouse boom. Stephen Starr recently shuttered his highly touted **Striped Bass** to retool the Center City landmark into **Butcher & Singer,** a posh '40s-style supper club–cum–beefery set to open in fall 2008. Slated for late 2008 are a Center City branch of the elegant **Del Frisco's Double Eagle Steak House,** and the homegrown **Union Trust,** a multilevel meatery near Washington Square.

Latin American cuisine is also having a love affair with the City of Brotherly Love. Jose Garces, who conquered Spain with **Amada** and **Tinto** (and who is of Ecuadorian ancestry), is dipping into South America for an early 2009 rollout of **Chifa,** a stylish fusion of Chinese and Peruvian cuisines, near Washington Square. On a similar note, our surveyors indicated they would like to see more Mexican *comidas* in their neighborhoods, and restaurateurs are happy to oblige. The refined **Las Bugambilias** on South Street typifies Philly's Mexican renaissance, as chef Carlos Molina (ex **Los Catrines/Tequila's**) creates inventive dishes and cocktails. A slew of cantinas has also popped up around town. Witness Wash West's **Azul,** Center City's **José Pistola's** and a Pennsauken outpost of **Tortilla Press.** In Northern Liberties, **Cantina Dos Segundos** (a second spot from the **Cantina Los Caballitos** crew) recently debuted and **El Camino Real,** a Texas border roadhouse from **Bar Ferdinand**'s Owen Kamihira, is set for a late summer 2008 debut.

In contrast to the upswing in high-end enterprises, some longtime favorite luxe establishments are giving patrons more wallet-friendly choices thanks to menu redos. Georges Perrier added à la carte options to his prix fixe French superstar **Le Bec-Fin,** which boosted consumer traffic and dropped tariffs considerably (though the signature pastry cart still wheels through the dining room). And Perrier and partner Chris Scarduzio also lightened up the approach at Center City's **Brasserie Perrier.**

Top Food Ratings

Excludes places with low votes. Top places outside Philadelphia appear on page 14.

29 | Fountain | *Continental/French*

28 | Little Fish | *Seafood*
Birchrunville | *French/Italian*
Amada | *Spanish*
Le Bar Lyonnais | *French*
Gilmore's | *French*
Lacroix | *French*

27 | Vetri | *Italian*
Le Bec-Fin | *French*
John's Roast Pork | *Sandwiches*
Paloma | *French/Mexican*
Rest. Alba | *American*
Tinto | *Spanish*
Swann Lounge | *Amer./French*
Blue Sage | *Vegetarian*
La Bonne Auberge | *French*
Sola | *American*

26 | Bluefin | *Japanese*
Talula's Table | *European*
Buddakan | *Pan-Asian*

Morimoto | *Japanese*
Sovana Bistro | *French/Med.*
Tiffin Store | *Indian*
Blackfish | *Seafood*
Mercato | *American/Italian*
Rist. San Marco | *Italian*
L'Angolo | *Italian*
Alison/Blue Bell | *American*
Zento | *Japanese*
Matyson | *American*
Oishi | *Pan-Asian*
Horizons | *Vegan*
Majolica | *American*
Modo Mio | *Italian*
Osteria | *Italian*
August | *Italian*
Barclay Prime | *Steak*
Capital Grille | *Steak*
Fioravanti | *Continental*
Mainland Inn* | *American*

BY CUISINE

AMERICAN (NEW)

27 | Rest. Alba
Swann Lounge
Sola
26 | Alison/Blue Bell
Matyson

AMERICAN (TRAD.)

26 | Mercato
25 | Kimberton Inn
General Warren
24 | Standard Tap
23 | Old Guard House

BARBECUE

23 | Bomb Bomb BBQ
22 | Rib Crib
21 | Sweet Lucy's
20 | Abner's BBQ
19 | Devil's Alley

CHEESE STEAKS

25 | Tony Luke's
24 | Dalessandro's
Steve's Prince/Steaks
22 | Jim's Steaks
Campo's Deli

CHINESE

25 | Sang Kee Duck House
Shiao Lan Kung
Yangming
Duck Sauce
24 | Sang Kee Asian

CONTINENTAL

29 | Fountain
26 | Fioravanti
25 | Bridgetown Mill
Yangming
Duling-Kurtz House

ECLECTIC

25 | Citrus
Carman's Country
Sabrina's Café
24 | Umbria
Totaro's

FRENCH

29 | Fountain
28 | Birchrunville Store
Gilmore's
Lacroix
27 | Le Bec-Fin

FRENCH (BISTRO)

- 28 Le Bar Lyonnais
- 26 Sovana Bistro
- 23 Spring Mill
- Supper
- 22 Brasserie 73

GREEK

- 25 Dmitri's
- 23 Estia
- Olive Tree Med. Grill
- 21 South St. Souvlaki
- Athena

INDIAN

- 26 Tiffin Store
- 24 Palace of Asia
- 23 Karma
- 22 Bindi
- 21 Palace/Ben

ITALIAN

- 27 Vetri
- 26 Mercato
- Rist. San Marco
- L'Angolo
- Modo Mio

JAPANESE

- 26 Bluefin
- Morimoto
- Zento
- Oishi
- 25 Ooka

LATIN/S. AMERICAN

- 25 Alma de Cuba
- 23 Fogo de Chão
- 22 Tierra Colombiana
- 21 Cuba Libre
- Mixto

MEDITERRANEAN

- 26 Sovana Bistro
- 24 Rest. Taquet
- Tangerine
- 23 Arpeggio
- Figs

MEXICAN

- 27 Paloma
- 25 Lolita
- 24 Los Catrines
- Las Cazuelas
- 23 Taq. La Michoacana

PAN-ASIAN

- 26 Buddakan
- Oishi
- Nectar
- 23 Pod
- 22 Trio

PIZZA

- 26 Osteria
- 25 Tacconelli's
- 24 Celebre's
- 23 Arpeggio
- Mama Palma's

PUB FOOD

- 24 Standard Tap
- 22 N. 3rd
- Monk's Cafe
- Abbaye
- Good Dog

SEAFOOD

- 28 Little Fish
- 26 Blackfish
- 25 Dmitri's
- Bobby Chez
- 24 Radicchio

SOUL/SOUTHERN

- 25 Honey's Sit 'n Eat
- 23 Geechee Girl
- 20 Marsha Brown
- Warmdaddy's
- Abner's BBQ

STEAKHOUSES

- 26 Barclay Prime
- Capital Grille
- 25 Fleming's Prime
- Morton's Steak
- Prime Rib

THAI

- 25 Nan
- Chabaa Thai
- Thai Orchid
- 24 Teikoku
- Cafe de Laos

VIETNAMESE

- 25 Vietnam
- 24 Pho Xe Lua
- Nam Phuong
- 23 Vietnam Café
- Vietnam Palace

BY SPECIAL FEATURE

BREAKFAST
25 Honey's Sit 'n Eat
   Carman's Country
   Sabrina's Café
24 Morning Glory
   Shank's & Evelyn's

BRUNCH
29 Fountain
28 Lacroix
27 Swann Lounge
26 Mainland Inn
25 Kimberton Inn

BYO
28 Little Fish
   Birchrunville Store
   Gilmore's
27 Rest. Alba
   Blue Sage

CHILD-FRIENDLY
23 Mama Palma's
20 Jones
18 Four Dogs
   Down Home
13 Abbraccio

CLASSIC PHILLY
23 Reading Term. Mkt.
21 Villa di Roma
19 Old Orig. Bookbinder's
   City Tavern
16 Melrose Diner

HOTEL DINING
29 Fountain
   (Four Seasons)
28 Lacroix
   (Rittenhouse Hotel)
27 Swann Lounge
   (Four Seasons)
25 General Warren Inne
   Prime Rib
   (Radisson Warwick)

LATE DINING
27 Tinto
   Swann Lounge
25 Shiao Lan Kung
   Tony Luke's
24 Dalessandro's

MEET FOR A DRINK
27 Tinto
   Swann Lounge

26 Horizons
   Osteria
   Capital Grille

NEWCOMERS (RATED)
24 Cochon
   Azie
23 Vietnam Café
   Supper
22 Bindi

OFFBEAT
26 Morimoto
25 Honey's Sit 'n Eat
   Tacconelli's
   Carman's Country
24 Ota-Ya

PEOPLE-WATCHING
27 Tinto
   Swann Lounge
25 Shiao Lan Kung
   Tony Luke's
24 Dalessandro's

POWER LUNCH
29 Fountain
28 Amada
   Lacroix
27 Le Bec-Fin
26 Buddakan

PRIVATE ROOMS
28 Lacroix
27 Le Bec-Fin
   La Bonne Auberge
26 Rist. San Marco
   Capital Grille

QUICK BITES
27 John's Roast Pork
26 Tiffin Store
   Zento
25 Naked Chocolate
   Bobby Chez

QUIET CONVERSATION
29 Fountain
28 Birchrunville Store
   Gilmore's
   Lacroix
27 Swann Lounge

SLEEPERS
28 Shinju Sushi
27 Masamoto

26 Mercer Café
Uzu Sushi
Le Virtù

SMALL PLATES

28 Lacroix (French)
26 Modo Mio (Italian)
25 Honey (American)
24 Ansill (Eclectic)
23 Chick's (Eclectic)

TEEN APPEAL

25 Tacconelli's
Tony Luke's
22 Jim's Steaks
20 Jones
19 Geno's Steaks

TRANSPORTING EXPERIENCES

28 Birchrunville Store
Gilmore's

Lacroix
27 Vetri
Le Bec-Fin

TRENDY

28 Amada
27 Vetri
Tinto
26 Buddakan
Morimoto

WINNING WINE LISTS

29 Fountain
28 Amada
Le Bar Lyonnais
Lacroix
27 Vetri

BY LOCATION

AVENUE OF THE ARTS

27 Vetri
26 Capital Grille
25 Naked Chocolate
Morton's Steak
Bobby Chez

BUCKS COUNTY

27 Blue Sage
La Bonne Auberge
26 Oishi
25 Bridgetown Mill
Honey*

CENTER CITY EAST (EAST OF BROAD ST.)

26 Morimoto
Mercato
25 Lolita
24 Raw Sushi
23 Reading Term. Mkt.
Tria
Valanni
22 Maoz Vegetarian
Rist. La Buca
Tampopo

CENTER CITY WEST (WEST OF BROAD ST.)

29 Fountain
28 Le Bar Lyonnais
Lacroix

27 Le Bec-Fin
Tinto
Swann Lounge
26 Matyson
Barclay Prime
25 Dmitri's
Prime Rib

CHESTER COUNTY

28 Birchrunville Store
Gilmore's
26 Talula's Table
Sovana Bistro
Majolica

CHESTNUT HILL

25 Citrus
24 CinCin
23 Osaka
21 Cake
Roller's/Flying Fish

CHINATOWN

25 Sang Kee Duck Hse.
Shiao Lan Kung
Vietnam
24 Lee How Fook
Pho Xe Lua

DELAWARE COUNTY

25 Bobby Chez
24 Teikoku

Azie
22 Marg. Kuo's Media
Rose Tree Inn

FAIRMOUNT

25 Sabrina's Café
24 Umai Umai
23 L'Oca
Figs
22 Rose Tattoo

LANCASTER/BERKS

27 Gibraltar
26 Green Hills Inn
Gracie's
24 Lily's on Main
22 Five Guys

MAIN LINE

27 Rest. Alba
Sola
26 Fioravanti
Nectar
25 Bunha Faun

MANAYUNK

25 Chabaa Thai
Jake's
23 La Colombe
Il Tartufo
22 Bella Trattoria

MONTGOMERY COUNTY

26 Bluefin
Blackfish
Rist. San Marco
Alison/Blue Bell
Mainland Inn

NORTHEAST PHILLY

27 Paloma
24 Steve's Prince/Steaks
22 Jim's Steaks
Pho 75
21 Sweet Lucy's

NORTHERN LIBERTIES/ OLD CITY

28 Amada
26 Buddakan
Tiffin Store
Zento
Modo Mio

QUEEN VILLAGE/ SOUTH STREET

26 Horizons
25 Gayle
Dmitri's
Django
24 Cochon

SOUTH PHILLY

28 Little Fish
27 John's Roast Pork
26 L'Angolo
August
25 Scannicchio's

UNIVERSITY CITY

25 Nan
24 Marigold Kitchen
Abyssinia
23 Vientiane Café
Pod

NEW JERSEY

27 Mélange
Little Café
Sagami
26 Giumarello's
Ritz Seafood

DELAWARE

26 Krazy Kat's
25 Culinaria
Moro
Green Room
24 Domaine Hudson
Mikimotos*

Top Decor Ratings

28 | Fountain

27 | Nineteen
Water Works
Buddakan
Nectar
Swann Lounge
Lacroix
Le Bec-Fin
Tangerine

26 | Azie
Bridgetown Mill
Duling-Kurtz House
Kimberton Inn
Morimoto
La Bonne Auberge

25 | Bella Tori
Alma de Cuba
Savona
Oceanaire
Cuba Libre

Barclay Prime
Moshulu
Prime Rib
Pod
Dilworthtown Inn
City Tavern
Los Catrines

24 | Amada
Inn/Phillips Mill
Palace/Ben
Simon Pearce
Estia
Pond
Teikoku
Supper
Osteria
Joseph Ambler
James
Positano Coast
Bar Ferdinand

OUTDOORS

Bay Pony Inn
Chart House
Continental Mid-town
Moshulu
Nineteen

Oceanaire
Pond
Savona
Twenty Manning
Water Works

ROMANCE

Anton's/Swan
Barclay Prime
Birchrunville Store
Honey
Inn/St. Peter's

James
Lacroix
Tangerine
10 Arts
Vetri

ROOMS

Buddakan
Chima
Lacroix
Nectar
Nineteen

Oceanaire
Osteria
Teikoku
10 Arts
Zahav

VIEWS

Bistro St. Tropez
Chart House
Fountain
King George II
La Veranda

Moshulu
Nineteen
Pond
Simon Pearce
Water Works

Top Service Ratings

__28__ Fountain
Gilmore's

__27__ Birchrunville Store
Swann Lounge
Le Bec-Fin
Vetri
Paloma
La Bonne Auberge
Lacroix

__26__ Le Bar Lyonnais
Talula's Table
Kimberton Inn

__25__ Barclay Prime
Dilworthtown Inn
Mainland Inn
General Warren
Duling-Kurtz House
Amada
Rest. Alba

__24__ Fleming's Prime

Sola
Fogo de Chão
Capital Grille
Morimoto
Prime Rib
Majolica
James
Tinto
Osteria
Morton's Steak
August
Mamma Maria
Buddakan
Davio's
Abacus

__23__ Savona
Charles Plaza
Parc Bistro
Zento*
Bridgetown Mill

Best Buys

In order of Bang for the Buck rating.

1. La Colombe
2. Brew HaHa!
3. Naked Chocolate
4. Bonté Wafflerie
5. John's Roast Pork
6. Maoz Vegetarian
7. Five Guys
8. Dalessandro's
9. Nan Zhou
10. Nifty Fifty's
11. Steve's Prince/Steaks
12. Pink Rose
13. Campo's Deli
14. Jim's Steaks
15. Bitar's
16. 10th St. Pour House
17. Pho 75
18. Baja Fresh Mex.
19. Tony Luke's
20. Qdoba
21. Shank's & Evelyn's
22. Reading Term. Mkt.
23. Celebre's
24. Geno's Steaks
25. Honey's Sit 'n Eat
26. Tampopo
27. Pat's Steaks
28. AllWays Café
29. Ardmore Station
30. Cake
31. Morning Glory
32. La Lupe
33. Isaac's
34. Mayfair Diner
35. Hank's Place
36. Taq. La Veracruzana
37. New Delhi
38. Carman's Country
39. Vientiane Café
40. Abner's BBQ

OTHER GOOD VALUES

Abyssinia
Banana Leaf
Beijing
Ben & Irv Deli
Cafe de Laos
Dahlak
Day by Day
Down Home
Fergie's Pub
Good Dog
Harmony Veg.
Izzy & Zoe's
Johnny Brenda's
K.C.'s Alley
Kibitz in City
Lee How Fook
Little Pete's
Mama Palma's
McGillin's
Melrose Diner
Mizu
More Than Ice Cream
Nam Phuong
Pho Xe Lua
Rangoon
Rib Crib
Royal Tavern
Ruby's
Sabrina's Café
Sang Kee Duck Hse.
Sitar India
Sweet Lucy's
Tacconelli's
Taq. La Michoacana
Thai Orchid
Tiffin Store
Trolley Car
Vietnam
Vietnam Café
Vietnam Palace

PRIX FIXE BARGAINS

DINNER ($35 & UNDER)

Alisa Cafe/NJ $35	Little Marakesh 25
Back Burner/DE 25	Ly Michael's 25
Bay Pony Inn 28	Manon/NJ 30
Bistro Cassis 32	Marrakesh 25
Bistro St. Tropez 30	Meridith's 30
Brasserie Perrier 35	Miller's Smorgas./LB 22
Cafe Fresko 32	Modo Mio 30
Caribou Cafe 29	Moonstruck 29
Casablanca 27	Museum Rest. 27
Cedars 25	My Thai 18
CinCin 30	Ortlieb's Jazz 20
Derek's 30	Paradigm 30
Devon Seafood 35	PTG 30
Fayette St. 32	Rist. La Buca 31
Fez Moroccan 25	Roux 3 20
Filomena/NJ 24	Roy's 35
Fleming's Prime 34	Rx 25
Gilmore's 35	Rylei 30
Gnocchi 30	Slate Bleu 33
Good 'N Plenty/LB 18	Summer Kitchen 20
Green Hills Inn/LB 30	Supper 35
High St. Caffé 30	Thai Singha 11
Il Cantuccio 28	Twenty Manning 30
Italian Bistro 27	Twin Bays 30
Jasper 35	Victor Café 25
Konak 25	Washington Cross. 19
Krazy Kat's/DE 35	Water Lily/NJ 30
La Locanda/Ghiottone 35	Xochitl 35

LUNCH ($25 & UNDER)

Bay Pony Inn $16	Ly Michael's 13
Bistro Cassis 20	Mamma Maria 20
Bistro St. Tropez 10	Nectar 10
Bliss 23	Nineteen 19
Brasserie 73 25	Paradigm 12
Caribou Cafe 16	Pattaya 9
Cedars 25	Pho Thai Nam 9
Derek's 20	Rist. La Buca 17
Estia 17	Susanna Foo 23
Haydn Zug's/LB 20	Sweet Basil Thai 11
Il Cantuccio 11	Thai Orchid 8
Jack's Firehouse 18	Thai Singha 9
J.L. Sullivan's 12	Valentino/Square 25
Joseph Ambler 25	Water Lily/NJ 10
Lemon Grass 9	Zocalo 10

All restaurants are in the Philadelphia area unless otherwise noted (LB=Lancaster/Berks Counties; NJ=New Jersey Suburbs; DE=Wilmington/Nearby Delaware).

RESTAURANT DIRECTORY

Philadelphia

Abacus ⓜ *Chinese* | 24 | 19 | 24 | $28 |

Lansdale | North Penn Mktpl. | 1551 S. Valley Forge Rd. (Sumneytown Pike) | 215-362-2010

For "as-good-as-it-gets" Chinese "in the 'burbs", locals count on this central Montco strip-mall BYO for "gourmet" eats "presented with flair"; factor in the "awesome fish tank" and "entertaining" host Joe Chen's one-liners ("a riot" even if they're "the same each time you dine") and it adds up to a "fun evening out."

Abbaye *Belgian* | 22 | 15 | 19 | $24 |

Northern Liberties | 637 N. Third St. (Fairmount Ave.) | 215-627-6711

Everyone from "high-maintenance vegans" to "carnivorous" types find "delicious" options at this "low-key", pet-friendly Northern Liberties Belgian gastropub, where "old-timers" and "hipsters" mingle over an "amazing" beer selection; just "don't expect lightning" service from the "easy-on-the-eyes" staffers – they're "just hanging out" too; N.B. it's a natural for weekend brunch.

Abbraccio *Italian* | 13 | 16 | 17 | $26 |

University City | 820 S. 47th St. (Warrington Ave.) | 215-727-8247 | www.abbracciorestaurant.com

Its name means 'hug' in Italian and it aptly describes the "cozy" "family" atmosphere at this University City trattoria; critics carp about "pedestrian" eats, but prices are moderate and the "hospitable" owners, "toasty" fireplace, alfresco porch and "quirky" touches like rooster-shaped wine pitchers fill seats – especially since there's "not much competition in the area."

Abner's Authentic Bar-B-Que ⓜ *BBQ* | 20 | 9 | 17 | $15 |

Jenkintown | Jenkintown Square Shopping Ctr. | 505 Old York Rd. (Hillside Ave.) | 215-885-8600 | www.abnersbbq.com

"Yeehaw! – down-home barbecue in Jenkintown" rave boosters of the "real-deal" slow-smoked meats found ("who would've thought?") in a BYO strip-mall joint whose "aroma" stirs "cravings" from "two blocks" away; given the "consistent" 'cue and "cool" staff, "who cares" about the "campy", cafeteria-style setup?

Abyssinia ◗ *Ethiopian* | 24 | 12 | 13 | $16 |

University City | 229 S. 45th St. (Locust St.) | 215-387-2424

"Hearty" Ethiopian fare is "finger-licking good – literally" ("you eat with your hands") at this University City traditional African in a converted row house; sure, the faux wood-paneled decor may "remind you of your parents' basement" and the "sweet" staff can work at "a snail's pace" ("bring a book") but it's a "good value" and the upstairs bar with its various theme nights is a "treasure."

Adobe Cafe *Southwestern* | 18 | 15 | 19 | $24 |

Roxborough | 4550 Mitchell St. (Leverington Ave.) | 215-483-3947

Surveyors are split on this "quirky, little" Southwestern "hideaway" in Roxborough: while some say *olé* to the "tasty" *comidas* (with "extensive veg" options), "amazing" margaritas and "convenient parking", the-less-than-impressed attest the "chief virtues" here are "low prices" and a "festive" atmosphere; N.B. a South Philly outpost is slated for summer 2008.

Agave Grille & Cantina *Southwestern*   16 | 17 | 17 | $27

Ambler | 110 E. Butler Ave. (York St.) | 215-641-1420 | www.agavegrille.com

For most, the "simple" "cantina" atmosphere and "solid" grub at this Montco Southwestern make it a "reasonable" stop when headed next door for a movie at the Ambler Theater; still, some have a pricklier reaction ("passably good", "spotty service") and note that it can get "a little noisy."

Al Dar Bistro *Mediterranean*   17 | 16 | 15 | $31

Bala Cynwyd | 281 Montgomery Ave. (Levering Mill Rd.) | 610-667-1245 | www.aldarbistro.com

This "popular" Main Line Mediterranean storefront serves as a "comfortable" "neighborhood" "meeting ground" that most surveyors find "reliable" for a bite (kebabs, salads) and a brew ("good beers on tap"); service can be "speedy" or "neglectful when it's crowded, which it often is", and a few feel the "prices don't match the food."

Alfa ● *American*   16 | 19 | 17 | $29

Center City West | 1709 Walnut St. (17th St.) | 215-751-0201 | www.alfa-bar.com

It's all about "the scene" at this "chill" New American "beautiful people" magnet with a chichi Rittenhouse address (conveniently located downstairs from the Walnut Room nightclub); while dinner draws mixed reviews, partyers find it's "fantastic" for happy-hour festivities, with "funky" "1970s-themed" libations and "tasty" "light" bites.

⊠ Alison at Blue Bell ⊠⊠⇄ *American*   26 | 16 | 22 | $47

Blue Bell | 721 Skippack Pike (Penllyn-Blue Bell Pike) | 215-641-2660 | www.alisonatbluebell.com

A "hot spot" in the 'burbs, chef-owner Alison Barshak's Blue Bell "destination" will "rock your taste buds" with "clever" twists on seafood-centric New American fare; yes, it's "cramped" and "noisy" (forget "private conversation" unless the patio is open) and doesn't take credit cards despite "upscale pricing", but the food, served by an "efficient" staff, "wins out."

AllWays Café, The ⊠ *Eclectic*   22 | 11 | 17 | $15

Huntingdon Valley | Bethayres Shopping Ctr. | 634 Welsh Rd. (Huntingdon Pike.) | 215-914-2151 | www.allwayscafe.com

"Back-to-nature" fans order "tasty", veggie-friendly Eclectic vittles (e.g. sweet potato quesadilla, plus fish and poultry dishes) "at the counter" of this "tiny" strip-mall spot in Huntingdon Valley, and the "generous portions" are delivered by a "patient" staff with a socially conscious edge: there are charity collection jars "in lieu of tipping"; N.B. no alcohol allowed.

| | FOOD | DECOR | SERVICE | COST |

☑ Alma de Cuba *Nuevo Latino*   25 | 25 | 23 | $48

Center City West | 1623 Walnut St. (bet. 16th & 17th Sts.) |
215-988-1799 | www.almadecubarestaurant.com

For Cuban "flair" near Rittenhouse Square, follow the "fashionistas"
and foodies to this "swanky" tri-level extravaganza from Stephen
Starr and celeb chef Douglas Rodriguez, which fuses "fabulous"
Nuevo Latino food and drink with a "sexy" "old-time" Havana ambiance complete with "attentive" waiters in white jackets; in-Fidels
find it "noisy" and "expensive" but most maintain it's well "worth it."

Almaz Café *Ethiopian*   ▽ 22 | 15 | 24 | $14

Center City West | 140 S. 20th St. (Sansom St.) | 215-557-0108

You'll find "affordable", "authentic" Ethiopian food at this "interesting" addition to Rittenhouse Square that doubles as a "quaint" coffee-
house; run by a "pleasant" East African couple that "works hard" to
serve tables "quickly", it's considered a "charming" "winner."

Alyan's *Mideastern*   ▽ 21 | 10 | 19 | $15

South St. | 603 S. Fourth St. (South St.) | 215-922-3553

"Even the simplest food" (falafel, hummus, fries) can be "dreamy" at
this long-running Middle Eastern BYO oasis off South Street; the
"bare-bones" setup is less dreamy, except for the "pretty, skylit back
room" that romeos recommend for a touch of "romance."

☑ Amada *Spanish*   28 | 24 | 25 | $52

Old City | 217 Chestnut St. (bet. 2nd & 3rd Sts.) | 215-625-2450 |
www.amadarestaurant.com

"Tapas of the heap" sums up the sentiment on Jose Garces' "sexy"
"sublime" Spaniard in Old City, where armadas of amigos ("book way
in advance") share small plates of "awesome", "cutting-edge" *comidas* and "primo" sangria served by an "informative" staff; it may be
"pricey" but the $45 tasting menu helps contain costs, and if "noise"
is a concern, come early (or for lunch) and pass on the "loud" though
"super-fun" flamenco shows on Wednesdays and Fridays.

America Bar & Grill *American*   17 | 17 | 17 | $32

Chester Springs | Shops at Lionville Station | 499 Uwchlan Ave.
(bet. Lionville Station Rd. & Rte. 113) | 610-280-0800
Glen Mills | Shoppes at Brinton Lake | 981 Baltimore Pike (Brinton Lake Rd.) |
610-558-9900
www.americabargrill.com

The menu "goes on for days" at these "comfortable", "reliable" New
American strip-mall sibs in the western suburbs, so folks from five
to 50 can find "plentiful" options as well as "prompt" service;
P.S. there's a "bargain" Sunday brunch ($15.95 for adults) and
entertainment on weekends.

Anastasi Seafood *Seafood*   22 | 9 | 17 | $30

South Philly | Italian Mkt. | 1101 S. Ninth St. (Washington Ave.) |
215-462-0550

"Fresh" rises to "a new level" at this "no-frills" seafooder – family-
owned for 100 years – in the back room of an Italian Market fish

store (it's one place "where 'cheap' and 'seafood' don't make me nervous" declares one devotee); expect "loud", "friendly" service from "South Philly" folks who "care."

Anjou ● *Asian Fusion*
19 | 18 | 18 | $36

Old City | 206-208 Market St. (bet. 2nd & 3rd Sts.) | 215-923-1600
Encompassing "creative" sushi plus Korean dishes (and French influences), the menu at this bi-level Asian fusion in Old City "seems random, but somehow it works", though maybe not all the time ("a bit disappointed"); if service can be "slow", people-watching helps pass the time, whether in the downstairs lounge, a "fun" late-night option with entertainment on weekends, or when dining alfresco.

Ansill *Eclectic*
24 | 19 | 22 | $46

South St. | 627 S. Third St. (Bainbridge St.) | 215-627-2485 | www.ansillfoodandwine.com
"Adventurous palates" can sample "unique" small plates – offal, shirred duck's egg and other "cutting-edge" "taste sensations" – at David Ansill's "trendy", eponymous Eclectic in a Queen Village "corner nook", where meals are enhanced by "great wines" suggested by "friendly", "informed" bartenders; "dudes with big appetites" might prefer dining here on Sundays, when the traditional menu from Ansill's former bistro, Pif, is offered.

Aoi *Japanese*
∇ 16 | 11 | 15 | $28

Center City East | 1210 Walnut St. (bet. 12th & 13th Sts.) | 215-985-1838
"All-you-can-eat sushi" is the draw at this long-running Japanese in Center City with a "biker-bar atmosphere" and a staff that "watches you like a hawk if you want to share your food"; though some call it a "get-what-you-pay-for bargain" ("good in theory" – "much rice, little fish"), "your prayers are answered" if you want to eat until you "almost burst."

Apamate ⓜ⚐ *Spanish*
23 | 16 | 19 | $27

Center City West | 1620 South St. (17th St.) | 215-790-1620 | www.cafeapamate.com
This "charming" northern Spanish BYO in the Graduate Hospital area Basques in the praise of "small-plates" fans who "eat their way through the whole menu" of "wildly delicious" pintxos and picas (mini-tapas) "without breaking the bank"; "made-to-order" churros and "spicy" hot chocolate are best enjoyed on the "cute" back patio; N.B. there's brunch on Saturdays and Sundays.

NEW Apothecary Bar + Lounge ●ⓜ *American*
- | - | - | M

Center City East | 102 S. 13th St. (Drury Ln.) | 215-735-7500 | www.apothecarylounge.com
Mixologists get downright pharmaceutical at this modern, bi-level Center City lounge, where high-minded cocktails with medicinal-sounding ingredients accompany the midpriced menu of New American small plates; N.B. a roof deck affords a view of happening 13th Street.

	FOOD	DECOR	SERVICE	COST

Aqua ☒ *Malaysian/Thai*

| 19 | 16 | 19 | $27 |

Center City East | 705 Chestnut St. (7th St.) | 215-928-2838

"Before checking out Washington Square and the Liberty Bell" (a block and a half away), take a seat by the "soothing waterfall" at this "casual" BYO Malaysian-Thai and savor the freedom to order a "variety" of "tasty nibbles" ("old favorites" and "new adventures") at "cheap prices"; also dependable is the "fast", "friendly" service.

Ardmore Station Cafe *Diner*

| 19 | 9 | 19 | $15 |

Ardmore | 6 Station Ave. (bet. Lancaster & Montgomery Aves.) | 610-642-2683

"Watch the choo choos go by" at this "spartan" Main Line diner that's on track for "solid" breakfasts ("pancakes to die for"), "decent" lunches and "filling" weekend brunches; it's "good and cheap" and the service is "friendly" so "get there early" to beat rush hour.

Ariana *Afghan*

| 20 | 15 | 19 | $24 |

Old City | 134 Chestnut St. (bet. Front & 2nd Sts.) | 215-922-1535

"Tasty", "comforting" Afghan "flavor combinations" in "snug" surroundings make this "affordable" BYO an "oasis of calm" in bustling Old City; if some feel there's "little atmosphere unless you get the window seat", for most it's a "pleasant change" of pace complete with servers who "never rush you" out.

Arpeggio *Italian/Mediterranean*

| 23 | 17 | 21 | $25 |

Spring House | 542 Spring House Village Ctr. (bet. Bethlehem Pike & Norristown Rd.) | 215-646-5055 | www.arpeggiobyob.com

"It's worth the wait – and you will wait" at this no-reservations Italian-Med BYO in a central Montco strip mall, where a "discriminating" clientele always "finds fabulous" *ciao* ("specialty" pizzas, "oh-so-creamy" hummus); a staff that's "dying to please" and "great-deal" pricing add to its appeal.

NEW Ashoka Palace ☒ *Indian*

| - | - | - | I |

Center City West | 38 S. 19th St. (Market St.) | 215-564-6466

Diners are in the pink – literally – with the blushing color everywhere at this cavernous, humbly decorated Indian BYO quick-serve near Rittenhouse Square; chef-owner Kinder Jit Singh – a fixture on the Center City curry circuit – makes his debut as a restaurateur, turning out budget-friendly dishes of every stripe (goat, seafood, lamb, chicken) from the back counter.

NEW Asuka *Japanese*

| - | - | - | M |

Blue Bell | 1002 Skippack Pike (Valley Rd.) | 215-654-8900

Historic stonework contrasts with contemporary accents at this handsome Japanese – which shares an entrance and kitchen with Gaya, an enormous Korean BBQ spot next door – in a newly renovated Blue Bell landmark; there's the requisite sushi bar with the usual suspects and midpriced lunch and dinner menus brimming with tempura, teriyaki and sukiyaki.

	FOOD	DECOR	SERVICE	COST

Athena 🅜🚭 *Greek/Seafood*
| 21 | 16 | 20 | $25 |

Glenside | 264 N. Keswick Ave. (Easton Rd.) | 215-884-1777

Bring your appetite (and cash – no credit cards accepted) to this "quaint" Greek BYO "tucked in a bland strip mall" near the Keswick Theatre in Glenside; "bargain" "sampler" platters (served with "warm" pita) proffered by a "friendly" staff are the way to go, and it's even better on the "deck."

Audrey Claire 🚭 *Mediterranean*
| 22 | 17 | 20 | $35 |

Center City West | 276 S. 20th St. (Spruce St.) | 215-731-1222 | www.audreyclaire.com

Audrey Taichman's "minimalist" cash-only BYO on a corner near Rittenhouse Square might be "too noisy to be romantic", but fans prefer to focus on the kitchen's "dependably delicious" Med meals anyway; the "elbow-knocking" atmosphere (think "family gathering" with "adventurous" food) is "not for the misanthropic."

August 🅈🅜🚭 *Italian*
| 26 | 19 | 24 | $35 |

South Philly | 1247 S. 13th St. (Wharton St.) | 215-468-5926 | www.augustbyob.com

The kind of place "that everyone wants to have in their neighborhood", this "intimate" BYO Italian on an "unassuming" South Philly corner earns impressive ratings for its "soulful" cooking proffered by an "attentive" staff; it's "quiet enough for conversation" and a "nice first-date" place – just keep in mind the cash-only policy.

August Moon *Japanese/Korean*
| 23 | 17 | 21 | $34 |

Norristown | 300 E. Main St. (Arch St.) | 610-277-4008 | www.augustmoonpa.com

"Fantastic" sushi and Korean barbecue in a "not-so-fantastic" Norristown location (but "there is a parking lot") sums up this "austere"-looking Asian staffed by an "attentive, friendly" crew; even those who say the bill "can add up" because you'll "want to try" everything maintain "it's worth it" since you "can't go wrong" here.

🆕 Auspicious *Chinese*
| 19 | 19 | 20 | $24 |

Ardmore | 11 Cricket Ave. (Lancaster Ave.) | 610-642-1858 | www.mastersofkungfood.com

Main Liners applaud the "auspicious debut" of this "sleek" BYO Chinese offering an "extensive" menu of classic and contemporary dishes plus the likes of shiitake Swiss burgers and "build-your-own stir-fries"; "aim-to-please" staffers, a "relaxing" atmosphere and "reasonable" tabs are more reasons why it's "always packed."

Ava 🅜 *Italian*
| 24 | 17 | 20 | $35 |

South St. | 518 S. Third St. (bet. Lombard & South Sts.) | 215-922-3282 | www.avarestaurant.com

"How can you go wrong?" ask admirers of this "BYO-ers' dream", an Italian trattoria off South Street that spotlights Michael Campagna's "delicious", "thoughtful" meals; while the "intimate" setting gets "noisy", loyalists laud this "staple" that "treats its customers with a sense of pride" – and sends them off with "change in their wallets."

	FOOD	DECOR	SERVICE	COST

Avalon ▣ *Italian*

21 | 21 | 20 | $44

West Chester | 312 S. High St. (Union St.) | 610-436-4100 |
www.avalonrestaurant.org

This West Chester "mom-and-pop" storefront "charmer" attracts
with its "pleasant" setting – including a "romantic" fireplace and
"great" patio – and "always interesting" American-influenced
Northern Italian food (think braised short rib agnoletti); acolytes
aver "it's worth a trip to the boonies", and even the less enamored
consider it a "decent fallback."

Aya's Café *Egyptian*

20 | 17 | 20 | $28

Center City West | 2129 Arch St. (22nd St.) | 215-567-1555 |
www.ayascafe.net

"You can't go wrong" with the "heavenly falafel" and "tasty couscous" affirm admirers of this "comfortable" Egyptian BYO in a "re-
modeled pizza shop" off Logan Square; a "kids' menu" and a "warm"
staff make it "a wonderful addition" to the neighborhood.

⚡NEW Azie *Asian Fusion*

24 | 26 | 22 | $49

Media | 217-219 W. State St. (Orange St.) | 610-566-4750 |
www.azie-restaurant.com

Media's masses find Center City "hipness" at this sleek, Zen-like Asian
fusion arrival, where an "upscale" crowd grooves to the "upscale" food
(from a former Morimoto chef) and "happening" mood complete with
a "lively" bar "lit from underneath"; though some cite "lots of style,
not enough substance", the majority deems it a "lovely addition."

NEW Azul Cantina ● *Mexican*

- | - | - | I

Center City East | 941 Spruce St. (10th St.) | 215-627-5200 |
www.azulcantina.com

Dozens of tequilas and ambitious Mexican pub grub join forces at
this bustling, colorful restaurant/lounge enlivening a Wash West
corner; all but five of the entrees on the affordable, expansive menu
are small plates intended for sharing; N.B. weekend brunch options
include coconut pancakes and other south-of-the-border twists on
mid-morning fare.

Bahama Breeze ● *Caribbean*

17 | 19 | 17 | $27

King of Prussia | 320 Goddard Blvd. (Mall Blvd.) | 610-491-9822 |
www.bahamabreeze.com

The "islands meet suburbia" at these "kid-friendly" chainsters in
King of Prussia and Cherry Hill, where you can "almost feel the sand
between your toes"; while "giant" portions of Caribbean-style food
and "creative cocktails" (with requisite "umbrellas") please most,
critics contend the "touch of the tropics" vibe can be marred by
"long waits" and "hit-or-miss" service.

Baja Fresh Mexican Grill *Mexican*

17 | 10 | 14 | $11

Springfield | 1138 Baltimore Pike (Rte. 320) | 610-690-1064
King of Prussia | 340 DeKalb Pike (Pennsylvania Tpke.) |
610-337-2050
Abington | Abington Shopping Ctr. | 1437 Old York Rd. (London Rd.) |
215-885-4296

(continued)

Baja Fresh Mexican Grill

Conshohocken | Plymouth Square Shopping Ctr. | 200 W. Ridge Pike
(Butler Pike) | 610-828-4524
www.bajafresh.com

If you crave "fresh", "made-to-order" Mex and need it "fast", this
Wendy's-owned "fast-food" chain puts "Taco Bell to shame"; while the
"cafeteria-style" settings won't win awards, "cheap" tabs and "cheerful" service put many on the *camino* in; P.S. the salsa bar is a "plus."

Banana Leaf ● *Malaysian*   22 | 19 | 21 | $21

Chinatown | 1009 Arch St. (bet. 10th & 11th Sts.) | 215-592-8288
"Venture outside the box" for "beautifully prepared" Malay dishes at
this "unpretentious" BYO "bargain" in Chinatown (owned by a
former Penang employee); the "helpful" staff, "charming straw-hut"
vibe and "great prices" ("you feel more bamboo-ed than bamboo-
zled") make it the "real deal."

⊠ Barclay Prime *Steak*   26 | 25 | 25 | $74

Center City West | The Barclay | 237 S. 18th St. (Locust St.) |
215-732-7560 | www.barclayprime.com
"Choose your weapon" from the "pick-your-knife selection" and
"feast away" on "fantastic" beef (including "awesome" Kobe cheese
steaks) at Stephen's Starr's "expense-account extraordinaire"
meatery on Rittenhouse Square; a "posh" "library" setting and
"knowledgeable" servers enhance the city's top-rated non-chain
steakhouse (just remember to get your "credit limit increased" before you go); N.B. jackets suggested.

Bar Ferdinand ● *Spanish*   23 | 24 | 20 | $38

Northern Liberties | Liberties Walk | 1030 N. Second St. (George St.) |
215-923-1313 | www.barferdinand.com
"No bull!" squeal amigos of Owen Kamihira's "gorgeous" Spaniard
in Northern Liberties lined in "vibrant" mosaic murals; "hipsters"
and "romantics" "bravely fight the crowds" for "knock-your-socks-off"
tapas "with a twist" and "sensational" sangrias that won't make "a
dent in the wallet"; N.B. dinner-only, plus Sunday brunch.

Basil Bistro & Bar *American*   18 | 16 | 17 | $33

Paoli | 522 King Rd. (Lancaster Ave.) | 610-647-1500 | www.basilbistro.com
Main Line "moms" "duck out" for a "civilized lunch" at this "upbeat"
New American, whose ambiance may "not be for romantic nights" but
it still offers a "great variety" of food that "pleases the masses" and
a "kid-friendly" staff; those who deride "so-so" fare are overruled.

Bay Pony Inn ⓜ *American*   19 | 19 | 19 | $38

Lederach | 508 Old Skippack Rd. (Salfordville Rd.) | 215-256-6565 |
www.bayponyinnpa.com
"Take your grandmother" to the "splendid" brunch buffet at this "consistent" Traditional American in Montco, where there's "nothing out of
the ordinary", but nothing ordinary about the "elegant", "country" setting; while modernists believe both menu and decor could use an "update", "an older crowd" says the mare's "worth the ride."

	FOOD	DECOR	SERVICE	COST

Beau Monde ⓜ French
23 | 23 | 20 | $29

South St. | 624 S. Sixth St. (Bainbridge St.) | 215-592-0656 |
www.creperie-beaumonde.com

Fans of this Queen Village Breton-style bistro find "endless possibilities" on its menu of "sweet and savory" crêpes – "best this side of the Seine" claim addicts – offered by "flirtatious" (some say "quirky") servers in a "romantic" beaux arts ambiance complete with fireplace; P.S. the calorie-conscious can "dance it off" après dinner at the upstairs nightclub, L'Etage.

Beige & Beige ⓜ Eclectic
20 | 20 | 15 | $37

Huntingdon Valley | 2501 Huntingdon Pike (bet. Red Lion & Welsh Rds.) |
215-938-8600 | www.beigebeige.com

Covering "extensive" culinary ground ranging from "sushi to Russian to Mediterranean", this "elegant" Eclectic BYO in Huntingdon Valley wins mostly praise for its "interesting", "flavorful" fare; if service can be "slow", there's more time to enjoy the "relaxing" atmosphere.

Beijing Chinese
16 | 7 | 17 | $14

University City | 3714 Spruce St. (bet. 37th & 38th Sts.) | 215-222-5242 |
www.beijingatpenn.com

"Hospital workers" can be heard saying if only HUP "were run as efficiently" as this college-catering BYO near the Quad at Penn, a Chinese "staple" where Quakers "cram" in for "cheap", "reliably" "good" food delivered by "comically swift" servers; in fact, speed is no surprise given the staff's "hurry-up-you-go-now" hospitality.

NEW Belgian Café, The ● Belgian
15 | 16 | 17 | $26

Fairmount | 601 N. 21st St. (Green St.) | 215-235-3500 |
www.thebelgiancafe.com

Though the beer list is "first-rate" at this Belgian "hangout" "hidden in the woodwork of Fairmount" (the new sib of the popular Monk's Cafe), the food (e.g. mussels, frites) and service "need some work", judging by mixed reviews; the dining room decor is also debated – "bright and cheery" vs. "hospital cafeteria" – but the "neighborhood vibe" is a plus.

Ⓩ Bella Tori at the Mansion ⓜ Italian
19 | 25 | 20 | $51

Langhorne | 321 S. Bellevue Ave. (bet. Gilliam & Maple Aves.) |
215-702-9600 | www.bellatori.com

"Plenty" of "spectacular" atmosphere at this "beautifully restored" 19th-century Bucks mansion proffering "pricey" Northern Italian fare wins plaudits from admirers who deem it a "happy discovery" in Langhorne Borough; hopes are high that the new chef will allow the cuisine to "match the mood"; N.B. dinner only, plus Sunday brunch.

Bella Trattoria Italian
22 | 17 | 20 | $29

Manayunk | 4258 Main St. (bet. Rector St. & Roxborough Ave.) |
215-482-5556 | www.bellatrattoriapa.com

"Reliable", "reasonably" priced Italian food is what you expect and get at this "congenial", "simply decorated" trattoria on Manayunk's Main Street; those in-the-know "get a window seat" or "sit outside" for outstanding "people-watching"; N.B. a smaller bar menu offers light bites for the plasma TV–watching crowd.

Bellini Grill *Italian*   19 | 14 | 19 | $32

Center City West | 220 S. 16th St. (bet. Locust & Walnut Sts.) | 215-545-1191 | www.bellinigrill.com

For an Italian fix, try this "dependable" BYO around the corner from the Kimmel Center; given the affordable tabs, it's an "insurance salesman's Palm", with "good", albeit "basic" food and a "quaint" setting warmed by the presence of an "affable" owner.

Ben & Irv Deli Restaurant *Deli*   19 | 10 | 17 | $17

Huntingdon Valley | Justa Farm Shopping Ctr. | 1962 County Line Rd. (Davisville Rd.) | 215-355-2000 | www.benandirvs.com

"One of the last of a dying breed", this "typical Jewish deli" in a Montco strip mall is "always packed" with folks digging into "excellent soups, overstuffed sandwiches" and other "authentic" eats served by "prompt" (if sometimes "snippy") staffers amid lots of "hustle and bustle"; in sum, "your bubbe would approve."

NEW Beneluxx   20 | 16 | 21 | $29
Tasting Room ◑⊠Ⓜ *Belgian*

Old City | 33 S. Third St. (Market St.) | 267-318-7269 | www.beneluxx.com

"You won't mind" that your "meals are comprised of" samples of wines and beers paired with cheeses and chocolates (plus pizzas, panini and such) at this "subterranean" Old City Belgian brother of the nearby Eulogy Belgian Tavern; every table features a built-in glass rinser that "allows multiple tastings" from the "bargain-priced", "exhaustive menu" – you'll "feel worldly" and "educated" "without hurting your credit card."

Bensí *Italian*   18 | 16 | 17 | $25

North Wales | The Shoppes at English Vill. | 1460 Bethlehem Pike (Welsh Rd.) | 215-283-3222 | www.bensirestaurants.com

"For the money", supporters say *sí* to this "contemporary" red-sauce Italian bistro in a Montco shopping center (an offshoot of the North Jersey chain), citing it as "better than a lot of other pretenders" for "*buono*" lunches or dinners, even if some say it's "format" fare; N.B. the new Wyomissing outpost has a warm, modern look.

Bertolini's *Italian*   18 | 18 | 18 | $29

King of Prussia | Plaza at King of Prussia Mall | 160 N. Gulph Rd. (bet. DeKalb Pike & Mall Blvd.) | 610-265-2965 | www.bertolinis.net

"If you're shopping" in King of Prussia "and don't want to move the car", this Italian from the Morton's chain may be "worth" your time for fare that's a "step above" typical food court options; while the "inconsistent" service may chafe, the "contemporary" setting "pleases."

Big Fork ⊠Ⓜ *American*   ▽ 21 | 14 | 21 | $39

Chadds Ford | Olde Ridge Village Shoppes | 100 Ridge Rd. (Rte. 202) | 610-358-8008 | www.bigforkrestaurant.com

Le Bec-Fin alum Kevin Diskin's "quaint" BYO is "well worth the drive" to a Chadds Ford shopping center for "solid" New American flavors at "big-value" prices purveyed by a staff that "tries"; any quibbles about the "limited menu" are offset by proclamations that it's mostly "delightful."

NEW Bindi Ⓜ🚫 Indian   22 | 19 | 19 | $37

Center City East | 105 S. 13th St. (bet. Chestnut & Sansom Sts.) | 215-922-6061 | www.bindibyob.com

"Indian meets New American" at this "up-and-coming", cash-only Center City arrival across the street from Mex sib Lolita (where chef Marcie Turney does double-duty), where "ambitious" fare and "great drinks" created with BYO booze are served in "dark", "industrial"-looking digs; given the $18 per person minimum, you may have to "run to the closest ATM between courses."

Ⓩ Birchrunville   28 | 23 | 27 | $51
Store Cafe ⓈⓂ🚫 French/Italian

Birchrunville | 1403 Hollow Rd. (Flowing Springs Rd.) | 610-827-9002 | www.birchrunvillestorecafe.com

"Book early" and bring cash along with your best BYO bottle to Francis Trzeciak's "charming" Franco-Italian – "if you can find it" – in rural Chester County; its "superb" cuisine (including a $65 six-course tasting menu served Wednesdays and Thursdays), "attentive" service and a historic "country-inn" setting make high tabs and "impossible"-to-land reservations "worth it"; N.B. closed Sundays–Tuesdays.

Bistro Cassis Ⓜ French/Mediterranean   ▽ 20 | 19 | 18 | $43

Radnor | 175 King of Prussia Rd. (E. Lancaster Ave.) | 610-293-9521 | www.cassis-bistro.net

Proponents of Pond's less-formal New French-Med bistro next door report that it's "carrying on a good tradition", with "creative" cuisine and a "beautiful" location befitting a "special occasion"; a few critics deem the cuisine "average" but concur that the "lovely" alfresco terrace "overlooking the swans' pond" is a plus.

Bistro Juliana Ⓜ Italian   ▽ 23 | 16 | 20 | $30

Fishtown | 2723 E. Cumberland St. (Salmon St.) | 215-425-2501 | www.bistrojuliana.com

The Fishtown address is appropriate at this "cute" trattoria where "fish is king" (grilled octopus, farfalle with seafood, Dover sole); "good" service and "free parking" (in a lot across the street) also draw a local crowd to this "affordable" BYO run by the folks from Radicchio in Old City; P.S. there are no reservations so "go early" – it's "packed otherwise."

Bistro La Baia 🚫 Italian   20 | 14 | 19 | $27

Center City West | 1700 Lombard St. (17th St.) | 215-546-0496 | www.bistrolabaia.com

Its "smiling owner" keeps a "watchful eye" on his "dependable" cash-only Italian "shoebox" of a BYO in Center City where locals enjoy "yummy", "carb lover's" cooking and "charming" service; most admit the food is "good enough" to compensate for the "incredibly cramped", "awfully crowded" conditions.

	FOOD	DECOR	SERVICE	COST

Bistro La Viola 🅜 ⇱ *Italian*
24 | 14 | 21 | $30

Center City West | 253 S. 16th St. (bet. Locust & Spruce Sts.) | 215-735-8630

"Forced intimacy" at this "tiny" Center City BYO Italian near the Kimmel Center may have you "eating off your neighbor's plate", but given the "heavenly", "priced-just-right" victuals proffered by "enthusiastic" servers ("our little waiter had a big sense of humor"), loyalists "la-la-love" it; N.B. some find larger sibling La Viola Ovest across the street "less enervating."

Bistro Romano *Italian*
21 | 21 | 21 | $38

Society Hill | 120 Lombard St. (bet. Front & 2nd Sts.) | 215-925-8880 | www.bistroromano.com

Admirers of this "romantic" Italian in a restored Society Hill 18th-century granary can't get enough of the "solid" cooking ("best tableside" Caesar salad in the city), "intimate" setting (a "subterranean" dining grotto and "softly lit" wine cellar) and "super-friendly" service; N.B. the street-level barroom features a pianist Fridays and Saturdays.

Bistro 7 🅜 *American*
24 | 16 | 22 | $41

Old City | 7 N. Third St. (Market St.) | 215-931-1560 | www.bistro7restaurant.com

Loyalists laud Michael O'Halloran's "urban cool" New American BYO in Old City as a "must-visit" for "foodie-esque" "flashes of brilliance" (e.g. wild boar terrine with sun-dried cherries) emanating from an open kitchen; the digs are rather "small" and "plain", but "gracious", "informed" service and "great" prices help compensate; N.B. a five-course tasting menu ($35) is offered Tuesdays–Thursdays.

Bistro St. Tropez 🅈 *French*
20 | 18 | 19 | $41

Center City West | Marketplace Design Ctr. | 2400 Market St., 4th fl. (23rd St.) | 215-569-9269 | www.bistrosttropez.com

Window tables supply "spectacular views of the Schuylkill" from this "obscurely" situated Marketplace Design Center French bistro that "brightens up the landscape"; "compelling" and at times "innovative" food helps redeem "outdated" interiors and "inconsistent" service.

Bitar's 🅈 *Mideastern*
23 | 8 | 16 | $12

Germantown | 7152 Germantown Ave. (bet. Mt. Airy & Mt. Pleasant Aves.) | 215-242-4910
South Philly | 947 Federal St. (10th St.) | 215-755-1121
www.bitars.com

For "mouthwatering" Middle Eastern "so cheap" you "won't care" about the "bare-bones" ambiance, these family-run "takeouts" in South Philly (with a "fantastic" "grocery attached") and Germantown – plus stands at Penn and Drexel – "leave 'em happy"; if only they were "open on Sundays" sigh admirers.

🅉 Blackfish 🅈 *Seafood*
26 | 18 | 23 | $47

Conshohocken | 119 Fayette St. (bet. 1st & 2nd Aves.) | 610-397-0888 | www.blackfishrestaurant.com

"What a catch!" aver acolytes of Chip Roman's "lively", "minimalist" New American–influenced BYO seafooder in a "small" Conshy "storefront"; ok, it can get "cramped and noisy", but given the "cutting-edge" cuisine ("from fish to fowl") and "uncommonly knowledgeable" service, most maintain it's a "great addition to the neighborhood."

Black Sheep Pub ◑ *Pub Food*   16 | 15 | 16 | $23

Center City West | 247 S. 17th St. (Latimer St.) | 215-545-9473 | www.theblacksheeppub.com

This "comfy" Irish pub off Rittenhouse Square can become "your favorite hangout" if you like "slumming" over TV "soccer matches", "darts", "Guinness" and burgers; the cookin's "pretty good", and most report "you can really feel the back-home Irish airs."

Bliss Ⓢ *American*   22 | 21 | 21 | $50

Avenue of the Arts | 220-224 S. Broad St. (bet. Locust & Walnut Sts.) | 215-731-1100 | www.bliss-restaurant.com

"Apt name" say loyalists who laud this New American next to the Bellevue for its "excellent" (if "a bit pricey") food, "friendly" service and "serene" atmosphere (despite all the "air kisses"); it's "great for pre-theater" dinner before the Kimmel Center, with validated parking a plus; P.S. a recent change of ownership and chef may not be reflected in the above ratings.

Blue Bell Inn ⓈⓂ *American*   21 | 18 | 19 | $43

Blue Bell | 601 Skippack Pike (Penllyn-Blue Bell Pike) | 215-646-2010 | www.bluebellinn.com

It's "not jazzy by any means", but this 60-year-old, family-operated Traditional American in Montco has had a long run at delivering "good" food to generations of fans; the "sizzling", "swinging septuagenarian bar scene" on Friday nights and early-bird specials, though, reinforce perceptions that it's a "blue-hair" hang.

Ⓩ Bluefin Ⓢ *Japanese*   26 | 12 | 20 | $36

Plymouth Meeting | 1017 Germantown Pike (Virginia Rd.) | 610-277-3917 | www.sushibluefin.com

Yong Kim's Japanese BYO "pearl" in an "unassuming" Plymouth Meeting strip mall is "filled to the gills" ("make a reservation") with afishionados who'd "give up" their "first child" for its "stop-in-your-tracks" sushi; "sparse" digs and parking are offset by "good value" and a staff that "remembers" you.

Blue Horse Restaurant & Tavern *American*   17 | 20 | 17 | $40

Blue Bell | 602 Skippack Pike (Penllyn-Blue Bell Pike) | 215-641-9100 | www.thebluehorse.net

Despite a change in management and chef, this lively New American in Montco still draws mixed reviews: while some praise "fresh", "fine" fare and find it "posh enough" for "business lunches"; others cite "erratic" food and service; still, a "happy" vibe rules "at the bar."

Blue Pacific *Pan-Asian*   ▽ 21 | 14 | 18 | $30

King of Prussia | Plaza at King of Prussia Mall | 160 N. Gulph Rd. (bet. DeKalb Pike & Mall Blvd.) | 610-337-3078 | www.bluepacifickop.com

"You'd pass right by if you didn't know about it", but those who are savvy to this King of Prussia Pan-Asian say it serves "darn good sushi

FOOD | DECOR | SERVICE | COST

for a mall restaurant"; sure, the decor and service "could be a bit better", but it qualifies as "welcome relief" from the shopping "frenzy."

🆕 Blue Pear Bistro ⊠ *American*   ∇ 22 | 22 | 20 | $40

West Chester | 275 Brintons Bridge Rd. (Old Wilmington Pike) | 610-399-9812 | www.bluepearbistro.com

This "friendly", "lower-priced sibling" of the next-door Dilworthtown Inn is a "hot ticket" among West Chester "boomers" who rave about its "creative" New American fare and "warm" bar; while a few sing the blues about a "limited" menu, most maintain it's a "great addition" to the area; N.B. a warm-weather porch adds extra appeal.

☑ Blue Sage   27 | 15 | 23 | $27
Vegetarian Grille ⊠Ⓜ *Vegetarian*

Southampton | 772 Second St. Pike (Street Rd./Rte. 132) | 215-942-8888 | www.bluesagegrille.com

"Come hungry" for "huge" portions of "insanely delicious", "unique" vegetarian vittles served by a "fun, helpful" staff at Mike and Holly Jackson's "small", "crowded" Bucks strip-mall BYO; fans who dub it "my blue heaven" say "whether you're a veggie or not", it's "total nirvana" ("if you can get in"), that is – "reservations are a must" for dinner.

Blush *Eclectic*   20 | 21 | 20 | $49

Bryn Mawr | 24 N. Merion Ave. (bet. Montgomery & W. Lancaster Aves.) | 610-527-7700 | www.dineatblush.com

To many Main Liners, this "sophisticated" Eclectic in Bryn Mawr scores points for "elegance" and "romance" thanks to "solidly executed" dishes and an "accommodating" staff; still, dissenters point to "high prices" and "inconsistency" as drawbacks.

Bobby Chez Ⓜ *Seafood*   25 | 11 | 16 | $21

🆕 **Avenue of the Arts** | The Lofts | 1352 South St. (Broad St.) | 215-732-1003
🆕 **Glen Mills** | The Shoppes at Brinton Lake | 100 Evergreen Dr. (Rte. 1) | 610-358-5020
www.bobbychezcrabcakes.com

Watch "yuppies wrestling over the last crab cake" at these Philly and South Jersey take-out/eat-in seafooders that "set the standard" for local crabnoscenti; "scintillating sides" like lobster mashed potatoes also help trump any complaints about "crabby" counter staff; P.S. while most locations have only "a few tables" for dining in, the new Glen Mills outpost is a sit-down cafe with a bar.

Bocelli *Italian*   - | - | - | M

🆕 **Chestnut Hill** | 8630 Germantown Ave. (Bethlehem Pike) | 215-248-1980 Ⓜ⇪
Ambler | 521 Plymouth Rd. (Evans Rd.) | 215-646-9912
www.bocellidining.com

Chestnut Hillers are now in on a secret known to those who've tried this quaint Italian BYO at the central Montco original in the Gwynedd Valley SEPTA station; like its sibling, the new location, in a simply decorated storefront at the top of Germantown

	FOOD	DECOR	SERVICE	COST

Avenue, boasts a moderately priced menu, low-key airs and a welcome BYO policy.

☑ Bomb Bomb Bar-be-que Grill Ⓢ *BBQ* | 23 | 13 | 20 | $26 |
South Philly | 1026 Wolf St. (Warnock St.) | 215-463-1311

"You can't go wrong" at this "tiny" South Philly Italian-BBQ joint dishing up "serious" red-sauce "standards" and "great" ribs that are "made with love" and "won't bust your budget"; the "dive bar" digs take a back seat to a staff that's "clearly having a good time."

Bona Cucina Ⓜ⇪ *Italian*   ▽ | 25 | 17 | 26 | $33 |
Upper Darby | 66 Sherbrook Blvd. (Marshall Rd.) | 610-623-8811

Locals laud this "awesome little" BYO Northern Italian in Upper Darby for its "consistently" "fabulous", "down-to-earth" fare that "tastes like it comes from your mama's *cucina*"; if the decor seems somewhat "dated", "warm" service and "reasonable prices" help compensate.

Bonefish Grill *Seafood* | 21 | 19 | 20 | $34 |
Exton | 460 W. Lincoln Hwy. (Whitford Rd.) | 610-524-1010
NEW Newtown Square | 4889 West Chester Pike (Providence Rd.) | 610-355-1784
Willow Grove | Regency Sq. | 1015 Easton Rd. (Fitzwatertown Rd.) | 215-659-5854
www.bonefishgrill.com

"Can't believe it's a chain" say fans of these "slick" yet "family-friendly" Outback-backed seafooders whose "ultrafresh" fish, "great" drinks and "can't-do-enough-for-you" servers add up to "good value"; just arrive "early to avoid long waits."

Bonté Wafflerie & Café *Coffeehouse* | 19 | 12 | 15 | $9 |
Avenue of the Arts | 1315 Walnut St. (bet. Jupiter & 13th Sts.) | 215-732-3259
Center City East | 922 Walnut St. (bet. 9th & 10th Sts.) | 215-238-7407
Center City West | 130 S. 17th St. (bet. Sansom & Walnut Sts.) | 215-557-8510
www.bontewaffles.com

The "spectacular" Belgian waffles at this Euro-style threesome will "ruin your diet", but you'll be "going back for more" (or maybe for a "top-quality" sandwich); relax over a cuppa joe and a selection of papers and magazines, and though they're smack in the middle of the "land of a thousand coffee shops", they tend to attract a "following."

Bottom of the Sea *Seafood*   ▽ | 22 | 11 | 21 | $27 |
NEW South St. | 714 South St. (7th St.) | 215-627-9510 Ⓜ
West Philly | 327 S. 52nd St. (Delancey St.) | 215-471-5600 ◗⇪
West Philly | 700 N. 43rd St. (Fairmount Ave.) | 215-386-0550

These "no-frills" seafooders are tops with fans of "jumping-out-of-the-ocean-fresh" fish – from Dungeness crab to tilapia – served, for the cholesterol courageous, "swimming" in the signature garlic butter; they're takeout/delivery only except for the South Street locale, which has dine-in seating plus a bar.

	FOOD	DECOR	SERVICE	COST

Bourbon Blue *Cajun/Creole*

	19	19	18	$30

Manayunk | 2 Rector St. (Main St.) | 215-508-3360 |
www.bourbonblue.com

An "awesome" bar scene and live music may be the main attractions at this "trendy" Cajun-Creole in a renovated stable by the Manayunk Canal; if a few find the fare "misses the mark", most focus on that "taste of Mardi Gras without the beads", with "good" food to boot.

Brandywine Prime, Seafood & Chops *Steak*

	20	20	18	$47

Chadds Ford | 1617 Baltimore Pike (Rte. 100) | 610-388-8088 |
www.brandywineprime.com

Dan Butler (Wilmington's Toscana) heads the kitchen of this New American chophouse, a "bright", "hip" Colonial update of the 300-year-old Chadds Ford Inn; while loyalists laud the "hearty" steaks, "very good brunch" and "fabulous" redo, critics cite "costly", "uneven" dishes, but given the pedigree, it should "improve."

Branzino *Italian/Seafood*

	23	18	21	$39

Center City West | 261 S. 17th St. (bet. Locust & Spruce Sts.) |
215-790-0103

"Superb fish" – particularly the "must-have" eponymous catch – and "wonderful" osso buco are the calling cards of this bi-level BYO Italian seafooder near the Kimmel Center; yes, it gets "crowded" and "noisy", but that doesn't faze admirers of its "classy" yet "homey" ambiance, "reasonable prices" and "professional" staff that never "hovers."

ⓩ Brasserie Perrier *French*

	24	22	23	$58

Center City West | 1619 Walnut St. (bet. 16th & 17th Sts.) | 215-568-3000 |
www.brasserieperrier.com

You'll have a "swanky good time" at this "casually elegant", relatively "affordable" Center City "alternative" to nearby sib Le Bec-Fin, where Georges Perrier and Chris Scarduzio provide "relaxed" French brasserie fare that "hits the mark" (a switch to "lighter" dishes kicked in mid-Survey); a "polished" staff that aims to please adds to the appeal, as does "classy" art deco decor that works for "business", a "romantic rendezvous" or "people-watching" at the bar.

Brasserie 73 *French*

	22	22	21	$49

Skippack | 4024 Skippack Pike (Mensch Rd.) | 610-584-7880 |
www.skippackrestaurants.com

Respondents report a pre-Survey change of chef and management hasn't affected the "thoroughly enjoyable" food and drink at this "high-end" French bistro in "quaint" Skippack that attracts a "see-and-be-seen" crowd; dine indoors or out but "whoosh – watch out for traffic", as you're "essentially on Route 73."

Brew HaHa! *Coffeehouse*

	18	17	21	$9

Center City East | 212 S. 12th St. (bet. Locust & Walnut Sts.) |
215-893-5680 | www.brew-haha.com

"Java me up, baby!" say satisfied surveyors of this local coffee mini-chain, a "great alternative" to the big-name beaneries where

FOOD DECOR SERVICE COST

"friendly", "knowledgeable" baristas wait "patiently" as customers consider which "delicious" sweets, sandwiches and beverages to order before "getting comfy" on an oversized sofa.

Brick Hotel, The *American* 18 | 20 | 18 | $39

Newtown | The Brick Hotel | 1 E. Washington Ave. (State St.) | 215-860-8313 | www.brickhotel.com

The "historical setting" in an 18th-centry building and "elegant" atmosphere are "still charming after all these years" according to fans of this Newtown New American; if some report "spotty" service and food (a mid-Survey chef change may help), most give a thumbs-up to the "good Sunday brunch" as well as the "lovely" porch and garden seating; N.B. there's live music on weekends.

Bridget Foy's ● *American* 19 | 17 | 18 | $31

South St. | 200 South St. (2nd St.) | 215-922-1813 | www.bridgetfoys.com

They've got "location, location, location" going for them at this New American, a "friendly neighborhood tavern" where the "bartenders know what they're doing" and regulars dig into "solid" grub while watching the South Street "parade" from a "street-level deck"; P.S. a post-Survey renovation should help quiet gripes about a "tired" look.

☒ Bridgetown Mill House ☒Ⓜ *American* 25 | 26 | 23 | $58

Langhorne | 760 Langhorne-Newtown Rd. (Bridgetown Pike) | 215-752-8996 | www.bridgetownmillhouse.com

"Old-world charm" thrives at this "romantic" New American-Continental in an 18th-century Bucks mansion, where diners take a "step back in time" for "deliciously prepared" "feasts" served on "fine china and crystal"; whether it's a "candlelit" dinner by a "blazing" fireplace in winter or tapas and drinks on the patio that's "perfect in warm weather", the experience is "sublime."

Bridgets 8 West Ⓜ *American/Steak* 22 | 21 | 20 | $48

Ambler | 8 W. Butler Pike (Main St.) | 267-465-2000 | www.bridgets8west.com

This "upscale" "steakhouse for the suburbs" in Ambler wins praise for its "very good" fare (now with a New American twist), "terrific wine list" and service that "exceeds expectations"; if some find it "too costly" and "loud", more consider it a "great local place"; N.B. an expanded barroom with an enhanced casual menu is scheduled for a summer 2008 debut.

Bridgid's *Eclectic* 21 | 14 | 20 | $27

Fairmount | 726 N. 24th St. (Meredith St.) | 215-232-3232 | www.bridgids.com

"When you want to get close to your date", it's worth "squeezing" into this "dark" Fairmount Euro-Eclectic "bistro" for "home-style" chow off a "chalkboard" menu and an "incredible" beer selection; in sum, you'll feel as comfortable as if "your best friend invited you over for dinner", especially when you see the "unbelievably reasonable" prices.

	FOOD	DECOR	SERVICE	COST

Buca di Beppo *Italian*   15 | 17 | 17 | $27

Center City West | 258 S. 15th St. (bet. Latimer & Spruce Sts.) |
215-545-2818
Exton | 300 Main St. (Bartlett Ave.) | 610-524-9939
East Norriton | 1 W. Germantown Pike (DeKalb Pike) | 610-272-2822
www.bucadibeppo.com

It can be "fun" to "bring the family" to *mangia* at this "goofy" Italian
chain for "amusement-park" decor "tacky" enough to "induce sei-
zures", a "cheery" staff that embraces the "cheesy" charm and stereo-
typically "gargantuan" portions of dishes including "meatballs as
big as your head"; while fans consider them "guilty pleasures",
many dis the eats as "an insult to Italians everywhere."

☑ Buddakan *Pan-Asian*   26 | 27 | 24 | $56

Old City | 325 Chestnut St. (bet. 3rd & 4th Sts.) | 215-574-9440 |
www.buddakan.com

"Everything you've heard" about Stephen Starr's "theatrical" "see-
and-be-seen" "scene" in Old City is "true": expect "large portions"
of "fabulous" Pan-Asian cuisine to "share" ("black cod? - cod bless
you"), "cool", "streamlined" surroundings, "spot-on" service "under
the smiling Buddha", a "who's who" crowd - and a "noise level" befitting "a construction site"; it's again Philly's Most Popular, so getting a reservation is "like scoring a date with Miss USA."

Bunha Faun *Asian/French*   25 | 12 | 21 | $35

Malvern | 152 Lancaster Pike (¼ mi. east of Morehall Rd.) |
610-651-2836

A transformed Dairy Queen houses this Malvern BYO, a French-
Asian "treasure" full of "locals" who've discovered its "incredible"
food and "attentive" service that "never let you down"; "dull", "minimal" digs, though, take some of the faun out of things.

NEW Buona Via *Italian*   ▽ 19 | 18 | 19 | $42

Horsham | 426 Horsham Rd. (Highland Ave.) | 215-672-5595

Italian food-loving Horshamites have followed the former
Ristorante Mediterraneo to its new location (about one mile away)
where dishes of "comparably" "fine quality" are served in "larger"
quarters; if the "noisy" dining room "feels like a cafeteria", at least
the (same) owners try to "please their clientele."

Butterfish *American*   25 | 20 | 22 | $38

West Chester | East Bradford Shops | 700 W. Nields St. (Bradford Ave.) |
610-738-8800 | www.butterfishrestaurant.com

"Melt-in-your-mouth" house-smoked fish plus other "interesting"
New American fare and "fine" service draw "quite the following" to
this "lovely" BYO (sibling of Spence Cafe) just outside West Chester;
bring your "sweetie" and "earphones" because it can get "very" loud.

Byblos ◐ *Mediterranean*   16 | 16 | 16 | $29

Center City West | 114 S. 18th St. (bet. Chestnut & Sansom Sts.) |
215-568-3050

At this "chill" Center City Mediterranean, you can sample "good,
simple" food at lunch and dinner, but "the scene changes quickly

later in the evening" when they crank up the music and "bring on the hookahs" for a "smokin' good time."

NEW Cafe Coláo ⊠ *Puerto Rican* — | — | — | I

Northern Liberties | 1305 N. Fifth St. (Thompson St.) | 215-232-0240
In this tidy, spartan storefront cafe on the edge of Northern Liberties, a homesick Puerto Rican chef cooks hearty breakfasts along with island specialties like *tostones* (fried green plantains), *mofongo* (green plantains smashed with garlic and gravy) and *chuleta* (fried pork chop); for the less adventurous, there's a small roster of sandwiches, burgers and cheese steaks.

Cafe de Laos *Laotian/Thai* 24 | 18 | 21 | $24

South Philly | 1117 S. 11th St. (bet. Ellsworth St. & Washington Ave.) | 215-467-1546
"Adventurous" Asia-philes are pleasantly "surprised" to find "real", "superb" Laotian and Thai cuisine at this "pretty" BYO in an "otherwise unappealing stretch" near South Philly's Italian Market; the "calming" interior is "like stepping into another world", and the servers "know the food and take pride in it, as they should."

NEW Café Estelle *American* — | — | — | I

Northern Liberties | 444 N. Fourth St. (Spring Garden St.) | 215-925-5080 | www.cafeestelle.com
On the Northern Liberties–Old City border, this sleek, industrial-looking mom-and-pop cafe in a business center just off the Ben Franklin Bridge is a convenient stop for a breakfast meeting, a quick panini lunch or an early casual (and inexpensive) dinner.

Cafe Fresko ⊠≠ *Mediterranean* 22 | 17 | 20 | $37

Bryn Mawr | 1003 W. Lancaster Ave. (Warner Ave.) | 610-581-7070 | www.cafefresko.com
Plan on bumping into "someone you know" at the Pappas family's snug, "homey" BYO, whose "Greek-diner friendliness and efficiency" and "rich", "delish" Med fare add up to a "welcome change for the Main Line"; some say it's best to "go on a weeknight" when it's not nearly as "hectic" and you can "hear yourself think."

Cafe Preeya Ⓜ *Eclectic* 21 | 15 | 21 | $35

Huntingdon Valley | Village Ctr. | 2651 Huntingdon Pike (Red Lion Rd.) | 215-947-6195 | www.cafepreeya.com
Here are three good reasons this "quiet" Thai-influenced Eclectic BYO in a Huntingdon Valley strip center is a longtime "favorite": "consistently excellent" food, "wonderful" service and parking; if some preeya they "update" the decor, more "can't wait to go back."

Cafe Spice *Indian* 20 | 19 | 19 | $31

Old City | 35 S. Second St. (bet. Chestnut & Market Sts.) | 215-627-6273
Cafe Spice Express *Indian*
Center City West | Liberty Pl. | 1625 Chestnut St. (16th St.) | 215-496-9580 | www.cafespice.com
"Young" and "beautiful" "hipsters" favor this "chic", "urban" Indian, an NYC import in Old City's "party district" known for its "helpful"

staff serving "delish", affordable fare and for late-night "dance club" action; the Liberty Place venue is more suited to quick meals.

Cafette *Eclectic*   20 | 15 | 19 | $23

Chestnut Hill | 8136 Ardleigh St. (Hartwell Ln.) | 215-242-4220 | www.cafette.com

"Awesome fried chicken" on Friday nights, "vegetarian options" aplenty and weekend brunch that's "a reason to get out of bed" explain why this "cute", "quirky" Eclectic BYO "on a Chestnut Hill backstreet" is always "packed with locals"; apart from some quibbles about service, most find it "charming", especially on the "lovely" patio.

Caffe Casta Diva ⊠Ⓜ⇎ *Italian*   24 | 17 | 21 | $37

Center City West | 227 S. 20th St. (Locust St.) | 215-496-9677

Among the multitude of Italian BYOs, this "jewel" in a "converted" apartment near Rittenhouse Square "stands out" with "beautiful" food and "friendly" service; it attracts a crowd, and bear in mind that "close", "intimate" quarters can mean "you hear everything your dinner neighbors have to say."

NEW Cake Ⓜ *Bakery*   21 | 23 | 18 | $19

Chestnut Hill | 8501 Germantown Ave. (Highland Ave.) | 215-247-6887

Housed in an "atriumlike", "sunny" "glass conservatory", this "adorable" Chestnut Hill bakery-cum-cafe is "packed" with locals for lunch, brunch and, Thursdays-only, BYO dinner; "come early" or "be prepared to wait" for "garden-fresh" salads, "creative" soups, sandwiches – and, natch, "great" cakes.

California Cafe *Californian*   20 | 19 | 19 | $35

King of Prussia | Plaza at King of Prussia Mall | 160 N. Gulph Rd. (bet. DeKalb Pike & Mall Blvd.) | 610-354-8686 | www.californiacafe.com

"When you need a civilized break from shopping", try this King of Prussia "safe house" vending "serious" Californian food and "liquid therapy" amid the Plaza's "madhouse" setting; it's a natural choice for those who also want "quality" in a sea of food court choices, though it is a "little pricey."

California Pizza Kitchen *Pizza*   19 | 14 | 17 | $23

Wynnefield | 4040 City Ave. (Monument Rd.) | 215-473-7010
King of Prussia | King of Prussia Mall | 470 Mall Blvd. (DeKalb Pike) | 610-337-1500
NEW Plymouth Meeting | 514 W. Germantown Pike (Hickory Rd.) | 610-828-8232
www.cpk.com

"Surprisingly good" food suits frazzled moods at this King of Prussia mall chain pizzeria providing an "escape from the crowds" in the food court; the "'80s" environs "sag a bit", but "tasty", "trendy" pizzas and salads "fortify" shoppers for the "traffic they'll face inside and outside"; P.S. fellow diners "don't mind your kids acting up because they brought theirs too"; N.B. Plymouth Meeting now has a slice of the California Pizza pie.

	FOOD	DECOR	SERVICE	COST

Campo's Deli ⊘ *Cheese Steaks* — 22 | 11 | 16 | $12

Old City | 214 Market St. (Strawberry St.) | 215-923-1000 |
www.phillyhoagie.com

Take "out-of-towners" or drop in on your own to the Campo family's
"affordable" Old City hoagiery for "great" sandwiches loaded with
"first-rate" fillings; they offer "arguably some of the best" goods
around, and "fast", yet "friendly" "whaddya-want" service helps
keep things moving.

Cantina Los Caballitos ● *Mexican* — 21 | 19 | 18 | $25

South Philly | 1651 E. Passyunk Ave. (bet. Morris & 12th Sts.) |
215-755-3550 | www.cantinaloscaballitos.com

NEW Cantina Dos Segundos *Mexican*

Northern Liberties | 931 N. Second St. (Wildey St.) | 215-629-0500 |
www.cantinadossegundos.com

South Philly's "growing" population of "young hipsters" "overruns"
this "festive", "campy" cantina for "innovative" Mexican *comidas*
and "killer cocktails"; "pretty darn good" prices extend to a "wonderful" tequila selection (40 varieties) that forms the basis of "great"
happy-hour $10 pitchers slung by "friendly" staffers; N.B. the
Northern Liberties outpost recently debuted.

⨅ Capital Grille, The *Steak* — 26 | 23 | 24 | $64

Avenue of the Arts | 1338 Chestnut St. (Broad St.) | 215-545-9588 |
www.thecapitalgrille.com

"You get what you pay for" at this "swanky", "old-school" Center
City beefery (one of the "best chain steakhouses, hands-down"), a
"Grand Central Station" for the city's "movers and shakers" who
gleefully "break out the platinum card" for "prime" cuts that "cost a
car payment" and "professional" service that meets "expectations";
the "always-packed" bar attracts a "suit-and-briefcase" crowd that
knows to "watch out" for those pineapple-infused Stoli Dolis and
other specialty drinks.

Carambola ⨅ *American* — 23 | 14 | 18 | $37

Dresher | Dreshertown Plaza | 1650 Limekiln Pike (Dreshertown Rd.) |
215-542-0900 | www.carambolabyo.com

This "grown-up" New American BYO in a Montco strip mall
makes its mark with "stylish" presentations of "amazing" food
that rivals what's offered at "some of Philly's finest"; while critics
condemn "noise", "attitude" and "no reservations" (dinner), the
majority reasons that the "consistently excellent" kitchen atones
for any negatives.

Caribou Cafe *French* — 19 | 19 | 18 | $33

Center City East | 1126 Walnut St. (bet. 11th & 12th Sts.) |
215-625-9535

"Ooh-la-la" rave Francophiles who flash back to "Paris vacations" at
this "classic" bistro in Wash West offering "hearty" Gallic "favorites" and "retro" aperitifs; if some suggest the service needs "an upgrade", the "affordable" prix fixe menu (three courses, $29), "lovely"
outdoor seating and weekend jazz help appease.

Carman's Country Kitchen ⊅ *Eclectic*   25 | 15 | 20 | $19
South Philly | 1301 S. 11th St. (Wharton St.) | 215-339-9613
"Bring your friends – not your parents" to Carman Luntzel's "funky",
R-rated South Philly breakfast/brunch BYO for "amazing" Eclectic
fare (the Food score rose four points in this Survey) that "tran-
scends" the "quirky" decor – a collection of phallic statues; the
"friendly" vibe extends to "personalized" service – and that's no
phallacy; N.B. open Fridays–Mondays, 8 AM–2 PM.

Carmine's Creole Cafe ⓜ *Cajun/Creole*   22 | 18 | 20 | $42
Bryn Mawr | 818 W. Lancaster Ave. (Bryn Mawr Ave.) | 610-520-9100 |
www.carminescafeonline.com
Those "lusting" for "authentic", "crazy good", "can-you-stand-the-
heat" Cajun-Creole cooking find it at John Mims' "sexy" salon in Bryn
Mawr that "always" "jumps" with "excitement" (there's a "full-
volume" blues band on weekends); the "unique experience" includes
a "noise level" that's sometimes reminiscent of "jackhammers."

Carversville Inn ⓜ *Southern*   ∇ 22 | 20 | 22 | $47
Carversville | 6205 Fleecydale Rd. (Aquetong Rd.) | 215-297-0900
"Authentically Colonial" is this "cozy" historic Bucks inn by the
Delaware in Carversville warming souls with a "lovely" fireplace for
"cold nights"; most feel rewarded with "reliable" Southern food and
"charming" service, and if you "need a bloodhound" to find it, many
agree it's "well worth" sniffing out.

Casablanca *Moroccan*   ∇ 21 | 23 | 23 | $36
Wynnefield | 7557 Haverford Ave. (City Ave.) | 215-878-1900 |
www.casablancarestaurants.com
Warrington | Warrington Mews Plaza | 1111 Easton Rd. (Bristol Rd.) |
215-343-7715 | www.casablancaone.com
These separately owned Moroccans are an "experience", offering
"amazing" seven-course feasts "eaten with your hands", and best
"worked off between courses" by joining "the belly dancer" (weekend nights only); "outstanding" service and "beautiful" decor seal
the deal; N.B. Warrington is BYO while Wynnefield serves alcohol.

Cassatt Tea Room & Garden *Tearoom*   ∇ 23 | 27 | 23 | $34
Center City West | Rittenhouse Hotel | 210 W. Rittenhouse Sq.
(bet. Locust & Walnut Sts.) | 215-546-9000 | www.rittenhousehotel.com
The "precious" atmosphere alone makes this "feminine" tearoom
(open 2–5 PM) just off the lobby of the "tony" Rittenhouse Hotel an
"amazing find" for fans craving "delightful" mini-sandwiches and
"decadent" scones, pastries and whatnot, all for a tuppence; "add
champagne" to the mix and "before you know it", you'll be in such a
swoon that you'll need to "rent a suite upstairs."

Catherine's ⓩⓜ *American*   24 | 21 | 23 | $45
Unionville | General Store | 1701 W. Doe Run Rd. (Rte. 82) |
610-347-2227 | www.catherinesrestaurant.com
You may "need the flashlight" supplied to diners to read the menu at
this dimly lit New American–Southwestern BYO in an "intimate"

converted general store in Chester County, but the effort is rewarded by "an eclectic mix" of "outstanding" fare served with a dose of "country-casual" "charm"; N.B. patio seating is a good bet.

Cebu ▣ *Eclectic*

− | 21 | 16 | M

Old City | 123 Chestnut St. (2nd St.) | 215-629-1100 | www.cebuphiladelphia.com

The "grand" atmosphere at this "high-ceilinged" "converted bank" in Old City hasn't changed, but recently the menu has, moving from Filipino to an Eclectic 'dipping grill' concept in which meat, fish and vegetable entrees are served with a choice of dipping sauce; an assortment of international appetizers remains for the bar and late-night crowd.

Cedar Hollow Inn *American*

20 | 19 | 19 | $39

Malvern | 2455 Yellow Springs Rd. (Rte. 29) | 610-296-9006 | www.cedarhollowinn.com

Locals know all about this Malvern New American for a "quiet lunch" "hidden away" near "corporate America"; many applaud "good" eats, while others opt to deal with "noise" from the bar that attracts an "after-work" following.

Cedars *Lebanese*

∇ 19 | 12 | 22 | $25

South St. | 616 S. Second St. (bet. Bainbridge & South Sts.) | 215-925-4950 | www.cedarsrestaurant.com

Word is the "price is right" for "solid" falafel and other Middle Eastern "comfort" food at this "quiet", "family-run" Queen Village Lebanese off South Street (a sibling of Fez and Byblos); the "no-frills" environs aren't an issue given that it's "great" for takeout.

Celebre's Pizzeria ◗ *Pizza*

24 | 10 | 17 | $14

South Philly | Packer Park Shopping Ctr. | 1536 Packer Ave. (Broad St.) | 215-467-3255

If you need a pizza "fix" with "the family" before a game at the sports complex, this "standby" purveying "tasty" pies is an obvious choice; you're assured of "friendly", "South Philly"-style service – and "strip-mall" decor that some may not celebrate, but many overlook.

Centre Bridge Inn, The *American*

∇ 19 | 20 | 20 | $48

New Hope | The Centre Bridge Inn | 2998 N. River Rd. (Upper York Rd.) | 215-862-9139 | www.centrebridgeinn.com

The "beautiful" fireplace on a "winter's night" and "nice view" of the Delaware from the warm-weather patio make this "rustic" New American in New Hope a destination for all seasons; most agree it's a "relative bargain" for the area, with a "cozy bar" and "great wine list" adding to the "enjoyable" experience.

Chabaa Thai Bistro *Thai*

25 | 22 | 21 | $28

Manayunk | 4371 Main St. (Grape St.) | 215-483-1979 | www.chabaathai.com

A "rare treat" is how devotees describe this Thai BYO on the Manayunk strip where the "creative" cooking of "smiling, hospitable" chef-owner Moon Krapugthong is "attentively" served in "cramped" but "cozy" surroundings with a "Zen"-like feel; the "work-of-art" dishes are complemented by an upper-level art gallery; N.B. reservations are a must.

Charles Plaza Chinese   23 | 13 | 23 | $25

Chinatown | 234-236 N. 10th St. (Vine St.) | 215-829-4383

"Light", "healthful" Mandarin meals and "impressive" service "with a smile" from "one-of-a-kind" chef-owner Charles Chen "himself" make this Chinatown BYO a "haven" for vegetarians ("lots of variety") and those who don't want "tons of grease"; though the atmosphere "could use updating", it's still a "favorite."

Charlie's Hamburgers ⊅ Burgers   ∇ 24 | 7 | 19 | $10

Folsom | 336 Kedron Ave. (Macdade Blvd.) | 610-461-4228

"Awesome", "cheap" burgers are "made fresh in front of you" at this "real-deal" Delco "no-frills" shack, where you belly up to the "friendly" counter, order "two" and wash 'em down with "high-grade" milkshakes; if it's "bad for you" who cares since it's "out of this world"; N.B. closed Tuesdays.

Chart House Seafood   18 | 22 | 18 | $49

Delaware Riverfront | Penn's Landing | 555 S. Columbus Blvd. (Lombard Circle) | 215-625-8383 | www.chart-house.com

Surveyors are split on this chain surf 'n' turfer on Penn's Landing; while fans claim "they know what they're doing" and urge "impressing a date" with "good food" and a "beautiful view" of the Delaware, detractors "walk the plank" over "average" eats and "slow" pacing; P.S. despite the disagreement, Sunday brunch "with mom" seems a safe bet.

Cheeseburger in Paradise Burgers   15 | 16 | 15 | $20

Langhorne | 750 Middletown Blvd. (Lincoln Hwy.) | 215-757-3179 | www.cheeseburgerinparadise.com

"Take the kids" for some "fun" at this Jimmy Buffett–inspired American hamburger specialist outside of the Oxford Valley Mall; most parrot the line it's also a "great place to hang at happy hour" amid island-esque digs, though some disagree whether the reasonably priced eats are "good" or "standard" enough to make you conclude "if this is paradise, I'm giving up religion."

⚡ Cheesecake Factory American   20 | 18 | 18 | $28

King of Prussia | Pavilion at King of Prussia Mall | 640 W. DeKalb Pike (bet. Allendale & Long Rds.) | 610-337-2200

NEW Willow Grove | Willow Grove Park Mall | 2500 W. Moreland Rd. (Easton Rd.) | 215-659-0270

www.thecheesecakefactory.com

"Tasty" options from an "encyclopedic" American menu served in "ginormous" portions ("enough to share") and capped by "awesome" cheesecake draw multitudes to this "mallish" "upscale-casual" chain for "gorgefests"; count on "enthusiastic" if "hit-or-miss" service and "interminable", "Rip van Winkle"-esque waits – so try "off-hours."

	FOOD	DECOR	SERVICE	COST

Chef Charin ☑ Continental
▽ 20 | 9 | 20 | $31

Bala Cynwyd | 126 Bala Ave. (bet. City & Montgomery Aves.) |
610-667-8680 | www.chefcharin.com

Those on their way to the flicks fuel up at this "tiny" Continental
BYO in a Bala storefront for "good" (if "acceptable" to some) dinners and service that "tries to please and often succeeds"; "lack of
frills" in decor strikes fans as "low-key" and others as a call to
"freshen things up."

Chestnut Grill & Sidewalk Cafe American
17 | 15 | 17 | $28

Chestnut Hill | Chestnut Hill Hotel | 8229 Germantown Ave.
(Southampton Ave.) | 215-247-7570 |
www.chestnuthillhotel.com

You'll "fit right in" if you "dress preppy" and sit outside on the patio to watch "the scene" at this "family-friendly" Traditional
American in the Chestnut Hill Hotel; they employ "some of the
friendliest and attentive" servers around (especially when
"smaller children" are present), and the "good", "consistent" comfort food is "affordable."

Chez Colette French
20 | 19 | 20 | $44

Center City West | Sofitel Philadelphia | 120 S. 17th St. (Sansom St.) |
215-569-8300 | www.sofitel.com

The few who've been to this "quiet", "unknown" New French in the
Sofitel describe an "easy place to linger and talk" over "tasty" fare at
"power breakfasts" or dinners amid a scene of "French travel post-
ers"; if it's just "ok" and "boring" to some, la majorité disagrees.

Chiangmai Thai
▽ 25 | 18 | 21 | $24

Conshohocken | 108 Fayette St. (1st Ave.) | 610-397-1757

Folks who've found this "charming" Thai in a "dressed-up" Conshy
BYO storefront report "excellent", "beautifully presented" dishes at
"reasonable" prices that never leave you "disappointed"; "good"
service "by family members" is a "plus" at this Thai Orchid offshoot.

Chiarella's Italian
▽ 19 | 16 | 20 | $30

South Philly | 1600 S. 11th St. (Tasker St.) | 215-334-6404 |
www.chiarellasristorante.com

Fans of this "charming" Italian BYO in the "heart" of South Philly off
Passyunk Avenue have "followed" the owners from their former digs
in Wildwood, NJ, for "monstrous" portions of "decent" red-gravy
dishes and service that "makes you feel like family"; though sometimes "loud", that's part of the "fun atmosphere."

☒ Chickie's & Pete's Cafe ☽ Pub Food
18 | 17 | 17 | $24

Northeast Philly | Roosevelt Plaza | 11000 Roosevelt Blvd. (bet. Red Lion &
Woodhaven Rds.) | 215-856-9890
Northeast Philly | 4010 Robbins Ave. (Frankford Ave.) |
215-338-3060 ⊞
South Philly | 1526 Packer Ave. (15th St.) | 215-218-0500
www.chickiesandpetes.com

"Roll up your sleeves" and "be prepared to get messy" over the signature crab fries with cheese and other beer-worthy "finger foods"

at this "classic" sports bar mini-chain, where "hot" waitresses roam the room and "endless plasmas" "rock" "da Iggles" – so for heaven's sake, "don't wear your Dallas jersey."

Chick's Café & Wine Bar *Eclectic*   23 | 22 | 23 | $34

South St. | 614 S. Seventh St. (Bainbridge St.) | 215-625-3700 | www.chickscafe.com

Many are "mesmerized" by the "quaint" Euro milieu at this "romantic" Eclectic "hideaway" in a restored "old men's bar" off South Street, and if a few find the "smartly edited menu" of "delicious" small plates "a bit pricey for the neighborhood", "fine" wines, "knowledgeable" servers and "great" sidewalk seating keep most content.

NEW Chima Brazilian   - | - | - | VE
Steakhouse *Brazilian/Steak*

Center City West | 1901 JFK Blvd. (20th St.) | 215-525-3233 | www.chimasteakhouse.com

Gaucho-suited waiters bearing sizzling meats patrol the swank dining room of this costly Brazilian churrascaria in the Kennedy House near Logan Square; the salad bar teems with vegetables, breads and soups, while the sexily appointed drinks bar lures the happy-hour crowds with light bites.

Chlöe ⊠ⓂⒻ *American*   25 | 16 | 22 | $38

Old City | 232 Arch St. (bet. 2nd & 3rd Sts.) | 215-629-2337 | www.chloebyob.com

The no-reservations/cash-only policy of this "teeny", "unpretentious" mom-and-pop New American BYO across from the Betsy Ross House in Old City doesn't deter devotees from "packing in like sardines" for "inspired" fare that "never disappoints"; just "go early" (and "with your whole party", please) to experience this "old faithful"; N.B. open only for dinner Wednesdays–Saturdays.

Chops *Steak*   19 | 18 | 20 | $52

Bala Cynwyd | 401 City Ave. (bet. Belmond Ave. & Monument Rd.) | 610-668-3400 | www.chops.us

"Power-lunching" Bala businessmen on "expense accounts" and Main Line "families" at dinner wear extra large pants to get their steak on at this "airy" meatery, where "flashy cars outside" betray the "lively" scene inside; the staff's pleasant, but disagreements over the food have fans describing it as "good" and foes labeling it "inconsistent."

Christopher's ☽ *American*   17 | 14 | 18 | $25

Wayne | 108 N. Wayne Ave. (Lancaster Ave.) | 610-687-6558 | www.christophersaneighborhoodplace.com

"Rowdy" kids run amok at this "super-kid-friendly" Wayne New American known as a "hangout for Main Line moms"; the location "is key", the food "inexpensive" and "reliable", and the floor crew "pleasant" (if "slow"), and to avoid the "screamers" who rule at lunch, it's advised to come later for a "more relaxing" setting at dinner or join the bar scene dominated by college students.

	FOOD	DECOR	SERVICE	COST

Chun Hing *Chinese*   22 | 10 | 19 | $22

Wynnefield | Pathmark Shopping Ctr. | 4160 Monument Rd. (City Ave.) | 215-879-6270

"Do not underestimate" this Wynnefield Chinese BYO, an "institution" "unchanged in 30 years" – and that pleases customers to no end; "consistent" offerings ("get the meat dumplings" already), "bargain" rates ("much better" than most in Chinatown) and "attentive" servers keep 'em coming.

CinCin *Chinese*   24 | 18 | 22 | $33

Chestnut Hill | 7838 Germantown Ave. (Springfield Ave.) | 215-242-8800 | www.cincinrestaurant.com

Come be "wowed" by the "downright cin-ful" Chinese cuisine (with a "pinch of French flair") at this "pleasant" mainstay on the Avenue, which "sets the standard" in Chestnut Hill for "creative" menu spins (no "egg foo yong here") and "coolly formal" service; just be "prepared to wait" for a table and a "parking" space.

Z Citrus ⊠Ⓜ⇗ *Eclectic*   25 | 14 | 18 | $34

Chestnut Hill | 8136 Germantown Ave. (bet. Abington Ave. & Hartwell Ln.) | 215-247-8188 | www.citrusbyob.com

"Even hard-core carnivores" find "delicious", "imaginative" vegetarian and seafood dishes ("no land-based meat") at this "tiny" Eclectic BYO in Chestnut Hill, though some find the "intense" political overtone (read: pro animal rights – no fur or shearling allowed on premises) less than peachy, wishing they'd "lose the 'tude, just serve the food."

City Tavern *American*   19 | 25 | 21 | $42

Old City | 138 S. Second St. (Walnut St.) | 215-413-1443 | www.citytavern.com

It's like "dining with George Washington" in this "pseudo-Colonial" Traditional American in a reconstructed "historic landmark" in Old City, replete with "enthusiastic", "period-clad" servers proffering 18th-century-style "comfort" food (e.g. lobster pot pie); whether you'll agree with those who find it "charming" or a "kitschy tourist trap" is debatable.

Clam Tavern *Seafood*   ▽ 21 | 15 | 23 | $31

Clifton Heights | 339 E. Broadway Ave. (Edgemont Ave.) | 610-623-9537 | www.clamtavern.net

When Delco fish fanciers seek "reasonably" priced seafood and "friendly" service, this "neighborhood hangout" (since '62) fills the bill; still, a few crabs carp that the "dark", "1959 diner"-like digs "need updating."

NEW Cochon ⊠Ⓜ⇗ *French*   24 | 18 | 23 | $41

Queen Village | 801 E. Passyunk Ave. (Catharine St.) | 215-923-7675 | www.cochonbyob.com

This "charming" mom-and-pop country French BYO (its name means pig *en français*) in a converted "old butcher shop" in Queen Village goes whole-hog with moderately priced Gallic classics like escargots and – fittingly – "excellent" pork belly and pork chop; the "care-about-their-customers" attitude and "casual" vibe – porcine knickknacks, open kitchen – also help it earn a "thumbs-up."

Cock 'n Bull *American* | 17 | 18 | 20 | $34 |

Lahaska | Peddler's Vill. | Rte. 263 & Street Rd. | 215-794-4010 | www.peddlersvillage.com

This Traditional American comfort-fooder "still holds up" as an ideal spot to "unwind after shopping" in the Peddler's Village and the "proper place to take auntie" for a "terrific" "bargain" brunch; while "fun"-seekers enjoy "murder mystery" theater on weekends, negativists nix the operation as "average" 'n' "touristy."

Coleman Restaurant *American* | 20 | 21 | 21 | $47 |

Blue Bell | Normandy Farm | 1431 Morris Rd. (DeKalb Pike) | 215-616-8300 | www.normandyfarm.com

A "picturesque" setting at Blue Bell's Normandy Farm gives admirers reason to visit "celeb-chef" Jim Coleman's "rustically elegant" New American, and once there, his followers consider the "innovative" meals "calories well spent"; though some look past the "expense", others opine the experience doesn't "match ambitions or prices."

☒ Continental, The *Eclectic* | 22 | 19 | 19 | $36 |

Old City | 138 Market St. (2nd St.) | 215-923-6069 | www.continentalmartinibar.com

The "cornerstone" of Stephen Starr's "empire" still "gets it right", delivering "small plates" of "well-prepared", "trendy" Eclectic eats (the Sichuan shoestring fries are "a tower of deliciousness") plus "killer" martinis (e.g. out-of-this-world "Buzz Aldrins") in a "funky former diner" in Old City complete with booths and sidewalk seats; some snipe "you'll fit right in" "if you're beautiful" – and if you're not they'll "make sure you know it."

☒ Continental Mid-town *Eclectic* | 21 | 23 | 19 | $35 |

Center City West | 1801 Chestnut St. (18th St.) | 215-567-1800 | www.continentalmidtown.com

Stephen Starr's "super-hip", multi-tiered Center City small-plater is a "frenetic" "hangout" for "trendy twentysomethings" drawn by its "groovy" *Jetsons* vibe" and "affordable" Eclectic "comfort food" with a "twist", served by "efficient" "part-time models" and washed down with "lethal drinks" (careful on those "swinging" seats); whether this offspring of the Old City original is "funkier" is debatable, but it's nonetheless a "scene" – especially on the "rooftop deck" – and has more "elbow room."

Copabanana ● *American/Mexican* | 16 | 12 | 15 | $22 |

Northeast Philly | Grant Plaza | 1619 Grant Ave. (Welsh Rd.) | 215-969-1712

South St. | 344 South St. (4th St.) | 215-923-6180

University City | 4000 Spruce St. (40th St.) | 215-382-1330

www.copabanana.com

The "holy trinity" of margaritas, burgers and Spanish fries keeps this "upbeat" Mexican-American bar mini-chain in business; it's "the place to be whether it's noon or midnight", and for those who think the original's digs "look and smell like a frat house", the newer outposts (Grant Avenue and Spruce Street) may address decor shortcomings.

Copper Bistro M *American*
| 22 | 18 | 22 | $37 |

Northern Liberties | 614 N. Second St. (bet. Fairmount Ave. & Spring Garden St.) | 215-627-9844 | www.copperbistro.net
Fans of this "homey" New American BYO in Northern Liberties find it "hard to believe" such "well-prepared", "moderately adventurous" fare from a "concise menu" can come out of Dan Connelly's "teeny" open kitchen; an "attentive", "courteous" staff "and "fresh, simple" atmosphere help make it a "great find" for most.

Coquette Bistro & Raw Bar *French*
| 18 | 20 | 17 | $38 |

South St. | 700 S. Fifth St. (Bainbridge St.) | 215-238-9000 | www.coquettephilly.com
Neighborhood Francophiles aren't coy in their praise for this "low-key" French bistro in Queen Village, citing "tried-and-true" dishes and an "awesome" raw bar; the less convinced point to issues such as "spotty" service, but boosters say with "some tweaks" it could be "what South Street has been waiting for."

Core De Roma M *Italian*
| ▽ 23 | 17 | 24 | $36 |

South St. | 214 South St. (2nd St.) | 215-592-9777 | www.corederoma.us
Locals and tourists roam in to this "welcoming" South Street BYO to savor midpriced Roman-Italian "comfort food "at its best" (try the "sautéed artichokes"); the "*paisan* patter" from chef-owner Luigi Papa Gigi Pinti – who "greets you and seats you" – and the rest of his "incredibly friendly" family are part of the "amazing charm."

Cosimo *American*
| 22 | 19 | 20 | $42 |

Malvern | 209 Lancaster Ave. (Malin Rd.) | 610-647-1233 | www.cosimorestaurant.com
"*In vino veritas*" is the mantra among wine fanciers attracted to the "flights and tastings" of vino (at "various price levels") paired with "imaginative" dishes at this "minimalist" New American in Malvern; what it may lack in "feng shui" it makes up for in an "educated, attentive" staff.

Coyote Crossing *Mexican*
| 20 | 21 | 17 | $36 |

West Chester | 102 E. Market St. (Walnut St.) | 610-429-8900
Conshohocken | 800 Spring Mill Ave. (8th Ave.) | 610-825-3000
At these "lively" Mexicans in the 'burbs, aficionados say "delish margaritas" and "interesting" (if a bit "pricey") *comidas* add up to a "feast", one that's best enjoyed on the porch in Conshy or "must-see" rooftop in West Chester; ambivalent *muchachos* report "clue-less" service and advise "don't believe the hype", but "big crowds" prove they're outvoted.

NEW Cravings ☒ *American*
| 21 | 15 | 17 | $31 |

Lansdale | Station Sq. | 155 Pennbrook Pkwy. (Church Rd.) | 215-855-4500
Admirers feel this New American in Lansdale "lives up to its name" with "substantial" servings of "ambitious" fare; while some laud the

move to roomier quarters (complete with bar) in Station Square, others opine the "open" dining room could use more "warmth"; an adjacent cafe offers coffee, desserts and a take-out area.

Creed's Seafood & Steaks ◪ *Seafood/Steak*   23 | 21 | 22 | $52

King of Prussia | 499 N. Gulph Rd. (Pennsylvania Tpke.) | 610-265-2550 | www.creedskop.com

For "first-class" dining in King of Prussia, check out this "somewhat hidden", white-tablecloth surf 'n' turfer, where a "leisurely" meal of "excellent" steaks and seafood is "worth the trip" according to admirers; yes, it's "pricey", but "very good" service and "entertaining" weekend music are compensations.

Cresheim Cottage Cafe Ⓜ *American*   18 | 22 | 18 | $35

Mount Airy | 7402 Germantown Ave. (Gowen Ave.) | 215-248-4365 | www.cresheimcottage.com

An "inviting" setting in a "secluded" circa-1706 cottage is the main draw at this "cozy" Mount Airy New American with an "amazing" summer patio and "roaring" winter fireplace; while the midpriced menu garners mixed marks ("innovative" vs. "hit-or-miss"), it's nonetheless deemed a "charming" stop for locals and "the wayward traveler."

Criniti *Italian*   19 | 17 | 20 | $26

South Philly | 2611 S. Broad St. (Shunk St.) | 215-465-7750

Fans of this "traditional" South Philly Italian in a "former church" reflect on a "divine experience" in the form of "attentive" servers and "heaping portions" of "reliably good" "old-fashioned" food; fairly "close" proximity "to the stadiums" also answer prayers.

◪ Cuba Libre *Cuban*   21 | 25 | 20 | $41

Old City | 10 S. Second St. (bet. Chestnut & Market Sts.) | 215-627-0666 | www.cubalibrerestaurant.com

Aficionados say *viva* to the "colorful" tropical setting that "transports you" to "pre-Castro Cuba" at this Latin star in Old City, where a "beautiful-people" crowd digs into the "tempting" dishes of Guillermo Pernot (ex ¡Pasión!) and downs "must-have" mojitos that inspire lots of "hip-wiggling" to salsa on weekends; P.S. bring "extra ka-ching" if you plan to explore the "rum menu."

Cucina Forte Ⓜ *Italian*   24 | 14 | 21 | $34

South Philly | 768 S. Eighth St. (Catharine St.) | 215-238-0778

Insiders claim "you don't know gnocchi" until you've tried Maria Forte's at her old-world BYO in a "cute, little" converted row house; for fans, it's South Philly Italian "at its best" – "like eating at mom's", including good "value" and "pleasant" service.

Cuttalossa Inn, The ◪ *American*   ▽ 16 | 22 | 16 | $41

Lumberville | 3487 River Rd. (Cuttalossa Rd.) | 215-297-5082

A "gorgeous" setting in Upper Bucks is the main claim to fame of this "cozy", circa-1758 Traditional American inn; the "decent" food takes a back seat to the surroundings and some say "you're paying a premium for the location", but romantics conclude it's "worth it", especially in summer on the "wonderful" patio overlooking a 30-ft. waterfall.

	FOOD	DECOR	SERVICE	COST

Dahlak *Eritrean*

22	16	20	$20

Germantown | 5547 Germantown Ave. (Maplewood Ave.) | 215-849-0788 **M**

University City | 4708 Baltimore Ave. (bet. 47th & 48th Sts.) | 215-726-6464

www.dahlakrestaurant.com

East African enthusiasts "eat with their hands" at these West Philly and Germantown Eritrean siblings dishing out "family-style" food; sit at "low tables" and soak up "fantastic", fairly priced eats and an ambiance warmed by "courteous" service, then hang with a "diverse" crowd at the bar in back.

Dalessandro's Steaks ● ☒ ⌿ *Cheese Steaks*

24	6	17	$10

Roxborough | 600 Wendover St. (Henry Ave.) | 215-482-5407

"If they serve cheese steaks in heaven" they must order them from this Roxborough "hole-in-the-wall" cheer fans who venture away from "touristy" Ninth Street for these "meaty", "awesome" sandwiches slathered in "fried peppers" and served by the "coolest rushed staff around"; N.B. scores don't reflect a post-Survey ownership change

D'Angelo's Ristorante Italiano ● ☒ *Italian*

18	15	19	$42

Center City West | 256 S. 20th St. (bet. Locust & Spruce Sts.) | 215-546-3935 | www.dangeloristorante.com

This Italian red-sauce "staple" off Rittenhouse Square pleases an "older crowd" with "basic" but "good" fare ("lots of garlic") and a staff that "makes you feel like part of the family"; if the decor's "outdated", compensations include an active "bar scene" and DJ nights that conjure up images of *"Saturday Night Fever."*

Dante & Luigi's ☒ ⌿ *Italian*

23	16	21	$37

South Philly | 762 S. 10th St. (Catharine St.) | 215-922-9501 | www.danteandluigis.com

This "red-gravy", cash-only Italian is still strong after more than 100 years, serving "delicious" veal among a "reliable" lineup of classics; yeah, the setting is *"Godfather"*-esque and it may get flak from some who think it "lives on reputation", but for the majority, it's "great" because it's "what South Philly is all about."

Dark Horse Pub ● *Pub Food*

17	15	18	$26

Society Hill | 421 S. Second St. (Pine St.) | 215-928-9307 | www.darkhorsepub.com

Hardly a dark-horse choice if seeking an "easygoing neighborhood" hang, this "friendly", multiroom British pub on Head House Square provides the requisite brews plus "unpretentious" bar food and TVs for watching the likes of "Arsenal vs. Man U"; the "fun crowd" of "regulars" equals "entertainment at no extra charge."

Dave & Buster's *American*

13	15	12	$26

Delaware Riverfront | Pier 19 N. | 325 N. Columbus Blvd. (bet. Callowhill & Spring Garden Sts.) | 215-413-1951

FOOD | DECOR | SERVICE | COST

(continued)

Dave & Buster's

Northeast Philly | Franklin Mills Mall | 1995 Franklin Mills Circle
(Woodhaven Rd.) | 215-632-0333
www.daveandbusters.com

"Stay in your kids' good graces" and "bring a bundle of money" for all the video games and other entertainment to this behemoth chain of a playground-cum-eatery on the Delaware Riverfront; sure, since it's the "Chuck E. Cheese's for adults", the American fare is "a passing thought", and if the "sensory overload" starts to kick in, there's beer just in case; N.B. a Plymouth Meeting outpost is slated for summer 2008.

Davio's *Italian*

23 | 22 | 24 | $52

Center City West | Provident Bank Bldg. | 111 S. 17th St. (bet. Chestnut & Sansom Sts.) | 215-563-4810 | www.davios.com

"Get spoiled" along with the "power" crowd at this "clubby" Center City Northern Italian steakhouse in a historic bank building, where an "impeccable" staff proffers "outstanding" food and wine for "expense-account" dinners or "special occasions"; yes, some find it "over the top" – and not just because of the "soaring" ceilings – but others say if you "want to impress, go here."

Day by Day *American/Eclectic*

21 | 11 | 21 | $18

Center City West | 2101 Sansom St. (21st St.) | 215-564-5540 | www.daybydayinc.com

Fans rave about the "freshly prepared" weekday lunches and "even better" Sunday brunches chosen from an "imaginative" Eclectic-American menu at this "informal" BYO "institution" (27 years and counting) near Rittenhouse Square, where "speedy" service is the norm; "large" windows, a new paint job and twinkle lights brighten the "funky charm"; N.B. closed Saturdays.

Delmonico's Steakhouse *Steak*

∇ 20 | 19 | 20 | $56

Wynnefield | Hilton Philadelphia City Ave. | 4200 City Ave. (Stout St.) | 215-879-4000

"Your bovine desires" will be fulfilled at this "traditional" chophouse exuding "old-world charm", which flies under the radar in the Hilton Philadelphia on City Avenue; if some have found it "inconsistent", adherents report "superb" steaks, a "quiet, leisurely" pace and "attentive" staff.

Derek's *American*

19 | 19 | 19 | $37

Manayunk | 4411 Main St. (bet. Gay & Levering Sts.) | 215-483-9400 | www.dereksrestaurant.com

Admirers of Derek Davis' Manayunk New American "standby" applaud its "creative menu" showcasing "well-crafted" "tasty" small plates; the digs offer some of the best "people-watching" in the area, with bars on each floor catering to the clientele with fancy drinks and half-price wines on Sundays; still, some say to expect "some inconsistency", noting that service is "friendly" if at-times "overwhelmed."

	FOOD	DECOR	SERVICE	COST

Devil's Alley *BBQ*

19 | 16 | 18 | $24

Center City West | 1907 Chestnut St. (19th St.) | 215-751-0707 |
www.devilsalleybarandgrill.com

Fans of this barbecue joint near Rittenhouse Square find the "finger-lickin' good" ribs, burgers (beef or veggie) and other "modernized" "bar food" right up their alley; if some deem it "uneven" and call the digs "rough around the edges", a "cute" "hipster" staff, "happy-hour specials" and tabs that "won't break the bank" compensate.

🆕 Devil's Den ❶ *American*

– | – | – | M

South Philly | 1148 S. 11th St. (Ellsworth St.) | 215-339-0855

Beer aficionados needn't sell their souls to savor the flavors at this rustic New American in South Philly where 16 taps spout a thoughtful selection of drafts and dozens of arcane brews are available by the bottle; the midpriced noshes run from the usual fried suspects to more ambitious gastropub grub.

Devon Seafood Grill *Seafood*

23 | 20 | 20 | $44

Center City West | 225 S. 18th St. (bet. Locust & Walnut Sts.) |
215-546-5940 | www.devonseafood.com

This "upscale" Rittenhouse Square chain seafooder is "first-class all the way", with "fish so fresh you can imagine the wiggle" and "must-order" crab cakes dispensed by a "smart", "witty" staff; "people-watching" around the "raw bar" is part of the happening "happy-hour" "experience" – as is the "loud din."

Dilworthtown Inn *American*

25 | 25 | 25 | $62

West Chester | 1390 Old Wilmington Pike (bet. Pleasant Grove & Street Rds.) | 610-399-1390 | www.dilworthtown.com

This "grande dame" of "destination-dining" near West Chester is guaranteed to "impress" with "impeccable" New American cuisine and wine proffered by "professionals" in a "romantic" circa-1758 "country"-inn setting; some find it too "formal" (read: jackets suggested) and "expensive", but believers boast that this "timeless classic" is well "worth the price."

DiNardo's Famous Seafood *Seafood*

19 | 12 | 17 | $35

Old City | 312 Race St. (bet. 3rd & 4th Sts.) | 215-925-5115 |
www.dinardos.com

Crabs good enough "to dive for" is the hook at this "kitschy" "family favorite" of a seafooder in a "nondescript" Old City building, where fans hit the "awesome" hard shells and servers "give you a lesson in cracking"; in sum, it's "the best you're going to get this side of Baltimore."

🆕 Distrito *Mexican*

– | – | – | M

University City | 3945 Chestnut St. (40th St.) | 215-222-1657 |
www.distritorestaurant.com

As we go to press, chef Jose Garces (Amada, Tinto) goes south of the border with this high-energy, bi-level 250-seat Mex in University City featuring contemporary takes on classic *comidas* from Mexico City, complemented by cocktails and 60 varieties of tequila; decor details include a wall showcasing 600 masks worn by professional Mexican wrestlers and a booth made from a VW Beetle.

Divan Turkish Kitchen *Turkish*
21 | 15 | 19 | $30

South Philly | 918 S. 22nd St. (Carpenter St.) | 215-545-5790 | www.divanturkishkitchen.com

You'll find "hearty" helpings of "flavorful", "reasonably priced" Turkish cuisine at this "delight" in the "transitional" Graduate Hospital area; "charming" staffers "keep the pita" and kebabs coming amid "warm" decor; N.B. there's a liquor license but you can BYO (no corkage fee Mondays–Thursdays; $10-a-bottle corkage fee Fridays–Sundays).

Django *European*
25 | 19 | 21 | $44

South St. | 526 S. Fourth St. (South St.) | 215-922-7151

"Spot on, as always" sizes up the sentiment on Ross Essner's "funky", "delightful" Euro storefront BYO, a Queen Village "destination" that has acolytes djazzed over "innovative" cuisine that's "still full of surprises"; alas, even with reservations, the wait can be "unfathomable", so "bring an extra bottle of wine" to help cope.

☒ Dmitri's *Greek*
25 | 14 | 20 | $31

Center City West | 2227 Pine St. (23rd St.) | 215-985-3680
Queen Village | 795 S. Third St. (Catharine St.) | 215-625-0556 ⌐

For "heavenly" Hellenic seafood (e.g. "Jules Verne"-size octopus) suitable for the "Greek gods", Dmitri Chimes' "bare-bones" "stalwarts" "set the standard"; the "no-rez" policies and "tight" quarters (you're practically on your neighbor's "lap") are worth it since you'll waddle out "with a full belly" – and wallet; N.B. Queen Village is BYO and doesn't take credit cards.

NEW Dock Street ☒ *Pub Food*
18 | 12 | 15 | $19

University City | 701 S. 50th St. (Baltimore Ave.) | 215-726-2337 | www.dockstreetbeer.com

"Inventive" beers (at least six on tap) brewed on-premises are the calling card of this "edgy", "up-and-coming" West Philly pub in an old firehouse also offering "cool-looking" growlers-to-go and "crispy" wood-fired pizzas and such; all in all it's a "great hangout" for Penn Quakers, even if the "slow kitchen" can mean "long waits."

Doc Magrogan's Oyster House *Seafood*
16 | 17 | 15 | $34

West Chester | 117 E. Gay St. (Walnut St.) | 610-429-4046 | www.docmagrogans.com

Surveyors are split on this "old-time"-y pub and oyster house in West Chester (from the folks behind Kildare's Irish pub chain): while fans cheerfully "drop in" for a "low-key", "ocean-inspired" evening (particularly at the "upstairs bar", open Thursdays–Saturdays), tepid ratings side with those who find it "run-of-the-mill."

Dolce ☒☒ *Italian*
21 | 20 | 19 | $38

Old City | 241 Chestnut St. (3rd St.) | 215-238-9983 | www.dolcerestaurant.com

Admirers have a sweet spot for this "trendy" Old City ristorante-cum-nightclub fusing "authentic", "above-average" Italian fare with "hip", "dark" decor distinguished by a floor with changing colored lights; it can get "noisy" on weekends but the "twentysomethings don't seem to mind."

Down Home Diner ∌ *Southern*
18 | **11** | **16** | **$17**

Center City East | Reading Terminal Mkt. | 51 N. 12th St. (Filbert St.) | 215-627-1955

"When you miss that truck stop in Georgia", Jack McDavid's "Philly classic" in the "buzzing" Reading Terminal Market comes a callin' with "stick-to-your-ribs" Southern goods and "excellent" breakfasts; as with the chow, the name aptly describes the "what-can-I-get-you, dear" service and "plain" decor.

Drafting Room *American*
18 | **14** | **19** | **$28**

Exton | Colonial 100 Shops | 635 N. Pottstown Pike (Ship Rd.) | 610-363-0521
Spring House | 900 N. Bethlehem Pike (Norristown Rd.) | 215-646-6116
www.draftingroom.com

Brewhounds "come to worship" at these "rocking" suburban "shrines to beer" (with 16 national microbrews on tap) that also offer "tasty spins" on "adventurous" New American and pub food; yes, some feel "makeovers" are in order, but for most they're a suds lover's "dream."

Duck Sauce Ⓜ *Chinese*
25 | **17** | **22** | **$26**

Newtown | 127 S. State St. (bet. Mercer & Penn Sts.) | 215-860-8873

All of Bucks goes daffy for the "interesting" mix of "classic" Chinese and "ambitious" Pan-Asian creations at this "trendy", well-priced BYO in Newtown that's considered "two cuts above" the norm; regulars suggest you bring "an extra bottle" for "while you wait for a table."

🇿 Duling-Kurtz House & Country Inn *Continental*
25 | **26** | **25** | **$52**

Exton | Duling-Kurtz House & Country Inn | 146 S. Whitford Rd. (Lincoln Hwy.) | 610-524-1830 | www.dulingkurtz.com

"Old-time elegance" and "European charm" abound at this "posh" Chesco Continental destination delivering "top-notch", "special-occasion" dining complemented by a "fine" wine list and "impeccable" service; it's "a sure winner" in a "beautiful" setting (jackets suggested); N.B. a new chef arrived post-Survey.

Earl's Prime *Seafood/Steak*
24 | **24** | **23** | **$59**

Lahaska | Peddler's Vill. | Rte. 202 & Street Rd. | 215-794-4020 | www.peddlersvillage.com

"Outstanding" steaks and seafood are complemented by a "surprisingly sophisticated" setting at this Bucks County carnivorium plopped inside the "rural" "tourist haven" of Peddler's Village; though some are nonplussed by the "prime prices", others feel the "attentive" service, "upscale" atmosphere ("beautiful artwork everywhere") and "excellent" wine list help make it "worth it."

| | FOOD | DECOR | SERVICE | COST |

Ecco Qui ⊠ *Italian* — 17 | 14 | 17 | $22
University City | Left Bank | 3200 Chestnut St. (32nd St.) | 215-222-3226 | www.eccoqui.com
This "value"-oriented Italian (with Latin influences) set amid the "chaos" of University City caters to Drexel and Penn students and staff with brick-oven pizzas and other "well-prepared" staples; on warm days, the patio is a "lively" place for happy-hour deals.

Effie's *Greek* — 21 | 15 | 19 | $26
Center City East | 1127 Pine St. (Quince St.) | 215-592-8333
"Get the sampler platter" because "you'll want to try everything" at the Boukidis family's "quaint" and "cute" Greek BYO in Center City; "unbelievably low" tabs accompany the "hands-down delicious" fare served "with love" by people who "take pride" in what they do; P.S. the "waits are worthwhile", especially in the "lovely" courtyard.

El Azteca *Mexican* — 18 | 10 | 17 | $20
Northeast Philly | 1710 Grant Ave. (Bustleton Ave.) | 215-969-3422
El Azteca II ⊠ *Mexican*
Center City East | 714 Chestnut St. (bet. 7th & 8th Sts.) | 215-733-0895 | www.elazteca2.net
For "straightforward" Mexican, it's hard to top these separately owned cantinas dishing out "overflowing" helpings; those who can abide decor and food "heavy on the cheese" are in the money, since these spots are "cheap"; N.B. Grant Avenue serves alcohol.

Elephant & Castle ● *Pub Food* — 11 | 12 | 15 | $24
Center City West | Crowne Plaza Philadelphia Center City | 1800 Market St. (18th St.) | 215-751-9977 | www.elephantcastle.com
If you're looking for an "after-work hangout" with "good beers on tap", these Philly and Jersey links in the "English-style pub" chain may satisfy; still, critics cite "so-so everything" and conclude "convenience is the main attraction."

NEW El Portal ⊠ *Mexican* — - | - | - | I
West Chester | 39 W. Gay St. (bet. Church & High Sts.) | 610-436-1110
Vegetarians and carnivores with hearty appetites are well served at this festive, low-cost Mexican BYO in the heart of West Chester; expect an assortment of *tortas* (sandwiches) plus huge sharing platters along with the staples – burritos, quesadillas and tacos.

NEW El Ranchito Ⓜ *Mexican* — - | - | - | I
North Philly | 1356 N. Second St. (Master St.) | 215-426-7946
Mexican émigrés have set up this simply stylish, Veracruz-influenced BYO on a North Philly corner just two blocks from Northern Liberties' Girard Avenue main drag; budget-priced seafood is the specialty – everything is under $13, whether it's ceviche, stew or tacos – and it's served by an eager-to-please crew.

El Sarape *Mexican* — 23 | 19 | 21 | $31
Blue Bell | 1380 Skippack Pike (DeKalb Pike) | 610-239-8667 | www.elsarapebluebell.com

(continued)

(continued)

Los Sarapes *Mexican*

Chalfont | 17 Moyer Rd. (E. Butler Ave.) | 215-822-8858 | www.lossarapes.com Ⓜ

Horsham | Horsham Center Sq. | 1116 Horsham Rd. (Limekiln Pike) | 215-654-5002 | www.lossarapeshorsham.com

"As close to Mexico as you can get" "north of the (Philadelphia) border" is the consensus on this trio of cantinas, boasting a "mind-numbing selection of tequilas" and "true" cuisine served by a "knowledgeable" staff; pssst, amigo: "the waitress says it's spicy."

𝗭 El Vez *Mexican*   21 | 23 | 20 | $37

Center City East | 121 S. 13th St. (Sansom St.) | 215-928-9800 | www.elvezrestaurant.com

"Bring on the margaritas – and your earplugs" at Stephen Starr's "hip" 'n' "kitschy" Center City Mex, where "high-energy" servers deliver "killer" guacamole and other *delicioso* eats to a "young, jumpy crowd" "partying" amid "quirky", "deco-velvet" decor ("Elvis would love it"); while *mucho* aficionados find it a "fabulous" "fantasy", dissenters dub it "style over substance" (though even they'd concede "the bar crowd is worth watching").

Epicurean, The *American*   21 | 15 | 19 | $31

Phoenixville | Village at Eland | 902-8 Village at Eland (Kimberton Rd.) | 610-933-1336 | www.americabargrill.com

New American fare prepared with "flair" and a "great" beer selection are to be savored at this Phoenixville venue in the Village at Eland; if it "tries to be upscale without making it", many rely on it as a "sports bar" and find it more useful as a place to "meet" over drinks.

Ernesto's 1521 Cafe 𝗦Ⓜ *Italian*   21 | 16 | 20 | $38

Center City West | 1521 Spruce St. (bet. 15th & 16th Sts.) | 215-546-1521 | www.ernestos1521.com

"They know how to get you to the concert on time" at this "serene", "warm" and "welcoming" Italian favored by both Kimmel Center "orchestra members and goers"; hats off to the "fine", "reasonably" priced food that's paired with a small but "good" wine list and "attentive" service – overall, "bravo!"

Estia *Greek*   23 | 24 | 22 | $52

Avenue of the Arts | 1405-07 Locust St. (bet. Broad & 15th Sts.) | 215-735-7700 | www.estiarestaurant.com

"Like taking a trip to Santorini", this "stunningly beautiful" Greek taverna in a "key" spot across from the Academy of Music wows surveyors with "ethereal" fish that you "choose from an awesome display on ice" – and pay for by the "pricey" pound; all considered, it's "worth it", given "well-informed" servers who "materialize from nowhere" and a "bargain" pre-theater prix fixe (three courses for $30).

Eulogy Belgian Tavern ◑ *Belgian*   18 | 13 | 18 | $26

Old City | 136 Chestnut St. (2nd St.) | 215-413-1918 | www.eulogybar.com

"You could drink your way to Belgium" (though the "fab" mussels here aren't from Brussels) at this small, "Gothic" Old City tavern

FOOD DECOR SERVICE COST

where beerheads come alive over a list so "outstanding" it should be "studied"; mavens of the macabre kick back in the upstairs coffin room, "one of Philly's more unusual drinking spots."

Fadó Irish Pub ● *Pub Food*
15 | 17 | 15 | $24

Center City West | 1500 Locust St. (15th St.) | 215-893-9700 | www.fadoirishpub.com

"Have beer with your breakfast boxty" as you hang with friends and "football" fans amid the "nooks and crannies" of this "dependable" Center City Celtic pub; it's "cookie-cutter" to some ("Irish bars should never become chains"), but chances are you'll be happy if you're looking for "a full belly and to satisfy a thirst for a few dollars."

Famous 4th Street Delicatessen *Deli*
22 | 12 | 16 | $21

South St. | 700 S. Fourth St. (Bainbridge St.) | 215-922-3274

Evoking a "NYC deli" well enough that "you can picture Meg Ryan faking", this "stark" Queen Village institution famed for "larger-than-life" portions of "awesome" "Jewish soul food" attracts matzo ball mavens for "stacked-to-the-sky" sandwiches, "outrageous" chocolate-chip cookies and the "best stuffed cabbage this side of Poland"; if the service is questionable "that's part of the charm."

Farmicia Ⓜ *Continental*
20 | 20 | 18 | $35

Old City | 15 S. Third St. (bet. Chestnut & Market Sts.) | 215-627-6274 | www.farmiciarestaurant.com

"Locally raised", "farm-fresh" food is the focus at this "beautifully simple", veggie-friendly Old City Continental, where the "cooking seems to be getting better" (reflected in a rising Food rating); prices that won't "break your wallet" – particularly the "bargain" brunch served in the restaurant and on-premises Metropolitan Bakery Cafe – help compensate for the occasionally "inconsistent" service.

Fatou & Fama Ⓜ *African/Soul Food*
∇ 16 | 6 | 11 | $19

University City | 4002 Chestnut St. (40th St.) | 215-386-0700 | www.fatouandfama.com

"Want a cab? you can always find a driver" chowing down on "interesting" eats at this University City Senegalese–soul fooder; yes, the service is "lax" and there's "no decor to speak of", but the "food is worth it" – and you can always "get it to go."

Fayette Street Grille *American*
23 | 14 | 22 | $35

Conshohocken | 308 Fayette St. (bet. 3rd & 4th Sts.) | 610-567-0366 | www.fayettestreetgrille.com

Devotees of this "popular" New American BYO in a Conshy storefront suggest making a reservation on account of food that's a "bargain" considering the "excellent" quality (especially the $32 prix fixe dinner) and "amiable" staff; the "bare-bones" quarters may be "tight", but it doesn't matter since many loyalists just lovette.

Fellini Cafe *Italian*
21 | 12 | 17 | $26

Ardmore | 31 E. Lancaster Ave. (bet. Cricket Ave. & Rittenhouse Pl.) | 610-642-9009

(continued)

(continued)

Fellini Cafe
Downingtown | 84 W. Lancaster Ave. (bet. Downing & Manor Aves.) |
610-518-1015 ⓢ
Fellini Cafe Newtown Square Ⓜ *Italian*
Newtown Square | St. Albans Shopping Ctr. | 3541 West Chester Pike
(Rte. 252) | 610-353-6131
"Show up hungry" or plan on a "doggy bag" given the "overflowing"
plates of "solid" Italian fare dished out at these separately owned
Italian BYOs; service can be "spotty" and you may have to endure
"noise", "tight tables" and "long waits", but the "price can't be beat";
P.S. some cite it's "tacky", others say "you don't eat the decor."

Fergie's Pub ❶ *Pub Food*   17 | 16 | 18 | $19
Center City East | 1214 Sansom St. (bet. 12th & 13th Sts.) |
215-928-8118 | www.fergies.com
"A real slice of Ireland" sums up this "atmospheric" Center City taproom where fans find "perfectly poured pints", "surprisingly decent"
(if "standard") grub and a "cool vibe"; extras like quizzo and live music add to its "hangout" appeal.

Fez Moroccan Cuisine *Moroccan*   ▽ 21 | 23 | 20 | $39
South St. | 620 S. Second St. (bet. Bainbridge & South Sts.) |
215-925-5367 | www.fezrestaurant.com
Plop down on "pillows" and "dig" into "authentic" Moroccan at this
"novelty" off South Street, owned by the crew from Byblos, Cedars
and Vango; "veggie"-friendly seven-course feasts come "complete
with belly dancers" (on weekends) and exotic hookahs – so "go with
the gang" or a "date" for an "entertaining night out."

NEW **Field House** *American*   ▽ 13 | 18 | 17 | $23
Center City East | 1150 Filbert St. (12th St.) | 215-629-1520 |
www.fieldhousephilly.com
Fans of this "roomy" new sports bar "conveniently" located next to
the Convention Center concur that the "very cool" "amenities" –
pool tables and video games on giant TVs – make it a "fun stop"; so
even if some find the food (burgers, cheese steaks) "average" and
the service "slow", it's still a "great hangout."

Figs Ⓜ⇱ *Mediterranean*   23 | 17 | 19 | $31
Fairmount | 2501 Meredith St. (25th St.) | 215-978-8440 |
www.figsrestaurant.com
As "cute" and compact as a "crib", this Fairmount Mediterranean
BYO purveys a "delicious" mix of flavors, from the "exotic" (Moroccan)
to the "down-home" (American); the "fabulous" weekend brunches
and "attentive" service are more reasons to celebrate – just bring
cash to do so, since they only take green.

Fioravanti ⓢ *Continental*   26 | 18 | 23 | $32
Downingtown | 105 E. Lancaster Ave. (bet. Beach St. & Brandywine Ave.) |
610-518-9170 | www.fioravantibyob.com
It "smells divine" inside this "unpretentious" BYO in Downingtown
thanks to the "excellent" Continental fare from Dave Wassel's "open

| | FOOD | DECOR | SERVICE | COST |

"kitchen" (that gained three points for Food since the last Survey); the "intimate" environs mean you'll "eavesdrop" on "fellow diners" even if you don't want to, but if you're in the area it's "worth a try."

Five Guys Famous Burgers & Fries *Burgers* | 22 | 9 | 15 | $10 |

Center City West | 1527 Chestnut St. (15th St.) | 215-972-1375
NEW **Warminster** | 864 W. Street Rd. (York Rd.) | 215-443-5489
Clifton Heights | 500 W. Baltimore Ave. (Delmar Dr.) | 610-622-5489
Glen Mills | 1810 Wilmington Pike (Old Baltimore Pike) | 610-358-5489
Bala Cynwyd | 77 E. City Ave. (Monument Rd.) | 610-949-9005
Wayne | 253 E. Swedesford Rd. (W. Valley Rd.) | 610-964-0214
www.fiveguys.com

"Stock up on napkins" at this "no-nonsense" chain 'cause "you're sure to make a mess" chowing down on its "fresh, fantastic", "made-to-order" burgers and "mountains" of "boardwalk-style" fries; so what if they're "unapologetically bare-bones" – this is one "calorie splurge" that's "worth risking a gall-bladder attack" for.

Fleming's Prime Steakhouse & Wine Bar *Steak* | 25 | 23 | 24 | $59 |

Wayne | 555 E. Lancaster Ave. (Radnor-Chester Rd.) | 610-688-9463 | www.flemingssteakhouse.com

Main Liners welcome this "classy", "pricey-but-worth-it" wood-adorned beefery off the Blue Route in Radnor, home of "perfectly cooked" steaks, 100 wines by the glass and "perky" servers who "know" their stuff; for best results, go on an "expense account", and if you have a need to "be seen", try the "hopping bar."

☑ Fogo de Chão *Brazilian* | 23 | 22 | 24 | $61 |

Avenue of the Arts | Widener Bldg. | 1337 Chestnut St. (bet. Broad & Juniper Sts.) | 215-636-9700 | www.fogodechao.com

A Center City "carnival for carnivores", this "cavernous", "energetic" Brazilian churrascaria chain outpost is where "aim-to-please" gauchos "race" to serve an "endless array" of meats "on swords" until you cry for mercy (flip your table card to the red side for a breather); just "don't fill up on the salad bar" – and bring "your Lipitor."

☑ Fork *American* | 24 | 21 | 22 | $47 |

Old City | 306 Market St. (bet. 3rd & 4th Sts.) | 215-625-9425 | www.forkrestaurant.com

Grown-ups "escape the Old City madness" at this "polished but not overly formal" New American "institution" that's still at "the forefront" of Philly's "dining scene", and for "good reason": "consistent" fare "refreshed with creativity" that "never disappoints" and "pleasant" servers who display a "sense of humor" as they navigate the "smallish" space; Fork: etc., the casual offshoot next door, is fine for a quick bite or takeout.

☑ Fountain Restaurant *Continental/French* | 29 | 28 | 28 | $86 |

Center City West | Four Seasons Hotel | 1 Logan Sq. (Benjamin Franklin Pkwy.) | 215-963-1500 | www.fourseasons.com

"Ask and you shall receive" at this "staggeringly good" New French-Continental "splurge" in Center City's Four Seasons Hotel (again

FOOD DECOR SERVICE COST

rated No. 1 for Food, Decor and Service) showcasing Martin Hamann's "exquisite" tasting menus that "bubble over" with "creativity"; the "sumptuous" quarters overlook the namesake fountain on Logan Square, and the "stately" though "nearly invisible" staff is "so attentive I expected a pedicure with dessert"; N.B. jacket required.

Fountain Side American/Italian
19 | 14 | 19 | $33

Horsham | 537 Easton Rd. (Meetinghouse Rd.) | 215-957-5122 | www.fountainsidegrill.com

"Ignore the tacky entrance in a strip mall" advise admirers who say this "large" Italian-American BYO near Willow Grove Naval Air Station can be counted on for "generous portions" of "very good" steaks, seafood and such served by "attentive" staffers at "reasonable" prices; "nondescript" decor is a nonissue for most.

Four Dogs Tavern American
18 | 17 | 18 | $26

West Chester | 1300 W. Strasburg Rd. (Telegraph Rd.) | 610-692-4367

Surveyors sniff out some "very good" pub fare at this "secluded" converted barn near West Chester; it's an easy "drop in" for "unpretentious" dining and music (Thursdays and Sundays), and you can bring Rover to the pooch-friendly patio; inside, it's all "funky" dog decor.

Four Rivers Chinese
∇ 24 | 11 | 19 | $22

Chinatown | 936 Race St. (bet. 9th & 10th Sts.) | 215-629-8385

"Spicy", "delicious" dishes overflowing with "flavor" "make you feel confident" that this Chinatown BYO provides a "true" Sichuan experience; considering that low tabs mean you can order "freely", many maintain "bare-bones" decor is just water under the bridge.

Fox & Hound ❶ Pub Food
12 | 14 | 13 | $22

Center City West | 1501 Spruce St. (15th St.) | 215-732-8610
King of Prussia | King of Prussia Mall | 160 N. Gulph Rd. (Mall Blvd.) | 610-962-0922
www.totent.com

"Football diehards" rush in for the "plethora" of TVs and beer – not the "passable" pub grub and "marginal" service – at these "huge" "hangouts" ("great" for "big groups") in Center City and KoP; just remember "if you aren't a sports fan, don't go on a sports night."

Franco's HighNote Cafe Ⓜ Italian
∇ 23 | 22 | 23 | $31

South Philly | 1549 S. 13th St. (Tasker St.) | 215-755-8903 | www.francoluigis.com

Franco Borda's "charming" South Philly Italian BYO is one of the "best" in the aria thanks to "singing waiters" whose tunes make a "wonderful combination" with the "generous portions" of "red-gravy" fare that's not "second to the entertainment"; the experience is "truly a treat" for "out-of-towners" who want a real taste of Downtown.

Franco's Trattoria Italian
20 | 18 | 20 | $35

East Falls | 4116 Ridge Ave. (Kelly Dr.) | 215-438-4848 | www.francostrattoria.net

A "warm" atmosphere, "friendly" staff and "homey" Italian eats ("scrumptious" pastas, "not-to-be-missed" desserts) have locals raving about owner Franco Faggi's "outstanding addition" to East Falls; add on "reasonable" prices and a "pleasant" terrace and it's no wonder they keep coming back.

Freight House, The *American*   19 | 23 | 19 | $48

Doylestown | Doylestown SEPTA Station | 194 W. Ashland St. (Clinton Ave.) | 215-340-1003 | www.thefreighthouse.net

"Train buffs" make a whistle stop for the "trendy" bar scene and "unique" decor at this classy New American in Doylestown's SEPTA station; though some feel railroaded by "hit-or-miss" food and "above-average" prices, they make do with what's arguably the "only hot spot" around; N.B. live music Wednesdays, DJs Thursdays–Saturdays.

Friday Saturday Sunday *American*   23 | 19 | 22 | $41

Center City West | 261 S. 21st St. (bet. Locust & Spruce Sts.) | 215-546-4232 | www.frisatsun.com

Weaver Lilley's "romantic" Traditional American in a corner brownstone near Rittenhouse Square is Philly's "Energizer Bunny" (since 1973), providing "excellent" (even "sexy") vittles, "affordable" wines and "super-efficient" service any day of the week; P.S. folks "get close" at the upstairs Tank Bar.

Fuji Mountain ● *Japanese*   22 | 17 | 20 | $32

Center City West | 2030 Chestnut St. (bet. 20th & 21st Sts.) | 215-751-0939 | www.fujimt.com

"Inventive" rolls of "surprising quality" can be had at this tri-level Japanese sushi specialist in Center City, but it's the sake bar and lounge that folks are floating to; you'll "feel like you traveled halfway around the world" for "rockin'" karaoke.

Full Plate Café, A *Eclectic*   ∇ 21 | 16 | 19 | $17

Northern Liberties | 1009 Bodine St. (George St.) | 215-627-4068 | www.afullplate.com

"Good ol' Southern cooking" with plenty of "creative options" for vegetarians makes this "funky" Eclectic BYO in Northern Liberties a solid "brunch alternative", "fun lunch place" or "novelty" dinner spot: just pair "chicken and waffles" with "fried pickles" for an "instant but blissful coronary."

Funky Lil' Kitchen ⊠Ⓜ *American*   ∇ 23 | 15 | 23 | $42

Pottstown | 232 King St. (Penn St.) | 610-326-7400 | www.funkylilkitchen.com

The "name says it all" at Michael Falcone's "intimate" BYO in Pottstown, offering "thoughtfully inspired", "slightly eccentric" New American comfort food that patrons "can relate to"; if some find the decor too offbeat (e.g. use "actual wine glasses" as opposed to "down-home" tumblers), "relaxed, helpful" servers keep it mellow.

FuziOn *Asian Fusion*   23 | 17 | 22 | $33

Worcester | Center Point Shopping Ctr. | 2960 Skippack Pike (Valley Forge Rd.) | 610-584-6958 | www.fuzionrestaurant.com

"Artfully prepared" French-Asian fare and "personal" service explain the "following" at this BYO, a "local favorite" in a Central

FOOD | DECOR | SERVICE | COST

Montco strip center (and sibling of Chinatown's Ly Michael's); those who insist it's "cramped" and lacks ambiance might prefer "dining outside" on the pleasant patio.

Gables at Chadds Ford, The *American* | 20 | 21 | 20 | $57 |

Chadds Ford | 423 Baltimore Pike (Brintons Bridge Rd.) | 610-388-7700 | www.thegablesatchaddsford.com

Brandywine Valley day-trippers and locals alike endorse this "civilized" New American seafooder in a former 1897 barn; aside from the "chic" "rusticity" of its setting, there's "good" fare, and many know to "ask for a table outside" on the "beautiful" patio and "listen to the sounds from the nearby waterfall."

NEW Gaya *Korean* | - | - | - | M |

Blue Bell | 1002 Skippack Pike (Valley Rd.) | 215-654-8300

Dark-wood tables topped with high-tech grills for smokeless Korean BBQ are firing up both the Korean community and other locals at this big, bright DIY specialist in Blue Bell, twinned with neighboring Asuka in a renovated landmark; some diners leave the cooking to the kitchen.

Gayle 🛇 Ⓜ *American* | 25 | 19 | 23 | $59 |

South St. | 617 S. Third St. (bet. Bainbridge & South Sts.) | 215-922-3850 | www.gaylephiladelphia.com

Thanks to the signature New American style of Daniel Stern (Rae), dining is "never dull" at this "shoebox"-size "splurge" off South Street, where fans enjoy "cutting-edge" meals in a "casual" atmosphere amid "family photos" or on the patio; servers who "know the menu" and a "quality" wine list also "delight."

Geechee Girl Rice Café Ⓜ⊘ *Southern* | 23 | 17 | 19 | $26 |

Germantown | 6825 Germantown Ave. (Carpenter Ln.) | 215-843-8113 | www.geecheegirlricecafe.com

There's "down-home" Southern soul "with a dose of sophistication" on the menu of this newly relocated BYO in Germantown that has adherents praising its "fabulous" "Low Country" cooking (particularly the "best" greens "north of the Mason-Dixon"); service is appropriately "hospitable" and "slow."

General Lafayette Inn & Brewery *American* | 15 | 17 | 16 | $29 |

Lafayette Hill | The General Lafayette Inn | 646 Germantown Pike (Church Rd.) | 610-941-0600 | www.generallafayetteinn.com

"Phenomenal" beers, "standard" pub grub and "relaxed" vibe come together in a historical "General-Lafayette-slept-here" setting at this Lafayette Hill Traditional American reportedly inhabited by the spirits of Revolutionary War soldiers; nowadays, "young professionals" haunt the bar, while an "older crowd" favors the dining room.

General Warren Inne 🛇 *American* | 25 | 24 | 25 | $50 |

Malvern | General Warren Inne | Old Lancaster Hwy. (Warren Ave.) | 610-296-3637 | www.generalwarren.com

This "quaint", circa-1745 Traditional American inn warrants praise from Malverners for "impeccably prepared" "classics" (beef

Wellington, Châteaubriand) suitable for everything from "business" dinners to "special occasions"; factor in "white-tablecloth", "old-world charm" and "top-notch" service and admirers find it "outstanding in every regard."

Genji *Japanese* | 21 | 15 | 18 | $37 |

Center City West | 1720 Sansom St. (bet. 17th & 18th Sts.) | 215-564-1720

"People come from all over" to "roll up to the sushi bar", "chat with the chefs and chow down" at this "upscale" Center City Japanese proffering fish "so fresh you'd think it had a pulse"; it's perhaps a bit "pricier than others", so if someone else is paying, take advantage and "go omakase."

Geno's Steaks ●⇄ *Cheese Steaks* | 19 | 8 | 12 | $11 |

South Philly | Italian Mkt. | 1219 S. Ninth St. (Passyunk Ave.) | 215-389-0659 | www.genossteaks.com

The eats are "cheese-alicious" at Joey Vento's neon-ringed 24/7 cheese steak "institution" in South Philly, which even at "3 AM" draws a "cultlike following" craving the "euphoric" sensation of "cholesterol-clogging" sandwiches in a "clean", "nothing fancy" joint; "worry about your health the next day" advise regulars (and be ready to order, preferably in English) at this local "rite of passage" that partisans prefer over that "place across the street."

Georges' M *Eclectic* | 20 | 23 | 20 | $48 |

Wayne | 503 W. Lancaster Ave. (Conestoga Rd.) | 610-964-2588 | www.georgesonthemainline.com

Most Main Liners find Georges Perrier's "cozy" Eclectic in Wayne an "oasis of civility", citing a "lovely" dining room, "lively" bar scene and food "that holds its own"; still, dissenters who "expected better" "given the source" suggest it hasn't "found its way"; P.S. check it out on Sundays, when the buffet brunch is "a real treat" and dinner, starting at 5:30 PM, is BYO ($5 corkage fee).

⊿ Gilmore's ⊠M *French* | 28 | 22 | 28 | $55 |

West Chester | 133 E. Gay St. (bet. Matlack & Walnut Sts.) | 610-431-2800 | www.gilmoresrestaurant.com

Francophiles in Downtown West Chester gush over Peter Gilmore's "fantabulous" BYO, citing "mouthwatering" Gallic fare served by a staff that "feels like family" (the chef also "comes out" to chat) in a "romantic" if "slightly cramped" setting; if you crave Gay Paree, "save yourself the flight time" – and euros – and head here (just be sure to "book way in advance"); N.B. there's a $35 four-course prix fixe.

Giwa ⊠ *Korean* | ▽ 25 | 18 | 20 | $14 |

Center City West | 1608 Sansom St. (16th St.) | 215-557-9830

It's a "tight squeeze" at this "simple" Korean "lunch joint" in a Center City storefront, but it's worth it for "awesome" bibimbop in a "blisteringly hot stoneware bowl" washed down with "hot ginger tea"; "great prices" and a "friendly" staff "draw you in" – and "keep you coming back for more."

	FOOD	DECOR	SERVICE	COST

Gnocchi ⊅ *Italian*
22 | **16** | **20** | **$28**

South St. | 613 E. Passyunk Ave. (bet. Bainbridge & South Sts.) | 215-592-8300

"Go for the namesake" dish and come away happy at this affordable, no-reserving Italian BYO operating in "tight", exposed-brick quarters off South Street; the "attentive" staff "screaming" over the "noise" is "part of the fun", even if the cash-only policy isn't.

Golden Pheasant Inn Ⓜ *French*
▽ **23** | **23** | **21** | **$50**

Erwinna | Golden Pheasant Inn | 763 River Rd. (Dark Hollow Rd.) | 610-294-9595 | www.goldenpheasant.com

"French country dining at its best" is the specialty of this "special-occasion" destination north of New Hope in Upper Bucks that's "worth the ride" for its "simply excellent" cuisine and "charm"; regulars regale with tales of "romance" given both its inn setting and location near the Delaware Canal.

NEW goodburger *Burgers*
– | – | – | I

Center City West | 1725 Chestnut St. (18th St.) | 215-569-4777 | www.goodburgerny.com

This bright, modern Center City outpost of the NYC burger joint has more to recommend it than its ground-on-premises burgers and fresh-cut fries – there's a civilized touch, as eat-in orders are served on real china with real cutlery; there's beer, wine and Ben & Jerry's shakes.

Good Dog ❶ *Pub Food*
22 | **12** | **17** | **$20**

Center City West | 224 S. 15th St. (bet. Locust & Walnut Sts.) | 215-985-9600 | www.gooddogbar.com

Fans of this Center City "hole-in-the-wall" pub lick their chops over the signature blue cheese–stuffed burger and other "ambitious" "comfort foods" worth "slobbering over"; the canine-filled atmosphere (photos of pooches abound) and upper-level game room are perfect for "hipster-watching", so "get to know" the "friendly" staff and join the pack; N.B. under-21 not permitted after 9 PM.

Grace Tavern ❶ *American*
19 | **12** | **16** | **$20**

Center City West | 2229 Grays Ferry Ave. (23rd St.) | 215-893-9580 | www.gracetavern.com

"Love this place" sizes up the appeal of this "bohemian" neighborhood tavern in emerging Grays Ferry slinging up "cheap" and "tasty" bar chow such as blackened green beans on its N'Awlins-accented New American slate; beerwise, qualified quaffers confess the on-tap selection is "very good."

Grey Lodge Pub ❶ *Pub Food*
18 | **13** | **17** | **$22**

Northeast Philly | 6235 Frankford Ave. (bet. Harbison Ave. & Robbins St.) | 215-825-5357 | www.greylodge.com

A "phenomenal", "ever-changing draft selection" – handily available at two bars – "complements" a "solid" menu of grub at this Northeast Philly brewpub that's a "fun place to go" with "like-minded beer fans"; it's "nothing fancy" but "friendly" folks make it "worth the trek" – as do the lower level dartboards and TVs.

	FOOD	DECOR	SERVICE	COST

Gullifty's *American* | 15 | 13 | 15 | $24 |

Rosemont | 1149 Lancaster Ave. (bet. Franklin & Montrose Aves.) | 610-525-1851 | www.gulliftys.com

The main draw at this "casual" Main Line sports bar is a "stealth" beer list and "decent" pub food that attracts a "college crowd" ("brews, cheese steaks and a 'Nova game . . . priceless'"), though families also stop in for a "quick bite" served by a "young, enthusiastic" staff; N.B. a new patio adds another dimension to the basic digs.

Gypsy Saloon *American/Italian* | 22 | 19 | 21 | $35 |

Conshohocken | 128 Ford St. (1st Ave.) | 610-828-8494 | www.gypsysaloon.com

"It's a great place to be a regular" say West Conshyites who find "great" Italian-American food with a twist (e.g. mussels margarita, lobster mac 'n' cheese) at this "cozy" bistro in an "unassuming" location – though whether it's a "bargain" or "overpriced" is debatable; N.B. there's valet parking at nearby sister restaurant Stella Blu.

Half Moon Saloon ⊠ *American* | 20 | 16 | 17 | $31 |

Kennett Square | 108 W. State St. (Union St.) | 610-444-7232 | www.halfmoonrestaurant.com

The "loud" downstairs of this Kennett Square New American features a long bar dispensing "exceptional" brews, while the "airy" deck upstairs is a sure bet "for sure" in the summer; they call it a "saloon", but who knew a place like this could have "good" food?

Ha Long Bay *Vietnamese* | ▽ 22 | 12 | 16 | $24 |

Bryn Mawr | 816 W. Lancaster Ave. (Bryn Mawr Ave.) | 610-525-8883

"Fresh", "delicious" Vietnamese fare and a "convenient" location make this "unpretentious" Bryn Mawr BYO a "nice alternative" for pho fans who "don't want to head into the city"; although some grouse the staff is "still learning the ropes", the "quick kitchen makes up for any delays" in service, and besides, it's "big on portions and value."

Hank's Place ⊅ *Diner* | 19 | 11 | 18 | $15 |

Chadds Ford | 1410 Baltimore Pike (Creek Rd.) | 610-388-7061 | www.hanks-place.net

They crank out "awesome" breakfasts for some of the "best prices in the state" at this "friendly", "down-home" Traditional American diner in Chadds Ford; you'll have to "tolerate the lines" on weekends, but whether you're fighting a "hangover" or preparing to visit Brandywine Valley, it's a tough act to beat.

Happy Rooster *Pub Food* | 17 | 12 | 16 | $34 |

Center City West | 118 S. 16th St. (Sansom St.) | 215-963-9311 | www.thehappyrooster.com

Beyond a "dive-bar" facade is this small and "offbeat" Center City spot still pulling off "good" French-American pub food amid a "dark" "supper-club" setting that's pure "vintage '60s"; in all, it's a testament to its success that many have come to roost here for nearly 40 years; N.B. there was a post-Survey change in ownership, though the same chef remains.

Hard Rock Cafe *American*
14 | 20 | 16 | $28

Center City East | 1113-31 Market St. (12th St.) | 215-238-1000 | www.hardrock.com

This Center City outpost of the "touristy" rock 'n' roll–themed American chain "gives customers exactly what they ask for" – "huge burgers", "guitars on the walls" and "fun music memorabilia" amid a "deafening" "din"; some detractors who deem it a "much better museum than meal" just "buy the T-shirt" instead.

Harmony Vegetarian *Chinese*
20 | 12 | 19 | $17

Chinatown | 135 N. Ninth St. (bet. Cherry & Race Sts.) | 215-627-4520

Admirers of this Chinese veggie specialist in Chinatown attest it "works magic" ("you'll never know it's not the real thing") with its all-you-can-eat dim sum ($24 for two) that's a "dream come true"; even meat eaters are in sync about "not missing the beef" when there's this much "flavor" going around.

Haru *Japanese*
21 | 22 | 20 | $39

Old City | 241-243 Chestnut St. (3rd St.) | 215-861-8990 | www.harusushi.com

Fans "love the SoHo feel" at this "classy" Old City link of the NYC-based Japanese chain, where there's "plenty of seating" in the "upscale" former bank space with a "great" upstairs lounge; "wonderfully fresh", "orca-size" sushi and "innovative" cooked items are "served elegantly", and if it's a "little pricey", many agree it's "worth the cost."

NEW Harusame ◑ *Japanese*
- | - | - | M

Ardmore | 2371 Haverford Rd. (Wynnewood Rd.) | 610-649-7192

The humble Japanese rice bowls with toppings known as *donburi* – a classic fast food in the motherland – are a specialty at this lively if utilitarian Ardmore strip center Asian across from the Wynnewood Road train station; separate sushi and drinking bars add to the din in the open, wood-paneled dining room – as does a bounty of brews.

Havana *American/Eclectic*
15 | 15 | 16 | $30

New Hope | 105 S. Main St. (bet. Mechanic & New Sts.) | 215-862-9897 | www.havananewhope.com

Everyone's Havana blast at this New Hope "mainstay" where the "people-watching" pumps up the "energy" of the "outside patio scene"; for most the "big attraction is the live music", although many are hoping that a mid-Survey chef change (which may not be reflected in the above Food score) will improve Eclectic–New American eats that critics find merely "so-so."

Hibachi *Japanese*
18 | 17 | 19 | $28

Delaware Riverfront | Pier 19 N. | 325 N. Columbus Blvd. (Callowhill St.) | 215-592-7100
Springfield | 145-147 S. State Rd. (bet. Bobbin Mill Rd. & Dora Dr.) | 610-690-4911
Berwyn | 240 W. Swedesford Rd. (Valley Forge Rd.) | 610-296-4028

(continued)

Hibachi

Downingtown | 985 E. Lancaster Ave. (Rte. 30) | 610-518-2910
Jenkintown | Benjamin Fox Pavillion | 261 Old York Rd.
(Township Line Rd.) | 215-881-6814

"You know the drill" ("flip, flip, catch the shrimp in your mouth") at this "festive" Japanese steakhouse chain that "entertains you as it feeds you" "decent" grilled fare; while some find the routine "corny" and "tired", "kids love it", and the "early-bird" specials can save you "several hundred yen"; P.S. check out the Delaware Riverfront location for "beautiful views" of the water.

High Street Caffé ⓜ Cajun/Creole

| 24 | 18 | 22 | $38 |

West Chester | 322 S. High St. (Dean St.) | 610-696-7435 |
www.highstreetcaffe.com

"What's not to like" about this "crazy" West Chester Cajun-Creole offering "awesome", "authentic" fare and "exceptional" service in a "cramped", "New Orleans–inspired" space complete with beaded chandeliers, large mirrors and a "spirited" vibe; N.B. although it now has a liquor license, you can still BYO wine for a $10 corkage fee.

Hikaru Japanese

| 21 | 17 | 19 | $32 |

Manayunk | 4348 Main St. (Grape St.) | 215-487-3500
South St. | 607 S. Second St. (bet. Bainbridge & South Sts.) | 215-627-7110
Even "sushi snobs" salute the "good" raw fare at these twins in Queen Village and near the canal in Manayunk (the latter sporting a "nice" river view); while adults admit the food's a bit "pricey", kids are "entertained" by the "overlooked" cooked dishes dispensed from the grills.

H.K. Golden Phoenix ❶ Chinese

| 20 | 11 | 15 | $20 |

Chinatown | 911 Race St. (bet. 9th & 10th Sts.) | 215-629-4988
The dim sum's "yum" and the prices "low" at this huge Chinese eatery in Chinatown specializing in family-style offerings fit for "banquets" and offering a "varied" selection of fare ("I can't remember how many dishes I tried"); on some nights the "waits can be long", and on most nights the service "isn't exactly classy."

Hokka Hokka Japanese

| 20 | 18 | 20 | $32 |

Chestnut Hill | 7830 Germantown Ave. (bet. Moreland &
Willow Grove Aves.) | 215-242-4489

"Fresh", "reliable" sushi, "awesome" noodle dishes and "plenty of other (cooked) items" comprise the menu at this Chestnut Hill Japanese where a "friendly" staff presides over the "comfortable", "refreshingly open" space with an "elegant" fireplace; a few find the tabs "a tad high", but many others feel it's still "worthwhile."

Honey ⓩ American

| 25 | 22 | 23 | $43 |

Doylestown | 42 Shewell Ave. (Main St.) | 215-489-4200 |
www.honeyrestaurant.com

Fans are abuzz over Amy and Joe McAtee's "romantic" New American near the Bucks County Courthouse in Doylestown, thanks to its "outrageously enjoyable" small plates and a limited selection

FOOD | DECOR | SERVICE | COST

of "specialty cocktails" served in an "austere", "modern" setting that comes off "warm and cool" "at the same time"; while it's a "little pricey" for some, it's a welcome "escape from the ordinary" for many others.

☑ Honey's Sit 'n Eat ⊘ *Jewish/Southern*   25 | 18 | 20 | $18
Northern Liberties | 800 N. Fourth St. (Brown St.) | 215-925-1150
"Who knew that Southern + Jewish = delicious?" marvel mavens of this "diner-esque" Bubba-meets-bubbe BYO in Northern Liberties where "hungover hipsters" "wait an hour" in line for "heavenly challah French toast" and other "unique twists on comfort food"; critics kvetch about what they call "slacker" help, while many savvy to its "secret" skip the AM rush and opt for dinner instead.

Horizons ⊠Ⓜ *Vegan*   26 | 21 | 22 | $36
South St. | 611 S. Seventh St. (Kater St.) | 215-923-6117 |
www.horizonsphiladelphia.com
"Vegan? really?" is the response of many, including "those who shudder at the word 'tofu'", to Rich Landau and Kate Jacoby's "mind-boggling" creations at their "upscale" meatless "haven" off South Street; the service is "pleasant" in the "relaxing" lodgelike upstairs dining room, as well as the "cute" first-floor bar, where even the "outstanding" "drinks are cruelty-free – at least until the next morning."

Hostaria Da Elio Ⓜ *Italian*   20 | 11 | 20 | $31
South St. | 615 S. Third St. (bet. Bainbridge & South Sts.) | 215-925-0930
"Don't judge a small Italian eatery by its decor", since the pastas are "delicious" and the other dishes "skillfully prepared" at Elio Sgambati's "intimate" BYO trattoria just off South Street; P.S. if "cramped" isn't quite your style, skip the dining room for the "quaint" patio.

Hotel du Village Ⓜ *French*   ▽ 22 | 24 | 23 | $49
New Hope | Hotel du Vill. | 2535 River Rd. (Phillips Mill Rd.) |
215-862-9911 | www.hotelduvillage.com
"Solid", "classic" country French food lures city slickers to this eatery in a 20-room lodgelike inn outside of New Hope; the "elegant", "Tudor-style" dining room, "old-world" airs and "helpful" service make "perfect romantic evenings" a sure thing; N.B. dinner only, and closed Mondays and Tuesdays.

Hunan *Chinese*   ▽ 21 | 15 | 21 | $25
Ardmore | 47 E. Lancaster Ave. (Rittenhouse Pl.) | 610-642-3050
"Flashier competitors" have little on this "quiet" Ardmore Chinese BYO where adherents gather for "interesting", "reasonably" priced food including some of "the best hot-and-sour soup anywhere"; the staff aims to "please", and they "never rush you" either.

Hymie's Merion Deli *Deli*   17 | 9 | 13 | $19
Merion Station | 342 Montgomery Ave. (Levering Mill Rd.) |
610-668-3354 | www.hymies.com
Servers in "bad moods" "yell" and dole out "pounds" of pastrami and other "reliable" deli gut busters at this Merion mainstay frequented by Main Line "seniors" and "families"; "long lines at all hours" are to

be expected, so "don't dillydally" when ordering; P.S. many are "so in love" with the pickle bar.

Ida Mae's Bruncherie ⋈⚲ *American/Irish* ▽ 22 | 18 | 21 | $16

Fishtown | 2302 E. Norris St. (Tulip St.) | 215-426-4209 | www.idamaesbruncherie.com

"Rub elbows" with "locals" at this "cute" BYO breakfast/bruncherie in "up-and-coming" Fishtown, where you bring your appetite (and cash – no credit cards are accepted) for "mouthwatering" Irish breakfasts, "filling" burritos and such sourced from local farms; P.S. the homemade soda bread is "highly recommended."

Il Cantuccio ⋈⚲ *Italian* 23 | 16 | 20 | $32

Northern Liberties | 701 N. Third St. (Fairmount Ave.) | 215-627-6573

"Bring a bottle of wine" to this "tiny", "bustling" and "friendly" neighborhood BYO fave in Northern Liberties, and they'll pair it with "superior" Italian food that's a "bargain"; "reservation times can be pure fiction" (you'll likely "wait" even if you made one), and "don't ask for coffee" because "someone is always waiting for your seat."

Illuminare *Italian* 18 | 21 | 17 | $31

Fairmount | 2321 Fairmount Ave. (bet. 23rd & 24th Sts.) | 215-765-0202 | www.illuminare2321.com

Whether you're up for a "casual" meal or a "romantic" rendezvous, this Italian near the Art Museum is a bright option; while things dim a bit with "spotty" service, the "excellent" brick-oven pizzas shine, as does the "gorgeous" wood-and-glass decor and "beautiful" courtyard.

Il Portico *Italian* 20 | 20 | 21 | $50

Center City West | 1519 Walnut St. (bet. 15th & 16th Sts.) | 215-587-7000 | www.il-portico.com

An "old-school" "class act", this chandeliered Walnut Street Italian provides an "upscale dining experience" via "well-prepared" food and a "knowledgeable staff"; still, some find it "overpriced" – unless "you're on an expense account."

Il Tartufo ⚲ *Italian* 23 | 17 | 19 | $40

Manayunk | 4341 Main St. (Grape St.) | 215-482-1999 | www.iltartuforestaurant.com

The "food's for savoring" at this "charming" cash-only Manayunk Tuscan (part of the Il Portico and Tira Misu family) that proves "you don't need to drive into the city" for "wonderful" Italian dining; come summer, some say sidewalk seating allows for prime "people-watching" on Main Street.

Imperial Inn ● *Chinese* 20 | 13 | 19 | $22

Chinatown | 146 N. 10th St. (bet. Cherry & Race Sts.) | 215-627-5588

Heaven is a bowl of dim sum is the word on this imperially resilient, "banquet"-size Chinatown landmark, whose "consistent", "quality" Chinese fare gives the place "street cred" even if decor that "hasn't changed in three decades" doesn't; the staff generally "takes good care of you", even if service is sometimes "slower" if you can't speak the language.

	FOOD	DECOR	SERVICE	COST

Inn at Phillips Mill ⊄ *French* | 24 | 24 | 22 | $48 |

New Hope | Inn at Phillips Mill | 2590 River Rd. (Phillips Mill Rd.) |
215-862-9919 | www.theinnatphillipsmill.com

Romantics are enamored of this French BYO in a "charming" circa-
1756 inn along a "curvy" stretch of River Road in New Hope, calling
it "worth the trip" for a "lovely" meal in the "beautiful" garden or
antiques-filled dining room (it's also a "great" overnight "getaway");
N.B. bring cash or personal checks, as no credit cards are accepted
for either supping or sleeping.

Inn at Saint Peter's Village Ⓜ *French* | ▽ – | 25 | 22 | E |

Saint Peters | 3471 St. Peter's Rd. (Ridge Rd.) | 610-469-2600 |
www.innatsaintpeters.com

Chef Francis Trzeciak of Birchrunville Store Cafe took over the
kitchen post-Survey at this "hard-to-find", "lovingly restored" inn in
a "breathtaking" setting by the French Creek in northern Chesco;
he's installed a French menu while keeping the "attentive, young"
staff known for "heartfelt" service.

Iron Hill Brewery & Restaurant *American* | 18 | 18 | 18 | $27 |

Phoenixville | 130 E. Bridge St. (Church Ave.) | 610-983-9333
West Chester | 3 W. Gay St. (High St.) | 610-738-9600 ◗
Media | 30 E. State St. (bet. Jackson & Monroe Sts.) | 610-627-9000
North Wales | Shoppes at English Vill. | 1460 Bethlehem Pike (Welsh Rd.) |
267-708-2000
www.ironhillbrewery.com

"High-quality" microbrews and "consistent" New American "comfort
food" (even works for "picky eaters") at "reasonable" prices make
this local brewpub chain a "no-brainer favorite" among suburban-
ites; "service with a smile" comes with the "totally family-friendly"
atmosphere – and "noise."

Isaac Newton's *American* | 16 | 14 | 16 | $24 |

Newtown | 18 S. State St. (Washington Ave.) | 215-860-5100 |
www.isaacnewtons.com

"Mommies", "kids" and young adults gravitate to this New American
pub in the middle of Newtown to chow down on "better-than-average"
fare from a "huge", reasonably priced menu; all the "meeting and
greeting" generates lots of "noise" that's further abetted by a "lively"
late-night bar scene and beer from a list so large it "boggles the mind."

Isaac's Restaurant & Deli *Deli* | 17 | 13 | 16 | $14 |

Exton | Crossroads Sq. | 630 W. Uwchlan Ave. (Pottstown Pike/Rte. 100) |
484-875-5825
West Chester | Commons at Thornbury | 1211 Wilmington Pike
(Rte. 202) | 610-399-4438
www.isaacsdeli.com

"This place isn't for the birds" even if the "healthy, tasty" sandwiches (including "interesting" versions on signature pretzel-buns)
at this kid-friendly deli chain bear aviary appellations; it's "nothing
fancy" but it's "fun" – and for most, "more adventurous than your
average roast beef on rye."

	FOOD	DECOR	SERVICE	COST

Italian Bistro *Italian*
16 | 15 | 17 | $29

Avenue of the Arts | 211 S. Broad St. (bet. Locust & Walnut Sts.) | 215-731-0700

Northeast Philly | 2500 Welsh Rd. (Roosevelt Blvd.) | 215-934-7700 www.italianbistro.com

For a "reliable" Italian meal at "reasonable prices", many head to this "bright", "comfortable" chain that's seemingly "been around forever"; maybe it offers "no surprises" but it works for a "quick" "business lunch" or pre-theater meal – and whether you think it's "better-than-average" or just plain "average", at least "they try."

Izzy & Zoe's *Deli*
15 | 12 | 11 | $13

University City | Hamilton Village Shops | 224 S. 40th St. (bet. Locust & Walnut Sts.) | 215-382-2328

"Convenience" counts for Penn students who praise the "ridiculous amount" of options (from bagels to corned beef sandwiches) at this on-campus deli, whose new owners still offer "free" pickles; if lackluster scores side with those who find it "not very satisfying" ("getting your order" without a "headache" is a challenge), it's still the "only bagel place around."

Jack's Firehouse *Southern*
19 | 20 | 19 | $35

Fairmount | 2130 Fairmount Ave. (bet. 21st & 22nd Sts.) | 215-232-9000 | www.jacksfirehouse.com

Most find this "local" "staple" in a "fabulous", "high-ceilinged" former firehouse in Fairmount a hot spot for "inventive" Southern specialties that sate "hungry meat eaters"; those who deem the eats "overrated" head for the "cool-looking" bar; N.B. former owner-chef Jack McDavid currently consults for the place.

Jake's *American*
25 | 21 | 23 | $50

Manayunk | 4365 Main St. (bet. Grape & Levering Sts.) | 215-483-0444 | www.jakesrestaurant.com

"Excellent as ever" affirm acolytes of Bruce Cooper's "classic" New American in Manayunk, where an "eager-to-please" staff offers "reliably high-end" dishes; it's still "the place to go in the area", particularly given an expansion planned for summer 2008 (to be called Cooper's Brick-Oven Wine Bar) that should solve gripes about "tight" seating.

Jamaican Jerk Hut *Jamaican*
20 | 13 | 14 | $20

Avenue of the Arts | 1436 South St. (15th St.) | 215-545-8644

Yes, Nicola Shirley's BYO, Avenue of the Arts Jamaican may look "low budget", and "slow" service "isn't always on the ball", but if you bring your own rum and sit out back for "good", "authentic" goat curry, oxtail and jerk chicken, you'll think you're in paradise; P.S. it's no longer a "best-kept secret" since its appearance in the movie *In Her Shoes.*

James 🗗 *American*
25 | 24 | 24 | $59

South Philly | 824 S. Eighth St. (bet. Catharine & Christian Sts.) | 215-629-4980 | www.jameson8th.com

Foodies swoon over Jim Burke's "bold" flavors at his "stunning", "minimalist" New American in South Philly, where the mood is "ro-

FOOD | DECOR | SERVICE | COST

mantic" and "stellar" drinks "enliven" the "hip" bar scene; count on culinary "surprises" (with a focus on local produce and humanely raised meats) and "hospitable" treatment from an "attractive" staff; N.B. tasting menus available by reservation.

Jasper 🗷 Ⓜ *American* ▽ 25 | 21 | 21 | $37

Downingtown | 78 W. Lancaster Ave. (Downing Ave.) | 610-269-7776 | www.jasperdowningtown.com

Nick Di Fonzo's "outstanding" New American menu and "quaint", art deco environs in a restored Victorian house in Downingtown add up to one of Chesco's "better" "romantic" BYO experiences; prix fixe deals on Wednesdays and Thursdays help make it a "rare find" (there's a dinner tasting menu too).

J.B. Dawson's *American* 18 | 17 | 19 | $28

Langhorne | Shoppes at Flowers Mill | 92 N. Flowers Mill Rd. (Rte. 213) | 215-702-8119

Drexel Hill | Pilgrim Garden Shopping Ctr. | 5035 Township Line Rd./ Rte. 1 (Fairway Rd.) | 610-853-0700
www.jbdawsons.com

Dawson's *American*

Plymouth Meeting | 440 Plymouth Rd. (Germantown Pike) | 610-260-0550
"Solid" ribs and other "satisfying" pub fare make these "midpriced" area Traditional Americans a "decent" choice for a family "night out" or a friendly "gathering place" in "dark" ("even during the day") digs; "friendly", "hurry-up" servers work as a "team" to "turn tables"; in summation, it's "nothing fabulous, nothing terrible"; N.B. Plymouth Meeting's ownership split off post-Survey.

Jim's Steaks ⦿ *Cheese Steaks* 22 | 9 | 14 | $11

Northeast Philly | Roosevelt Mall | 2311 Cottman Ave. (Bustleton Ave.) | 215-333-5467

South St. | 400 South St. (4th St.) | 215-928-1911 ⊄

West Philly | 431 N. 62nd St. (bet. Callowhill St. & Girard Ave.) | 215-747-6615 ⊄

Springfield | Stony Creek Shopping Ctr. | 469 Baltimore Pike (Sproul Rd.) | 610-544-8400
www.jimssteaks.com

"What decor? what service?" ask fans who "drool" in line at "almost any hour of the day" at this "bare-bones", "cafeteria-style" Philly cheese steak foursome for "awesome" creations "cooked in front of your eyes"; be sure to order "with Whiz" – and bring "Rolaids for dessert."

NEW J.L. Sullivan's Speakeasy *Pub Food* - | - | - | M

Avenue of the Arts | Bellevue Bldg. | 200 S. Broad St. (Walnut St.) | 215-546-2290 | www.jlsullivans.com

Sophistication meets sports bar at this swanky subterranean grotto located beneath the Bellevue in Center City; lunchers and happy hour-hunters should appreciate the 34 flat-screens, 80-ft.-long bar and upmarket pub grub, while dinner crowds can sate themselves with New American entrees and old-time cocktails befitting the 1920s vibe.

	FOOD	DECOR	SERVICE	COST

NEW Joe Pesce *Italian/Seafood* | 18 | 18 | 18 | $40

Center City East | 1113 Walnut St. (11th St.) | 215-829-4400
Piscine pleasures proffered by "amiable" waiters appeal to acolytes of these "affordable", "no-nonsense" Italian seafooders in Philly and South Jersey from Joseph Tucker (ex Joseph's) and brother Robert Liccio (ex Pompeii); the milieu is "bright" and "modern" – Center City has a "relaxing" "circular" bar while Collingswood is BYO.

Johnny Brenda's ● *American/Eclectic* | 21 | 17 | 15 | $21

Fishtown | 1201 Frankford Ave. (Girard Ave.) | 215-739-9684 | www.johnnybrendas.com
This Fishtown "joint" from the crew behind Standard Tap revels in its "dive bar" appearance, "interesting" American-Eclectic "pub grub" (with an "expanded menu") and "excellent" beer selection; jukebox tunes and bands geared toward "thirtysomethings" plus "laid-back", "attentive" service from "self-styled hipsters" are part of the package.

Johnny Mañana's *Mexican* | 15 | 17 | 16 | $24

East Falls | 4201 Ridge Ave. (Midvale Ave.) | 215-843-0499 | www.johnnymananas.com
An "extensive list" of "amazing margaritas" helps explain why this "cute" East Falls Mexican is "always packed"; despite debate over the food ("solid" vs. "nothing special"), most agree it's a "fun place" to "meet up with friends" over a "pitcher of drinks" and nachos; outdoor seating and weekend mariachi music are pluses.

Z John's Roast Pork ⊠⊄ *Sandwiches* | 27 | 5 | 16 | $10

South Philly | 14 E. Snyder Ave. (Weccacoe Ave.) | 215-463-1951 | www.johnsroastpork.com
This "real-deal" "shack" buried in South Philly is a top-rated sandwich spot for "to-die-for" roast pork topped with "sharp provolone" ("don't cut your fingers on it") and cheese steaks that will impress even the "jaded"; "who cares if they yell at you to keep the line moving?" – the only "negative" is the "limited" daytime hours.

Jonathan's American Grille *American* | 17 | 18 | 18 | $31

Jenkintown | Jenkintown Train Station | 95 West Ave. (Greenwood Ave.) | 215-885-9000 | www.jonathansamericangrille.com
"Watch the trains go by" at this Traditional American, a "cool" "hangout" inside Jenkintown's SEPTA station serving "very good" pizza and other "comfort" food, "generous pours" from the bar and "friendly" attention to kids; a few derail the happy talk with regrets that "it empties out too early" and is "still searching for an identity."

Jones ● *American* | 20 | 21 | 19 | $30

Center City East | 700 Chestnut St. (7th St.) | 215-223-5663 | www.jones-restaurant.com
Cross *The Brady Bunch* with a little "Frank Lloyd Wright", then throw in some mac 'n' cheese and meatloaf, and you've got Stephen Starr's "campy" Washington Square American, a "retro" den complete with cork flooring and a "Chevy" vibe; the comfort food's "done right" and the servers "genuinely peppy" – ain't that swell?

	FOOD	DECOR	SERVICE	COST

Jong Ka Jib *Korean* — | - | - | - | I |

East Oak Lane | 6600 N. Fifth St. (66th Ave.) | 215-924-0100
"It's sure to please" assert advocates of this "authentic" BYO Korean
in the Olney section of Koreatown, serving "wonderfully" "satisfying" barbecue, bibimbop and "non-spicy" dishes; just "forget about
much communication with the staff" and focus on "food that's terrific for the price."

Joseph Ambler Inn *American* — 23 | 24 | 23 | $46

North Wales | Joseph Ambler Inn | 1005 Horsham Rd. (bet. Stump &
Upper State Rds.) | 215-362-7500 | www.josephamblerinn.com
"Creative" fare and a "bucolic setting" keep patrons "coming back"
to this "inviting" New American in a historic North Wales inn for
"special occasions" and "business lunches", most notably on the
summer patio ("a real treat"); it may be "pricey" but the staff seems
to "care that you have an excellent experience."

NEW José Pistola's ◐ *Mexican* — 16 | 13 | 16 | $19

Center City West | 263 S. 15th St. (Spruce St.) | 215-545-4101 |
www.josepistolas.com
It's not the margaritas but an extensive list of Belgian brews on the
"eclectic" beer list that attracts locals to this "funky", "bare-bones"
Center City Mex; "edgy takes" on traditional fare is another selling
point, but detractors slam "frustrating" service and "three-story
hikes to restrooms"; N.B. prix fixe beer dinners are on tap.

Joy Tsin Lau ◐ *Chinese* — 20 | 12 | 16 | $20

Chinatown | 1026 Race St. (bet. 10th & 11th Sts.) | 215-592-7226
"Dynamite dim sum" generates "long lines on weekends" at this
Chinatown "classic" that also dishes up other "reliable" "cheap
eats"; service can be "lacking" ("take a translator"), ditto the decor,
but it's "very popular" so brace for "crowds" and "noise."

Kabobeesh *Pakistani* — ▽ 23 | 6 | 15 | $12

University City | 4201 Chestnut St. (42nd St.) | 215-386-8081 |
www.kabobeesh.us
"Rub shoulders with half the cabbies in the city" at this "no-frills"
BYO, a University City Pakistani kebab-ery where you step up to the
"counter" for the "real deal" at "unbeatable" prices; there's "nothing
more filling", and the service is "friendly" to boot.

Kabul *Afghan* — 22 | 15 | 19 | $26

Old City | 106 Chestnut St. (bet. Front & 2nd Sts.) | 215-922-3676 |
www.kabulafghancuisine.com
This "understated" long-running BYO "sleeper" takes you out of
"loud and sceney" Old City via "delectable" Afghan dishes and a setting that "charms"; there's nothing more you can ask for besides an
"excellent value" and a staff that is "as attentive as possible."

NEW Kanella Ⓜ *Greek* — | - | - | - | M |

Center City East | 266 S. 10th St. (Spruce St.) | 215-922-1773
The chef behind South Philly's erstwhile Meze transplants his
Greek-Cypriot fare to a rustic, airy space carved out of a former

diner in Wash West; patrons armed with BYO booze cram into close-spaced tables for gently priced meat and fish dishes, as well as creative yogurt-based dips.

Karma *Indian* | 23 | 15 | 20 | $28 |

Old City | 114 Chestnut St. (bet. Front & 2nd Sts.) | 215-925-1444 | www.thekarmarestaurant.com

"Philadelphia must have done something good in a previous life" to deserve this "exceptional" Old City Indian (that also spun off a South Jersey satellite); while the colorful setting sparks some debate ("unremarkable" or "attractively sexy"), the "consistently excellent" fare and "eager" staff create good vibes.

K.C.'s Alley *Pub Food* | 17 | 15 | 19 | $18 |

Ambler | 10 W. Butler Pike (Main St.) | 215-628-3300 | www.kc-alley.com

"Great" burgers and "awesome" fries have a "cult following" at this "quaint", bi-level "neighborhood" pub in Ambler lauded for "fun" happy hours and "family dinners"; N.B. complaints about "cigarettes" no longer apply since the recent smoking ban kicked in.

Khajuraho *Indian* | 21 | 14 | 17 | $29 |

Ardmore | Ardmore Plaza | 12 Greenfield Ave. (Lancaster Ave.) | 610-896-7200 | www.khajurahoindia.com

Supplying "manna" in Ardmore is this Indian BYO serving "superb" (if "slightly pricey") fare that's perfect for vets and "neophytes" (i.e. "spicy" or not); those put off by "patchy" service and sometimes "tiny" portions head to the "highly recommended" "bargain" of a buffet; P.S. "distracting" images of characters striking "sensual poses" are naught for the weak.

Kibitz in the City ⓧ *Deli* | 21 | 8 | 16 | $15 |

Center City East | 703 Chestnut St. (7th St.) | 215-928-1447

"What deli food should look, smell and taste like" is the consensus on this "cafeteria-style" standard near Washington Square cranking out "fabulous", "ridiculously overstuffed" sandwiches ("my jaw hurts just thinking about them") and chopped liver to make "your bubbe cry"; N.B. unaffiliated with the Cherry Hill spot of the same name.

Kildare's ⓞ *Pub Food* | 16 | 19 | 17 | $25 |

Manayunk | 4417 Main St. (Green Ln.) | 215-482-7242
South St. | 509-511 S. Second St. (bet. Lombard & South Sts.) | 215-574-2995
West Chester | 18-22 W. Gay St. (High St.) | 610-431-0770
King of Prussia | 826 W. DeKalb Pike (N. Gulph Rd.) | 610-337-4772
www.kildarespub.com

The Guinness flows and the "social scene" throbs at this local "Irish flair" pub chain, where many go for "dependable bar food" and "adept" service even when it's "jammed"; N.B. a mid-Survey migration to an upscale gastropub menu may affect the above Food and Cost scores.

	FOOD	DECOR	SERVICE	COST

⊠ Kimberton Inn ⓜ *American* — 25 | 26 | 25 | $48

Kimberton | 2105 Kimberton Rd. (Hares Hill Rd.) | 610-933-8148 | www.kimbertoninn.com

"Excellent all the way around" is the consensus on this Traditional American in a "beautifully renovated" historic house in Chester County's "countryside"; "top-notch" dinners and "tasty" brunches by the "cozy" fire supply "all the charm you would expect", and the "prompt", "pleasant" staff pays "attention to detail."

Kingdom of Vegetarians *Chinese* — ▽ 19 | 10 | 18 | $17

Chinatown | 129 N. 11th St. (bet. Arch & Race Sts.) | 215-413-2290

Just say "all-you-can-eat dim sum" and savor the flavors to come at this humble Chinatown BYO, a "palace" for vegans and vegetarians that "even pleases carnivores"; not only is the menu big, but with prices this low, you'll think you're in paradise.

King George II Inn ⓜ *American* — 21 | 22 | 20 | $42

Bristol | 102 Radcliffe St. (Mill St.) | 215-788-5536 | www.kginn.com

Bristol colonists seem smitten by this circa-1681 Traditional American "landmark" near the Riverside Theater offering a "beautiful" view of the Delaware; while commoners find the fare "reliable", Tories tout it as "fit for a king" and add "good" service isn't too far behind.

Kisso Sushi Bar ⊠ *Japanese* — 22 | 14 | 21 | $35

Old City | 205 N. Fourth St. (Race St.) | 215-922-1770

"All sushi, all the time" could be the catchphrase of this "calming", orange-walled Japanese BYO on the fringe of Old City, a "mecca" for fanatics endeared by "expert", "lovingly prepared" fish; while some complain about "minuscule" portions and "limited" options (there's no cooked fare here), many swim away happy.

Knight House *American* — 21 | 20 | 21 | $50

Doylestown | 96 W. State St. (Clinton St.) | 215-489-9900 | www.theknighthouse.com

Loyalists laud this Doylestown New American as the "best dining experience" in the area, complete with a "bar menu" that's a "great value"; even if some snipe that a culinary "knight in shining armor" is in order, they're easily outvoted and most agree the outside patio is a "must" for a "special night out."

NEW Knock *American* — 19 | 23 | 20 | $39

Center City East | 225 S. 12th St. (Locust St.) | 215-925-1166 | www.knockphilly.com

Knock, knock – this New American is here, a "crowd magnet" "classing up" a corner in Wash West with "Aspen ski lodge" environs that permit "conversation without screaming"; "stunningly handsome" bartenders "provide major eye candy" at the "cozy" bar while "tasty" comestibles ferried by a "pleasant" staff greet those in the dining room.

	FOOD	DECOR	SERVICE	COST

Koi ⊠ *Japanese/Korean* ▽ 23 | 17 | 20 | $27

Northern Liberties | 604 N. Second St. (bet. Fairmount Ave. & Green St.) | 215-413-1606

Afishionados aren't coy about their feelings for the "consistently executed", "solid" sushi (plus "huge" bento-box lunch specials) at this "modern, sleek" Northern Liberties Japanese-Korean, considered a "go-to" spot for "creative" Asian; add on "relatively speedy takeout" and "what more could you need?"

Konak ⓜ *Turkish* 20 | 19 | 21 | $34

Old City | 228 Vine St. (bet. 2nd & 3rd Sts.) | 215-592-1212 | www.konakturkishrestaurant.com

"A sultan" would be happy enough to swing in this "cavernous" Turkish "bringing the Bosphorus" to Old City with "authentic" food and decor; "pleasant" service and "reasonable" prices delight all, and there's live music and belly dancing (Fridays) for a taste of "something different."

Kotatsu *Japanese* ▽ 22 | 15 | 22 | $30

Ardmore | 34 Greenfield Ave. (bet. Lancaster & Spring Aves.) | 610-642-7155

"Good-natured chefs" make the "shrimp fly" at the hibachi tables and sushi chefs roll 'em "with love" at this "family-fun" BYO Japanese (with Chinese accents) in Ardmore; "go hungry" Mondays–Wednesdays for the "above-average" all-you-can-eat sushi.

Kristian's Ristorante *Italian* ▽ 25 | 19 | 23 | $50

South Philly | 1100 Federal St. (11th St.) | 215-468-0104 | www.kristiansrestaurant.com

"Not your typical South Philly pasta and gravy joint" is this "elegant" yet "homey" Italian showcase for chef-owner Kristian Leuzzi's "beautiful" food supported by service as "gracious" as can be; suburban partisans pine "if only it were closer" so it could become their neighborhood haunt.

La Belle Epoque Café ⓜ *French* ▽ 19 | 14 | 17 | $33

Media | 38 W. State St. (Olive St.) | 610-566-6808 | www.labelleepoquecafe.com

"When they get it right, it's a beautiful thing" at this Media enterprise featuring crêpes and other assorted hits from the French bistro repertoire; all in all, it's a "good" value and a "welcome bit of France" for the neighborhood.

☑ La Bonne Auberge ⓜ *French* 27 | 26 | 27 | $72

New Hope | 1 Rittenhouse Circle (River Rd.) | 215-862-2462 | www.bonneauberge.com

"After all these years", Gerard Caronello's "formal" French "in the middle" of a condo development in New Hope still ranks among "the best" "special-occasion" venues in Bucks County; boosters note it's "priced accordingly" so "be prepared to open your wallet" for "perfect" eats in a country "dollhouse atmosphere" aided by a "professional" staff; N.B. dinner only, Thursdays–Sundays.

	FOOD	DECOR	SERVICE	COST

La Cava ⓜ *Mexican*   21 | 13 | 19 | $35

Ambler | 60 E. Butler Ave. (bet. Cavalier Dr. & Ridge Ave.) |
215-540-0237 | www.lacavarestaurantpa.com
There's nary a taco or fajita in sight marvel gringos who dine at this
"upscale" Mexican BYO in "understated" Ambler digs, where chef-
owner Carlos Melendez is "on a crusade" to change the "American
definition" of south-of-the-border fare by delivering "true", "mouthwatering" creations to "gourmets"; "personable" service is part of
the secret to its success.

La Collina ⓩ *Italian*   23 | 19 | 23 | $53

Bala Cynwyd | 37-41 Ashland Ave. (Jefferson St.) | 610-668-1780 |
www.lacollina.us
This "old-world" Italian mainstay on a hilltop "overlooking" the
Schuylkill River in Bala Cynwyd affords a "pricey", "high-quality experience" thanks to "delicious" Northern Italian dishes, "efficient"
service and a recent "face-lift"; entertainment Wednesdays–
Saturdays is another plus, and if some find it "a little out of date",
advocates affirm they're still "doing a great job after all these years."

La Colombe ⓟ *Coffeehouse*   23 | 15 | 16 | $8

Center City West | Rittenhouse Sq. | 130 S. 19th St. (bet. Sansom &
Walnut Sts.) | 215-563-0860
Manayunk | 4360 Main St. (bet. Grape & Levering Sts.) |
215-483-4580
www.lacolombe.com
"Starbucks who?" ask devotees of these "relaxed", "faux-boho"
"java" joints (Philadelphia's Top Bang for the Buck) near Rittenhouse
Square and in Manayunk, where the "best-looking" "baristas" with
a "too-hip-for-you attitude" "know how to sling the beans" for "full-
bodied brews" that will "satisfy the pickiest coffee lovers"; despite
"hit-or-miss" snacks ("there's food? who knew?") and a "lacking"
atmosphere, it's still the "place to see and be seen."

ⓩ Lacroix at The Rittenhouse *French*   28 | 27 | 27 | $83

Center City West | Rittenhouse Hotel | 210 W. Rittenhouse Sq.
(bet. Locust & Walnut Sts.) | 215-790-2533 | www.lacroixrestaurant.com
Ardent admirers find "a spot of heaven" overlooking the Square
at the Rittenhouse's "handsome", "special-occasion" French,
where chef Matthew Levin creates "memorable" tasting menus
of "micro-gastronomic" feats that "explode on your taste buds"
(plus a "divine" Sunday brunch), augmented by a "great wine
list" and "impeccable" service; "bring your expense-account
card", "sit near a window" and experience one of Philly's "wows";
N.B. jacket suggested.

La Famiglia ⓩ *Italian*   24 | 21 | 22 | $63

Old City | 8 S. Front St. (bet. Chestnut & Market Sts.) | 215-922-2803 |
www.lafamiglia.com
The "quickest way from Philadelphia to Palermo" is via this Old City
"grand Italian dining" destination, catering to "big spenders" with
"impeccable" specialties and a "voluminous wine list" that "knocks

	FOOD	DECOR	SERVICE	COST

your socks off"; the "black-tie service" is "attentive", though some encounter "stodgy" airs and insist you get the star treatment only "if they know you."

La Fontana Della Citta *Italian*   20 | 18 | 20 | $34

Center City West | 1701 Spruce St. (17th St.) | 215-875-9990 | www.lafontanadellacitta.com

"Bring your favorite vino" and "sweetie" to this "welcoming" Center City West "jewel box" for a "reasonably priced", pre-theater Italian dinner – it's "consistent" and offers "soooo many options"; sidewalk dining with an occasional "impromptu aria" from passing Academy of Vocal Arts students is an alternative to the "noise" inside.

Lai Lai Garden *Pan-Asian*   22 | 20 | 21 | $32

Blue Bell | 1144 DeKalb Pike (Skippack Pike) | 610-277-5988 | www.lailaigarden.com

Blue Bell's "high-end" Pan-Asian has its devotees who dig the "varied" and "fresh" Chinese, Thai and Japanese selections (and some of the "best sushi in the 'burbs"); though dinner is slightly "pricey" ("stick to lunch!"), a "caring" staff and "pretty" decor make the package ever more "yum yum."

La Locanda del Ghiottone Ⓜ⇥ *Italian*   23 | 15 | 21 | $33

Old City | 130 N. Third St. (Cherry St.) | 215-829-1465

This "cramped" Old City locanda of all things Italian is where lovers come for "intimacy" and foodies arrive to partake of "awesome" fare in portions "hearty" enough to make a glutton blush; the "entertaining", "friendly" waiters are "real pros" and are also adept at keeping tables turning (i.e. they'll "rush you" on weekends if necessary).

La Lupe ◐ *Mexican*   22 | 11 | 14 | $15

South Philly | 1201 S. Ninth St. (Federal St.) | 215-551-9920

Fans say this "super-authentic" Mexican BYO "passes the tamale test" for "cheap" *comidas* near the cheese steak joints in South Philly; count on comfort food "like your *abuela* made" "without the flash of the chains", and "warm" if "haphazard" service; P.S. there's "no ambience" but they're open late.

La Na Thai-French Cuisine *French/Thai*   21 | 15 | 18 | $32

Media | 33 W. State St. (bet. Jackson & Olive Sts.) | 610-892-7787

For most, this "tiny" Thai-French BYO in a Media storefront gets "a thumbs-up" for cuisine that displays an "amazing array" of "flavors, colors and textures"; if the menu's a "bit stale", many more focus on the quality of the fare and are also sold on "good" service and "reasonable" prices.

Landing, The *American*   16 | 19 | 18 | $38

New Hope | 22 N. Main St. (Bridge St.) | 215-862-5711 | www.landingrestaurant.com

For most, the "wonderful" patio view of the Delaware River is "the thing" at this New Hope New American offering "basic" sandwich-to-entree eats; while some dismiss it as a summer "tourist" attraction, regulars regard as it a "nice local place" to while away the hours.

	FOOD	DECOR	SERVICE	COST

☒ L'Angolo Ⓜ Italian
26 | **16** | **23** | **$35**

South Philly | 1415 W. Porter St. (Broad St.) | 215-389-4252

First "squeeze to get into" this "charming" South Philly Italian BYO owned by the Faenzas of Center City's Salento, then "squeeze to get out" after "filling up" on "affordable", "outstanding" antipasto and "divine" pasta proffered by "vivacious" servers who "aim to please"; just be sure to "reserve early" – "the food is plentiful, the space is not."

La Pergola Mideastern
19 | **11** | **17** | **$24**

Jenkintown | 726 West Ave. (Old York Rd.) | 215-884-7204

"Plentiful" portions of "consistently good" Middle Eastern and Eastern European "comfort food" earn "loyal customers" for this Jenkintown BYO; the "minimalist" setting may leave "much to be desired", but "reasonable prices" work in its favor.

NEW Las Bugambilias Ⓜ Mexican
▽ **26** | **22** | **23** | **$35**

South St. | 148 South St. (2nd St.) | 215-922-3190 | www.lasbugambiliasphilly.com

It's "the real deal" on South Street at this "new star" of Philly's Mexican "renaissance" where chef Carlos Molina (ex Los Catrines/Tequila's) creates "innovative" dishes complemented by "interesting" tequila cocktails; "hospitable" servers deliver the goods in a "casual", "tight" setting with "culturally faithful" decor including Mexican art and cinematic memorabilia.

LaScala's Old World Italian Italian
20 | **15** | **18** | **$30**

Center City East | 615 Chestnut St. (7th St.) | 215-928-0900 | www.lascalasphilly.com

"Feels like a chain, eats like a neighborhood joint" is the lowdown on this "affordable" red-gravy house near the Liberty Bell, known for "hearty" Italian "basics" and equipped with a bar, "blaring TVs" and a "helpful" staff; validated parking after 3 PM weekdays and all day weekends is a plus.

Las Cazuelas Mexican
24 | **19** | **21** | **$26**

Northern Liberties | 426 W. Girard Ave. (bet. 4th & 5th Sts.) | 215-351-9144 | www.lascazuelas.net

A "roaming" mariachi serenades faithful fans and helps bring the house down at this "cozy" and "colorful" Northern Liberties Mexican BYO, though the "authentic", affordable fare that'll "knock your socks off" probably takes center stage; in all, it's got charm and then some.

La Terrasse ☒ American/French
18 | **18** | **18** | **$35**

University City | 3432 Sansom St. (bet. 34th & 36th Sts.) | 215-386-5000 | www.laterrasserestaurant.com

Penn grads like "coming home" to this French-American "standby" for "low-key" lunches, "chic" dinners and winsome scenes of "fraternity boys trying to impress their dates" with "Daddy's Amex"; the "wine list" has graduated to Ivy League and the olive tree still grows in the airy dining room, but many find the service "snooty."

	FOOD	DECOR	SERVICE	COST

Latest Dish, The American
24 | 15 | 20 | $31

South St. | 613 S. Fourth St. (bet. Bainbridge & South Sts.) |
215-629-0565 | www.latestdish.com
"Creativity meets yummy" at this "hip", date-friendly New
American off South Street where "the chef is a quiet genius", craft-
ing "sophisticated", "imaginative", veggie-friendly fare; a "diverse"
beer selection fuels midnight "noshes"; N.B. night owls flock to
Fluid, the club upstairs.

La Vang Bistro Ⓜ French/Vietnamese
▽ 22 | 16 | 20 | $33

Willow Grove | Moreland Shopping Plaza | 101 E. Moreland Rd.
(York Rd.) | 215-659-4504 | www.lavangbistro.com
Admirers say "refined Vietnamese" cooking with a "French influ-
ence" yields "fabulous flavors" at this "lovely" BYO near Willow
Grove Park; some find it a bit "expensive", but it's a "nice change of
pace" that includes a staff "genuinely concerned about pleasing."

La Veranda Italian
23 | 20 | 23 | $57

Delaware Riverfront | Penn's Landing, Pier 3 | 5 N. Columbus Blvd.
(bet. Arch & Market Sts.) | 215-351-1898 |
www.laverandapier3.com
"Romantics" profess their love for this "top-of-the-line" Italian overlooking the Delaware and boasting "superb" "wood-grilled" steaks
and fish served by "attentive" waiters who've "been there forever";
some say you could take a "date" "to Italy" and "spend less", but this
Philly "classic" promises a "fine experience."

La Viola Ovest ⌖ Italian
23 | 16 | 22 | $33

Center City West | 252 S. 16th St. (Locust St.) | 215-735-8630
This "gem" of an "authentic" Italian from Ram Hima draws "long
lines" of Center City theatergoers for "outstanding", "bargain" fare
in a "plain" BYO setting; though "more refined" than its big sister,
Bistro La Viola, across the street, it "leaves the 'I'm-out-to-impress-
you' stuff to other places"; N.B. cash only.

☒ Le Bar Lyonnais ⓼ French
28 | 23 | 26 | $61

Center City West | 1523 Walnut St. (bet. 15th & 16th Sts.) |
215-567-1000 | www.lebecfin.com
A "delight on all accounts", Georges Perrier's "cozy boîte" beneath
Le Bec-Fin might be the "best bargain" around for "those who like
the kitchen but not the prices upstairs"; with "top-notch" service
and "clubby", "intimate" surroundings (including a small, "sexy"
bar) it works for a "lovers' rendezvous", and though wine prices "can
negate savings", for most it's "worth every penny."

☒ Le Bec-Fin ⓼ French
27 | 27 | 27 | $122

Center City West | 1523 Walnut St. (bet. 15th & 16th Sts.) |
215-567-1000 | www.lebecfin.com
Georges Perrier's "euphoric" French "gold standard" in a "fin de
siècle"–style Center City brownstone got with the times and revamped
to a lower-priced à la carte menu post-Survey (bring the "platinum
card" now, not the "titanium"), while still serving "exquisitely

crafted" prix fixe tasting menus at lunch (five courses, $54) and dinner (seven courses, $140); count on the "all-you-care-to-try" dessert cart (it "never disappoints") and "assiduous" service that "anticipates your every need."

Le Castagne 🛇 *Italian* — 22 | 21 | 20 | $51

Center City West | 1920 Chestnut St. (20th St.) | 215-751-9913 | www.lecastagne.com

The Sena family's "upscale", "contemporary" Northern Italian in Center City has regulars talking up the "delicious" food on par with crosstown relative La Famiglia and chalking up its "charming" ambiance to a "knowledgeable" staff that oozes "tons of class without pretension" – even if a few point out the pace can run a little "slow" (i.e. "they don't rush you").

Lee How Fook 🅼 *Chinese* — 24 | 11 | 19 | $22

Chinatown | 219 N. 11th St. (bet. Race & Vine Sts.) | 215-925-7266 | www.leehowfook.com

"It's always a pleasure" say regulars who bank on this "unpretentious" Cantonese BYO in Chinatown for the "best" "hot pots" and "salt-baked seafood" at "unbeatable" prices; there "really is no decor" but given its longevity (25 years) it's a nonissue – nobody really seems to mind.

Legal Sea Foods *Seafood* — 20 | 19 | 18 | $40

King of Prussia | King of Prussia Mall | 680 W. Dekalb Pike (Mall Blvd.) | 610-265-5566 | www.legalseafoods.com

Afishionados' "prayers were answered" when this "contemporary" Boston seafooder docked at King of Prussia, turning out "fishtastic" chowder and "generous portions" of "tastily prepared" seafood served against a "cool bubble wall" backdrop; still, some carp this link in the chain "doesn't do the name justice."

Lemon Grass Thai *Thai* — 22 | 15 | 17 | $24

University City | 3626-30 Lancaster Ave. (36th St.) | 215-222-8042

King of Prussia | Henderson Sq. | 314 S. Henderson Rd. (Pennsylvania Tpke.) | 610-337-5986

Lunch specials are "a steal" at this "low-key" Thai threesome that "endures" "despite competition" (and "spotty" service) thanks to "authentic" cooking and "eccentric" dish names (e.g. Young Girl on Fire, Evil Jungle Princess); N.B. both the Lancaster (separately owned) and King of Prussia branches are BYO.

NEW Les Bons Temps *Cajun/Creole* — - | - | - | E

Center City East | 114 S. 12th St. (Sansom St.) | 215-238-9100 | www.lesbonstempsonline.com

The sights, sounds and scents of N'Awlins permeate this high-style, tri-level Cajun-Creole – the Downtown offspring of Carmine's Creole Cafe in Bryn Mawr – located in an urbane, art deco Wash West building; a high-rolling roster of appetizers, small plates and entrees helps fuel the *bons temps* scene that rolls both downstairs at the bar and upstairs in a Mardi Gras–theme lounge.

	FOOD	DECOR	SERVICE	COST

NEW Le Virtù *Italian* ▽ 26 | 23 | 24 | $38

South Philly | 1927 E. Passyunk Ave. (Juniper St.) | 215-271-5626 |
www.levirtu.com

This "awesome jewel" on South Philly's "busy" Passyunk Avenue
strip imparts a "creative" take on Italian cuisine with "intriguing offerings" (fazzoletti with duck ragu, rabbit ravioli) from a "well-
studied" chef "imported" from Abruzzo; "wonderful" staffers "really
know their wines", and warm weather brings the experience outside
to the handsome patio.

Liberties *Pub Food* 14 | 14 | 15 | $22

Manayunk | 4439 Main St. (bet. Carson St. & Green Ln.) | 215-483-9222
Northern Liberties | 705 N. Second St. (Fairmount Ave.) | 215-238-0660
Hulmeville | 11 Beaver St. (Bellevue Ave.) | 215-752-9878 ◐
www.libertiesrestaurant.com

You'll have a "blast" as long as you stick with the "great" fries and
expect nothing more at these area saloonlike Americans; while loyalists laud the longevity of the "original" in Northern Liberties, the
latest Manayunk and Hulmeville outposts also keep the beer flowing.

☑ Little Fish *Seafood* 28 | 13 | 22 | $37

South Philly | 600 Catharine St. (6th St.) | 215-413-3464 |
www.littlefishphilly.com

Loyalists laud this "fintastic" South Philly BYO where the seafood
"melts in your mouth" and "troubles disappear" thanks to the "heart"-
felt cooking by new chef-owner Mike Stollenwerk; the Sunday five-
course prix fixe is a "steal" in the small, "enticing" dining room.

Little Marakesh ☑ *Moroccan* ▽ 21 | 22 | 22 | $32

Dresher | 1825 S. Limekiln Pike (Twining Rd.) | 215-643-3003 |
www.littlemarakesh.com

"If you have all night for a feast" and have the urge to "get up and
dance with the belly dancer", this "cozy" Moroccan "den" in a
Dresher strip mall is sure to make for an "amazing" experience;
bring "friends" and be prepared to eat "authentic" food "with your
hands" and take in a touch of North African "culture."

Little Pete's *Diner* 16 | 8 | 16 | $14

Center City West | 219 S. 17th St. (Chancellor St.) | 215-545-5508 ◐⊟
Fairmount | The Philadelphian | 2401 Pennsylvania Ave. (bet. 24th &
25th Sts.) | 215-232-5001

These "legendary" egalitarian Greek diners and "ports of call after
last call" are "always packed" with "off-duty truckers", "the mayor",
"millionaires", twentysomethings and seniors seeking "comfort
food" and "free-flowing" coffee poured by "waitresses who call you
'hon'"; N.B. 24/7 eats at the 17th and Chancellor location.

L'Oca ☑ *Italian* 23 | 18 | 18 | $33

Fairmount | 2025 Fairmount Ave. (Corinthian Ave.) | 215-769-0316 |
www.locafairmount.com

Chef Luca Garutti treats "nouvelle" Northern Italian cookery "with
reverence" (goose ragu, gnochetti) at this modern, "minimalist"
BYO in Fairmount that's "low on decor, high on quality"; "everyday

prices" and reservations (a "huge upgrade") are pluses, as is the state store down the block for last-minute vino.

Loie Ⓜ *American/French* | 17 | 15 | 15 | $31 |
Center City West | 128 S. 19th St. (bet. Sansom & Walnut Sts.) | 215-568-0808 | www.loie215.com
Lounge lizards keep crawling to this regularly "packed" French-American club-cum-eatery off Rittenhouse Square selling "reliable" bistro cooking and a "hot", "trendy" vibe; enter after 9 PM "at your own risk", as the music is pumped and the place rocks.

Ⓩ Lolita ⊅ *Mexican* | 25 | 19 | 21 | $36 |
Center City East | 106 S. 13th St. (bet. Chestnut & Sansom Sts.) | 215-546-7100 | www.lolitabyob.com
Bring your own tequila for "fabulous" custom margaritas "the way nature intended" at this "very hot" "New Age" Mex in Wash West, where Marcie Turney's "nouvelle" kitchen creates "Latino-fusion" in "noisy", "tight squeeze" quarters; N.B. reservations accepted Sundays–Thursdays (cash only).

London Grill *American* | 18 | 16 | 16 | $34 |
Fairmount | 2301 Fairmount Ave. (23rd St.) | 215-978-4545 | www.londongrill.com
"Is it a bar or is it a restaurant?" is the question, but it doesn't matter since the "soul of Fairmount", Michael and Terry McNally's "long-running" New American hangout, still produces "reliable" "pub" fare suited for "imbibers and noshers", and more "gourmet" items for Art Museum denizens; despite "haphazard" service, nearly all agree this place offers "just what you need sometimes."

Los Catrines/Tequila's *Mexican* | 24 | 25 | 23 | $41 |
Center City West | 1602 Locust St. (16th St.) | 215-546-0181 | www.tequilasphilly.com
"Come hungry" to this "high-end" Center City Mexican boasting an "exuberant", "elegant" setting, "giant portions" of "mouthwatering", "non-Americanized" dishes and a "library list" of 100-plus tequilas (including Siembra Azul, the house brand); the "entertaining", "circus"-like vibe extends to "friendly" waiters who serve "amazing" margaritas "balanced on their heads."

Lourdas Greek Taverna Ⓜ⊅ *Greek* | 21 | 13 | 19 | $32 |
Bryn Mawr | 50 N. Bryn Mawr Ave. (Lancaster Ave.) | 610-520-0288 | www.lourdasgreektaverna.com
This "upscale" Greek BYO near the Bryn Mawr train station provides "reliably good" meals ("especially the seafood") in a "small, intimate" space that, alas, can get "noisy"; fans feel it's "well worth the money", but you might need "an ATM card" given the cash-only policy.

L2 Ⓜ *American* | 17 | 17 | 19 | $34 |
Center City West | 2201 South St. (22nd St.) | 215-732-7878 | www.l2restaurant.com
Supporters rally 'round this "romantic" Traditional American, talking up "enormous" portions of "memorable" comfort food at "bar-

gain prices" and a staff that "pays just enough attention"; those who find the menu "limited" may find more interest in a "cozy corner to cuddle in" and the "must"-see live jazz on Thursdays (7–11 PM).

Ly Michael's *Asian Fusion*   ∇ 21 | 15 | 18 | $32

Chinatown | 101 N. 11th St. (bet. Arch & Cherry Sts.) | 215-922-2688 | www.lymichaels.com

FuziOn's newer Asian fusion sib across from the Convention Center flies mostly below the radar, but there's talk of "quality" Chinese and Vietnamese cooking at "reasonable prices", "friendly" help and "Zen-like" environs, and "well-made" drinks are a highlight.

Maccabeam *Israeli*   18 | 4 | 13 | $15

Center City East | 128 S. 12th St. (bet. Chestnut & Walnut Sts.) | 215-922-5922

Fans insist this "storefront" kosher Israeli in Center City "proves you don't need too much ambiance" when you're dishing out such "satisfying" eats at "such low prices"; still, others feel the "nondescript" digs could use a "makeover"; N.B. it's closed for Sabbath (sundown Friday–sundown Saturday).

Madame Butterfly *Japanese*   ∇ 22 | 19 | 21 | $37

Doylestown | 34 W. State St. (Main St.) | 215-345-4488

"Consistently fresh" sushi "prepared in fantastic ways" and "above-average" cooked offerings are served in an "attractive", "uncramped" space with a "Zen cool" vibe at this "reliable" Doylestown Japanese; while some report a "language barrier", the "commendable" staff tries to be "helpful" when you "ask for suggestions."

⊠ Maggiano's Little Italy *Italian*   20 | 18 | 19 | $33

Center City East | 1201 Filbert St. (12th St.) | 215-567-2020
King of Prussia | King of Prussia Mall | 205 Mall Blvd. (Gulph Rd.) | 610-992-3333
www.maggianos.com

"Bottomless plates" of "tasty" Italian "favorites" are served "family-style" at this "casual" red-sauce chain, where "old photos" and the sounds of "Sinatra" create a "nostalgic" feel in "loud" rooms; the staff goes the "extra mile" for big groups, and though purists find the fare merely "ordinary", that doesn't deter the "crowds."

Maggio's *Italian/Pizza*   17 | 15 | 17 | $25

Southampton | Hampton Sq. | 400B Second St. Pike (bet. Madison & Rozel Aves.) | 215-322-7272 | www.maggiosrestaurant.com

Just about "everyone leaves with a doggy bag" at this "affordable", "family"-friendly Bucks Italian where the portions are "huge", the menu "vast" and the eats "above-average"; regulars report the move in 2006 to its current location, which includes a sports bar and banquet hall, "hasn't hurt" its popularity.

NEW Maia *European*   - | - | - | M

Villanova | 789 E. Lancaster Ave. (Rte. 476) | 610-527-4888

Big is the byword at this enormous, rustic Euro off the Blue Route in Villanova that spans an assortment of food concepts and price points – there's a gourmet market/bistro, coffee/pastry bar and bar/ lounge on one level and a polished dining room on the second floor – all focused on made-from-scratch products from locally sourced ingredients; the restaurant menus lean toward Scandinavian and Alsatian fare with an emphasis on seafood; N.B. open for breakfast, lunch and dinner.

Mainland Inn *American*

| 26 | 21 | 25 | $52 |

Mainland | 17 Main St. (Sumneytown Pike) | 215-256-8500 | www.themainlandinn.com

Considered the Mainland "gold standard" for "special"-occasion dining by many, this "fine" farmhouse-style inn off the turnpike in Central Montco delivers "excellent" New American cuisine boasting "big, bold flavors", a "terrific wine list" and "professional" service; while the "romantic" setting is a draw for "Jaguar- and BMW-driving yuppies", others find it "worth the trip" for the early-bird specials.

Majolica 🅂🅼 *American*

| 26 | 19 | 24 | $45 |

Phoenixville | 258 Bridge St. (bet. Gay & Main Sts.) | 610-917-0962 | www.majolicarestaurant.com

Andrew Deery and Sarah Johnson "create magic every night" at their "intimate", "upscale" BYO New American that's "well worth a drive" to "old steel town" Phoenixville, thanks to "top-notch", "sophisticated" fare served by a staff that "really cares"; though the "stark" decor leaves some critics "cold", most agree this "hideaway" "continues to set the high bar" for the area; P.S. "book early", as the owners have cut back hours since the birth of their daughter.

Mama Palma's 🅼�'t *Italian*

| 23 | - | 18 | $21 |

Center City West | 2229 Spruce St. (23rd St.) | 215-735-7357

The "crispy" brick-oven pizzas that come with "creative topping combinations" at this "family-friendly", cash-only BYO Italian in Center City are some of the "best in the city" according to pie-zani; while the service can be "hit-or-miss", they're "nice to kids"; N.B. the space was renovated after a post-Survey fire.

Mamma Maria *Italian*

| 22 | 18 | 24 | E |

South Philly | 1637 E. Passyunk Ave. (bet. 11th & 12th Sts.) | 215-463-6884 | www.mammamaria.info

"You'll think your friend's mama had you over for dinner" at this "homey" South Philly Italian where the "outstanding", "old-world" seven-course dinner and three-course lunch prix fixes are "must-have" experiences; between the complimentary wine and "homemade" cordials, you and your "group" will "leave full and tipsy", so *amici* advise "take a cab."

Manayunk Brewery & Restaurant ❷ *Pub Food*

| 18 | 18 | 18 | $28 |

Manayunk | 4120 Main St. (Shurs Ln.) | 215-482-8220 | www.manayunkbrewery.com

"Pour me another one" cry "yuppie" loyalists of this "lively" Manayunk brewhouse "staple" in a refurbished textile mill; the "diverse" burgers-

FOOD   DECOR   SERVICE   COST

to-sushi slate is "straightforward", "good" and "reasonably priced" plus the "bumping" scene is abetted by scores of "beautiful people" and, best of all, a "wonderful" outdoor dining area overlooking the canal; N.B. there's a late-night menu on Fridays and Saturdays.

Mandarin Garden *Chinese*   20 | 13 | 20 | $25

Willow Grove | 91 York Rd. (Davisville Rd.) | 215-657-3993
This "reliable" 20-year-old Chinese opposite the Willow Grove train station is "still at the top" of its game with "friendly" service and "terrific" fare that consistently delivers; while "drab" digs are no Garden of Eden, the majority concludes this one surpasses other "typical" joints in its genre.

Manny's Place Ⓜ *Seafood*   ▽ 22 | 10 | 18 | $21

Chestnut Hill | 8229 Germantown Ave. (Southampton Ave.) | 215-242-4600 🅂
Bala Cynwyd | 140 Montgomery Ave. (Penbroke Rd.) | 610-771-0101 🅂
Wayne | Gateway Shopping Ctr. | 251 E. Swedesford Rd. (Rte. 202, exit Valley Forge) | 610-688-1000
www.mannyscrabcakes.com
"Especially good" crab cakes and a "nice selection of comfort foods" at "reasonable prices" are the draw at this BYO seafood trio; a "friendly" staff provides "quick" counter service, and while the Wayne location sports a bit of "storefront chic", limited seating translates into "mostly take-out" traffic.

Mantra 🅂 *Pan-Asian*   19 | 20 | 18 | $34

Center City West | 122 S. 18th St. (Sansom St.) | 215-988-1211 | www.mantraphilly.com
Feel the "tranquil" vibe "as soon as you walk through the door" at Albert Paris' "quirky", "down-to-earth" restaurant/lounge near Rittenhouse Square, a popular venue for "dates" or "girls' night out" thanks to "offbeat" but "comfortable" quarters, "appealing" Pan-Asian eats and a "friendly" staff; what's more, "you won't get hit over the head by the prices."

Maoz Vegetarian *Mideastern*   22 | 9 | 15 | $10

NEW **Center City East** | 1115 Walnut St. (11th St.) | 215-922-3409
South St. | 248 South St. (3rd St.) | 215-625-3500 ◗
www.maozveg.com
Some of the "best falafel" "this side of Jerusalem" and other "guilt-free", "delicious" eats can be found at these "closet-size" Center City and South Street links of an Amsterdam-based Middle Eastern/vegetarian chain; "no seats, no service, no problem" gush "hipsters" who gladly "eat standing up" at the "bottomless salad bar" they say "beats the hell out of waiting in line for pizza."

Marathon Grill *American*   18 | 14 | 16 | $21

Avenue of the Arts | 1339 Chestnut St. (Juniper St.) | 215-561-4460
Center City East | 927 Walnut St. (bet. 9th & 10th Sts.) | 215-733-0311 ◗
Center City West | 121 S. 16th St. (Sansom St.) | 215-569-3278
Center City West | 1818 Market St. (18th St.) | 215-561-1818 🅂
(continued)

(continued)

Marathon Grill

University City | 200 S. 40th St. (Walnut St.) | 215-222-0100
www.marathongrill.com

The "foodies' answer to Starbucks" is what some dub this "Philly staple", an "inexpensive" chain dishing out "gigantic" portions of
"gourmet-esque" "all-American food" in "minimalist" settings; critics
report "marathon" waits in spite of "move-'em-in-move-'em-out" service, and quip that the noise level may deliver "free hearing loss with
your meal", but others find it "fantastic for the price" nonetheless.

Marathon on the Square *American*   19 | 15 | 16 | $26

Center City West | 1839 Spruce St. (19th St.) | 215-731-0800 |
www.marathongrill.com

Marathon Grill's "bustling", "furniture"-filled Rittenhouse Square
outpost (and brunch "staple") has "something for everyone" on its
menu, namely "uniformly good" gourmet diner standards (even at
"11 PM") at "fair" prices; "congenial" staffers help make it a "home
away from home" for the Square's hip "twentysomethings";
N.B. there's a late-night menu Fridays and Saturdays.

Marco Polo *Italian*   19 | 14 | 18 | $35

Elkins Park | Elkins Park Sq. | 8080 Old York Rd. (Church Rd.) |
215-782-1950 | www.mymarcopolo.com

Diners point their compasses to this "dependable", "workmanlike"
Elkins Park Italian seafooder serving "delectable" pasta and "excel-
ling" at fish; adventurers who've journeyed here compliment its "relaxed" vibe and "sports-bar-ish" atmosphere.

Margaret Kuo's *Chinese/Japanese*   23 | 23 | 20 | $39

Wayne | 175 E. Lancaster Ave. (Louella Ave.) | 610-688-7200 |
www.margaretkuos.com

Upscale Chinese and Japanese dishes are prepared with "equal exper-
tise" at Margaret Kuo's "beautiful", stately Wayne mansion, where
Main Liners marvel at the "waterfall by the stairs" while "trying not
to drool" over the signature Peking duck downstairs, or the "surprisingly good" sushi in the redecorated second-floor room; for some, the
"best part" is the owner herself, as she "welcomes you personally."

Margaret Kuo's Mandarin *Chinese/Japanese*   23 | 18 | 18 | $32

Frazer | 190 Lancaster Ave. (Malin Rd.) | 610-647-5488 |
www.margaretkuos.com

"Far above the usual neighborhood Chinese place", Margaret Kuo's
BYO "mainstay" in Frazer provides "excellent Mandarin for the
'burbs" (sushi and tempura too) in "pleasant", "upscale" environs;
though service draws mixed reviews, it's nonetheless a "long-lasting
favorite"; P.S. check out the "great lunch buffet."

Margaret Kuo's Media *Chinese/Japanese*   22 | 20 | 19 | $34

Media | 6 W. State St. (Jackson St.) | 610-892-0115 |
www.margaretkuos.com

"Fine Chinese and Japanese dining" in a "quiet, lovely atmosphere"
is what you can expect at this Margaret Kuo outpost in Downtown

Media; a few complaints about service and cost notwithstanding, it's deemed "one of the better" bets in the area when hankering for the likes of "mouthwatering Peking duck" and "inventive" sushi.

Margaret Kuo's Peking *Chinese/Japanese* | 22 | 21 | 20 | $32 |
Media | Granite Run Mall | 1067 W. Baltimore Pike (Middletown Rd.) | 610-566-4110 | www.margaretkuos.com
The "innovative twists on standard" Chinese fare and "wonderful" Japanese offerings at Margaret Kuo's "cool"-looking Media stalwart are "not your typical mall food", and the "classy" digs are an "unlikely" fit in the aging Granite Run Mall; "attentive" service is another plus, but some find it "a little pricey."

Margot 🗷🅼 *American/Eclectic* | 20 | 17 | 20 | $40 |
Narberth | 232 Woodbine Ave. (Hampden Ave.) | 610-660-0160 | www.margotbyob.com
"Consistently fine" New American–Eclectic offerings are served "mighty quick" in a "welcoming" setting at this "quaint", "reasonably" priced BYO "hidden away on a side street" in Narberth, though locals would just as soon "keep this spot a secret."

Maria's Ristorante on Summit 🅼 *Italian* | ▽ 21 | 15 | 21 | $31 |
Roxborough | 8100 Ridge Ave. (Summit Ave.) | 215-508-5600
Amid pizzeria-heavy Roxborough dwells the D'Alicandra family's affordable Italian "treasure", a quintessential "neighborhood" spot that charms with its "excellent" slate of classic dishes along with "welcoming" service that echoes the sunny, golden decor; P.S. it's a "solid" choice when "taking the parents to dinner."

Marigold Kitchen 🅼 *American* | 24 | 18 | 23 | $45 |
University City | 501 S. 45th St. (Larchwood Ave.) | 215-222-3699 | www.marigoldkitchenbyob.com
Surveyors report this "grown-up" BYO "gem" in University City is "still worth a trip" after the mid-Survey arrival of chef Erin O'Shea, who does "Southern comfort" cuisine "darn well"; fans would "feel good about taking a NY food snob" for the five-course tasting menus and Sunday night prix fixe, served by a "pleasant" staff in a "charming" Victorian house setting; in sum, "long may it bloom."

Marrakesh 🎝 *Moroccan* | 23 | 23 | 22 | $38 |
South St. | 517 S. Leithgow St. (South St.) | 215-925-5929
"Bring an appetite" – and cash – to this "sultry" Moroccan just off South Street, where diners use their "fingers" to tuck into "abundant" $25 seven-course feasts of "melt-in-your-mouth" fare while sitting on cushions and watching belly dancers perform on weekends in the "opium den–like" setting; some find it a bit "kitschy", but others insist that "you can't beat the experience."

Marra's 🅼 *Italian* | 22 | 14 | 18 | $22 |
South Philly | 1734 E. Passyunk Ave. (Moore St.) | 215-463-9249 | www.marras1.com
"Incredible" thin-crust pies and classic "red-gravy" chow draw "visitors" and regulars to this "homey" pizza/pastaria that's so "quint-

essentially" South Philly "it's almost a caricature of itself"; "bring a thick skin" for "gruff" (yet "lovable") service and a "big appetite", and you'll see why this "tradition" has been around for four generations.

Marsha Brown *Creole/Southern*

20 | 24 | 21 | $57

New Hope | 15 S. Main St. (Bridge St.) | 215-862-7044 | www.marshabrownrestaurant.com

Stained-glass windows, pews and a choir loft are part of the "fabulous" decor at this New Hope spot housed in a "dramatically renovated" church, where "solid" Cajun-Creole and Southern victuals are served in "close but friendly quarters"; naysayers, though, find it "overpriced" and "more about the decor than the food."

NEW Masamoto Asian Grill & Sushi Bar *Pan-Asian*

∇ 27 | 16 | 20 | $32

Glen Mills | Keystone Plaza Shopping Ctr. | 1810 Wilmington Pike (Woodland Dr.) | 610-358-5538 | www.masamotosushi.com

Johnny Cia's "colorful" BYO Pan-Asian is a "welcome" "addition" to the "suburban sushi wasteland" that is Glen Mills according to aficionados; "swimmingly good" seafood, "interesting chef's specials" and "ample portions" at "bargain" prices are quickly making it a "popular spot."

☑ Matyson ⊠ *American*

26 | 18 | 23 | $45

Center City West | 37 S. 19th St. (bet. Chestnut & Ludlow Sts.) | 215-564-2925 | www.matyson.com

Regulars report that new chef-owners Brian Lofink and Ben Puchowitz "haven't changed" the "delicious" New American cuisine at this "high-class" Center City BYO near Rittenhouse Square – in fact, a rising Food score suggests it may be "getting better"; "bring a special wine", brace yourself for "tight seating" in the "not-too-formal" room and "trust" the staff that "understands the concept of dining"; P.S. the "tasting menus" (Mondays–Thursdays) are an "amazing bargain."

NEW Max & David's *Mediterranean*

∇ 23 | 18 | 20 | $36

Elkins Park | Yorktown Plaza | 8120 Old York Rd. (Church Rd.) | 215-885-2400 | www.maxanddavids.com

"Religious and secular" diners alike get their fill of "terrific" kosher Med and Eastern Euro fare and "friendly", "old-fashioned" service at this "gourmet" spot in Elkins Park, where you can BYO as long as it's Kashrut-compliant; while some may find the decor "cheesy", fromage and other dairy are strictly *treif* here, and remember it's closed for Sabbath; N.B. now open for lunch Mondays–Fridays.

Max & Erma's *American*

15 | 12 | 15 | $20

Downingtown | 1205 E. Lancaster Ave. (Quarry Rd.) | 610-873-0473
Oaks | 180B Mill Rd. (Egypt Rd.) | 610-650-8014
www.maxandermas.com

Crayons and "great" burgers mean you can expect to "dine with a zillion kids" at these suburban chainsters, an American duo that is "a step up from TGI Friday's, but not much of a step up"; still, with the "scoop-your-own-sundae bar" and "warm", "delicious" chocolate chip cookies, some say the places are even "safe for your fourth date."

	FOOD	DECOR	SERVICE	COST

Mayfair Diner ◗ Diner
`15` `13` `19` `$15`

Northeast Philly | 7373 Frankford Ave. (bet. Bleigh Ave. & Tudor St.) | 215-624-4455

Feeding hungry hordes, 24 hours a day, seven days a week is this "landmark" "stainless-steel"–decorated Northeast diner, a "pillar of the community" "holding its own" by serving "classic" Americana for nearly 75 years; some even enjoy going here just to get a picture of "what diner life used to be like" way back when.

McCormick & Schmick's Seafood
`21` `20` `21` `$49`

Avenue of the Arts | 1 S. Broad St. (Penn Sq.) | 215-568-6888 | www.mccormickandschmicks.com

"Seafood lovers" are hooked on the "endless menu" of "fresh" fin fare that "changes daily" at these Philly and NJ links in the "elevated" maritime chain; "pleasant" service "without drama" in a "clubby", "white-tablecloth" setting and "great" "happy-hour" specials help make it a "reliable", albeit "costly", choice for many.

McFadden's Pub Food
`13` `14` `14` `$24`

Northern Liberties | 461 N. Third St. (bet. Spring Garden & Willow Sts.) | 215-928-0630 | www.mcfaddensphilly.com
South Philly | Citizens Bank Park | 1 Citizens Bank Way (Pattison Ave.) | 215-952-0300 | www.mcfaddensballpark.com ◗

"College kids dig" these "crowded" restaurant/sports bars in Northern Liberties and at Citizens Bank Park, which some describe as a "frathouse" "decorated for Philly sports fans"; backers insist the pub grub is "better than ballpark food", but some warn of the "crowds."

McGillin's Olde Ale House ◗ Pub Food
`16` `18` `18` `$20`

Center City East | 1310 Drury St. (bet. Chestnut & Sansom Sts.) | 215-735-5562 | www.mcgillins.com

Kickin' it "olde"-school is this circa-1860 Irish alehouse tucked away in a Center City back alley; everyone "feels right at home" over beers, wings and other "standard, but good" pub grub in the "friendliest joint this side of the Atlantic" – no wonder it's a Philly "favorite."

Melrose Diner ◗ Diner
`16` `13` `18` `$16`

South Philly | 1501 Snyder Ave. (15th St.) | 215-467-6644

Fans of this "classic", 24/7 South Philly "institution" "still go" for "solid" diner chow served with "extra salt from the waitresses" ("everyone needs to be called 'hon' at least once a year") and the "interesting experience" of "sharing your booth" with a stranger; others suggest the "long-term effects" of new ownership "remain to be seen."

Melting Pot Fondue
`20` `19` `21` `$46`

Center City East | 1219 Filbert St. (bet. 12th & 13th Sts.) | 215-922-7002
Chestnut Hill | 8229 Germantown Ave. (Southampton Ave.) | 215-242-3003
King of Prussia | 150 Allendale Rd. (bet. Court Blvd. & DeKalb Pike) | 610-265-7195 | www.meltingpot.com

"Fun-do fondue" is the name of the game at this trio of "interactive" chain eateries where you "dip, dip, dip" your food into "amazing se-

| | FOOD | DECOR | SERVICE | COST |

lections" of chocolate, cheese or oil; so "bring a date", the "family" or the "girls" for a "relaxed" "evening" aided by staffers who "make you feel special" – even if frugal-minded types wonder why "it costs so much to cook my own food."

NEW Memphis Taproom ● *Pub Food*

| – | – | – | M |

Port Richmond | 2331 E. Cumberland St. (Memphis St.) | 215-425-4460
Beer-loving barflies are lighting on Port Fishington – the border of Port Richmond and Fishtown – where this polished, old-fashioned–looking corner tap dispenses nearly a dozen brews on draft and plenty more by the bottle; chef Jesse Kimball (ex Lacroix at The Rittenhouse) turns out a gastropub menu with lots of vegetarian options.

Mendenhall Inn *American*

| 21 | 23 | 22 | $45 |

Mendenhall | Clarion Inn at Mendenhall | 332 Kennett Pike (Rte. 1) | 610-388-1181 | www.mendenhallinn.com
This "refined" New American "landmark" in the Brandywine Valley is a "favorite" for "elegant dining", with nightly "live music" and a "delicious" prix fixe Sunday champagne brunch; P.S. it's also a "great place to stay for the weekend."

☑ Mercato ⊘ *American/Italian*

| 26 | 18 | 22 | $38 |

Center City East | 1216 Spruce St. (Camac St.) | 215-985-2962 | www.mercatobyob.com
"If you can get into" this "hip", "minimalist" BYO bistro in a Center City storefront, you surely will "love, love, love" R. Evan Turney's "amazingly fresh" American-Italian fare (and "flights of olive oil"), delivered by an "efficient" staff that gracefully "navigates the cramped quarters"; N.B. reservations are accepted Sundays–Fridays between 5-6:30 PM for parties no larger than six (cash only).

Mercer Café *American/Italian*

| ▽ 26 | 17 | 25 | $15 |

Port Richmond | 2619 E. Westmoreland St. (Mercer St.) | 215-426-2153 | www.mercerstreetcafeonline.com
"The hipsters haven't found" this "great little" "neighborhood" luncheonette in Port Richmond serving "especially good", "made-from-scratch" American-Italian breakfast, lunch and – on Fridays only – dinner; best of all, "there's no line to get in"; N.B. it's BYO.

Meridith's *Eclectic/Mediterranean*

| 22 | 18 | 20 | $35 |

Berwyn | 10 Leopard Rd. (Lancaster Ave.) | 610-251-0265 | www.meridiths.com
"Find a place to park" then join the crowds that flock to this "lively" Berwyn Med-Eclectic BYO warmed by "friendly" service and "charming" Tuscan-influenced decor; look for "delicious" breakfasts and lunches (Saturday and Sundays only) and daily dinners from a place just "perfect for the neighborhood."

Meritage Philadelphia ☒ *American*

| 23 | 21 | 22 | $53 |

Center City West | 500 S. 20th St. (Lombard St.) | 215-985-1922 | www.meritagephiladelphia.com
"Well-presented" food, a "terrific" wine list and "feel-right-at-home" bar make a "successful combination" at this "calm", "ele-

	FOOD	DECOR	SERVICE	COST

gant" New American near Graduate Hospital; fans say the newest owners merit praise for having "broadened the appeal" of the place.

Mexican Post *Mexican*
	17	14	16	$22

Center City West | 1601 Cherry St. (16th St.) | 215-568-2667
Old City | 104 Chestnut St. (Front St.) | 215-923-5233 ◗
www.mexicanpost.com

Every day is "Cinco de Mayo" at this "affordable" cantina mini-chain, packed with "noisy", "happy-hour" crowds inhaling "decent though pedestrian" grub; those who find service "s-l-o-w" – it feels like "they're waiting for the tomatoes for the salsa to ripen" – opt for "amazin'" margaritas at the bar.

Mezza Luna ⓜ *Italian*
	21	17	19	$40

South Philly | 763 S. Eighth St. (Catharine St.) | 215-627-4705

"Old-world charm" is at work at this "classic" Roman-style South Philly Italian hailed for its "warmth" "from the minute you walk in" and "gratifying" Italian cooking, especially "gnocchi that'll change the way you look at gnocchi"; aside from "parking" woes, just about everyone who goes here ends up "moonstruck."

Mikado *Japanese*
	▽ 22	17	19	$37

Ardmore | 66 E. Lancaster Ave. (bet. Rittenhouse Pl. & Simpson Rd.) | 610-645-5592

This "cute" Japanese is "always packed" with Main Liners settling into "interesting" sunken seats for "consistently solid" if "a little pricey" sushi and tempura accompanied by wine, beer and the "bonus" of being able to order from Thai Pepper, the relative next door; N.B. unrelated to the Mikado trio in New Jersey.

Mimosa Restaurant ⓜ *Eclectic*
	▽ 24	15	20	$41

West Chester | 2 Waterview Rd. (West Chester Pike) | 610-918-9715 | www.mimosa-restaurant.com

Gilles Moret's "stunning" Eclectic cuisine "keeps them coming back" to his "quaint", "often overlooked" Tuscan-style BYO "tucked away" in a shopping center outside of West Chester; other assets include "attentive" service and crowd-pleasing, three-course early-birds (Wednesdays, Thursdays and Sundays, 5–7 PM); N.B. also closed Tuesdays.

ⓝⓔⓦ Minar Palace Ⓢ *Indian*
	-	-	-	I

Center City East | 1304 Walnut St. (13th St.) | 215-546-9443

As we go to press, the Singh family's beloved, humble Indian BYO, uprooted from its Rittenhouse hole-in-the-wall digs by redevelopment, is expected to resurface in summer 2008 in Wash West with much of the same budget-priced cuisine and sweet, brisk service; the key difference is aesthetics – while not fancy, it should be date-friendly.

Mio Sogno *Italian*
	▽ 23	19	20	$37

South Philly | 2650 S. 15th St. (bet. Oregon Ave. & Shunk St.) | 215-467-3317

Don't say "gravy house" when describing this "refeshing change from typical South Philly Italians", a "quality" place "worth the effort" of visiting on account of "good" cooking and a "feel-good" atmosphere; though a "tad pricey", chances are you'll come away "impressed."

Mirna's Café *Eclectic/Mediterranean*   22 | 16 | 20 | $32
Blue Bell | Village Sq. | 758 DeKalb Pike (Skippack Pike) | 610-279-0500
Jenkintown | 417 Old York Rd. (West Ave.) | 215-885-2046 Ⓜ
www.mirnas.com

You "get your money's worth" of "fab", "zesty" Eclectic-Med fare at these suburban BYO twins; ok, the tables are "close together" and the noise can be "unbearable", but the service is "attentive", and overall, fans think things here make for a "winning" formula.

Misconduct Tavern ❶ *Pub Food*   17 | 14 | 18 | $24
Center City West | 1511 Locust St. (15th St.) | 215-732-5797 | www.misconduct-tavern.com

It's all hands on deck at this "better-than-standard" Center City pub with "solid" "daily specials" and a "comforting" nautical theme; despite middling ratings, there's "plenty of screens" "to watch sports", the bartenders "know how to make a drink" – and it's a "real value."

Mission Grill Ⓩ *Southwestern*   21 | 21 | 19 | $38
Center City West | 1835 Arch St. (bet. 18th & 19th Sts.) | 215-636-9550 | www.themissiongrill.com

"Interesting" Southwestern is the mission of the "kitchen that cares" at this "trendy" corner spot near Logan Square, and since it's a sib of the Public House and Field House rest assured there's a "happening bar scene"; some insist the "slow" service "needs seasoning" but add "the wait is worth it."

NEW Misso *Japanese*   - | - | - | M
Avenue of the Arts | 1326 Spruce St. (Broad St.) | 215-546-2355 | www.missosushi.com

Bruce Kim, who wowed Blue Bellites at Sushikazu, has moved on, taking over the ground floor of a condo building off the Avenue of the Arts with a peaceful, comfy Japanese BYO featuring his signature rolls and other raw-fish creations, as well as cooked dishes, notably seafood; reasonable prices and efficient service make it a decent choice before the theater.

Mixto *Pan-Latin*   21 | 21 | 18 | $31
Center City East | 1141 Pine St. (bet. Quince & 12th Sts.) | 215-592-0363 | www.mixtophilly.com

Fans admit the *comida* at this "sexy", brick-walled Center City Latin is so "yummy" and the vibe so "lively" you'll feel "like doing the salsa mid-meal"; the scene's enhanced by "fabulous" sangrias and a bar on the second floor ("bring earplugs"), and it's probably safe to expect service that ranges from "good" to "where's my waiter?"

Mizu Ⓩ *Japanese*   19 | 11 | 18 | $17
Center City West | 133 S. 20th St. (Moravian St.) | 215-563-3100
NEW Old City | 220 Market St. (bet. 2nd & 3rd Sts.) | 215-238-0966

(continued)

Mizu

University City | 111 S. 40th St. (bet. Chestnut & Sansom Sts.) | 215-382-1745
www.mizusushibar.com

This "totally unassuming" trio of Philly sushi bars turns out "great quick fixes" of "grab-and-go" or sit-down Japanese specialties at "amazing prices"; N.B. no liquor allowed at University City, though Center City and Old City are BYO.

Modo Mio ☒Ⓜ⇌ *Italian*

26 | 16 | 20 | $36

Northern Liberties | 161 W. Girard Ave. (Hancock St.) | 215-203-8707 | www.modomiorestaurant.com

Accolades abound for the "absolutely first-rate", "imaginative" Italian fare of Peter McAndrews at his "warm" BYO on the edge of Northern Liberties – particularly for the "outrageously underpriced" $30 four-course prix fixe dinner with "just the right amount to eat"; the cooking supercedes gripes about the "noise level" ("bring ear-plugs"), "cash-only" policy and front-of-the-house "glitches."

Monk's Cafe ❶ *Belgian*

22 | 14 | 17 | $27

Center City West | 264 S. 16th St. (bet. Latimer & Spruce Sts.) | 215-545-7005 | www.monkscafe.com

"It's hard to go wrong" at this "dark", "overcrowded" Belgian "classic" in the heart of Center City where a "knowledgeable" but "frenzied" staff serves a selection of beers "the size of a small-town phone book" abetted by "the best mussels" (and "frites" and "burgers"); visit during "off-hours" to avoid becoming "awash in a sea of youthful humanity."

Moonstruck *Italian*

21 | 20 | 21 | $47

Northeast Philly | 7955 Oxford Ave. (Rhawn St.) | 215-725-6000 | www.moonstruckrestaurant.com

Claire Di Lullo and Toto Schiavone's "old-world" Italian in Fox Chase has long been beloved as an "oasis in a desert of concrete and traf-fic" (in other words, Northeast Philly); aside from "tasty" food, both a layout that provides "intimacy" and "knowledgeable" service im-bue the place with "class", and even those struck by somewhat "high prices" call this one their "home away from home."

More Than Just Ice Cream *Dessert*

20 | 11 | 18 | $17

Center City East | 1119 Locust St. (bet. Quince & 12th Sts.) | 215-574-0586

"Bring your sweet tooth but leave your pancreas at home" before dig-ging into the "delightfully obscene" ice creams and "heavenly" deep-dish apple pies at this "chill", "diner-type" American joint in Wash West; since "yummy" burgers and sandwiches round out the rest of a "comfort-food-central" menu that's "much better than you'd expect", don't be surprised if you catch yourself noshing the night away.

Moriarty's ❶ *Pub Food*

19 | 15 | 17 | $22

Center City East | 1116 Walnut St. (Quince St.) | 215-627-7676 | www.moriartysrestaurant.com

"Beer, burgers, wings – that's all you need to know" about this "reli-able", "no-fuss" Center City pub "favorite" popular with "Forrest

	FOOD	DECOR	SERVICE	COST

Theatre"–goers and the "Jefferson Hospital crowd"; some like to "chase it all down" with a shot of "Saturday night karaoke."

☑ Morimoto *Japanese*
26 | 26 | 24 | $76

Center City East | 723 Chestnut St. (bet. 7th & 8th Sts.) | 215-413-9070 | www.morimotorestaurant.com

"Exquisite" "everything" sums up sentiment on this Japanese "foodie temple" in Center City fronted by *Iron Chef* Masaharu Morimoto and "dream-maker" Stephen Starr, where sushionados "splurge" for "sublime" creations "worth every penny" in "ultramodern" quarters suggesting the *"Star Trek* control room"; though the master toque is rarely on-premsies, a staff of "very knowledgeable" servers and ever-present sushi "geniuses" help ensure an "exceptional" experience; P.S. the seven-course omakase tasting menu ($80) is a "must."

Morning Glory Diner ⊄ *Diner*
24 | 12 | 17 | $17

South Philly | 735 S. 10th St. (Fitzwater St.) | 215-413-3999

"Everything is wonderful except the wait" at this "tiny", cash-only South Philly breakfast-luncher known for "awesome" "comfort food" ("the best reason to get up in the morning") and a "friendly" vibe; a post-Survey renovation may have addressed thoughts of dated decor.

☑ Morton's The Steakhouse *Steak*
25 | 21 | 24 | $66

Avenue of the Arts | 1411 Walnut St. (Broad St.) | 215-557-0724
King of Prussia | Pavilion at King of Prussia Mall | 640 W. DeKalb Pike (bet. Allendale & Long Rds.) | 610-491-1900
www.mortons.com

Bring your "appetite" and your "Lipitor" for the "manly sized" steaks in a "manly setting" at this meatery chain whose "high standards" extend to outposts in Center City and KoP; just don't forget your "corporate expense card" for the "pricey", "second-to-none" porterhouses and seafood hustled out by a "can-do" staff – even if the pre-dinner "raw" meat presentation isn't your thing.

Moshulu *American*
22 | 25 | 22 | $52

Delaware Riverfront | Penn's Landing | 401 S. Columbus Blvd. (Spruce St.) | 215-923-2500 | www.moshulu.com

"Terrific views" of the water from the dining room and deck of this "historic" 100-year-old four-masted ship–cum–New American restaurant berthed at Penn's Landing accompany Ralph Fernandez's "consistently good", Polynesian-accented New American fare, including "luxurious" $35 buffet Sunday brunches; it's all anchored by an "entertaining" crew; N.B. it serves alcohol but BYO is allowed ($25 corkage fee, bottles cannot be on their wine list).

Mother's Rest. & Wine Bar *American*
▽ 18 | 15 | 19 | $30

New Hope | 34 N. Main St. (bet. Bridge & Randolph Sts.) | 215-862-5857 | www.mothersnewhope.com

"Basics are done well" at this "casual" Traditional American "standby" on Main Street in New Hope, favored by "locals" who enjoy "people-watching" from sidewalk seats and bantering with the "very social staff"; weekend brunch and "frequent wine events" are additional draws.

	FOOD	DECOR	SERVICE	COST

Mr. Martino's Trattoria Ⓜ⊄ *Italian* | 22 | 19 | 23 | $28 |

South Philly | 1646 E. Passyunk Ave. (bet. Morris & Tasker Sts.) | 215-755-0663

"If feels like you're eating with family" declare devotees of Maria and Marc Farnese's "quaint", "cash-only" Italian BYO in an old hardware store "deep in the heart" of South Philly; the "limited menu" of "made-with-love" "home cooking" is, alas, served only at dinner Fridays–Sundays (they're closed the rest of the week).

Ms. Tootsie's *Soul Food* ▽ 21 | 16 | 19 | $27 |

South St. | 1314 South St. (13th St.) | 215-731-9045

Ms. Tootsie's Restaurant Bar Lounge ⓈⓂ *Soul Food*

South St. | 1312 South St. (13th St.) | 215-985-9001
www.kevenparker.net

KeVen Parker's "authentic" soul fooders in adjacent South Street storefronts – one's a lively restaurant, bar and lounge (open weekends), the other a more casual cafe – "win high acclaim" for "incomparable fried chicken and catfish" and other Southern-style eats; "you will not leave hungry", Tootsie.

Murray's Deli ⊄ *Deli* | 19 | 7 | 14 | $18 |

Bala Cynwyd | 285 Montgomery Ave. (Levering Mill Rd.) | 610-664-6995

"Unhinge your jaw" for "great" "overstuffed" sandwiches and other chow at this Bala "staple" locked in a "battle" for Main Line deli supremacy with Hymie's across the street; adherents simultaneously love the "grungy charm" that "never disappoints" yet blast both "tight quarters" and "service without a smile"; N.B. changed hands post-Survey (not necessarily reflected in the above scores).

ⓃⒺⓌ Murray's Deli/bistro M Ⓜ *Deli* | 19 | 16 | 19 | $28 |

Berwyn | 575 Lancaster Ave. (Lakeside Ave.) | 610-644-1010 | www.murraysmainline.com

Main Liners "welcome" this "pleasant surprise" in Berwyn, combining a Jewish deli counter for "blissfully noshing" on corned beef on rye with an industrial-looking BYO bistro next door serving an "exciting" Eclectic menu for breakfast, lunch, dinner and brunch; clearly "this is not your parents' deli."

Museum Restaurant Ⓜ *American* | 19 | 19 | 16 | $36 |

Fairmount | Philadelphia Museum of Art | 2601 Benjamin Franklin Pkwy. (Spring Garden St.) | 215-684-7990 | www.philamuseum.org

After being "cultured", stop in for "tasty" fare at the Philadelphia Museum of Art's "understated" eatery, a New American providing both "lovely interludes" for art fans and a "good", "creative" menu that mimics the exhibit (e.g. Cézanne-wich); overall, most find it a "treat", even if they think it costs a little too much Monet.

Mustard Greens *Chinese* | 21 | 15 | 21 | $27 |

Queen Village | 622 S. Second St. (bet. Bainbridge & South Sts.) | 215-627-0833

"Fresh, light" and "clean" is the word on the "nouvelle" cuisine at Bon Siu's "serene" Chinese in "charmingly spare" Queen Village

PHILADELPHIA

FOOD DECOR SERVICE COST

quarters; forget about "gloppy sauces" – this is a "healthy" alternative to "greasy" joints, and it's all enhanced by "pleasant" servers who hand out "steamed towels at the end."

My Thai *Thai* 18 | 15 | 20 | $24

Center City West | 2200 South St. (22nd St.) | 215-985-1878
"Thai one on" at this "peaceful retreat" "tucked away" near Graduate Hospital offering "dependably delicious and affordable" Thai that's "fresh and authentic", including popular three course prix fixes ($14.95 weekdays, $17.95 Fridays–Saturdays); while the "interior could use a face-lift", "warm welcomes" make it a good choice for most.

Naked Chocolate Café *Dessert* 25 | 18 | 19 | $12

Avenue of the Arts | 1317 Walnut St. (13th St.) | 215-735-7310 | www.nakedchocolatecafe.com
It may be "just a dessert cafe", but this Center City spot is a "chocoholic's heaven", offering "amazing cupcakes", "sinfully rich" "drinking chocolate" and other "wickedly delicious" delights in a "warmly lit" "adorably European" setting; it's "perfect for daytime dates and escaping the winter blues", though some complain there's "not enough seating" in the "tiny" space; N.B. a new Rittenhouse outpost is due in fall 2008.

Nam Phuong *Vietnamese* 24 | 9 | 17 | $19

South Philly | 1100-1120 Washington Ave. (11th St.) | 215-468-0410
This "always crowded", "warehouse-size" Vietnamese near the Italian Market turns out "delightful" pho and other "authentic" dishes at "bargain-basement" prices; while it adheres to the "restaurant school" dictum "get 'em in, get 'em out", and meals here are "like eating in a mess hall", all told, it offers up some of the best food "this side of Saigon."

Nan ⊠ *French/Thai* 25 | 15 | 21 | $40

University City | 4000 Chestnut St. (40th St.) | 215-382-0818 | www.nanrestaurant.com
Kamol Phutlek "knows what he's doing" at his BYO "oasis" near Penn in University City, serving up "well-executed", "beautifully presented" French-Thai "fusion" cuisine at prices that are "affordable enough for every day"; a "polite" staff works the "quiet", "minimalist" room, and while a few feel it's "time to change the menu", for many it "consistently delivers high value" and is "worth a trip."

Nan Zhou Hand Drawn Noodles ⋈ *Noodle Shop* 22 | 7 | 15 | $10

Chinatown | 927 Race St. (bet. 9th & 10th Sts.) | 215-923-1550
"If you want decor and service, don't come here", but "if you want the best bowl of noodle soup in Chinatown" then head to this cash-only BYO vending "miraculously" good noodles at "criminally" "cheap" prices ("I would have paid double"); P.S. watching the "experienced" staff at work provides a "good show."

	FOOD	DECOR	SERVICE	COST

National Mechanics ●⍟Ⓜ *Pub Food* ▽ 17 | 19 | 19 | $19

Old City | 22 S. Third St. (Market St.) | 215-701-4883 |
www.nationalmechanics.com

Boosters boast this "chill" pub "hangout" in a 19th-century bank
building is a "nice break from the tragically hip, trendy pretentiousness of Old City" with its "moody", Goth vibe, "weird art" and
"friendly" servers who are "a little bit punk"; expect "solid, standard" bar fare, a "great beer selection" served in "glasses imprinted
with famous Philly folk" and "unbeatable" prices.

☒ Nectar *Pan-Asian* 26 | 27 | 23 | $51

Berwyn | 1091 Lancaster Ave. (Manchester Ct.) | 610-725-9000 |
www.tastenectar.com

It's "oh-so-chic" ("there's not a GM car on the lot") at Michael Wei and
Scott Morrison's Berwyn Pan-Asian "destination", a "Buddakan clone"
that's "full of energy" and "yuppies" "carrying on" over "amazing",
"sophisticated" eats and "special" nectars in a "gorgeous" David
Rockwell–designed space; service is generally "attentive", and any
complaints about "pretense" are drowned out by the "noise"; P.S. the
$9.95 two-course lunches are some of the best "deals" around.

New Delhi Ⓜ *Indian* 20 | 13 | 17 | $16

University City | 4004 Chestnut St. (40th St.) | 215-386-1941 |
www.newdelhiweb.com

Adherents of this long-running University City Indian sing praises for
the "much-needed" "redecoration" ("works wonders") while digging
into the "same amazing" "bargain" buffets of "comfort food"; it's
popular with the "college crowd", hence "textbooks on the table."

New Samosa *Indian* ▽ 16 | 9 | 12 | $13

Center City East | 1214 Walnut St. (bet. 12th & 13th Sts.) | 215-546-2009

You "can't beat the price" at this "basic" all-veg Indian BYO in Center
City, which "fills a niche for hungry vegetarians" who enjoy its "full
menu" as well as the "tasty" buffets for "sampling" a "wide range of
foods"; still, a few miss its "old" incarnation.

New Tavern, The ⍟ *American* 16 | 16 | 18 | $33

Bala Cynwyd | 261 Montgomery Ave. (Levering Mill Rd.) | 610-667-9100 |
www.thetavernrestaurant.com

"It never changes – which is a good thing" according to fans of Nick
Zarvalas' "friendly neighborhood" place in Bala that provides "reasonably priced" Greek-influenced Traditional American fare along
with "great personal attention"; if it leaves a few unimpressed, it's "still
a treat" for an "older crowd" that finds it "like being at the club."

Newtown Grill *Italian/Steak* 21 | 19 | 21 | $45
(fka Alberto's)

Newtown Square | 191 S. Newtown Street Rd. (½ mi. south of
West Chester Pike) | 610-356-9700 | www.italiansteakhouse.com

"Outstanding steaks" and "above-average" Italian dishes are complemented by a "nice" wine list at this "huge" Newtown Square es-
tablishment; while some report "lower prices" and a "more casual"

FOOD | DECOR | SERVICE | COST

feel since the name change, it remains an "upscale" destination that's still popular among "business" diners; P.S. for "special occasions", regulars recommend reserving the "wine cellar."

New Wave Café ❶ *American* 18 | 12 | 18 | $26

Queen Village | 784 S. Third St. (Catharine St.) | 215-922-8484 | www.newwavecafe.com

"Everybody knows your name" at this "quintessential" "sports bar" in Queen Village, drawing "young professionals" who "grab a beer" to go with the new chef's "tasty" New American chow; even those who cite "hit-or-miss" grub agree it's a "good hangout"; P.S. a post-Survey spruce-up may address "dive bar" labels.

NEW Nicholas Ⓜ *American* - | - | - | M

South Philly | 2015 E. Moyamensing Ave. (Emily St.) | 215-271-7177 | www.nicholasphilly.com

Two vets of Striped Bass and Morimoto – both named Nick – teamed up for this tiny, cheerful New American located in a former gelateria in South Philly's emerging Pennsport neighborhood; studded with bargains, the menu changes with the marketplace, and mixers are available for those who bring their own spirits.

Nifty Fifty's ⊘ *Diner* 19 | 19 | 19 | $13

Northeast Philly | 2491 Grant Ave. (Blue Grass Rd.) | 215-676-1950
Bensalem | 2555 Street Rd. (Knights Rd.) | 215-638-1950
Folsom | 1900 MacDade Blvd. (Kedron Ave.) | 610-583-1950
www.niftyfiftys.com

Nostalgists take a "time-machine" ride back to the "happy days" of Ike at these "neon" diners "with a Philly twist", known for "upbeat" service, "street-corner doo-wop flowing from the speakers" and "fresh" burgers, fries and shakes "worth every calorie"; better still, the "trip down Memory Lane" is "cheap", but be sure to "bring cash", "daddy-o."

Ⓩ Nineteen (XIX) *American/Seafood* 23 | 27 | 23 | $58

Avenue of the Arts | Park Hyatt at the Bellevue | 200 S. Broad St., 19th fl. (Walnut St.) | 215-790-1919 | www.parkhyatt.com

The Park Hyatt's "luxurious", "modern" "aerie" will "impress your date or client", from its "stunning" 19th-story Center City "views" to the menu of "amazing" New American seafood (including "brunch elevated to lofty heights") and "charming" service; it's the "kind of indulgence" that might "break the bank", and while some find the "swanky" setting "over the top", where else can you wear your "mother's pearls and match the decor?"

Nodding Head Brewery & Restaurant ❶ *Pub Food* 18 | 14 | 17 | $23

Center City West | 1516 Sansom St., 2nd fl. (bet. 15th & 16th Sts.) | 215-569-9525 | www.noddinghead.com

There's appeal beyond the "bobblehead collection" at this "relaxed" pub on Sansom Street, namely "good" and somewhat "fancified" bar food that's inevitably washed down or preceded by "kick-butt"

	FOOD	DECOR	SERVICE	COST

brews (and "thank God they're cheap"); what with "comfy" booths and "rock" on the sound system, "dude, it's a hip place."

North by Northwest ◩ *American* | 16 | 15 | 15 | $29 |

Mount Airy | 7165 Germantown Ave. (Mt. Airy Ave.) | 215-248-1000 | www.nxnwphl.com

"Good food, good tunes, good times" are what fans find at this Mount Airy restaurant/nightclub outfitted with exposed brick and tin ceilings; even if some are less taken with the Traditional American fare ("average"), it's a "great place to catch a show" or "go swinging after dinner."

N. 3rd ◑ *American* | 22 | 18 | 19 | $26 |

Northern Liberties | 801 N. Third St. (Brown St.) | 215-413-3666 | www.norththird.com

The term 'pub grub' "doesn't do justice" to the New American dishes (from pierogi to quesadillas) at this "trendy" Northern Liberties corner spot that "sets the standard for great bar food"; you'll likely "never have a bad meal" here, and the "eclectic" decor (featuring "Christmas-tree" lights and "interesting" artwork for sale) works.

Oceanaire Seafood Room *Seafood* | 22 | 25 | 22 | $58 |

Center City East | 700 Walnut St. (Washington Sq.) | 215-625-8862 | www.theoceanaire.com

The "large on wow" factor impresses even landlubbers at this "elegant", "nautically" themed, "ocean liner"-like chain seafooder in a former bank on Washington Square, where "real pros" purvey "fresh-off-the-boat fish" befitting the evening's "big-ticket" tabs; those who deem it "style over substance" are in the minority; N.B. there's nothing fishy about the $30 three-course prix fixe (5–6:30 PM daily).

Ocean Harbor *Chinese* | 20 | 11 | 14 | $21 |

Chinatown | 1023 Race St. (bet. 10th & 11th Sts.) | 215-574-1398

Carts "loaded" with "every shape, size and flavor" of "top-notch dim sum" explain why this Chinatown Chinese is a "madhouse on weekends" ("arrive early" or expect a "long wait"); the decor "leaves a lot to be desired" and "ordering can be a challenge", but "at these prices, who cares?"

◪ Oishi *Pan-Asian* | 26 | 19 | 20 | $34 |

Newtown | 2817 S. Eagle Rd. (Durham Rd.) | 215-860-5511

Newtowners "storm" this "first-rate" BYO Pan-Asian for what many consider the "best sushi in Bucks" – plus "excellent hibachi fun" and "creative" Thai and Korean fare; though the strip-mall setting "doesn't do it justice", it's considered a "scene" by local standards.

Old Guard House Inn ◩ *American* | 23 | 20 | 22 | $50 |

Gladwyne | 953 Youngsford Rd. (Righters Mill Rd.) | 610-649-9708 | www.guardhouseinn.com

This "old-world" "Colonial" "throwback" "keeps the glad in Gladwyne", turning out "consistent" American-Germanic comfort food "with a flair"; you may need a "flashlight" in the "dark", "wooden" environs to view the menu but "there's a reason it's always crowded"; N.B. liquor is served but BYO is allowed – with a $20 per bottle corkage fee.

Old Original Bookbinder's *Seafood* | 19 | 20 | 19 | $54 |

Old City | 125 Walnut St. (2nd St.) | 215-925-7027 | www.bookbinders.biz
Tourists and locals say this Philly seafood "institution" in Old City "still feels like home" after a "trendy" redo, taking it a "step up from the old rubber-lobster" days with an "updated menu" that "revamps old favorites" while adding "eccentricities such as oyster shots"; still, a nostalgic few sigh it's "not what it used to be."

Olive Tree Mediterranean Grill ⊠ *Greek* | 23 | 14 | 20 | $28 |

Downingtown | 379 W. Uwchlan Ave. (Peck Rd.) |.610-873-7911 | www.olivetreegrill.com
Surveyors have recently "discovered" this casual Downingtown Greek BYO operating in strip-mall digs and serving "wonderful" homespun food (think Greek salads, souvlaki and calamari); reports indicate that the "welcoming" service is as pleasing as the "authentic" eats.

Ooka Japanese *Japanese* | 25 | 20 | 21 | $36 |

Doylestown | 110 Veterans Ln. (Main St.) | 215-348-8185
Willow Grove | 1109 Easton Rd. (Fitzwatertown Rd.) | 215-659-7688
www.ookasushi.com
"Ooh, ooh, Ooka" is the mantra at Benny and Lenny Huang's suburban Japanese twins (Willow Grove is BYO, while Doylestown added a sake bar post-Survey); "reservations" are a must given the "sinfully sublime" sushi and "delicious" hibachi fare dispensed by an "attentive" staff in "modern", "peaceful environs" ("except for the noise from the kids in the grill room").

Orchard, The Ⓜ *American* | - | - | - | E |

Kennett Square | 503 Orchard Ave. (Rte. 1) | 610-388-1100 | www.theorchardbyob.com
This Kennett Square BYO near Longwood Gardens changed hands post-Survey and is now under the helm of chef-owner Gary Trevisani (ex The Restaurant School at Walnut Hill College), who's turning out Continental–Regional American fare in "intimate", "understated" environs; N.B. there's a $5 corkage fee, capped at $10.

Ortlieb's Jazzhaus ● *Cajun* | - | - | - | M |

Northern Liberties | 847 N. Third St. (Poplar St.) | 215-922-1035 | www.ortliebsjazzhaus.com
Get a taste of the "past" at this "old-time" Cajun eatery-cum-jazz house in Northern Liberties, a Philly "must" that's been serving up "great" live acts for nearly 20 years; N.B. the full impact of mid-Survey changes in ownership, menu and decor remains to be seen.

Osaka *Japanese* | 23 | 18 | 18 | $36 |

Chestnut Hill | 8605 Germantown Ave. (Evergreen Ave.) | 215-242-5900 | www.osakachestnuthill.com

(continued)

Osaka

Wayne | 372 W. Lancaster Ave. (Strafford Ave.) | 610-902-6135
"High-quality", "beautifully" presented Japanese cuisine – particularly the "amazing" sushi – is the hallmark of this piscine-centric duo; they further appeal with "fabulous" sakes for adults, a fish tank (Lancaster Avenue) that "entertains" the kids and "wonderfully accommodating" (though sometimes "slow") service.

Ⓩ Osteria *Italian*

26 | 24 | 24 | $56

North Philly | 640 N. Broad St. (Wallace St.) | 215-763-0920 | www.osteriaphilly.com
"Bravo" declare devotees of chef Marc Vetri and Jeff Benjamin (the Vetri team) who've "done it again" with partner-chef Jeff Michaud at this "spectacular", "industrial"-style North Philly Italian "destination" distinguished for its "cutting-edge" cuisine, including "sublime" brick-oven pizzas, complemented by an "interesting" wine list; though less expensive than its celebrated sibling, many say it's still a "splurge."

Ota-Ya *Japanese*

24 | 14 | 20 | $35

Newtown | 10 Cambridge Ln. (Sycamore St.) | 215-860-6814 Ⓜ
Warrington | 638 Easton Rd. (Street Rd.) | 215-918-2900
www.ota-ya.com
Fans say "ya" to these casual Japanese BYOs known for "unique" sushi and cooked dishes ("the hibachi tables are a hit"); the digs may "need updating" but the "kind", "friendly" staff helps smooth the rough edges.

Otto's Brauhaus *German*

20 | 14 | 19 | $26

Horsham | 233 Easton Rd. (Pine Ave.) | 215-675-1864 | www.ottosbrauhauspa.com
"*Wunderbar*" is the word for the Teutonic treats at this circa-1930 German "institution" in Horsham that "raises the stein" to "perfectly prepared", "hearty classics" and "rare" imported brews; for most, "the real draw" is the "lovely summer beer garden", though the "delicious" Sunday buffet (4–8 PM, $18.95) is also an "excellent call"; N.B. new owners came onboard post-Survey.

Pace One *American*

21 | 22 | 22 | $44

Thornton | 341 Thornton Rd. (Glen Mills Rd.) | 610-459-3702 | www.paceone.net
There's "romance in the air" at this New American in an 18th-century farmhouse in Thornton, so "take a date" to the "intimate bar" and enjoy the "wonderful country inn atmosphere"; though distinguished for its "great brunch" (and steaks), the jaded complain the "menu's a little dated."

Palace at the Ben *Indian*

21 | 24 | 18 | $39

Center City East | Ben Franklin Hse. | 834 Chestnut St. (9th St.) | 267-232-5600 | www.palace-of-asia.com
This "swanked-out" Indian "hot spot" in the "stately" Ben Franklin House is undeniably "beautiful", and for many the "refined" menu and "specialty cocktails and wines" set it above the crop of "bare-

bones" "buffet" joints; still, a dissenting faction reports it's "over-priced" for "average" food and "haphazard" if "friendly" service.

Palace of Asia *Indian*   24 | 17 | 20 | $25
Fort Washington | Best Western Inn | 285 Commerce Dr. (Delaware Dr.) | 215-646-2133

"Delicious and ambitious" Indian fare awaits Eastern Montco curry connoisseurs who sate "hankerings" for "authentic" flavors at this "pleasant" spot in the Best Western in Fort Washington; just don't go "for the ambiance" or "if you're in a rush", given the "friendly" if "slow" service; P.S. there's an "awesome" $9.95 lunch buffet.

Palm *Steak*   23 | 19 | 22 | $62
Avenue of the Arts | The Bellevue | 200 S. Broad St. (Walnut St.) | 215-546-7256 | www.thepalm.com

"The powers that be" can be themselves at this "bustling" meatery "mainstay" in The Bellevue, chowing down on "enormous portions" of "top-flight" steaks and seafood amid caricatures of the "famous" on the walls; "expense accounts" come in handy at this "oldie but goodie" with "no surprises" – and for most that's a "good thing."

ⓩ Paloma ⓈⓂ *French/Mexican*   27 | 20 | 27 | $50
Northeast Philly | 6516 Castor Ave. (bet. Hellerman St. & Magee Ave.) | 215-533-0356 | www.palomafinedining.com

"It's always a pleasure" for fans of this "surprise" French-Mexican "sleeper" on an "unlikely" block in Northeast Philly, purveying "sublime", "magnificently presented" cuisine that's "worth the trip if you want a classy meal"; "wonderful" service (the owner "takes a personal interest in your satisfaction") and a "quaint" atmosphere add to the "wow" factor; N.B. open for dinner Thursdays–Saturdays.

Paradigm ⓈⓂ *American*   18 | 20 | 18 | $39
Old City | 239 Chestnut St. (bet. 2nd & 3rd Sts.) | 215-238-6900 | www.paradigmrestaurant.com

A "hip crowd" makes "the scene" at this "trendy", "clubby" Old City American with "*très chic*" decor; the food may "vary", ditto the service, but the cocktails are "great", and some say it's "worth the trip just for the ultracool bathrooms."

Paradiso Ⓜ *Italian*   23 | 22 | 23 | $44
South Philly | 1627-29 E. Passyunk Ave. (Tasker St.) | 215-271-2066 | www.paradisophilly.com

There's a "Center City flair" that makes this "upscale" Italian a piece of paradise on South Philly's East Passyunk strip; it may be a "bit pricey" but it's a "good value" when you consider chef-owner Lynn Rinaldi's "creative" cuisine and "extensive" wine list that comes complete with a "knowledgeable" staff.

NEW Parc *French*   - | - | - | M
Center City West | Parc Rittenhouse | 227 S. 18th St. (Locust St.) | 215-545-2262 | www.parc-restaurant.com

Stephen Starr's airy though intimate brasserie in the Parc Rittenhouse brings a big touch of Paris to Rittenhouse Square; not only does sidewalk dining along both the 18th and Locust Street sides add to the feeling of joie de vivre, so do bistro favorites from chef Dominique Filoni (ex Savona and Bianca in the 'burbs, Four Seasons Hotel in DC) served at the zinc bar and throughout the antiques-filled lounge and dining room.

Parc Bistro *American* | 25 | 22 | 23 | $43 |

Skippack | 4067 Skippack Pike (bet. Church & Store Rds.) | 610-584-1146 | www.parcbistro.com

"Innovative" New American cuisine and "not-to-be-missed" brick-oven pizza are "worth the trip" to this "charming" eatery in a refurbished 19th-century roadside inn located in Downtown Skippack; factor in an "inviting" vibe (with summer patio dining) and "knowledgeable" service and fans say it "rivals any restaurant in Center City."

Passage to India *Indian* | 19 | 13 | 17 | $21 |

Avenue of the Arts | 1320 Walnut St. (Juniper St.) | 215-732-7300

"Delicious" treats at "terrific values" is a rite of passage for devotees of this "friendly", spacious Center City Indian near the theaters; the "fabulous" buffets – $8.99 lunch, $10.99 dinner – offer "a nice sampling" (with many "vegetarian choices"), and if the "no-frills" decor is a bore, a weekend piano player helps brighten things up.

Patou 🅼 *French/Mediterranean* | 18 | 17 | 17 | $42 |

Old City | 312 Market St. (bet. 3rd & 4th Sts.) | 215-928-2987 | www.patourestaurant.com

The "Côte d'Azur" comes to Old City via Patrice Rames' "hip", "high-ceilinged" nautically themed French-Med; but surveyors seem adrift on its attributes, with some praising the "thought and care" put into the fare and point out it "won't break the bank", while others are "disappointed" with "inconsistent" eats and service and think the interior more "waiting area than restaurant."

Pat's King of Steaks ◐⇲ *Cheese Steaks* | 20 | 7 | 12 | $11 |

South Philly | 1237 E. Passyunk Ave. (9th St.) | 215-468-1546 | www.patskingofsteaks.com

"All hail the king" say aficionados of this 24/7 South Philly cheese steak "institution" that "defines the genre" (and whose Food rating just beats the "competition" across the street), doling out "authentic" "mm-mm greasy" sandwiches with a "side of attitude"; the "tourists" and "pilgrims" who join the "long lines" "better know" what they want when they order – "wit'" means "wit' onions" – and keep their wits about them.

Pattaya Grill *Thai* | 19 | 15 | 17 | $21 |

University City | 4006 Chestnut St. (40th St.) | 215-387-8533 | www.pattayacuisine.com

Pennsters swear by this "quaint" University City Thai for "reliably tasty" cooking from an "extensive" menu, albeit one "without surprises"; "you can bring anyone" to this place, and they'll probably come away pleased on account of "budget"-friendly tabs and a glass-enclosed sunroom that gives a "wonderful sense of the outdoors."

NEW Pearl *Pan-Asian* — — — M
Center City West | 1904 Chestnut St. (19th St.) | 215-564-9090 | www.pearlphilly.com
This modern bistro/lounge near Rittenhouse Square shimmers with multicolor lighting, beaded curtains and sumptuous banquette seating, a sexy backdrop for its ambitious Pan-Asian menu from Ari Weiswasser (ex Striped Bass); the upstairs bar features a DJ booth and private rooms for bottle service.

Penang ● *Malaysian* 22 18 18 $24
Chinatown | 117 N. 10th St. (bet. Arch & Cherry Sts.) | 215-413-2531 | www.penangusa.com
"Adventurous" foodies look to this "bustling", "contemporary" Malaysian chain link in the middle of Chinatown for "big", "bold" dishes that "please all the senses"; "eat quickly and talk elsewhere", since servers who try to keep up work at the "speed of light" amid a "continuous din"; N.B. now accepting major credit cards.

Penne *Italian* 18 19 19 $38
University City | Inn at Penn | 3611 Walnut St. (36th St.) | 215-823-6222 | www.pennerestaurant.com
Watching the "heavenly" pastas being made before your eyes gives this "fancified" Italian in the Inn at Penn the nickname "penne campus"; though some insist the "hit-or-miss" service is "out of its (Ivy) League" and suggest "South Philly" for the "real" deal when it comes to food, many maintain this spot is a "surprisingly good" option to "typical campus fare."

NEW Peppercorns Ⓜ *American* — — — M
South Philly | 1401 E. Moyamensing Ave. (Reed St.) | 267-322-3000
This airy, contemporary newcomer on a quiet South Philly corner draws locals after a movie at the Riverview for straightforward, mid-priced New American fare; after-work and late-night crowds are already gathering at its well-stocked bar.

Pepper's Cafe Ⓢ⊘ *Italian* ▽ 23 5 21 $19
Ardmore | 2528 Haverford Rd. (Eagle Rd.) | 610-896-0476 | www.pepperscafe.net
Main Liners seek out Kate Rapine's "tiny hut" for "yummy" pastas and other "superb" Italian food dished out by "caring", "friendly" folks; with just a few seats and not much decor inside, most head for the patio or opt for takeout, the latter a "working mom's dream" come true.

Persian Grill *Persian* 20 11 19 $29
Lafayette Hill | 637 Germantown Pike (Crescent Ave.) | 610-825-2705
Instantly recognized by its "turquoise" pond out front and easily mistaken for a "small diner" from its exterior is this "low-key" Montco mainstay that has fans "purring" over "very good" Persian cooking; what's more, the prices are "good" and the service "gracious."

	FOOD	DECOR	SERVICE	COST

☒ P.F. Chang's China Bistro *Chinese* | 21 | 21 | 19 | $31 |

NEW **Warrington** | Valley Sq. | 721 Easton Rd. (Street Rd.) |
215-918-3340
Glen Mills | Shoppes at Brinton Lake | 983 Baltimore Pike (Brinton Lake Rd.) |
610-545-3030
NEW **Plymouth Meeting** | 510 W. Germantown Pike (Hickory Rd.) |
610-567-0226
www.pfchangs.com

"Hefty portions" of "reliably consistent" Chinese food – including
"lettuce wraps" and "dumplings to die for" – plus "polite" service
draw "long lines" to this "glitzy" mid-market chain that "raises the
concept on takeout"; while some find the "uptempo" scene "noisy"
and others "energetic, most say it's "fun."

Philadelphia Fish & Co. *Seafood* | 21 | 17 | 20 | $40 |

Old City | 207 Chestnut St. (2nd St.) | 215-625-8605 |
www.philadelphiafish.com

Although the "name may sound boring", the fare at Kevin and Janet
Meeker's Old City seafooder provides a useful example of how "excellent" "simple preparations from quality products" can be; "pleasant" service and a bar menu that's "the best bargain in town" mean
this longtimer's still a "keeper"; P.S. their burgers are a "favorite."

Phillips Seafood *Seafood* | 19 | 16 | 19 | $48 |

Center City West | Sheraton City Center Hotel | 200 N. 17th St.
(Race St.) | 215-448-2700 | www.phillipsseafood.com

Respondents report the "to-die-for" crab cakes make this outpost of
a "venerable" Maryland seafood chain in the Sheraton City Center
worth a visit; while detractors dis "oversized prices" and "bland" decor, count on "an excellent wine selection."

Pho 75 ⊅ *Vietnamese* | 22 | 7 | 17 | $12 |

Chinatown | 1022 Race St. (10th St.) | 215-925-1231
Northeast Philly | 823 Adams Ave. (Roosevelt Blvd.) | 215-743-8845
South Philly | 1122 Washington Ave. (12th St.) | 215-271-5866

"Fragrant", "soul-satisfying" Vietnamese noodle soups and service
"faster than the speed of light" are what you get at these local "lino-
leum" "ca-pho-terias"; so what if they're "dives" – "for these prices,
who cares how the place looks?" N.B. cash-only.

Pho Thai Nam Ⓜ *Thai/Vietnamese*   ▽ | 21 | 9 | 20 | $22 |

Blue Bell | Whitpain Shopping Ctr. | 1510 DeKalb Pike (Yost Rd.) |
610-272-3935 | www.phothainam.com

Though the Vietnamese menu is "limited" at this "modest" Thai-
Vietnamese BYO in a Blue Bell strip mall, surveyors claim some of
the "best pho in the suburbs" comes out of the kitchen; N.B. the
$8.95 lunch special includes two courses and a drink.

Pho Xe Lua *Vietnamese* | 24 | 8 | 15 | $16 |

Chinatown | 907 Race St. (9th St.) | 215-627-8883

It's "all aboard" the 'pho train' – its name in Vietnamese – pho fans
of some of the "best" noodle soups in Chinatown; "slurp" away while
you "bump your neighbors' elbows" and deal with the "hit-or-miss"

service and "dismal" atmosphere that are part of the experience (including a "neon train" in the window); N.B. closed Wednesdays.

Picasso Ⓜ *Italian/Spanish* ▽ 17 | 16 | 16 | $41

Media | 36 W. State St. (Olive St.) | 610-891-9600 | www.picasso-bar.com
Small plates of "good" Italian-Spanish food provide a "nice complement" to the fare at the next-door (and related) La Belle Epoque at this wine-focused Media bar with a "bistro-like" vibe; the "people-watching" possibilities are "great", and the overall scene is enhanced by live music some nights.

Piccolo Trattoria *Italian* 21 | 15 | 18 | $30

Newtown | 32 West Rd. (Eagle Rd.) | 215-860-4247 |
www.piccolotrattoria.com
"Good", "homemade" Italian cookery trumps the "strip-mall" locale of this "small" Bucks BYO where "waits" and "friendly", "brisk" service are the norm; the "exceptionally varied" menu including "extensive" daily specials help generate popularity.

Pietro's Coal Oven Pizzeria *Pizza* 19 | 15 | 16 | $23

Center City West | 1714 Walnut St. (bet. 17th & 18th Sts.) | 215-735-8090
South St. | 121 South St. (bet. Front & Hancock Sts.) | 215-733-0675
www.pietrospizza.com
"Mouthwatering" "thin-crust" pies and "humongous" salads sate "the entire family" at this "rustic" Italian trio considered "heaven" by pizza pros; ok, the service ranges from "passable" to "slow", and so what if they're "too loud" (go ahead and "bring your baby") to carry on a conversation?

🆕 Pietro's Prime *Steak* ▽ 24 | 19 | 19 | $55

West Chester | 125 W. Market St. (Darlington St.) | 484-760-6100 |
www.pietrosprime.com
"Delicious" steaks, well-made Cosmos and overall "hustle and bustle" sum up this stylish midrange steakhouse down the street from the Chester County Courthouse in West Chester, noted for live jazz and soft rock later in the week and weeknight happy-hour specials; "cheerful" management walks around tables to "make sure everything is good", though a few note it's "still growing into itself."

Pink Rose Pastry Shop *Bakery* 21 | 16 | 16 | $13

South St. | 630 S. Fourth St. (Bainbridge St.) | 215-592-0565
With "too many delicious desserts" to choose from, it's "hard not to have your sweet-tooth life changed" after walking out of this "local blessing" of a Queen Village bakery purveying "rich, enticing" pastries to fans who tend to "indulge"; some even like the "froufrou" "Victoriana" of the decor, which seems to suit the mood and "homey" goods.

Pistachio Grille Ⓜ *American/Mediterranean* ▽ 19 | 15 | 18 | $33

Maple Glen | 521 Limekiln Pike (Norristown Rd.) | 215-643-7400 |
www.thepistachiogrille.com
Locals who laud the "wonderful" New American-Med eats at this BYO "find" in Maple Glen are willing to "overlook the strip-mall loca-

tion" and "funky decor"; a minority reports service might improve with "more staff."

Pizzicato *Italian*   20 | 16 | 19 | $30

Old City | 248 Market St. (3rd St.) | 215-629-5527

The "reasonably" priced "quality" food shows a "surprising consistency" and encourages "repeat visits" to these "understated", "laid-back" Italians good for "quick bites" at lunch or dinner before or after the theater (Old City) or shopping (Marlton, which is BYO).

P.J. Whelihan's ● *Pub Food*   15 | 14 | 15 | $21

Blue Bell | 799 Dekalb Pike (Skippack Pike) | 610-272-8919 | www.pjspub.com

"Lots of options" keep crowds "hanging out" at this expanding pub chain in Blue Bell and South Jersey, considered a "reliable standby" for "bar food" ("must-try" "hot and honey wings", a "good beer selection"), a "fun" crowd and "watching sports" on TV; if some find the service "slow", at least it provides "plenty of eye candy."

Plate *American*   16 | 16 | 16 | $32

Ardmore | Suburban Sq. | 105 Coulter Ave. (Anderson Ave.) | 610-642-5900 | www.platerestaurant.com

You'll say "Center City" to yourself after paying a visit to this "contemporary" Traditional American comfort-fooder in Suburban Square; though some cite "uneven" fare and service "snafus", for others, it "doesn't disappoint" as they cater to everyone from "families with finicky kids" to "trendy" types.

Plough & the Stars *Pub Food*   18 | 19 | 19 | $33

Old City | 123 Chestnut St. (2nd St.) | 215-733-0300 | www.ploughstars.com

"When the city's snowed in", it's comforting that the fireplace "burns bright", the "Guinness" flows and bands play "wonderful" music at this "authentic" Irish pub inside a high-ceilinged converted bank in Old City; fans also favor the "good" fare, "friendly", "gabby" staffers and "lively", "people-watching" atmosphere.

Plumsteadville Inn Ⓜ *American*   19 | 21 | 20 | $38

Plumsteadville | Plumsteadville Inn | Rte. 611 & Stump Rd. (4 mi. north of Doylestown) | 215-766-7500 | www.theplumsteadvilleinn.com

"Bucks County charm" abounds at this Traditional American eatery located in a circa-1751 inn; maybe its "basic menu" won't excite foodies, but partisans say it offers "good" meals at "prices that won't offend" in a "historic setting" that works for anything from "birthdays" to a "quiet dinner."

Pod *Pan-Asian*   23 | 25 | 20 | $44

University City | 3636 Sansom St. (bet. 36th & 37th Sts.) | 215-387-1803 | www.podrestaurant.com

"Beam me up, Stephen Starr" to this "groovy", "futuristic" Pan-Asian plotted on the Penn campus, which takes "taste buds on a journey of delight" (perhaps to "the set of *Star Trek*") with "swimmingly fabu-

FOOD DECOR SERVICE COST

lous" "conveyor-belt" sushi and "inventive" dishes; it draws "mon-
eyed" types who like to reserve a "multicolor pod" where they can
"play with the lights" ("a blast"), but a few earthlings find the "sci-fi"
experience "a little too hip" for its "own good."

Pond Restaurant 🅾🅼 *French/Mediterranean* 21 | 24 | 19 | $58

Radnor | 175 King of Prussia Rd. (E. Lancaster Ave.) | 610-293-9411 |
www.pondrestaurant.com

Whether you dine in the "elegant" interior or on the "terrace and
watch the swans" glide by, this "gorgeous" Main Line French-Med
"pleases" for "fancy" lunches or "special-occasion" dinners; yes, it's
"pricey" but the tranquil setting and "friendly" staff help soothe ruf-
fled feathers; N.B. tasting menus available.

Porcini 🅾 *Italian* 22 | 11 | 20 | $34

Center City West | 2048 Sansom St. (bet. 20th & 21st Sts.) |
215-751-1175

"Amazing" homemade pastas make up for the "tight squeeze" at
this "romantic", "smaller-than-a-shoebox" Italian BYO "bargain"
"tucked away" near Rittenhouse Square, where the Sansone
brothers make you "feel like part of the family"; if it's "crowded
and loud", most find it "part of the fun" – and are delighted they
now take reservations.

Portofino *Italian* 20 | 18 | 19 | $41

Center City East | 1227 Walnut St. (bet. 12th & 13th Sts.) | 215-923-8208 |
www.portofino1227walnut.com

Get a "very good" meal in before seeing a show at this "nicely re-
furbed", longstanding Center City Italian whose "delightful"
servers are skilled at the art of "getting you to the theater on
time"; even though it's a moderately "upscale" kind of place, fans
applaud the 20% discount on your meal when you show the
staff your ticket.

Positano Coast *Italian* 21 | 24 | 20 | $40

Society Hill | 212 Walnut St., 2nd fl. (2nd St.) | 215-238-0499 |
www.lambertis.com

This "evocative" Lamberti family Italian is like an "instant spa vaca-
tion" ("without the massage") with a "dreamy coastal" feel;
"Euro-philes" enjoy the "first-rate", "creative" small plates "prepared with care" and "attentive" service that "takes you away" to a
happy point between "the banging drums of Old City and the quiet
spots of Society Hill."

Primavera Pizza Kitchen *Pizza* 18 | 19 | 16 | $29

Ardmore | 7 E. Lancaster Ave. (Cricket Ave.) | 610-642-8000
Downingtown | Ashbridge Shopping Ctr. | 853 E. Lancaster Ave.
(Plaza Dr.) | 610-873-6333 | www.primaverapk.com

These "affordable" Italians (one in a "hangar"-size space in
Downingtown and the other occupying a former Ardmore bank
building) attract "kids", "adults" and those on "dates" with "well-
prepared" pastas and pizzas and bar scenes; N.B. the properties are
now separately owned.

	FOOD	DECOR	SERVICE	COST

Prime Rib *Steak*

25 | 25 | 24 | $65

Center City West | Radisson Plaza-Warwick Hotel | 1701 Locust St. (17th St.) | 215-772-1701 | www.theprimerib.com

"Old-fashioned supper club" meets "classy" steakhouse at this "sophisticated" "temple" to beef in the Radisson Warwick, where "Fred Flintstone–size slabs" of "expensive-but-worth-it" prime rib come complete with all the "trimmings" – plus "nightly music", a "well-schooled staff" and on Sundays, a three-course "bargain" prix fixe; N.B. jackets required only in main dining room (other areas business-casual).

PTG Ⓜ *Italian*

▽ 20 | 15 | 22 | $40

Roxborough | 6813 Ridge Ave. (Parker Ave.) | 215-487-2293 | www.ptgrestaurantandcaterers.com

"You feel like part of the family" at this "nicely redone" "neighborhood" Italian BYO in Roxborough; most agree that the "hunt for parking" pays off with "well-prepared" food served by "down-home, friendly" folks (just "don't let it get around").

Public House at Logan Square *American*

15 | 17 | 15 | $31

Center City West | 1801 Arch St. (18th St.) | 215-587-9040 | www.publichousephilly.com

"What a meat market" marvel followers of the action at this "upscale" Center City American bar "loaded" with "after-work attorneys" and other "young professionals" who congregate for the "hot" happy hour in the "cool", "warehouselike" space; "passable" fare suggests more "social scene" than cuisine here, and some note "shaky" service in this house.

Pub of Penn Valley *Eclectic*

19 | 12 | 19 | $28

Narberth | 863 Montgomery Ave. (Iona Ave.) | 610-664-1901 | www.pubofpennvalley.com

"Bump into someone you know" at this "low-key", *"Cheers"*-like Main Line Tudor-style taphouse, whose staff "greets customers with a smile"; it's "popular", so "expect to wait" for "satisfying" Eclectic pub fare ("who knew?") that's "a cut above" the norm.

Pumpkin Ⓜ🍽 *American*

24 | 17 | 22 | $39

Center City West | 1713 South St. (17th St.) | 215-545-4448

Ian Moroney's "refined cooking" from a "daily changing menu" has carved a niche among "adventurous eaters" who "squeeze" into the "quirky", "shoebox-size" New American BYO he runs near Graduate Hospital with partner Hilary Bor; though it has all of 28 seats, the "sweet" room "brims with character."

Pura Vida ⓈⓂ🍽 *Pan-Latin*

▽ 24 | 13 | 21 | $18

Northern Liberties | 547 Fairmount Ave. (6th St.) | 215-922-6433

"More attention" should be paid to this rustic Pan-Latin BYO "corner joint" on the edge of Northern Liberties that "produces some of the best fusion *comidas* around" (e.g. gaucho-grilled flank steak with tequila shrimp and roasted potatoes in chimichurri); "friendly service" and "great value" make it "always worth a visit."

	FOOD	DECOR	SERVICE	COST

Qdoba Mexican Grill *Mexican* — 17 | 9 | 14 | $11

Center City West | 1528 Walnut St. (16th St.) | 215-546-8007
Center City West | 1900 Chestnut St. (19th St.) | 215-568-1009
North Philly | 1600 N. Broad St. (W. Oxford St.) | 215-763-4090
University City | 230 S. 40th St. (Locust St.) | 215-222-2887
Springfield | 1054 Baltimore Pike (Riverview Rd.) |
610-543-4104
Bala Cynwyd | Bala Cynwyd Shopping Ctr. | 33 E. City Ave.
(Conshohocken State Rd.) | 610-664-2906
www.qdoba.com

They're "not gourmet" but for "solid, cheap" "made-to-order" burritos and other "addictive" Mex munchies most amigos favor these "fresh fast-food" chain links with "cafeteria-style dining" and counter help that moves *"muy rapido"* – so what if it's a "dieter's nightmare?"

Radicchio *Italian* — 24 | 17 | 22 | $35

Old City | 402 Wood St. (4th St.) | 215-627-6850 |
www.radicchio-cafe.com

"Outstanding" fish filleted tableside by "skilled waiters" before a "standing-room-only" crowd and "skinny prices" are the hook at this "tiny", "rustic" Old City BYO trattoria; it's "worth circling the block 10 times" for a parking space, but many find the "no-reservations" policy "problematic": "get there early – or be willing to wait."

Rae *American* — 22 | 21 | 19 | $54

University City | Cira Ctr. | 2929 Arch St. (30th St.) | 215-922-3839 |
www.raerestaurant.com

Devotees of Daniel (Gayle) Stern are wowed by his "modern", "urbane" New American "destination" near Amtrak's 30th Street Station in the Cira Centre, where the "well-heeled" savor "innovative and unlikely combinations" (e.g. smoked rabbit nachos); even so, some suggest it "doesn't live up to the hype", citing service "lapses" and "sky-high prices" befitting the "skyscraper" surroundings.

Ralph's ⊄ *Italian* — 22 | 15 | 20 | $32

South Philly | Italian Mkt. | 760 S. Ninth St. (bet. Catharine & Fitzwater Sts.) | 215-627-6011 | www.ralphsrestaurant.com

"Still fun after all these years" – about 100 – the Rubino family's "quaint" South Philly "classic" Italian keeps on rolling, with "big portions" of "reasonably priced", "red-gravy" eats (including "forever-amazing pasta"), waiters who "make you feel welcome" and "checkered tablecloths"; in other words, it's "the whole nine yards" – and the "ATM in the dining room" is handy (it's cash-only).

Rangoon *Burmese* — 24 | 14 | 22 | $21

Chinatown | 112 N. Ninth St. (bet. Arch & Cherry Sts.) |
215-829-8939

"For something totally different" the intrepid rally 'round this "must-try" Burmese in Chinatown offering "well-seasoned", "wallet-friendly" dishes ("delicious" thousand-layer bread, "filling" noodles) amid "cozy" Asian-accented surroundings; "swift", "solicitous" service seals the deal.

	FOOD	DECOR	SERVICE	COST

Raw Sushi & Sake Lounge *Japanese* | 24 | 23 | 20 | $40 |

Center City East | 1225 Sansom St. (bet. 12th & 13th Sts.) |
215-238-1903 | www.rawlounge.net

"Sushi lovers should shimmy on over" to this "sexy", "upscale" Center
City Japanese "resto-lounge" in an old "Stetson Hat factory" for
"creative" rolls and "sake flights" from a list that would "make Japan
proud"; "fast service" makes it a "nice lunchtime getaway", and the
"dressy" dinner crowd can "cozy" up in the "hip", "romantic" setting.

Ray's Cafe & Tea House 🗷 *Chinese* | ▽ 25 | 12 | 21 | $19 |

Chinatown | 141 N. Ninth St. (bet. Cherry & Race Sts.) | 215-922-5122 |
www.rayscafe.com

For "the best cup o' joe" in Philly fans flock to Grace Chen's "intimate", "minimal" Chinatown Taiwanese BYO, a "find" for "fancy
brewed coffee" (prepared in a glass siphon), "out-of-this-world"
dumplings and bubble tea; "kind, friendly people" who "go the extra
mile to see you're happy" help make it a "local" favorite.

🗷 Reading Terminal Market 🗷 *Eclectic* | 23 | 13 | 15 | $14 |

Center City East | 51 N. 12th St. (Arch St.) | 215-922-2317 |
www.readingterminalmarket.org

"This little piggy goes to market" say "grazers" who "regularly" em-
bark on a culinary "treasure hunt" within this "sprawling"
Philadelphia "landmark" next to the Pennsylvania Convention
Center; a "something-for-everybody" extravaganza, it boasts dozens of ethnic stalls and a "real farmer's market" (with Amish and
Mennonite vendors Wednesdays–Saturdays) plus "compelling"
people-watching amid the "frenzy" of food court seating, making it
a "favorite" pastime for locals and "a must for out-of-towners";
N.B. open daily.

Redstone American Grill ● *American* | 21 | 22 | 20 | $36 |

NEW **Plymouth Meeting** | Plymouth Meeting | 512 W. Germantown Pike
(N. Wales Rd.) | 610-941-4400 | www.redstonegrill.com
See review in the New Jersey Suburbs Directory.

Rembrandt's *American* | 20 | 18 | 19 | $34 |

Fairmount | 741 N. 23rd St. (Aspen St.) | 215-763-2228 |
www.rembrandts.com

Fans of this "long-running" Fairmount hangout paint a picture of
"hearty", "interesting" American fare and "friendly" service, even
when the occasional "kid" pops in; aside from the "down-to-earth"
atmosphere, the "great" bar and entertainment (quizzo and live
jazz) make it "worthwhile."

🗷 Restaurant Alba Ⓜ *American* | 27 | 22 | 25 | $46 |

Malvern | 7 W. King St. (Warren Ave.) | 610-644-4009 |
www.restaurantalba.com

"Serious cooking" from Sean Weinberg's "wood-fired grill" attracts
a "gourmet" crowd to this "warm" Malvern New American BYO for
locally driven, "nuanced" cuisine (including a five-course tasting
menu and "innovative" antipasto plates) proffered by "profession-

als"; quibbles about "noise" and "smoke" from the grill aside, "it doesn't get much better than this" in the 'burbs.

Restaurant Taquet ⊠ *French/Mediterranean* | 24 | 23 | 23 | $50 |

Wayne | Wayne Hotel | 139 E. Lancaster Ave. (Wayne Ave.) | 610-687-5005 | www.taquet.com

"Outstanding" French-Med fare is "well worth the hefty tariff" at this "romantic" Main Line "classic" in the Wayne Hotel; any complaints about a "stuffy" dining room are overshadowed by praise for a "great bar" and "welcoming" veranda; N.B. a post-Survey change of chef may alter the above Food score.

Rib Crib ●⊠Ⓜ∌ *BBQ* | 22 | 8 | 16 | $18 |

Germantown | 6333 Germantown Ave. (bet. Duval St. & Washington Ln.) | 215-438-6793

"Bone-sucking-good" BBQ ribs are the attraction at this "genuine" Germantown "hole-in-the-wall" where everything's "done the old-fashioned way", from the "white bread to sop up the sauce" to the service by "friendly" women with "huge" "biceps" from "cutting the" meat; N.B. open for takeout only Thursdays–Saturdays (cash only).

Ristorante Il Melograno Ⓜ *Italian* | ▽ 24 | 17 | 23 | $49 |

Doylestown | Mercer Sq. Shopping Ctr. | 73 Old Dublin Pike (Main St.) | 215-348-7707 | www.ilmelogranodoylestown.com

Bucks Countians enjoy "classic" Italian cookery in "plentiful" portions at this "small", white-tablecloth strip-mall "surprise" outside Doylestown; claims of "dependable" from "start to finish" extend to the "congenial" service, and it almost goes without saying reservations are highly suggested.

Ristorante La Buca ⊠ *Italian* | 22 | 16 | 23 | $49 |

Center City East | 711 Locust St. (bet. 7th & 8th Sts.) | 215-928-0556 | www.ristlabuca.com

"Classic", "old-world" Italian "at its best" still comes out of Giuseppe Giuliani's kitchen at his "been-here-forever" "time capsule" "basement" on Washington Square; fans never tire of "tuxedoed waiters" wheeling "carts" laden with "fresh fish and great cuts of meat" in an atmosphere that's "elegant without being showy."

Ristorante Panorama *Italian* | 24 | 22 | 22 | $52 |

Old City | Penn's View Hotel | 14 N. Front St. (Market St.) | 215-922-7800 | www.pennsviewhotel.com

"Light, fresh" gnocchi and other "traditional" Italian favorites are "enhanced" by "top-notch" "wine flights" at this "comfortable" trattoria in the Penn's View Hotel in Old City; it's clearly "La Famiglia's little brother" given the "classy" service.

Ristorante Pesto *Italian* | 22 | 18 | 21 | $32 |

South Philly | 1915 S. Broad St. (bet. McKean & Mifflin Sts.) | 215-336-8380 | www.ristorantepesto.com

"Bring some Chianti" and "come hungry" to this "upbeat" BYO across from St. Agnes; "wonderful" Italian food (and specials "longer than the regular menu") awaits you, as does a "friendly"

	FOOD	DECOR	SERVICE	COST

vibe and rustic setting filled with antiques and terra-cotta – all factoring in to its success.

Ristorante Primavera *Italian*
| 17 | 15 | 18 | $36 |

Wayne | 384 W. Lancaster Ave. (Conestoga Rd.) | 610-254-0200
Main Liners craving a "solid" Italian meal head for this "unpretentious" Wayne trattoria where a "quick, polite" staff makes folks feel as "comfortable in jeans" as "in a suit"; just stick to the "basics" and "don't let the regulars intimidate you."

☑ Ristorante San Marco ☒ *Italian*
| 26 | 22 | 22 | $51 |

Ambler | 504 N. Bethlehem Pike (Dager Rd.) | 215-654-5000 |
www.sanmarcopa.com
"Top-rate" Northern Italian seafood and "impressive" wines suitable for "celebrations" are the draw at this "upscale", "villa"-like "find" near Ambler; while the service may be "impersonal", it's "dedicated", in "old-school fine-dining fashion."

Rock Bottom Restaurant & Brewery *Pub Food*
| 16 | 14 | 15 | $24 |

King of Prussia | Plaza at King of Prussia Mall | 160 N. Gulph Rd. (DeKalb Pike) | 610-337-7737 | www.rockbottom.com
Women shoppers send their "husbands or boyfriends" to this Southwestern pub chain link in the Plaza at King of Prussia Mall; the boys ring up "great" brews and chow down on "standard" bar vittles, and while the place is "too busy for its own good" (i.e. the "service needs work"), at least there are "fewer whiny kids here than at TGI Friday's."

Roller's at Flying Fish Ⓜ☞ *Eclectic*
| 21 | 16 | 17 | $35 |

Chestnut Hill | 8142 Germantown Ave. (bet. Abington Ave. & Hartwell Ln.) | 215-247-0707 | www.rollersrestaurants.com
Fans find "creative cooking" that's "always spot-on" at chef-owner Paul Roller's "simple" Eclectic "staple" in Chestnut Hill ("want to know what's best? ask him!"); while the "neighborly atmosphere" feels "cramped" to some, by and large this "Philly classic" "still delivers"; N.B. cash-only.

Roselena's Coffee Bar *Italian*
| ▽ 21 | 23 | 21 | $30 |

South Philly | 1623-1625 E. Passyunk Ave. (bet. Morris & Tasker Sts.) | 215-755-9697
Though "good" Italian dishes are served at this "nostalgic Victorian"-style BYO on South Philly's East Passyunk strip, many stop in for the "divine" desserts (a "phenomenal selection of pastries", coffee and tea) "after dinner" nearby.

Rose Tattoo Cafe ☒ *American*
| 22 | 22 | 20 | $38 |

Fairmount | 1847 Callowhill St. (19th St.) | 215-569-8939 |
www.rosetattoocafe.com
"Sit on the balcony" and savor the "intimate", "greenhouse atmosphere" and "reliable", "delectable" "comfort food" at this "nonpretentious" New American "hideaway" near the Art Museum; it's "worth every penny" (particularly for a "romantic rendezvous").

	FOOD	DECOR	SERVICE	COST

Rose Tree Inn *American*   22 | 19 | 22 | $48

Media | 1243 N. Providence Rd. (Rte. 1) | 610-891-1205 |
www.rosetreeinn.net

"Class" abounds at this "old-fashioned" Media Traditional American
serving an "old-guard" crew "wonderful" dishes; while an "update"
of the "outdated" decor is called for, this mainstay is still "one of the
nicest places" to "impress business associates", "parents or grand-
parents" over a leisurely paced meal.

Rouge *American*   22 | 21 | 18 | $42

Center City West | 205 S. 18th St. (bet. Locust & Walnut Sts.) |
215-732-6622

This "Euro-sexy" New American boasts a "seductive", "Gothic"
"jewel-box" interior and some of Rittenhouse Square's best sidewalk "people-watching" along with what many consider the
"best burger" in town; even if some sigh that an "uppity" vibe and
"see-and-be-seen" scene come with the territory, it "won't stop
them from hanging."

Rouget *American*   - | - | - | M

Newtown | 2 Swamp Rd. (Sycamore St.) | 215-860-4480

The name refers to the fish (rather than the pinkish-red walls) at this
Frenchified New American in Central Bucks, where the quaint, sub-
dued atmosphere is matched by prices that won't shock;
N.B. there's an assortment of breakfast/brunch and dinner prix
fixes from which to choose.

Roux 3 *American*   21 | 19 | 18 | $46

Newtown Square | 4755 West Chester Pike (Crum Creek Rd.) |
610-356-9500 | www.roux3.com

Main Liners seeking something "Center City" turn to this "modern"
Newtown Square New American that features "creative", at
times "terrific" fare and a "hip" vibe (and a "bargain" of a prix
fixe dinner); but for the "slow" service, overall, this place is doing
a "commendable" job.

Royal Tavern ● *American*   23 | 17 | 19 | $22

South Philly | 937 E. Passyunk Ave. (bet. Carpenter & Montrose Sts.) |
215-389-6694

Add up "fantastic" "twists to comfort food" – with lots of veggie
options – a "killer jukebox", "decent beer list" and "year-round
Christmas lights" and the sum is this "hip", "chill" Old English–style
"gastropub" "hangout" in Bella Vista; "bring friends" and "relax" in
what many consider "the best neighborhood bar in the city."

Roy's *Hawaiian*   23 | 22 | 22 | $51

Center City West | 124-34 S. 15th St. (Sansom St.) | 215-988-1814 |
www.roysrestaurant.com

This "bustling" Center City link in Roy Yamaguchi's "modern"
Hawaiian fusion chain gets solid marks for "fresh" seafood, "romantic lighting", "island music" and "attentive but not intrusive" service
from waiters whose "advice" you should "trust"; the budget-conscious

	FOOD	DECOR	SERVICE	COST

tout the prix fixe option – and everyone leaves room for the "molten" hot chocolate soufflé.

Ruby's *Diner* | 16 | 16 | 17 | $16 |

Glen Mills | Brinton Lake | 919 Baltimore Pike (Brinton Lake Rd.) | 610-358-1983
King of Prussia | Plaza at King of Prussia Mall | 160 N. Gulph Rd. (DeKalb Pike) | 610-337-7829
Ardmore | Suburban Sq. | 5 Coulter Ave. (Anderson Ave.) | 610-896-7829
www.rubys.com
Model trains run "round the track" above the "roomy" booths at this "classic" '40s-style diner chain where "students", "stay-at-home moms" and their tots feast on "good" burgers, fries and shakes while ignoring attendant "calories and cholesterol"; a few fuddy-duddies frown and say it's a "kidfest" and advise to get ready to fight the brigades of "strollers."

Ruth's Chris Steak House *Steak* | 23 | 21 | 22 | $61 |

Avenue of the Arts | 260 S. Broad St. (Spruce St.) | 215-790-1515 ◐
King of Prussia | 220 N. Gulph Rd. (DeKalb Pike) | 610-992-1818
www.ruthschris.com
"No fancy prep" – "just a great steak the way you want" (and topped with "sizzling" butter, "the not-so-secret ingredient") helps "please your inner carnivore" at this "class-act" chain meatery with branches on the Avenue of the Arts and in King of Prussia; if some find the fare "uneven for the price", adherents insist it's "worth" the "splurge."

Rx Ⓜ *Eclectic* | 23 | 18 | 19 | $31 |

University City | 4443 Spruce St. (45th St.) | 215-222-9590 | www.caferx.com
Set up in a former pharmacy is this "cute" University City BYO Eclectic where "arty" acolytes swear by the "natural-organic" approach to food, one that knits the "high-end" to the "homey"; the servers are as "warm" as the "laid-back" atmosphere, and the "amazing" Sunday brunch is prescribed to boost everyone's attitude.

Rylei Ⓢ Ⓜ *American* | ▽ 24 | 17 | 22 | $39 |

Northeast Philly | 7144 Frankford Ave. (bet. Friendship & St. Vincent Sts.) | 215-335-0414 | www.ryleirestaurant.com
Those who've discovered this "elegant" New American BYO in Mayfair marvel at the "innovative", "sophisticated" cuisine emanating from the kitchen of Jose Vargas; though some find the prix fixe dinner menu "limited", it's "well worth it" as "you get a lot for your money."

Sabrina's Café *Eclectic* | 25 | 16 | 20 | $21 |

Fairmount | 1802-1804 Callowhill St. (18th St.) | 215-636-9061
South Philly | 910 Christian St. (bet. 9th & 10th Sts.) | 215-574-1599
A "diverse" menu featuring "innovative" "comfort-food" "combinations" wins praise at these "adorable" New American twins in the Italian Market and Fairmount, where "awesome" brunches and "all-day" breakfasts are "worth the wait", and dinners are a "treat"; the

digs remind some of their "grandma's basement rec room", but it doesn't dampen the "creative" vibe, which extends all the way to the "friendly" staff's "hair color."

Salento ⓜ *Italian*   21 | 14 | 20 | $37

Center City West | 2216 Walnut St. (23rd St.) | 215-568-1314
Davide Faenza's "carefully prepared" southern Italian cuisine and wife Kathryn's "creative" desserts will "send you right into nirvana" at this Center City sibling of L'Angolo; service comes "with a smile", and though the "simple" interior strikes some as "spare", many consider this spot "one of the better" "additions" in the recent BYO "bumper crop."

Saloon Ⓢ *Italian/Steak*   24 | 22 | 21 | $63

South Philly | 750 S. Seventh St. (bet. Catharine & Fitzwater Sts.) | 215-627-1811 | www.saloonrestaurant.net
"Impress the clients" by taking them to join the crowd of "movers and shakers" at this "landmark" South Philly Italian steakhouse where "you can't go wrong" with its "memorable" *mangiare,* served by some of the "most attractive waitresses anywhere" in a "club-like" setting; regulars recommend: "eat upstairs", "come hungry" and be sure to "check the limit" on your Amex beforehand.

Salt & Pepper Ⓢⓜ *American*   ▽ 23 | 14 | 22 | $35

South Philly | 746 S. Sixth St. (Fitzwater St.) | 215-238-1920 | www.saltandpepperphilly.com
"Spice up your routine" at this "overlooked" New American BYO in Bella Vista urge fans of its "oh-so-delicious", "locally sourced" seasonal fare and "gracious" service; while some gripe about "limited" seating, the "teeny" digs "allow you to chat with the chef" at work in the open kitchen.

Sang Kee Asian Bistro *Chinese*   24 | 17 | 20 | $26

Wynnewood | 339 E. Lancaster Ave. (Remington Rd.) | 610-658-0618
Main Line mavens insist you "don't need to go to Chinatown anymore" for the "superb", "cheap" Chinese cuisine of the popular Ninth Street original, thanks to this "dependable" BYO offshoot in Wynnewood; "speedy" service, a setting that's "more upscale" than its counterpart's and "easier parking" are pluses, but cognoscenti caution "be prepared to stand in the vestibule and dodge the take-out patrons."

Ⓩ Sang Kee Peking Duck House ⏪ *Chinese*   25 | 10 | 18 | $21

Center City East | Reading Terminal Mkt. | 51 N. 12th St. (bet. Cuthbert & Filbert Sts.) | 215-922-3930
Chinatown | 238 N. Ninth St. (Vine St.) | 215-925-7532
"Get the duck" is the mantra at Michael Chow's "bargain" cash-only Chinatown Chinese (and its Reading Terminal Market take-out branch), where Sinophiles swear the "first-rate" Cantonese fare is "as close to Hong Kong as one can expect" in these parts; service is "extremely efficient", and even if there's "no decor to speak of", many insist "you can't go wrong" with this "old faithful."

	FOOD	DECOR	SERVICE	COST

Sassafras International Cafe ● *Eclectic* | – | – | – | M |

Old City | 48 S. Second St. (bet. Chestnut & Market Sts.) | 215-925-2317 | www.sassafrasbar.com

This romantic Victorian favorite in an Old City storefront has been refurbished to its former splendor, from the mirrored bar to the wild mural in the women's restroom upstairs; the original chef is also back, offering a menu of midpriced Eclectic fare such as sandwiches and various burgers (beef, lamb, ostrich and buffalo) and a small assortment of retro entrees, plus signature Mongolian dumplings.

Savona *French/Italian* | 25 | 25 | 23 | $70 |

Gulph Mills | 100 Old Gulph Rd. (Rte. 320) | 610-520-1200 | www.savonarestaurant.com

At this "much ballyhooed" "special-occasion" "classic" in Gulph Mills, the "superb" "Riviera-inspired" French-Italian cuisine and "magnificent" wine list are matched by a "refined" setting with "old-world charm" and "first-rate" service; though some find it "snooty" ("pretentiousness, thy name is Savona") and note that you may experience "sticker shock" from the bill, to most it's "worth every penny."

NEW Savor Saigon Ⓜ *Vietnamese* | ▽ 21 | 14 | 20 | $24 |

Levittown | H Mart | 1150 Oxford Valley Rd. (Woodbourne Rd.) | 215-943-4292 | www.savorsaigon.com

Phonatics are fond of the "authentic" Vietnamese "favorites" at this mom-and-pop BYO located in a Levittown strip mall, a "good value" with prices that are "just right" according to budget-conscious boosters; add homemade desserts such as the Grand Marnier flan and "what more can you ask for?"

Sazon Ⓜ *Venezuelan* | ▽ 21 | 13 | 21 | $23 |

North Philly | 941 Spring Garden St. (10th St.) | 215-763-2500 | www.sazonrestaurant.com

Aficionados aver "even a native would love" the "incredible" arepas and other "yummy" Venezuelan specialties (washed down with "the best hot chocolate" and "killer fruit shakes") at this "unpretentious" BYO on the western edge of Northern Liberties; "knowledgeable" service and "reasonable prices" add to its allure.

Scannicchio's *Italian* | 25 | 18 | 23 | $36 |

South Philly | 2500 S. Broad St. (Porter St.) | 215-468-3900 | www.scannicchio.com

"Superior" "red-gravy" Italian eats are "prepared with love" and served by "friendly" folks at this South Philly BYO outpost of the Atlantic City original, and the "healthy portions" will satisfy a "big table of friends"; regulars "hope not a lot of people find out" about it, for it's usually "crowded enough" already.

Scoogi's Classic Italian *Italian* | 19 | 16 | 20 | $28 |

Flourtown | 738 Bethlehem Pike (Arlingham Rd.) | 215-233-1063 | www.scoogis.com

There's a "good bang for the buck" at this "homey" Montco Italian with a "creative" menu that includes pizzas and "pub fare" (the

FOOD DECOR SERVICE COST

salmon wrap's a "winner every time"), served by a "pleasant" staff; regulars report the "awesome" bar "gets overcrowded" at happy hour and the "cozy" dining room fills up with early birds "around 5:30."

Seafood Unlimited *Seafood* | 20 | 11 | 18 | $30 |
Center City West | 270 S. 20th St. (Spruce St.) | 215-732-3663 | www.seafoodunlimited.com
Enjoying a "solid reputation for good, plain cooking", this "unassuming" seafooder off Rittenhouse Square may be "spare"-looking, but the fish is so "fresh" and prices so "reasonable" that few mind; regulars advise that you "stick to the simpler dishes" and consider the "close" seating an opportunity to make "new acquaintances."

Serrano *Eclectic* | 20 | 19 | 20 | $38 |
Old City | 20 S. Second St. (bet. Chestnut & Market Sts.) | 215-928-0770 | www.tinangel.com
"Carnivores" and "vegetarians" agree the food "doesn't disappoint" at this Old City Eclectic whose "narrow", "cozy" environs are "romance"-friendly and servers treat you like "you're being waited on by a close friend"; if you crave "great" live music, head upstairs to the Tin Angel.

Seven Stars Inn Ⓜ *Continental* | 23 | 19 | 23 | $49 |
Phoenixville | Hoffecker Rd. & Rte. 23 (W. Seven Stars Rd.) | 610-495-5205 | www.sevenstarsinn.com
"No one goes home without a doggy bag" from this "dependable" circa-1736 Continental steakhouse in Phoenixville, where the "enormous portions" are "fit for Fred Flintstone"; many consider it "special-occasion" worthy, even if a few find the fare "passé", and while fashionistas feel the "decor needs work", traditionalists insist the "dated" setting is "part of the charm."

Shanachie *Irish* | 17 | 18 | 18 | $29 |
Ambler | 111 E. Butler Ave. (Ridge Ave.) | 215-283-4887 | www.shanachiepub.com
A "pub in the truest sense of the word" is this "modern", "convivial" Ambler Irish venue favored for its "interesting" "more-than-just-potatoes" menu and "wonderful" live music; for a "change of pace", this hangout impresses.

Shangrila *Asian Fusion* | 20 | 19 | 21 | $33 |
Devon | 120 W. Swedesford Rd. (Valley Forge Rd.) | 610-687-8838 | www.shangrila120.com
Many Main Liners "recommend" this Asian fusion spot in Devon for its "bargain lunches", "professional", "consistently friendly" service and "pleasant", "modern" setting in a "converted Denny's"; while foes feel it has "little identity" because it "tries to do everything", it's "popular" among fans who regard it as a "step above your average Chinese."

Shank's & Evelyn's Luncheonette ⊄ *Italian* | 24 | 7 | 18 | $13 |
South Philly | 932 S. 10th St. (Carpenter St.) | 215-629-1093
"Don't ever $%#@* change!" is the war cry of "characters" who frequent this "hole-in-the-wall" South Philly luncheonette for the

	FOOD	DECOR	SERVICE	COST

"great" Italian home cooking, especially the "best sandwiches in the world"; the seats are "few and far between", and the setting brims with "attitude" (be prepared to be "yelled at" by the folks behind the counter).

Shiao Lan Kung ● *Chinese*   25 | 7 | 18 | $22

Chinatown | 930 Race St. (bet. 9th & 10th Sts.) | 215-928-0282
Devotees "dare you to find better pork dumplings", "hot pots" or "salt-baked dishes" than the "excellent" versions at this BYO Chinese "hole-in-the-wall" in Chinatown; the "basic" digs are "cramped", and since it's "no longer a secret", you may be "waiting outside", but the service is "smoking fast", and most agree the "old-timey" eats and "bargain" prices are "worth" the hardships.

Shinju Sushi *Japanese*   ▽ 28 | 21 | 24 | $30

Center City East | 930 Locust St. (Delhi St.) | 215-351-6265
A "superior find" in Wash West for Jefferson med students and others, this "affordable" BYO Japanese offers "creative", "very fresh" sushi that exhibits a "perfect balance" of "flavors and textures" amid simple surroundings; for "non-lovers" of raw fin fare, there's also a selection of cooked appetizers, such as dumplings, udon noodles and other crowd-pleasers.

Shiroi Hana *Japanese*   23 | 18 | 21 | $34

Center City West | 222 S. 15th St. (bet. Locust & Walnut Sts.) | 215-735-4444 | www.shiroihana.com
If you're in the market for "simple, fresh" sushi that "won't bust your budget", this "serene", "low-key" Japanese near the Kimmel Center "can't be beat"; just "don't expect fireworks" from the food – but pleased patrons who know "great" service and good grub when they see it.

Shula's 347 *American*   ▽ 21 | 17 | 18 | $51

West Conshohocken | Philadelphia Marriott West | 111 Crawford Ave. (Rte. 23) | 610-941-5600 | www.donshula.com
"Superb" steaks "huge enough for a linebacker's appetite" score points with fans at this manly New American from Hall-of-Fame coach Don Shula in West Conshy's Philadelphia Marriott West, where a touch of "formality" complements the "sports-bar" theme; still, despite solid ratings, critics sack the fare as "merely passable."

Siam Cuisine *Thai*   22 | 13 | 20 | $28

Chinatown | 925 Arch St. (bet. 9th & 10th Sts.) | 215-922-7135
Buckingham | Buckingham Green Shopping Ctr. | 4950 York Rd. (Hwy. 202) | 215-794-7209
Newtown | Village at Newtown | 2124 S. Eagle Rd. (bet. Durham & Swamp Rds.) | 215-579-9399
www.siamcuisinepa.com
There's a "party for all your senses" at this "reasonably priced" Thai trio where "flavorful", "well-prepared" dishes are served in a "pleasant" atmosphere; while some say "eh" to decor they describe as "recycled from the '80s", most just "ignore it" or get their food "to go"; N.B. Newtown is BYO.

Siam Cuisine at
The Black Walnut ⓜ *French/Thai*

▽ 23 | 18 | 23 | $47

Doylestown | 80 W. State St. (bet. Clinton & Hamilton Sts.) |
215-348-0708 | www.siamcuisinepa.com

"Lovely" servers deliver "imaginative" French-Thai offerings that
range from "good to superb" at this "upscale" eatery (the posh link
in the Siam Cuisine chain) on Doylestown's Restaurant Row; P.S. the
patio and garden "charm" in the warmer months.

Sidecar ⓜ *Eclectic*

19 | 13 | 18 | $23

South Philly | 2201 Christian St. (22nd St.) | 215-732-3429 |
www.thesidecarbar.com

Many swear they never sausage a gastropub menu in South Philly
like the one at this "cute" "urban hipster hangout" near Graduate
Hospital, where "excellent" house-smoked meats highlight the
"N'Awlins"-influenced Eclectic fare; the "friendly" vibe and "casual", "dimly lit" setting make it "perfect for those laid-back nights
when you are not seeking anything fancy."

Silk City ◗ *American*

20 | 19 | 17 | $24

Northern Liberties | 435 Spring Garden St. (bet. 4th & 5th Sts.) |
215-592-8838

A major "makeover" by the owner of N. 3rd has transformed a "landmark" "greasy spoon" diner in Northern Liberties into this "upscale", "urban-chic" destination for "honest", "nouveau" American
"comfort food"; it's attracting a young, "trendy" crowd that grooves
to DJs in the adjacent nightclub, although some purists sniff that it's
"missing" a "good shake" and "real diner waitresses."

Silk Cuisine *Thai*

▽ 23 | 14 | 21 | $29

Bryn Mawr | 656 W. Lancaster Ave. (bet. Lee Ave. & Penn St.) |
610-527-0590

En-thai-cing the Main Line is this "dependable" Bryn Mawr BYO
cooking up "yummy" Thai dishes (including an "ample" array of vegetarian options) at "best-buy" prices; it's "more than worth the
parking hassle" when you have that "curry craving."

Simon Pearce on the
Brandywine *American*

20 | 24 | 21 | $52

West Chester | 1333 Lenape Rd. (Pocopson Rd.) | 610-793-0948 |
www.simonpearce.com

The "romantic setting" "overlooking" the Brandywine River is the
chief attraction at this "pricey", "out-of-the-way" New American attached to a glassblowing factory and retail store near West Chester;
also pleasing are the "elegant" ambiance, "interesting" fare and wines
served in Simon's "blown glass", making it worthy of a "special occasion"; P.S. classical "musicians add a nice touch" at Sunday brunch.

Singapore Kosher Vegetarian *Chinese*

▽ 19 | 12 | 18 | $19

Chinatown | 1006 Race St. (bet. 10th & 11th Sts.) | 215-922-3288

"You won't miss the meat" given the "interesting menu" of kosher
vegetarian fare say supporters of this Chinatown option; it's not big

on decor but prices are modest too and "very nice servers" add to the "calm, soothing atmosphere."

Sitar India *Indian* | 20 | 9 | 16 | $15 |

University City | 60 S. 38th St. (bet. Chestnut & Market Sts.) | 215-662-0818
For a "deal" of a meal, hit this University City Indian buffet specialist, where Pennsters "come to feed" on "tasty" dishes for a few rupees ($7.95 at lunch, $10.95 at dinner); fans want to keep it a "secret."

NEW Sláinte *Pub Food* | ▽ 18 | 20 | 18 | $23 |

University City | 3000 Market St. (30th St.) | 215-222-7400 | www.slaintephilly.com
"Cira Centre lawyers", "Drexel employees" and "postal workers" all "can feel at home together" over "straightforward" pub grub and "happy-hour" specials at this "comfortable" University City Irish saloon across from 30th Street Station; commuters also commend it as a spot for "killing time" "before your train."

Slate Bleu *French* | ▽ 22 | 20 | 21 | $53 |

Doylestown | 100 S. Main St. (Green St.) | 215-348-0222 | www.slatebleu.com
Mark Matyas (of NYC's La Grenouille fame) heads this "sophisticated" French bistro "off-the-beaten-path" in Doylestown; "luscious" fare, "lovely" decor and a staff that "appears" and "vanishes" when "needed" add up to a "favorite hometown" "foodie destination."

Sly Fox Brewery *Pub Food* | 15 | 13 | 19 | $24 |

Phoenixville | 519 Kimberton Rd. (bet. Pothouse & Seven Stars Rds.) | 610-935-4540
Royersford | 312 N. Lewis Rd. (Royersford Rd.) | 610-948-8088
www.slyfoxbeer.com
These brewpub twins in Phoenixville and Royersford rock the 'burbs with a "wide sampling" of beers and "varied menu" of "decent" bar bites in a "family-friendly" setting with a "fox" motif; while cynics sneer at their chances of "winning any food awards", they remain popular "gathering spots" for those who crave a "growler" and a "snack."

Smith & Wollensky ● *Steak* | 22 | 20 | 21 | $61 |

Center City West | Rittenhouse Hotel | 210 W. Rittenhouse Sq.
(bet. Locust & Walnut Sts.) | 215-545-1700 | www.smithandwollensky.com
It's all about the "fabulous" "dry-aged" steaks "with all the trimmings" served by a "professional" staff at this "clubby", "high-end beef joint" in the Rittenhouse Hotel, where the "tab for the à la carte menu can add up quickly" warn wallet-watchers; with a "view of the Square" as a backdrop, "babes and studs" munch "burgers" at the bar "downstairs", while the "jacket-and-tie crowd" heads upstairs.

Snackbar ● *American* | 18 | 20 | 19 | $37 |

Center City West | 253 S. 20th St. (Rittenhouse Sq.) | 215-545-5655 | www.phillysnackbar.com
"Watch the Rittenhouse crowd" from the sidewalk or "grab a table by the fireplace" at this "trendy", "tiny" New American bistro off the

Square; a post-Survey chef change resulted in a menu that now includes full-size plates, which may address complaints about portions "for mice" (and may outdate the above Food score), although some feel the staff could downsize the "attitude" as well.

Snockey's Oyster & Crab House *Seafood*   18 | 11 | 18 | $30
South Philly | 1020 S. Second St. (Washington Ave.) | 215-339-9578 | www.snockeys.com

"Out of the sea into Snockey's" is on the lips of many an afishionado when talking about the "super-fresh" oysters and clams at this South Philly institution doing business since 1912; its "tried-and-true recipes" without the "fancy sauces" and "old-fashioned" service have helped it remain "unscathed by the big boys."

Society Hill Hotel ● *American*   18 | 15 | 18 | $26
Old City | Society Hill Hotel | 301 Chestnut St. (3rd St.) | 215-923-3711

The decor and menu "got fancied up" at this "quaint" Traditional American "landmark" serving "solid" bar fare downstairs from a 12-room Old City bed and breakfast; plenty of "people-watching" goes on at the outdoor tables, where tourists get to "rub elbows with the locals."

☑ Sola ⓢⓜ *American*   27 | 19 | 24 | $51
Bryn Mawr | 614 W. Lancaster Ave. (Penn St.) | 610-526-0123

"Ex-sola-nt" exclaim enthusiasts about this "intimate" New American BYO in Bryn Mawr, regarded by some as "the best-kept secret on the Main Line", where "superb", "refined" "city food" is served by an "attentive" staff in a "jewel box–size" space; "suburban prices" make it easier to "bring your finest" wine to pour into the "high-end" Schott Zwiesel stemware.

Solaris Grille *American*   16 | 18 | 16 | $29
Chestnut Hill | 8201 Germantown Ave. (Hartwell St.) | 215-242-3400 | www.solarisgrille.com

Dining on the "awesome" patio is the "main draw" at this popular New American "gathering spot" on the Avenue in Chestnut Hill, a favorite of "young crowds" and "families"; if the menu draws mixed marks ("commendable" vs. "so-so") and the interior is sometimes "loud", compensations include "well-presented", "substantial portions", "decent" service and a "heavenly" outside bar.

SoleFood *Seafood*   21 | 23 | 21 | $43
Center City East | Loews Philadelphia Hotel | 1200 Market St. (12th St.) | 215-231-7300 | www.loewshotels.com

"Way better than the average" hotel venue according to loyal sole-jahs, this "cosmopolitan" seafooder in the Loews in Center City leaves many "pleasantly surprised" by its "innovative", "beautifully presented" fin fare and "accommodating" service; it's a "little pricey", and some complain it's "not great for romantic dining" due to the "loud din from the bar", where folks "unwind after work" over "happy-hour" "specials."

	FOOD	DECOR	SERVICE	COST

Sotto Varalli *Seafood*   21 | 20 | 21 | $44

Avenue of the Arts | 231 S. Broad St. (Locust St.) | 215-546-6800 |
www.varalliusa.com

"Artfully prepared" seafood and a "helpful" staff that "goes out of its
way to get you to the show on time" are "equally outstanding" at this
"downstairs sister" to Upstares at Varalli in the heart of the Avenue
of the Arts; a "giant squid above the bar" "gives you something to
chat about" in the "inviting" space with "cool views" of the street,
and weekend "jazz combos" add to the "wonderful experience."

South St. Souvlaki Ⓜ *Greek*   21 | 14 | 18 | $22

South St. | 509 South St. (bet. 5th & 6th Sts.) | 215-925-3026
"Yummy" Greek eats at "easy-on-the-credit-card" prices are the
norm at this "unpretentious" South Street taverna; if you "don't have
time for a sit-down meal", order from the "take-out counter", chat
with the cooks and you'll come away "pleased."

Southwark Ⓜ *American*   22 | 20 | 22 | $46

South St. | 701 S. Fourth St. (Bainbridge St.) | 215-238-1888
A "convivial" vibe informs this "old-timey" spot in Queen Village
where Sheri Waide's "dependable", "imaginative" New American
cuisine "changes with the seasons" and "professional" bartenders
who know their "fine liquor" mix up "classic cocktails"; regulars recommend a table next to one of the "people-watching windows" or an
outdoor seat; N.B. no strollers allowed.

Sovalo Ⓩ *Californian/Italian*   25 | 21 | 23 | $45

Northern Liberties | 702 N. Second St. (bet. Brown St. & Fairmount Ave.) |
215-413-7770 | www.sovalo.com

"Classic Italian ideas" and "American ingredients" go into Joseph
Scarpone's "creative" Cal-Ital cuisine at this "sophisticated" "bit of
Napa" in Northern Liberties; "first-class" service from a "down-to-
earth" staff adds to a "relaxed" atmosphere in the "classy" space with
a "romantic" bar, and the Monday BYO nights are a "great value."

Ⓩ Sovana Bistro Ⓜ *French/Mediterranean*   26 | 20 | 22 | $40

Kennett Square | 696 Unionville Rd. (Rte. 926) | 610-444-5600 |
www.sovanabistro.com

Nicholas Farrell's "awesome" French-Med fare "floors" foodies at
his "upscale" BYO in Kennett Square, where a "combination of tried-
and-true and new twists" comprises the seasonal menu; "first-rate"
service and "reasonable" prices help quell kvetching about "jam-
packed" tables and the "shopping-center location."

Spamps *Eclectic/Steak*   17 | 15 | 17 | $37

Conshohocken | 16 E. First Ave. (George St.) | 610-825-4155 |
www.spampsrestaurant.com

Surf 'n' turf and sushi are featured on the "extensive" menu at this
"trendy" Conshy Eclectic steakhouse that attracts a "business"
lunch clientele and a "bar crowd" later on; critics feel it's trying to do
"too many cuisines" and "doesn't know what it wants to be", which
is why some just "go there to meet, not eat."

	FOOD	DECOR	SERVICE	COST

Spasso *Italian* — 23 | 17 | 23 | $38

Old City | 34 S. Front St. (bet. Chestnut & Market Sts.) | 215-592-7661 |
www.spassoitaliangrill.com

A "going-home" feeling fills this "casual" (and sometimes "loud")
Italian in Old City, where fans extol the "authentic" chow served in
"family-style" "portions large enough to share" at "reasonable
prices"; the kitchen is willing to "accommodate any request", and
the rest of the "entertaining" staff is "on top of everything."

Spence Cafe *Eclectic* — ∇ 23 | 17 | 19 | $42

West Chester | 29-31 E. Gay St. (bet. High & Walnut Sts.) |
610-738-8844 | www.spencecaferestaurant.com

"College students and profs" check off the merits of this West
Chester Eclectic, one of the "best" in the borough for its "interesting" menu served in "dark" quarters; that it morphs into a "late-
night" bar/club scene (with live bands) is cool with the kids.

Spotted Hog *American* — 17 | 16 | 18 | $26

Lahaska | Peddler's Vill. | Rte. 263 & Street Rd. | 215-794-4040 |
www.peddlersvillage.com

"Day-trippers" "take a break from shopping" for "quick" lunches and
dinners at this "family-friendly", "touristy" Traditional American in
Peddler's Village offering "good food at reasonable prices"; though
wags squeal it's "hogging a prime location", others insist it's "a perfect getaway from the city."

Spring Mill Café Ⓜ *French* — 23 | 20 | 21 | $46

Conshohocken | 164 Barren Hill Rd. (bet. Ridge Pike & River Rd.) |
610-828-2550 | www.springmill.com

How about a "Parisian bit of fresh air by way of Conshy" – that's the
story of this "quirky", "rustic" country French BYO tucked "out of the
way" on Barren Hill Road; owner Michele Haines' food is "worth the
caloric hit", and a "knowledgeable" staff maintains the "relaxing"
vibe; though a few debate the setting ("tired" or "charming"), most
agree it's still perfect for "lovers."

Ⓩ Standard Tap ❶ *American* — 24 | 17 | 18 | $26

Northern Liberties | 901 N. Second St. (Poplar St.) | 215-238-0630 |
www.standardtap.com

Fans insist the "inventive" American pub grub and "fab" beer selection at this "low-key" Northern Liberties "taproom" "set the standard" for Philly's new crop of pubs; an "eclectic" crowd packs into
the "comfortable" tavern digs with a "dive-bar" feel and "hipster"
staff, and while some find the service "inconsistent", many consider
this one a "classic."

NEW Station Bistro Ⓩ *American* — - | - | - | M

Kimberton | 1300 Hares Hill Rd. (Kimberton Rd.) | 610-933-1147 |
www.stationbistro.com

Urban escapees get another dining option in the Chester County
countryside with this New American bistro set in an 18th-century
inn outside of Phoenixville; its funky Colonial-meets–art deco atmo-

sphere suits its mission as a drop-in for morning coffee/danish and a lunch/dinner BYO.

Stefano's Ⓜ *Italian* ▽ 19 | 19 | 21 | $36

Huntingdon Valley | 2519 Huntingdon Pike (Red Lion Rd.) | 215-914-1224 | www.stefanos.us

It "holds a special spot" in the hearts of habitués who frequent this "old-fashioned" Italian Huntingdon Valley BYO, a "friendly" favorite; while the cooking ranges from "average" to "good", most at least sense the "romance" in the air.

Stella Blu Ⓢ *American* - | - | - | M

West Conshohocken | 101 Ford St. (Front St.) | 610-825-7060 | www.stellablurestaurant.com

A "recent makeover" has pumped up the mood and menu at this "sleek", "intimate" West Conshy New American "trying for trendiness", where diners lap up lobster mac 'n' cheese and lounge-lizards choose from a deep wine list (24 by the glass); parking is "a major challenge" so valet is the way to go.

Steve's Prince of Steaks ⊅ *Cheese Steaks* 24 | 8 | 16 | $11

Northeast Philly | 2711 Comly Rd. (Roosevelt Blvd.) | 215-677-8020 ◑

Northeast Philly | 7200 Bustleton Ave. (St. Vincent St.) | 215-338-0985 ◑

Langhorne | 1617 E. Lincoln Hwy. (Highland Pkwy.) | 215-943-4640 www.stevesprinceofsteaks.com

Boosters boast these steak stands "reign supreme" in Northeast Philly and Lower Bucks with their "awesome" cheese steaks of "sliced rib-eye" ("not chopped-up ground beef") served by royally "rude" counter guys; "you don't go there for decor", but regulars recommend it anyway for an "artery-clogging" experience without "driving to South Philly."

St. Stephens Green ◑ *Irish* 19 | 20 | 19 | $26

Fairmount | 1701 Green St. (17th St.) | 215-769-5000 | www.saintstephensgreen.com

Folks in Fairmount have fine things to say about this "happening" Irish pub boasting "warm woods", "big windows", fireplaces and "plenty of TVs", a "cozy" backdrop for "imaginative" "gastropub" fare and a "wonderful selection of beers", poured by bartenders who speak with a "desirable brogue"; regulars report it's like "hanging out" in your own "living room."

Sullivan's Steakhouse *Steak* 23 | 21 | 21 | $54

King of Prussia | King of Prussia Mall | 700 W. DeKalb Pike (Mall Blvd.) | 610-878-9025 | www.sullivansteakhouse.com

These KoP and Wilmington outposts of the "'40s-style" meatery chain offer "mouthwatering" steaks, a "killer wine list" and "caring" service to a "high-energy crowd" in an "elegantly retro" setting; "live jazz" can be heard in the "inviting bar", and while some find the scene "too noisy" and there's debate over the cost ("reasonably priced for an upscale steakhouse" vs. "overpriced"), most deem it a "good bet for a special night out."

	FOOD	DECOR	SERVICE	COST

Summer Kitchen ⓜ *Eclectic*   23 | 16 | 20 | $36

Penns Park | Rte. 232 & Penns Park Rd. | 215-598-9210 |
www.thesummerkitchen.net

Mario Korenstein's "exciting" Eclectic cooking is showcased in a
"unique menu" – ranging from paella to étouffée to strip steak – at
this casual 40-seat BYO in "the sticks" of Central Bucks; fans are
"charmed" by the outdoor patio, and bargain-hunters seek out the
prix fixe dinners offered Tuesdays, Wednesdays and Thursdays.

NEW Supper ⓜ *American*   23 | 24 | 22 | $60

South St. | 926 South St. (10th St.) | 215-592-8180 |
www.supperphilly.com

Fans declare Mitch Prensky "one of the more creative chefs in town"
thanks to his "intriguing" menu of "tasty" French-accented small
plates (paired with "pricey" wines) at this "beautiful" New American
brasserie and bar on South Street, where "artful items" hang from
the ceiling and patrons get a "clear view" of the open kitchen; service
is "charming", but wallet-watchers warn the bill can be "stunning."

ⓩ Susanna Foo *Chinese/French*   24 | 23 | 23 | $58

Center City West | 1512 Walnut St. (bet. 15th & 16th Sts.) |
215-545-2666 | www.susannafoo.com

"Every presentation is a visual feast" at this "smartly decorated",
"low-key" Center City Chinese-French that's "still in a class by itself" for "inventive" cuisine and "professional" service, suitable
for a "power meal", "wow-factor hot date" or "long lunch";
volume-minded critics sniff it's "too much Susanna and not enough
foo-d", but for others it remains a "go-to" choice whenever they
"have extra cash."

Susanna Foo's Gourmet Kitchen *Pan-Asian*   21 | 22 | 18 | $45

Wayne | Radnor Financial Ctr. | 555 E. Lancaster Ave. (Iven Ave.) |
610-688-8808 | www.susannafoo.com

"To-die-for dumplings" and other "haute" takes on Pan-Asian dishes
are served in a "luxurious" "modern" dining room at Susanna Foo's
Wayne outpost, which offers a kid-friendly ambiance as well as a
"hip" night scene; nitpickers find the TV at the bar a "noisy" "dis-
traction", however, and kvetch that service can be "choppy."

Sushikazu *Japanese*   ▽ 24 | 16 | 22 | $32

Blue Bell | 920 DeKalb Pike (Skippack Pike) | 610-272-7767 |
www.sushikazupa.com

"Creative", "super-fresh" sushi and "decent" cooked items attract
Central Montcoites to this "cozy" BYO Japanese in Blue Bell (and help
them "overlook the decor"); while the service can be "ver-ry slow", the
staff is "friendly" and "willing to put together whatever you fancy."

NEW Swallow ⓜ *European*   - | - | - | M

Northern Liberties | Liberties Walk | 1030 N. American St. (Wildey St.) |
215-238-1399

It's the first kitchen of their own for the husband-and-wife team behind
this midpriced Liberties Walk BYO bistro serving casual European

| | FOOD | DECOR | SERVICE | COST |

fare – e.g. bone marrow, steak frites – in a romantic candlelit setting; the name, incidentally, refers to the bird, not the verb

Swanky Bubbles ◐ *Pan-Asian* | 20 | 19 | 19 | $38 |

Old City | 10 S. Front St. (Market St.) | 215-928-1200 | www.swankybubbles.com

"Sushi and champagne" just might be the "new Brad and Angelina" predict fans of these "poppin'", "lounge-type" Pan-Asians in Old City and Cherry Hill; "swanky drinks", "seriously delicious" small plates and an "I'm-too-cool-to-be-Philly" vibe make them perfect for an "evening out with the girls" or gawking at "beautiful folk."

Z Swann Lounge ◐ *American/French* | 27 | 27 | 27 | $55 |

Center City West | Four Seasons Hotel | 1 Logan Sq. (bet. Benjamin Franklin Pkwy. & 18th St.) | 215-963-1500 | www.fourseasons.com

When you don't want to "brave" the Fountain's "formality", the Four Seasons' "bargain" "little sister" next door delivers "accessible elegance" in the form of "top-notch" New American cooking with a "French flair", "impeccable" service and "delicious views" of Swann Fountain; besides, it's fun to see the mix of "guests in their sweats and locals after a black-tie affair"; P.S. the $24.95 lunch buffet comes "highly recommended."

NEW Sweet Basil Thai Cuisine Ⓜ *Thai* | ▽ 21 | 16 | 18 | $28 |

Chadds Ford | 275 Wilmington-W. Chester Pike (Smith Bridge) | 610-358-4015

This family-owned Chadds Ford BYO provides a solid "introduction" to Thai cuisine with its "traditional", "spicy" offerings made with "fresh" ingredients, and neophytes can see "exactly" what they're "getting into", thanks to the menu's "good descriptions"; a "pleasant" atmosphere adds to the "excellent value."

Sweet Lucy's Smokehouse *BBQ* | 21 | 14 | 17 | $19 |

Northeast Philly | 7500 State Rd. (bet. Bleigh Ave. & Rhawn St.) | 215-333-9663 | www.sweetlucys.com

"Finger-lickin' good" Southern-style brisket, ribs and pork pull 'cuennoisseurs off I-95's Cottman exit to this Northeast BBQ BYO for aptly named platters such as the "quadruple bypass"; there are "plenty of paper towels" on hand in the "cafeteria-style" space in a "minimalist" "warehouse" setting, and while some find it "pricey" for what it is, others insist the $17.95 Monday night buffet is "worth the trip."

NEW Table 31 Ⓢ *Steak* | - | - | - | VE |

Center City West | Comcast Ctr. | 1701 JFK Blvd. (17th St.) | 215-567-7111 | www.table-31.com

Prime cuts of beef in assorted sizes star at Chris Scarduzio and Georges Perrier's sumptuous (and sumptuously priced) tri-level steakhouse in the landmark Comcast Center; the two-story-tall lounge offers a new after-work option for Comcast execs and Center City lawyers, while alfresco fans can dine at an outdoor cafe beside a fountain.

	FOOD	DECOR	SERVICE	COST

Tacconelli's Pizzeria Ⓜ⇄ *Pizza*   25 | 9 | 14 | $18

Port Richmond | 2604 E. Somerset St. (bet. Almond & Thompson Sts.) |
215-425-4983 | www.tacconellispizzeria.com

"Wacko for Tacco" pie-zani tout this "quirky", "no-frills" Port
Richmond "destination" and its Maple Shade offspring as home of
the "best thin-crust pizzas around", where the policy of "reserving
your dough" in advance (at the parent only) is "worth it" – otherwise, you might be "out of luck"; just remember to pack some dough
in your wallet (no plastic, *capice*?), and maybe "bring a cooler full of
beer and a bunch of friends" to settle in for "long waits."

Tai Lake ◑ *Chinese*   ▽ 24 | 11 | 17 | $23

Chinatown | 134 N. 10th St. (bet. Cherry & Race Sts.) | 215-922-0698
"Tanks of frogs and fish" greet you at the door of Sam Leung's "fabulous" Chinatown eatery prized for its "superb", "unbelievably
fresh" Chinese seafood; for an affordable, undeniably "authentic"
experience, "this is the place to go"; P.S. it's open till 3 AM.

ⓩ Talula's Table *European*   26 | 19 | 26 | $59

Kennett Square | 102 W. State St. (Union St.) | 610-444-8255 |
www.talulastable.com

By day, Bryan Sikora and Aimee Olexy's "cozy", shabby-chic BYO
Euro "gem" in Downtown Kennett Square is a takeaway cafe purveying an "excellent selection" of prepared sandwiches, cheeses,
breads and "homemade sausages"; scoring the "private" farmhouse
or kitchen table for the "fabulous", "imaginative" prix fixe dinners
($90 and up, evenings only) is "like hitting the lottery", where you
might have to "wait a year" – seriously – for the experience.

Tamarindo's Ⓜ *Mexican*   23 | 16 | 20 | $33

Broad Axe | Homemaker's Shopping Plaza | 36 W. Skippack Pike
(Butler Pike) | 215-619-2390

Some of the "finest" Mexican you'll find is on the menu at this "upscale" (it "isn't a rice 'n' bean" joint) Yucatán-style BYO "hidden" in
a Central Montco strip mall; most agree that the margaritas "soften
the long waits for a table" and help turn the place into a "party."

Tampopo ⓩ *Japanese/Korean*   22 | 11 | 18 | $15

Center City East | 719 Sansom St. (bet. 7th & 8th Sts.) | 215-238-9373
Center City West | 104 S. 21st St. (bet. Chestnut & Walnut Sts.) |
215-557-9593
www.tampoporestaurant.com

"Delicious", "high-quality" food for "so little cash" is the calling card of
these Japanese-Korean BYO twins in Jewelers Row and Rittenhouse;
they're touted for takeout, but their "cheerful" vibes may make you
want to "eat there", especially at the newer Sansom Street satellite.

Tandoor India *Indian*   ▽ 20 | 10 | 15 | $17

University City | 106 S. 40th St. (bet. Chestnut & Walnut Sts.) |
215-222-7122

Get past the im-penn-etrable "buffet line" and "try a little of everything" at this Indian BYO "standby" on Penn's campus; the all-you-

can-eat deals are the main attractions, and the stuff's "tasty" to boot, so chances are you "won't be disappointed."

☑ Tangerine *Mediterranean*   24 | 27 | 23 | $54
Old City | 232 Market St. (bet. 2nd & 3rd Sts.) | 215-627-5116 | www.tangerinerestaurant.com

Take a "chichi" trip to the "casbah" at Stephen Starr's "dark", "sensuous" Old City Med, where "creative", "exotic" "meals" and "fun plates to share" are served in an "amazing", "romantic" space aglow with twinkling "votive candles" and complemented by a "sexy" lounge; it's "not inexpensive", warn cognoscenti, as "hipness has its price."

Tango *American*   20 | 19 | 19 | $40
Bryn Mawr | 39 Morris Ave. (Lancaster Ave.) | 610-526-9500 | www.tastetango.com

Many Main Liners think this "busy", "convivial" New American at the Bryn Mawr train station stays on track with a "diverse" menu and "comfortable" rustic decor in the main room and a more casual, rail-station motif in the other; as long as you can deal with some "noise", you may find it "better than expected."

Taqueria La Michoacana *Mexican*   23 | 15 | 19 | $21
Norristown | 301 E. Main St. (Arch St.) | 610-292-1971

"Authentic" preparations (i.e. "Mexican food as Mexicans know it") of "well-prepared" fare have helped bring this "little-known" "gem" in Norristown a fair share of acclaim; it's wise to disregard the "questionable locale", since the "friendly" folks here "make every effort to please."

Taqueria La Veracruzana ● *Mexican*   22 | 6 | 14 | $13
South Philly | 908 Washington Ave. (9th St.) | 215-465-1440

Whether you "bring your Spanish phrasebook" or not, you'll still fill up on "fantastic" Mexican "soul food" at this BYO "diamond in the rough" in the Italian Market; the value is "incredible", but bring "Pepcid" for the plentiful portions and a pair of shades to blot out the "blinding" fluorescent lights.

Taqueria Moroleon *Mexican*   ∇ 24 | 9 | 17 | $18
Kennett Square | New Garden Shopping Ctr. | 345 Scarlet Rd. (W. Baltimore Pike) | 610-444-1210

"Bring your own tequila" and expect a "line out the door on weekends" at this Mexican BYO "jewel" in Kennett Square that's "not a secret anymore", thanks to the "authentic", "excellent" *alimento*; while some find the digs "a bit tacky" and service "slow", it's still a "great deal" and "very popular with the locals."

Taqueria Puerto   - | - | - | I
Veracruzano ●⏇ *Mexican*
South Philly | 1446 S. Eighth St. (Dickinson St.) | 215-334-7000

This South Philly taqueria near the Italian Market may "look like a dive" but devotees focus on the wide choice of "fabulously authentic" homespun Mex faves available daily (9 AM–midnight); N.B. any language problem is quickly overcome by pointing.

	FOOD	DECOR	SERVICE	COST

PHILADELPHIA

Tavern 17 ● *American* — 18 | 19 | 15 | $31

Center City West | Radisson Plaza-Warwick Hotel | 220 S. 17th St. (Chancellor St.) | 215-790-1799 | www.tavern17restaurant.com
"Ambitious" "twists" on American favorites, a 1,000-bottle wine cellar and a "good beer list" win praise for this "modern" tavern in Center City's Radisson Warwick, where an "after-work crowd" can be found "flanking the prominent bar"; critics, though, complain the "surly" staff "takes forever" to deliver orders, and wonder if the kitchen is "even farther than the bathrooms" that seem to be "nearly a block away."

Teca ●▣ *Italian* — 21 | 21 | 20 | $32

West Chester | 38 E. Gay St. (Walnut St.) | 610-738-8244 | www.tecawine.com
The "cool crowd" likes to "hang" and "chat" at this Italian "bistro" in West Chester, a "snacker's delight" serving "great panini", "artisanal cheese platters" and an "awesome" "range" of wines, with plenty of "people-watching" from "sidewalk tables"; the "small plates and big prices" don't add up to some critics, though, who also report a "snobby" vibe.

Ted's Montana Grill *Steak* — 16 | 16 | 16 | $32

Avenue of the Arts | 260 S. Broad St. (Spruce St.) | 215-772-1230
NEW Warrington | 1512 Main St. (bet. Hwy. 611 & Street Rd.) | 215-491-1170
www.tedsmontanagrill.com
Fans of Ted Turner's "family-oriented" steakhouse chain with links in Center City and Warrington applaud the "chirpy" staff and "Old West"–inspired space, though debates continue over the bison and beef-heavy menu ("it's like an Outback on steroids") – a "treat" for some, "average" for others.

Teikoku *Japanese/Thai* — 24 | 24 | 20 | $46

Newtown Square | 5492 West Chester Pike (bet. Delchester & Garrett Mill Rds.) | 610-644-8270 | www.teikokurestaurant.com
An "interesting blend" of Japanese cuisine ("top-notch" sushi) and "satay"-sfying Thai fare is served amid a handsome "visual experience" (waterfall, bamboo ceiling) and "techno background music" at this "serene" yet "dynamic" Newtown Square spot; sake and "ginger martinis" "enhance" the dining, and while some wince at the "NYC prices", it's "good enough" to keep the locals "coming back for more."

NEW 10 Arts *American* — - | - | - | E

Avenue of the Arts | Ritz-Carlton Hotel | 10 S. Broad St. (City Hall) | 215-523-8273 | www.10arts.com
Eric Ripert (of NYC's Le Bernardin) continues his Colonial expansion with this polished New American that takes advantage of the soaring lobby in Center City's Ritz-Carlton – a wine case dramatically fills the space beneath the 140-ft. skylit rotunda; the pricey menu focuses on local ingredients, with all-day options that cover everything from breakfast through late-night dining.

132   subscribe to ZAGAT.com

	FOOD	DECOR	SERVICE	COST

NEW Tennessee's BBQ & Grill *BBQ* — | — | — | I

Levittown | Langhorne Sq. | 1295 E. Lincoln Hwy. (Highland Park Way) | 215-949-1599

The smoker is puffing mightily at this built-for-speed barbecue joint (an offshoot of a Boston mini-chain) located in a strip center near Oxford Valley Mall; the inexpensive menu follows a familiar 'cue-print, offering ribs, chicken and brisket, plus a dozen or so sides, while the full bar and communal sink demonstrate amenities a few steps above the rib-shack norm.

Ten Stone *American* 18 | 15 | 16 | $22

Center City West | 2063 South St. (21st St.) | 215-735-9939 | www.tenstone.com

As "solid" as "neighborhood" bars go is this "convivial" Center Cityite near Graduate Hospital purveying a "wide selection" of "fabulous" brews on tap; no, the American food's "not spectacular", but it's "good" and certainly "worth the price", and the setting here is flexible enough for a "casual date" or night out with friends.

Tenth St. Pour House ⊘ *American* 21 | 11 | 16 | $13

Center City East | 262 S. 10th St. (Spruce St.) | 215-922-5626

The "first-rate" breakfasts and lunches at this "homey" no-dinner Traditional American in Center City are "better than aspirin" after a "long night"; it's an "inexpensive" standby for many (especially folks from the nearby Jefferson Hospital), so note that even before you "squeeze yourself in" you may have to "wait in the doorway" if you don't go early.

Teresa's Cafe of Wayne *Italian* 22 | 15 | 19 | $30

Wayne | 124 N. Wayne Ave. (Lancaster Ave.) | 610-293-9909

"If you don't mind getting cozy with your neighbors", this "modest", "family"-friendly Wayne "mainstay" is the "go-to" spot of many for "simple", "contemporary" Italian fare with "flair", served by an "attentive" staff; reports of "overwhelming" noise in the "close quarters" explain why some opt for lunch instead, when it's more "conversation-friendly"; N.B. no longer BYO.

Teresa's Next Door ● *Belgian* 20 | 18 | 20 | $29

Wayne | 124-126 N. Wayne Ave. (Lancaster Ave.) | 610-293-0119

Boosters boast that even folks in Brussels "would be jealous" of the "succulent" mussels, "don't-miss" pommes frites, "outrageous beer selection" and "interesting" wine list at this "classy" Belgian-influenced bar next to Teresa's Cafe in Downtown Wayne; "knowledgeable" service is another reason why many consider this spot way "more than a pub."

Tex Mex Connection *Tex-Mex* 20 | 18 | 20 | $27

North Wales | 201 E. Walnut St. (2nd St.) | 215-699-9552 | www.texmexconnection.com

"Strong margaritas" (and "so many flavors" of them) connect the dots as to the appeal of this "lively" Central Montco Tex-Mex eatery-cum-"barroom"; while some are impressed with the *comidas* ("amazing"), other's "skip it" and "save room" for the drinks.

Thai L'Elephant *Thai*   ∇ 23 | 18 | 23 | $27

Phoenixville | Kimberton Sq. | 277 Schuylkill Rd. (Hares Hill Rd.) | 610-935-8613 | www.thailelephant.com

"Be sure to make reservations" at this BYO "hidden gem" in Phoenixville counsel cognoscenti, for it's "rapidly being discovered" by locals thanks to "authentic", "expertly prepared" Thai cuisine, "great prices" and "accommodating", "efficient" service; the "ample-size" room is graced with likenesses of the eponymous pachyderm.

Thai Orchid *Thai*   25 | 19 | 22 | $27

Blue Bell | Blue Bell Shopping Ctr. | 1748 DeKalb Pike (Township Line Rd.) | 610-277-9376

Fans attest they've "never had a bad meal" at this "relaxing", "family-owned" Thai BYO in Blue Bell, where the "excellent" cuisine "goes beyond the standard", and "hot" waitresses provide "pleasant" service in the "cozy" "storefront" space; the $7.95 weekday lunches are a "must" for many wallet-watchers.

Thai Pepper *Thai*   19 | 15 | 18 | $29

Ardmore | 64 E. Lancaster Ave. (Argyle Rd.) | 610-642-5951

"High-quality ingredients" make for "low-risk" dining at this "small", "reliable" Ardmore Thai, where the "pleasing", "well-presented" fare earned it a bump in Food score since the last Survey; the mood is "warm" and the "kind" staff will even let you order Japanese dishes from Mikado next door.

Thai Singha House *Thai*   19 | 12 | 17 | $22

University City | 3939 Chestnut St. (39th St.) | 215-382-8001

A "student's budget" won't bust at this University City Thai, a Pennsters "favorite" that doles out "generous" servings of "basic" yet "good" foodstuffs from a "long" menu; the "gracious", "customer-friendly" staff helps to offset the "boring" decor.

Thomas' *Eclectic*   - | - | - | M

Manayunk | 4201 Main St. (Pensdale St.) | 215-483-9075 | www.thomasrestaurant.com

The "great bar atmosphere" makes this "corner spot" in Manayunk "a nice place to eat and chat", and "happy-hour deals" make it a "fun place for drinks"; still, the effects of mid-Survey chef and ownership changes, a new Eclectic menu and makeover remain to be seen.

333 Belrose ⧄ *American*   23 | 20 | 21 | $45

Radnor | 333 Belrose Ln. (King of Prussia Rd.) | 610-293-1000 | www.333belrose.com

"They do it right" at this "upscale" Radnor New American tucked in an office complex off the Blue Route, a triple threat for "adventurous" food, "responsive" service and a "classy" setting (complete with a popular patio and "busy bar" that draws its share of "Main Line Mrs. Robinsons"); if some find it "noisy" and "pricey", most maintain it "never fails to satisfy."

	FOOD	DECOR	SERVICE	COST

Tierra Colombiana *Colombian/Cuban*   22 | 16 | 18 | $24

North Philly | 4535-39 N. Fifth St. (3 blocks south of Roosevelt Blvd.) | 215-324-6086

Though "not in the nicest part" of the upper reaches of North Philly, this Cuban-Colombian mix off Roosevelt Boulevard dishes out "plenty" of "amazing", "hearty" food that's "as vibrant as the patrons"; prices are *"muy bueno"*, and a "helpful" staff makes sitting in the "well-appointed" room feel "like home."

Z Tiffin Store *Indian*   26 | 13 | 21 | $21

NEW Mount Airy | 7105 Emlen St. (W. Mt. Pleasant Ave.) | 215-242-3656

Northern Liberties | 710 W. Girard Ave. (Franklin St.) | 215-922-1297
www.tiffinstore.com

"Incredibly flavorful" naan and vindaloo, "butter chicken to die for" and other "excellent" dishes are a "revelation" at this Northern Liberties storefront, voted the city's top-rated Indian in this Survey; while its takeout "shines" ("delivery throughout Center City" by "guys in ties" just "says it all"), a seat in the "Ikea-furnished" "upstairs dining room" is like "eating at a friend's house", the location on a "transitional" stretch of Girard Avenue notwithstanding; N.B. a new branch in West Mount Airy opened in summer 2008.

NEW Time ◗ *Continental*   - | - | - | M

Center City East | 1315 Sansom St. (bet. Juniper & 13th Sts.) | 215-985-4800 | www.timerestaurant.net

The owners of City Center's Vintage clock in with this rustic, hipster-friendly Continental in Wash West, featuring a moderately priced menu of contemporary comfort food paired with brown liquors (ryes, bourbons, single malts); the watch-word is it gives off a happy retro vibe.

Z Tinto ◗ *Spanish*   27 | 22 | 24 | $53

Center City West | 114 S. 20th St. (Sansom St.) | 215-665-9150 | www.tintorestaurant.com

Basque-ing in superlatives such as "awesome" and "sublime", Jose Garces' "intimate" Spanish sibling of Amada near Rittenhouse Square offers an "ever-changing" assortment of "fantastic" small plates, backed by "pitchers of sangria" and "unusual wines"; the "knowledgeable" staff "makes solid suggestions", and even after an expansion of the "claustrophobia"-inducing space, some quip it'll still "cost your first born to get a reservation."

Tír na nÓg *Pub Food*   14 | 17 | 17 | $26

Center City West | 1600 Arch St. (16th St.) | 267-514-1700 | www.tirnanogphilly.com

"Yuppies" and expats swarm this "party" parlor of a pub opposite City Hall for "standard" but "good", "dressed-up" Irish fare, "excellent" ales and a scene so "packed with eligibles" you can "barely lift your elbow to drink your Guinness"; "friendly" barkeeps and "beautiful" people help keep the liveliness going, and note that weekend nights seem like "frat"-boy central; N.B. there's a daily late-night menu.

	FOOD	DECOR	SERVICE	COST

Tokyo Hibachi Steakhouse & Sushi Bar *Japanese*

▽ 17 | 17 | 18 | $38

Center City West | 1613 Walnut St., 2nd fl. (16th St.) | 215-751-9993 | www.tokyo1613.com

Sushi and hibachi are rarely seen together in Center City, but this dimly lit Japanese satisfies "groups that want both"; while the grill chefs' shtick may be "fun the first time", the jaded shrug it's "more about the show than the food", which they deem "ok but not spectacular."

☑ Tony Luke's Old Philly Style Sandwiches ✪ *Cheese Steaks*

25 | 7 | 14 | $12

South Philly | 39 E. Oregon Ave. (Front St.) | 215-551-5725 | www.tonylukes.com

The "amazing" cheese steaks are worth even a "wait in the cold and rain" at this "classic South Philly" stop off I-95 near the stadiums, where it's a given you'll "park in the median" amid truckers and watch "counter people" "yell at the drunk customers"; the "prices match" the "picnic-table" setting, but "who needs decor when you have the hot pork with greens?"

NEW Toscana 52 *Italian*

- | - | - | M

Feasterville | 4603 Street Rd. (Lincoln Hwy.) | 215-942-7770

Old-world Tuscany meets contemporary Bucks County at this sprawling Italian located near Route 1 in Feasterville and priced reasonably enough to draw families in addition to business diners (and a bar crowd); N.B. the number 52 refers to its weekly theme menus (a year's worth).

Totaro's *Eclectic*

24 | 12 | 21 | $50

Conshohocken | 729 E. Hector St. (bet. Righter & Walnut Sts.) | 610-828-9341 | www.totaros.com

Though it's "in the middle of nowhere" and looks like a "corner tappy" from the outside, this Conshy Eclectic is a "gem" (and one that's "pricier than it looks"), serving an "excellent variety" of "wonderful" Italian-influenced fare; you can "can hear yourself talk" in the "relaxed" setting where the staff "takes good care of you."

Trattoria Alberto ☒ *Italian*

▽ 21 | 17 | 23 | $44

West Chester | 116 E. Gay St. (bet. High & Matlack Sts.) | 610-430-0203

"Some of the servers have it down to perfection" at this "old-school" Italian in downtown West Chester where regulars "keep coming" back for "solid", "traditional" fare and "friendly" service in "elegant" "townhouse" surroundings; while some find it a "bit pricey", "live music" in the bar area can make for an "entertaining", if somewhat "noisy", evening.

Trattoria Primadonna *Italian*

17 | 13 | 17 | $38

Center City West | 1506 Spruce St. (15th St.) | 215-790-0171 | www.trattoriaprimadonna.com

Kimmel-goers in search of "good", "straightforward" Roman-influenced Italian food at a "reasonable" price would do well to search out this Center City trattoria whose "gregarious" staff guarantees a "warm reception"; N.B. though they serve wine, feel free to BYO.

Trattoria San Nicola *Italian*   22 | 19 | 22 | $36

Berwyn | 668 Lancaster Ave. (Main Ave.) | 610-296-3141 🏠
Paoli | 4 Manor Rd. (Lancaster Ave.) | 610-695-8990
www.tsannicola.com

The "super value" is part of the lure of these "dependable" Italians in Berwyn (the original) and Paoli (the roomier spin-off); the "good" cooking appeals to Main Liners too, though "crowded", "bustling" digs translate into "high noise levels."

Trax Café 🏠Ⓜ *American*   23 | 18 | 21 | $39

Ambler | Ambler SEPTA Station | 27 W. Butler Pike (Maple St.) | 215-591-9777 | www.traxcafe.com

Everything seems on the right track at Steve Waxman's "quaint" Traditional American BYO housed in the "converted" Ambler SEPTA station, where locals punch their ticket for "superb", "interesting" fare; some report that "crowding" and "noise" can sometimes "detract" from the "intimate" setting, a consequence of its "popularity."

Tre Scalini Ⓜ *Italian*   24 | 16 | 21 | $39

South Philly | 1915 E. Passyunk Ave. (bet. McKean & Mifflin Sts.) | 215-551-3870

This "quiet" Italian BYO trattoria on East Passyunk is "what South Philly is supposed to be" say fans who fete its "homemade pastas" and other "solid", "authentic" offerings; "they treat you right" here (especially if you're with "someone known to them"), but opinions are split over the 2007 relocation – some feel the current, "larger" space gives a "boost" to the ambiance while others complain that the staff's burgeoning "attitude matches the (new) dimensions."

Tria ● *Eclectic*   23 | 19 | 22 | $30

NEW Center City East | 1137 Spruce St. (12th St.) | 215-629-9200
Center City West | 123 S. 18th St. (Sansom St.) | 215-972-8742
www.triacafe.com

A "helpful" staff that "knows its stuff" will guide you to "fantastic" "pairings" of wine, cheese, beer and "beautifully executed" Eclectic small plates at this pair of "sophisticated" yet "unpretentious" Center City "oases"; "loitering is encouraged" in the "cramped" quarters full of "Gen-Yers" "looking to be seen"; P.S. the 'Sunday School' specials "provide great value."

Trinacria 🏠 *Italian*   ▽ 25 | 18 | 24 | $50

Blue Bell | 1016 DeKalb Pike (Sumneytown Pike) | 610-275-0505 | www.trinacria-pa.com

"Prepared just right" and "well-presented", the Sicilian fare is "always delicious" at this Blue Bell Italian where the service is "friendly" and "top-notch" (especially if you're a "regular"); it's "wonderful for large family groups", but critics contend that it's "too expensive for the location" and "atmosphere."

	FOOD	DECOR	SERVICE	COST

Trio *Pan-Asian* | 22 | 17 | 21 | $29 |

Fairmount | 2624 Brown St. (Taney St.) | 215-232-8746 | www.triobyob.com

Fairmounters "recommend" this "family-run" Pan-Asian BYO as a "secret" "worth discovering" for its "consistently delicious" fare, including "fancy-ish" Thai "staples"; "extremely nice" owners and staff work the "converted row house" space with a "pleasant roof deck", and most agree "for the price, you can't beat it."

Triumph Brewing Co. ◐ *American* | 19 | 20 | 18 | $29 |

Old City | 117 Chestnut St. (2nd St.) | 215-625-0855
New Hope | 400 Union Square Dr. (Main St.) | 215-862-8300
www.triumphbrewing.com

"Delicious beer brewed in-house" and a "party atmosphere" make this "snazzy" mini-chain of Traditional American microbreweries a "terrific" destination for a "date", "impromptu small parties" or just plain "hanging out"; fans note it "takes as much care with its food as it does with its brewing", and though it "tends to be noisy, once the brews start flowing you become part of the atmosphere."

Trolley Car Diner *Diner* | 14 | 14 | 17 | $16 |

Mount Airy | 7619 Germantown Ave. (Cresheim Valley Dr.) | 215-753-1500 | www.trolleycardiner.com

"Basic diner fare" makes this "kid-friendly" stainless-steel American in Mount Airy a "reliable" choice for breakfast and lunch, as it sports a "huge menu of solid, if not exceptional" chow, a new deli counter and an adjacent ice cream parlor in a refurbished trolley car; while it's "worth the trip" for some, others insist it's "not worth a trolley ride."

Twenty Manning *American* | 22 | 21 | 20 | $43 |

Center City West | 261 S. 20th St. (bet. Locust & Spruce Sts.) | 215-731-0900 | www.twentymanning.com

Rittenhouse Square "sophisticates" are enthralled by Audrey Claire Taichman's "nouveau chic" New American, where Kiong Banh brings "Asian flair" and a "masterful touch" to the "dependable", "upscale" fare; "classic movies" are shown behind the bar in the "sexy" space with "lots of windows" and "pleasing" outdoor seating, but some counsel "come at off-hours or you won't be able to hear yourself think."

Twin Bays Café 🗷🅼 *Eclectic* | ▽ 24 | 21 | 22 | $45 |

Phoenixville | 19 S. Whitehorse Rd. (Rte. 23) | 610-415-1300 | www.twinbayscafe.com

"Warm" servers, "lovely" owners and "great" Eclectic food work their charms on those who've dropped by this "Victorian" Phoenixville BYO in what was once a point on the Underground Railroad; while the tabs can be "expensive", "cocktails on the deck" help compensate.

211 York 🗷🅼 *American* | 22 | 17 | 21 | $43 |

Jenkintown | 211 Old York Rd. (bet. Greenwood & Washington Ln.) | 215-517-5117 | www.211york.com

Jenkintowners shrug off the "tight quarters" at Timothy Papa's "unassuming" New American and dig into the "reliable", "quality" fare at a "reasonable price"; a "gem hidden in plain sight" on the main drag, it boasts a "quaint" vibe and staff that "treats you like a regular", making it a "favorite" for "dates", "birthdays or anniversaries."

NEW Ugly American, The *American* ▽ 19 | 17 | 22 | $31

South Philly | 1100 Front St. (Federal St.) | 215-336-1100 | www.uglyamericanphilly.com

For South Philly folk who don't "subsist on cheese steak" this "casually chic" Pennsport gastropub near the Mummers Museum "holds great promise" by "elevating" "comfort food" with "amped-up" "regional American specialties" (Rochester-style garbage plates, anyone?); "charming" types serve the "unusual" grub, including brunch.

Umai Umai ⊠ *Asian Fusion* 24 | 18 | 22 | $35

Fairmount | 533 N. 22nd St. (Brandywine St.) | 215-988-0707

"Adventurous" eaters find "exciting tastes" at this "intimate", "date"-worthy Asian fusion BYO in Fairmount where "delicious" sushi and "imaginative" entrees are "beautifully prepared"; the "friendly" service can be "slow", so "go with patience"; N.B. the winter menu offers 'hot rocks' on which to cook your own Kobe beef.

Umbria ⊠M *Eclectic* 24 | 17 | 22 | $40

Mount Airy | 7131 Germantown Ave. (bet. Mt. Airy & Mt. Pleasant Aves.) | 215-242-6470

"Many regulars" savor "superb" Eclectic fare at this Mount Airy "storefront" "sleeper" brimming with "character" and "attentive" service; though it "rarely makes" changes, a welcome one is that it "finally accepts credit cards"; N.B. open only for dinner Wednesdays–Saturdays.

NEW Union Gourmet Market & Café M *American* - | - | - | I

Center City East | Western Union | 1113 Locust St. (11th St.) | 215-238-8800 | www.uniongourmetmarket.com

The longtime operators of Philly's Downtown Club have branched out into a bright, open gourmet marketplace/cafe on the first floor of a condo building around the corner from Thomas Jefferson University Hospital in Wash West; pick up budget-priced pizza, sandwiches and such to-go, or dine on-site (a communal table is an option).

Upstares at Varalli *Italian* 21 | 20 | 20 | $43

Avenue of the Arts | 1345 Locust St. (Broad St.) | 215-546-4200 | www.varalliusa.com

The "beautiful view" of the Broad Street "action" and proximity to theaters are the forces pulling patrons to this "cosmopolitan" Italian, the upstairs partner of Sotto Varalli; those who return count on the "enjoyable" meals and staff adept at "keeping everything moving" to accommodate curtain time.

NEW Urban Saloon ● *Pub Food* 16 | 16 | 18 | $21

Fairmount | 2120 Fairmount Ave. (21st St.) | 215-808-0348 | www.theurbansaloon.com

It's like a "high school reunion" for Fairmount's "Gen-Xers" at this "neighborhood" "nightspot" where "reasonably priced" "pub food" and drinks supplement sports on the tube; those who find the menu "overreaching" head for "the bar."

Uzu Sushi *Japanese* | ▽ 26 | 14 | 20 | $33 |

Old City | 104 Market St. (Front St.) | 267-639-3447 | www.uzuphilly.com
Bo Choi's 16-seat sushi bar in Old City gets "overrun" with afishiona-dos seeking "high-quality sashimi" and "creative rolls" at "incredible values"; some sniff they feel as if they're "eating in the vestibule" but find solace in the "reasonably quick" service.

Valanni ● *Mediterranean* | 23 | 19 | 20 | $40 |

Center City East | 1229 Spruce St. (bet. 12th & 13th Sts.) | 215-790-9494 | www.valanni.com
It's "hard to get bored" at this "chic" but "unpretentious" Med in Wash West that works both pre- and post-Kimmel with its "well-thought-out" "little- and large-plates" menu; the service is "friendly without crossing the line", and there's plenty of "people-watching" in a "bar scene" that some liken to "West Hollywood" (which is "not a bad thing"); a mid-Survey expansion may not be reflected in the above Decor score.

Valentino on the Square *Italian* | 19 | 17 | 18 | $36 |

Center City West | 267 S. 19th St. (Rittenhouse Sq.) | 215-545-0441
Valentino Ristorante *Italian*
Center City East | 1328 Pine St. (Juniper St.) | 215-545-6265
Caffe Valentino *Italian*
South Philly | 1245 S. Third St. (Wharton St.) | 215-336-3033
www.valentinoonthesquare.com
The "imaginative" "old-world" offerings at these "neighborhood" Italians lead to "regular" stops for many – the swankier Rittenhouse Square branch (which serves alcohol, offers live music and boasts a boosted atmosphere and menu, post-Survey) and the intimate Pine Street BYO are handy "before concerts" at Kimmel, while the more casual BYO Caffe works for trips to the Mummers Museum; despite debate over the service and cost, most consider them "pleasant" options.

NEW Vango Lounge & Skybar ● *Pan-Asian* | ▽ 16 | 21 | 15 | $35 |

Center City West | 116 S. 18th St. (bet. Sansom & Chestnut Sts.) | 215-568-1020 | www.vangoloungeandskybar.com
A fiber-optic chandelier, a wall of vodka bottles and a 15-ft.-tall vase are part of the "eye-catching" decor at this Pan-Asian "luxe lounge" in Rittenhouse, where a "young and fun" crowd can be seen "hanging out" on the "LA-style roof deck"; while the "delicious martinis" and other "expensive" libations "go down very smoothly", surveyors are split on the Japanese-influenced eats – "creative" vs. "average."

Vesuvio ● *Italian* | 17 | 17 | 15 | $31 |

South Philly | 736-38 S. Eighth St. (Fitzwater St.) | 215-922-8380 | www.vesuvio-online.com
A "warm" mood pervades this rustic South Philly Italian enjoyed for its "excellent" bar and staff that "tries hard"; but while some say the

food exhibits "good, straightforward" cooking, others judge it "pretty standard" and add the place seems in the midst of an "identity crisis" (is it a "fine-dining" spot or a "pool hall"?).

ⓩ Vetri ⌧ *Italian*   27 | 23 | 27 | $88

Avenue of the Arts | 1312 Spruce St. (bet. Broad & 13th Sts.) | 215-732-3478 | www.vetriristorante.com

Although "you're not under the real Tuscan sun", fans swear you're as good as there at Marc Vetri and Jeff Benjamin's "rustic" Italian "legend" in Center City, which "continues to amaze" with a menu of "sublime" "handmade everything" and "outstanding", "knowledgeable" service; it's "tough to get a table" in the "shoebox"-like space, and be prepared "to pay an arm and leg"; N.B. there's no à la carte on Saturdays.

Victor Café *Italian*   20 | 22 | 23 | $43

South Philly | 1303-05 Dickinson St. (bet. Dickinson & 13th Sts.) | 215-468-3040 | www.victorcafe.com

Those who "enjoy opera" "sing the praises" of this "quirky", "old-fashioned" South Philly Italian "treasure", where waiters "break into arias" while serving "Pavarotti"-sized "portions" of "good" red-gravy fare"; some sniff the "performances outshine the food", but most agree the "total experience" "can't be beat."

Victory Brewing Co. ☻ *Pub Food*   15 | 9 | 16 | $23

Downingtown | 420 Acorn Ln. (Chestnut St.) | 610-873-0881 | www.victorybeer.com

"Great beers in numerous styles" are "the star" at this "noisy", "up-beat", "family"-friendly brewpub in Downington where the bar food can be "good" but is "secondary" to the suds; N.B. extensive post-Survey renovations – including the addition of flat-screen TVs and an authentic BBQ pit – may outdate the above Food and Decor scores.

Vientiane Café ⌧⏚ *Laotian/Thai*   23 | 14 | 21 | $19

University City | 4728 Baltimore Ave. (bet. 47th & 48th Sts.) | 215-726-1095

Do what the "locals" do and join "vegetarian anarchists", "Penn students and their families", and "businesspeople" at this "tiny" storefront BYO in West Philly for "glorious", "cheap" Laotian-Thai eats; "don't let appearances fool you" – the food and "lovely" servers justify a trip here.

ⓩ Vietnam *Vietnamese*   25 | 20 | 21 | $26

Chinatown | 221 N. 11th St. (bet. Race & Vine Sts.) | 215-592-1163 | www.eatatvietnam.com

The "reputation" of Benny Lai's Chinatown "gem" for "affordable", "top-notch" Vietnamese eats is "well deserved" according to locals who steer their "out-of-town friends" here for the "don't-miss" BBQ platter and "divine" spring rolls, or "tie-curling" cocktails from the "intimate" third-floor bar; service comes at "supersonic" speeds in the "elegant", "lively" setting, where you can "expect a wait" for a table.

	FOOD	DECOR	SERVICE	COST

NEW Vietnam Café Ⓜ Vietnamese | 23 | 19 | 21 | $21 |

West Philly | 814 S. 47th St. (Baltimore Ave.) | 215-729-0260 |
www.eatatvietnam.com

Vietnam's BYO "satellite" in West Philly delights the Penn community with "outstanding", "reasonably priced" Viet eats, served by a
"professional" staff in "tasteful", albeit "tiny", quarters; although
some grouse that the menu is "limited" compared to the parent's,
many still feel it's the "new best thing" in the neighborhood.

Vietnam Palace Vietnamese | 23 | 18 | 19 | $22 |

Chinatown | 222 N. 11th St. (bet. Race & Vine Sts.) | 215-592-9596 |
www.vietnampalacephilly.com

It may have a "rival across the street", but Nhon T. Nguyen's
Chinatown Vietnamese more than holds its own with "quick" service, "delicious" fare off a "diner"-length menu and "comfortable"
quarters; overall, "you can't complain" – given the "cheap" check.

Viggiano's Italian | 19 | 17 | 20 | $34 |

Conshohocken | 16 E. First Ave. (Fayette St.) | 610-825-3151 |
www.viggianosrestaurant.com

"Family-style" describes the "big plates" of "red-sauce" fare as well as
the ambiance at this, yes, "family-run" Conshy Italian BYO; though a
renovation removed the booths fashioned from carriages, the kitchen
is "still working just fine", and if a few feel the menu "lacks inspiration",
they're outvoted by those who enjoy its "consistent", "solid" quality.

Villa di Roma ⌀ Italian | 21 | 10 | 17 | $29 |

South Philly | Italian Mkt. | 936 S. Ninth St. (bet. Christian St. &
Washington Ave.) | 215-592-1295

The Italian Market's "old", "homey" reliable keeps on churning out
"really good" Italiana that's "nonna"-certified; as the "red gravy"
adorns the "baseball-size meatballs", "lifers" for waitresses "treat you
like family", and though it's cash only, "it's a deal you can't refuse",
especially when this spot is as "real as South Philly gets", hon'.

Vincent's ⓩ Continental | ▽ 16 | 14 | 18 | $40 |

West Chester | 10 E. Gay St. (bet. High & Walnut Sts.) | 610-696-4262 |
www.vincentsjazz.com

"Holy 1957", this "white-tablecloth" West Chester "landmark" attracts a diverse roster of "regulars" with "ample portions" of "steady"
Continental cuisine, "incredible" jazz and blues Thursdays–Saturdays
and some of the "best bartenders in the state"; those who find
the fare just "fair" agree the "entertainment" is "well worth the trip."

Vinny T's of Boston Italian | 15 | 15 | 16 | $26 |

Wynnewood | Wynnewood Square Shopping Ctr. | 260 E. Lancaster Ave.
(bet. Church & Old Wynnewood Rds.) | 610-645-5400 |
www.vinnytsofboston.com

Bring a "doggy bag" for the "lotsa pasta" at this "roomy" Wynnewood
link of an Italian chainlet, where the over-*abbondanza* of food is complemented by din akin to a "school lunch room"; the "pleasant" servers are "efficient", which helps keep the "basic" fare flowing.

	FOOD	DECOR	SERVICE	COST

Vintage ● ⊠ French
| | 19 | 21 | 20 | $31 |

Center City East | 129 S. 13th St. (bet. Chestnut & Walnut Sts.) | 215-922-3095 | www.vintage-philadelphia.com

This "stylish", "sophisticated" wine bar makes an impression with its "interesting" French bistro fare and "informed" bartenders who offer "large pours" of some 60 selections by the glass beneath an "awesome wine-bottle chandelier"; any thoughts of fine "conversation", however, may go out the "window" (literally) during "happy hour."

Warmdaddy's ● M Soul Food
| | 20 | 21 | 20 | $30 |

South Philly | RiverView Plaza | 1400 S. Columbus Blvd. (Reed St.) | 215-462-2000 | www.warmdaddys.com

"Well-prepared" Southern "home cooking", some of the "best bartenders around" and "good ol' Delta blues" go together at this soul fooder in a South Philly "movie-plex strip mall"; while a few miss the "old location", others swear the "incredible" ("loud") music makes the grub "taste that much better", so if you want to "share a heart-to-heart conversation, look elsewhere" advise insiders.

Warsaw Cafe Polish
| | 18 | 14 | 17 | $34 |

Center City West | 306 S. 16th St. (Spruce St.) | 215-546-0204 | www.warsawcafephilly.com

Get in touch with your inner "Slav" at this "cheery" Center City mainstay proffering "authentic" Eastern European (read: pierogi and borscht) that both "sticks to your ribs" and is sold at "reasonable" tabs; while some think it's "time for a menu change" most maintain the food's "done right."

Washington Crossing Inn M American
| | 17 | 19 | 17 | $46 |

Washington Crossing | Washington Crossing Inn | Rtes. 32 & 532 | 215-493-3634 | www.washingtoncrossinginn.com

"Understandably touristy" (it's near the site of the legendary boat ride) is this Traditional American situated in a "historical" Washington Crossing inn, where the "charm" is "Colonial", the quarters "comfortable" and the setting "perfect"; foodwise, the fare is "good" – so, all told, "generally reliable" sums up the situation here.

⊠ Water Works M Mediterranean
| | 21 | 27 | 20 | $54 |

Fairmount | 640 Water Works Dr. (Kelly Dr.) | 215-236-9000 | www.thewaterworksrestaurant.com

"One of the city's best views" of the Schuylkill Falls and Boathouse Row serves as a backdrop to this "lovely", "romantic" Fairmount destination behind the Art Museum, where the "contemporary" Mediterranean fare is "well prepared"; while some feel "spotty service mars" the experience, sager sorts assert that the "beautiful" vistas will "soothe your soul" – at least "until the bill arrives."

Whip Tavern Pub Food
| | 20 | 22 | 20 | $34 |

Coatesville | 1383 N. Chatham Rd. (Springdell Rd.) | 610-383-0600 | www.whiptavern.com

Jolly good, this "cool interpretation of an old English pub" in the "horsey" "boondocks" of Chester County will "put a smile on your face" and sate any "cravings for bangers and mash", "amazing fish 'n' chips" or "fantastic" lagers and bitters; a "hands-on" owner and "friendly" staff are just "part of the charm" of this "pubby and clubby" "treasure."

✓ White Dog Cafe *Eclectic*

| 21 | 20 | 19 | $36 |

University City | 3420 Sansom St. (bet. 34th & 36th Sts.) | 215-386-9224 | www.whitedog.com

"Enviro-friendly", "locally sourced" "food with a conscience" is showcased at Judy Wicks' "pleasantly Bohemian" Eclectic "mainstay" in the heart of the Penn campus; while fans are smitten with the "creative", "delicious" "comfort food" and "cutesy" gift shop next door, it's hounded by foes who bark at the crunchy vibe and service they say is "slow."

White Elephant *Thai*

| 22 | 19 | 22 | $31 |

Huntingdon Valley | 759 Huntingdon Pike (bet. Cottman & Filmont Aves.) | 215-663-1495 | www.whiteelephant.us

It's hard to ignore the elephants in the room (i.e. the motif) of this "winning" pachyderm-themed Thai BYO in Huntingdon Valley that's a "good second bet" to going to Thailand; count on being "greeted warmly" before sitting down to "delicious" dishes in a place "you'd never expect."

William Penn Inn *American/Continental*

| 22 | 23 | 23 | $43 |

Gwynedd | William Penn Inn | 1017 DeKalb Pike (Sumneytown Pike) | 215-699-9272 | www.williampenninn.com

Its "staid", "blue-rinse-and-pearls" reputation notwithstanding, this "grand old" "special-occasion" "favorite" in Central Montco is a "class act all the way" according to fans who cite its "wonderful" American-Continental fare and "impeccable" service; while some quip that the "lovely" circa-1714 landmark can't be described "without a quill pen", others insist they don't call it "old faithful" for nothing.

Winberie's *American*

| 16 | 17 | 17 | $29 |

Wayne | 1164 Valley Forge Rd. (bet. Anthony Wayne Dr. & Valley Ford Rd.) | 610-293-9333 | www.selectrestaurants.com

Even if the "reliable" Traditional American menu at this "local standby" on the edge of Valley Forge National Historical Park won't "knock your socks off", many find it a "great alternative" to the usual "chain food" in the area; "reasonable" prices and "outside summertime seating" add to the "try-it" tag.

Winnie's Le Bus *American*

| 21 | 17 | 19 | $25 |

Manayunk | 4266 Main St. (bet. Green & Shurs Lns.) | 215-487-2663 | www.lebusmanayunk.com

Manayunk fans "could live on the bread alone" (it's "fabulous") at this "lively" "vegetarian" and "kid"-friendly "treasure" offering "excellent" New American cuisine, namely "great" baked goods and sandwiches, along with "savory" breakfasts and brunches; most surveyors say this is the kind of "comfort food you could eat" all the time.

	FOOD	DECOR	SERVICE	COST

Wooden Iron ⊠ *American* — 18 | 18 | 19 | $42

Wayne | 118 N. Wayne Ave. (Lancaster Ave.) | 610-964-7888 |
www.woodeniron.com

"Country club" dining comes "without the membership" fees at this
golf-themed, mahogany-embellished Traditional American in
Downtown Wayne; once you get past the "enormous bar crowd"
studded with "divorcées", you'll sit down to "reliably good" dishes
served by "courteous" staffers, even if some cite "costly" tabs.

World Café Live *American* — 14 | 19 | 16 | $25

University City | 3025 Walnut St. (bet. 30th & 31st Sts.) | 215-222-1400 |
www.worldcafelive.com

This "hip" split-level University City performance venue is the home
of Penn's WXPN station and the showcase for "terrific" live acts
backed by an "unbelievable sound system"; while some say it's suitable for a "sit-down" meal, the consensus is that the music here far
outshines the otherwise "decent" American eats.

Xochitl Ⓜ *Mexican* — 23 | 21 | 22 | $41

Society Hill | 408 S. Second St. (Pine St.) | 215-238-7280 |
www.xochitlphilly.com

"Innovative riffs" on Mexican *comidas* ("there's no burrito in sight")
sate hungry amigos at this "charming", "chic" regional "Haute-xa-can"
"addition" to Society Hill (pronounced 'SO-cheet'); the "fun staff"
"knows its way" around "the exotic menu", and some of the "hardest-
working bartenders in Philly" fix "specialty" drinks (e.g. "white sangria like rocket fuel") while DJs entertain on weekends; P.S. the Sunday
prix fixe dinners "deliver" – and at reasonable prices.

NEW Yakitori Boy ◗ *Japanese* — ▽ 22 | 23 | 23 | $24

Chinatown | 211 N. 11th St. (Race St.) | 215-923-8088 |
www.yakitoriboy-japas.com

"What more could you ask for" at this "swanky" Japanese in
Chinatown offering 'Japas' – Asian-style tapas – of "outstanding"
yakitori and "fantastic" sushi that are "great" for sharing, plus
"yummy" cocktails and Sapporo "on tap"; an upper level karaoke bar
with private booths is "where the action is."

NEW Yalda Grill *Afghan* — ▽ 20 | 8 | 19 | $21

Horsham | 222 Horsham Rd. (Easton Rd.) | 215-444-9502 |
www.yaldagrillandkabob.com

"You won't be disappointed" declare devotees of this "unpretentious"
family-owned BYO Afghan "surprise" off Route 611 in Horsham dispensing "large" portions of "simple", "well-prepared" fare (kebabs and
such, plus kid-friendly burgers and pizza) at "great-value" prices;
the "very friendly" staff "warms" the "charmless" atmosphere.

⊠ Yangming *Chinese/Continental* — 25 | 22 | 23 | $37

Bryn Mawr | 1051 Conestoga Rd. (Haverford Rd.) | 610-527-3200 |
www.yangmingrestaurant.com

"No Column A here" – this "stellar" Mandarin-Continental with "style"
in Bryn Mawr offers a "fine-dining" experience, with "well-crafted",

"unforgettable" meals (plus "awesome takeout") and "smiling faces" from the staff; if there's debate about the cost ("reasonable" vs." expensive"), at least "the quality" "never wavers."

Yardley Inn *American*   21 | 22 | 21 | $42

Yardley | 82 E. Afton Ave. (Delaware Ave.) | 215-493-3800 | www.yardleyinn.com

This "charming" New American by the Delaware in "picturesque" Yardley proffers "pleasant surprises" for "loyal" locals who tout its "wide-ranging" menu with "many pleasant surprises" including an "awesome" Sunday brunch; given the "dearth of fine restaurants" in the area, most agree "this is the one."

Yazmin Ⓜ *Pan-Asian*   ▽ 21 | 15 | 19 | $30

Warminster | Warminster Shopping Ctr. | 340-342 York Rd. (Henry Ave.) | 215-443-0800 | www.yazminrestaurant.com

Surveyors who've discovered this Pan-Asian BYO in a Warminster strip mall report being "surprised" by its "excellent" "fusion" of Thai, Vietnamese and Chinese cuisines and "careful", "attentive" service; a few suggest some "improvement" in the decor is in order "to match the quality of the food."

yello'bar ● *American*   ▽ 16 | 16 | 16 | $21

South Philly | 2425 Grays Ferry Ave. (Catharine St.) | 215-735-3533 | www.yell-obar.com

Most report this "lively", "bi-level" Irish-style pub across from the historic Naval Square condos in South Philly is a "good addition to the local scene", with "not fancy but well-prepared" bar food and a "great" beer selection; others cite "inconsistencies" in food and service but allow there's lots of "potential."

NEW Zacharias Creek Side Cafe Ⓢ *American*   21 | 18 | 23 | $42

Lansdale | Center Point Shopping Ctr. | 2960 Skippack Pike (Valley Forge Rd.) | 610-584-5650 | www.zachariascreeksidecafe.com

"Accommodating owners" and an "adventurous" menu attract an appreciative crowd to this "bright" New American BYO that "upgrades" the Skippack Pike Restaurant Row outside of Lansdale; while some find it "expensive" and "noisy", the majority rules it a "wonderful addition to the suburban dining scene."

NEW Zahav *Israeli*   - | - | - | M

Society Hill | 237 St. James Pl. (2nd St.) | 215-625-8800 | www.zahavrestaurant.com

Modern Middle Eastern tastes play out in a warm, stone-floor atmosphere recalling Old Jerusalem at this family-style Society Hill Israeli from Steven Cook and Michael Solomonov (Marigold Kitchen, Xochitl); classic fare includes hummus and fried eggplant, bread is baked in an Arabic *taboon,* fish and skewered meats are cooked over coal and creative cocktails boast names like Milk & Honey (vodka, date syrup and almond milk); N.B. a late-night menu is also served.

	FOOD	DECOR	SERVICE	COST

Zakes Cafe *American*

23 | 13 | 18 | $27

Fort Washington | 444 S. Bethlehem Pike (Lafayette Ave Connector) | 215-654-7600

"Don't let the exterior fool you" – this New American BYO "find" in Fort Washington is the "lifeblood of Montco moms" on account of its "excellent" breakfasts, lunches and dinners, and "deliciously decadent" desserts; the "small" space is always "jam-packed", and what's more, the "secret" is out, so expect to sit "elbow to elbow" in a scene akin to a "gossip-filled teahouse."

⊠ Zento *Japanese*

26 | 11 | 23 | $32

Old City | 138 Chestnut St. (2nd St.) | 215-925-9998 | www.zentocontemporary.com

"It's all about the fish" at Morimoto alum Gunawan Wibisono's "shoebox"-sized sushi "paradise" in Old City, home of the "mystically delicious" signature "square" rolls and other "standouts"; any quibbles over "heavy" cooked entrees and "minimal" decor are compensated by the "special karma" from a "cheerful", "quick" staff; N.B. it's BYO.

Zesty's *Greek/Italian*

20 | 17 | 18 | $36

Manayunk | 4382 Main St. (Levering St.) | 215-483-6226 | www.zestys.com

"Fresh" fish that's "simply prepared" is to be savored at this "homey" Greco-Roman outfit on Main Street; while testy types find it a bit "expensive for what you get", popular opinion swims in a favorable direction (it's a "nice change from the fussy Manayunk scene").

NEW Zhi Wei Guan ⊕ *Chinese*

- | - | - | I

Chinatown | 925 Race St. (10th St.) | 215-873-0808

Dumplings and noodle dishes star at this simple, white-lace-tablecloth Chinatown BYO focusing on the cuisine of Hangzhou, China, home of the chef and helpful staff; the menu caters to both adventurous and tame palates.

Zinc ⊠ *French/Seafood*

22 | 19 | 22 | $43

Center City East | 246 S. 11th St. (bet. Locust & Spruce Sts.) | 215-351-9901

"Why go to Paris" when you have this "romantic" New French seafooder in Wash West from Olivier de St. Martin (Caribou Cafe) that "delivers" on the bistro concept with "deliciously creative" cuisine in "cozy" quarters; while most maintain it's an "excellent experience", others insist "the jury's still out", citing dishes that lack a certain "je ne sais quoi."

Zocalo *Mexican*

20 | 18 | 19 | $34

University City | 3600 Lancaster Ave. (36th St.) | 215-895-0139 | www.zocalophilly.com

"If you love Taco Bell" you won't think much of chef-owner Gregory Russell's "upscale" University City Mex "favorite" that puts a "satisfying twist" on "authentic" south-of-the-border *comidas* and offers "sunny rooms" and a "great" patio in which to enjoy it; keep in mind

| | FOOD | DECOR | SERVICE | COST |

that "gourmet Mexican is not an oxymoron", and if it seems "pricey", it's possibly because you "can never stop at one margarita."

Zorba's Taverna Ⓜ *Greek*   20 | 11 | 18 | $26
Fairmount | 2230 Fairmount Ave. (bet. 22nd & 23rd Sts.) | 215-978-5990
There are "no frills but lots of love" at this "authentic" Fairmount Greek BYO, where a father-son team's "delectable" "comfort food" may inspire you to "jump up, wave a hankie and dance"; the "price is right", the service is "gracious" and overall, it's a "great neighborhood" place.

ZoT *Belgian*   20 | 18 | 17 | $36
Society Hill | 122 Lombard St. (2nd St.) | 267-639-3260 | www.zotrestaurant.com
Most find this "cool" Belgian "hangout" in Society Hill "gets it right", with "more types of mussels than the governor of California" and a "boffo" beer selection; those who've encountered "inconsistent" vittles and "clueless" servers say "stick to" the brew; P.S. its "goofy name" is Flemish for madman.

Lancaster/Berks Counties

TOP FOOD	TOP SERVICE
27 Gibraltar	26 Green Hills Inn
26 Green Hills Inn	24 Gibraltar
Gracie's	23 Lily's on Main
24 Lily's on Main	Good 'N Plenty
22 Five Guys	21 Gracie's

TOP DECOR	BEST BUYS
25 Gracie's	1. Five Guys
23 Gibraltar	2. Qdoba
22 Lily's on Main	3. Isaac's
Green Hills Inn	4. Good 'N Plenty
21 Haydn Zug's	5. Shady Maple Smorgas.

Bensí *Italian*

18	16	17	$25

NEW **Wyomissing** | Shoppes at Wyomissing | 700 Woodland Rd. (Rte. 422) | 610-375-3222 | www.bensirestaurants.com
See review in the Philadelphia Directory.

Bird-in-Hand
Family Restaurant 🖾 *PA Dutch*

18	14	19	$23

Bird-in-Hand | 2760 Old Philadelphia Pike (Ronks Rd.) | 717-768-1500 | www.bird-in-hand.com
"Bring your appetite" to this "classic" (35 years and counting) Pennsylvania Dutch in Lancaster County proffering "hearty", "homespun" Amish-style cooking (e.g. pork and sauerkraut, chicken-corn soup) via wallet-friendly, all-you-can-eat breakfast, lunch and dinner buffets; après dining, burn off some calories browsing the handy, on-site gift shop.

Cameron Estate Inn 🖽 *American*

-	-	-	E

Mt. Joy | 1855 Mansion Ln. (Donegal Springs Rd.) | 717-492-0111 | www.cameronestateinn.com
"Expect to dine like a king and queen" on fine New American cuisine at this "historic mansion" and B&B in "wonderful, out-of-the-way" Mount Joy; sup in the stately dining room or glass-enclosed 'sun porch' with a "country" view (you may decide to "stay the whole weekend").

Carr's 🖽 *American*

∇ 25	19	23	$48

Lancaster | Hager Arcade | 50 W. Grant St. (bet. King & Prince Sts.) | 717-299-7090 | www.carrsrestaurant.com
This "intimate" New American below the Hager Arcade in Lancaster is a "total joy" thanks to chef-owner Tim Carr's cuisine, inspired by local ingredients and proffered by "all-around" "super" servers; N.B. kitchen-made meals are available for takeout at Carr's Corner Grocery, a gourmet shop upstairs, open Tuesdays–Saturdays.

El Serrano *Nuevo Latino*

19	19	15	$29

Lancaster | 2151 Columbia Ave. (Rte. 741 S.) | 717-397-6191 | www.elserrano.com
This "little secret" – "one of the few good" Nuevo Latino destinations amid the starch lands in Lancaster – dishes up "traditional"

Peruvian *comidas* in "beautifully crafted", villa-like surround-ings; "wonderful" live music (mariachi, jazz, Latin) on weekends completes the experience.

Five Guys Famous Burgers & Fries *Burgers*
22 | 9 | 15 | $10

NEW Lancaster | 1962 Fruitville Pike (Rte. 30) | 717-569-7730
NEW Lancaster | 2090 E. Lincoln Hwy. (Rte. 30) |
717-299-4470
www.fiveguys.com
See review in the Philadelphia Directory.

☑ Gibraltar *Mediterranean/Seafood*
27 | 23 | 24 | $48

Lancaster | 931 Harrisburg Pike (Race Ave.) | 717-397-2790 |
www.dhollidays.com
A rock-solid "standout" for "innovative" seafood is the buzz on this "all-around excellent" Lancaster County Mediterranean, "miles from the water, but who can argue with the results?"; an "amazing" wine list, "pretty" open-air ambiance and "well-trained" staff en-hance this "divine" "find."

Good 'N Plenty ☒ *PA Dutch*
19 | 16 | 23 | $22

Smoketown | 150 Eastbrook Rd. (Rte. 30) | 717-394-7111 |
www.goodnplenty.com
"Dive into" "plenty" of "good" "down-home" Amish cooking at this Lancaster County "tourist attraction" in a Smoketown farmhouse, where you'll dine communally with "fellow travelers" (aka "strang-ers") "without the benefit of alcohol"; still hungry? –"stop by the bakery" before the ride home.

☑ Gracie's 21st Century Cafe ☒Ⓜ *Eclectic*
26 | 25 | 21 | $51

Pine Forge | 1534 Manatawny Rd. (King St.) | 610-323-4004 |
www.gracies21stcentury.com
Take a "step back in time" at Gracie Skiadas' "quirky" country "hide-away" tucked among landscaped gardens in Pine Forge for "imagi-native" Eclectic eats "infused" with "love and mystery"; it's like a "round-the-world tour" – and "worth the trip" to Berks County.

☑ Green Hills Inn ☒ *American/French*
26 | 22 | 26 | $58

Reading | 2444 Morgantown Rd. (Love Rd.) | 610-777-9611
"Romantics" head to this "cozy", "upscale" country inn on the out-skirts of Reading for "superb" French-American fare and "profes-sional" service that makes you "want to stay all night"; the food hasn't "changed much" over the years, but for most, "consistency" is a plus (and "reservations are a must"); N.B. there's a $29.95 three-course dinner prix fixe.

Haydn Zug's ☒ *American*
18 | 21 | 19 | $48

East Petersburg | 1987 State St. (Rte. 72) | 717-569-5746 |
www.haydnzugs.com
"Ask to sit by the fireplace" in the "lovely" "Colonial" setting of this "classy" East Petersburg mainstay set in an "old home" with "rustic

	FOOD	DECOR	SERVICE	COST

charm"; while some feel the Traditional American "standards" "lack creativity", others laud the "excellently prepared" fare, as well as the "New World"-centric wine list with "lots of good values."

Iron Hill Brewery & Restaurant *American* | 18 | 18 | 18 | $27 |

NEW Lancaster | 781 Harrisburg Pike (Race Ave.) | 717-291-9800 | www.ironhillbrewery.com
See review in the Philadelphia Directory.

Isaac's Restaurant & Deli *Deli* | 17 | 13 | 16 | $14 |

Ephrata | Cloister Shopping Ctr. | 120 N. Reading Rd. (Rte. 272) | 717-733-7777
Lancaster | Granite Run Sq. | 1559 Manheim Pike (Rte. 283) | 717-560-7774
Lancaster | Sycamore Ct. | 245 Centerville Rd. (Rte. 30) | 717-393-1199
Lancaster | 25 N. Queen St. (King St.) | 717-394-5544
Lancaster | The Shoppes at Greenfield | 565 Greenfield Rd. (Rte. 30) | 717-393-6067
Lititz | 4 Trolley Run Rd. (Rte. 501) | 717-625-1181
Strasburg | Shops at Traintown | 226 Gap Rd. (Rte. 896) | 717-687-7699
Wyomissing | Village Sq. | 94 Commerce Dr. (bet. Papermill & State Hill Rds.) | 610-376-1717
www.isaacsdeli.com
See review in the Philadelphia Directory.

J.B. Dawson's *American* | 18 | 17 | 19 | $28 |

NEW Lancaster | Park City Ctr. | 491 Park City Ctr. (Rte. 30) | 717-399-3996
Austin's *American*
Reading | 1101 Snyder Rd. (Van Reed Rd.) | 610-678-5500
www.jbdawsons.com
See review in the Philadelphia Directory.

Lemon Grass Thai *Thai* | 22 | 15 | 17 | $24 |

Lancaster | 2481 Lincoln Hwy. E. (Eastbrook Rd.) | 717-295-1621 | www.thailemongrass.com
See review in the Philadelphia Directory.

ⓩ Lily's on Main *American* | 24 | 22 | 23 | $39 |

Ephrata | Brossman Business Complex | 124 E. Main St. (Lake St.) | 717-738-2711 | www.lilysonmain.com
There's a "romantic" "hint of Manhattan in the air" at this "sleek", art deco New American in tiny Ephrata in the heart of Pennsylvania Dutch Country, where "inventive" cuisine "tickles the taste buds" and "continues to amaze" loyalists; friendly service and "small-town" prices also receive praise.

Mazzi *Italian* | - | - | - | E |

Leola | Inn at Leola Vill. | 46 Deborah Dr. (Main St.) | 717-656-8983 | www.mazzirestaurant.com
Located in the "heart" of Pennsylvania Dutch country, this "inno-vative" Leola Italian emphasizes produce from local farmers in

its cuisine, and while à la carte dishes suit some, those in-the-know deem the $99 seven-course tasting menu "one of the best"; you can also dine in the intimate lounge boasting a slate-topped bar.

Miller's Smorgasbord *PA Dutch*   18 | 15 | 18 | $25

Ronks | 2811 Lincoln Hwy. E. (Ronks Rd.) | 717-687-6621 | www.millerssmorgasbord.com

"Tried-and-true" defines this Pennsylvania Dutch all-you-can-eat "tourist" "bus-trip finale", dishing out course after course of "starchy", "home-cooked" "classics" (and signature shoofly pie for dessert) for 80 years; it's "well worth the money" – $21.95 for adults – so "plan on" "eating yourself to death" (or "leaving with unbuttoned pants").

Plain & Fancy Farm *PA Dutch*   ▽ 19 | 15 | 24 | $25

Bird-in-Hand | 3121 Old Philadelphia Pike (bet. N. Harvest & Old Leacock Rds.) | 717-768-4400 | www.millerssmorgasbord.com

Plainly speaking, "lots of home cooking" can be found at this communal, 700-seat Pennsylvania Dutchery in the heart of Lancaster County; diners can pick from an à la carte menu or the all-you-can-eat buffet ($14.95) featuring the likes of fried chicken, baked ham and shoofly pie.

Qdoba Mexican Grill *Mexican*   17 | 9 | 14 | $11

Lancaster | Park City Ctr. | 387 Park City Ctr. (Ring Rd.) | 717-299-4766 | www.qdoba.com

See review in the Philadelphia Directory.

Restaurant at Doneckers 🗷 *American*   19 | 19 | 20 | $54

Ephrata | The Doneckers Community | 333 N. State St. (Walnut St.) | 717-738-9501 | www.doneckers.com

"After a day of shopping", a stop at this "lovely" destination in an Ephrata retail complex satisfies with decent New American cuisine and a "spectacular" wine list; for some, there's a "disadvantage" with a relatively new chef getting "established", but the lack of "attitude" "prevalent in city restaurants" of this ilk is a big advantage.

Shady Maple Smorgasbord 🗷 *PA Dutch*   19 | 13 | 20 | $20

East Earl | 129 Toddy Dr. (28th Division Hwy.) | 717-354-4981 | www.shady-maple.com

"Eat yourself full" at this "busy, busy, busy" "smorgasbord-lover's dream" that's part of a retail complex in Lancaster County, where "wow is the first thing you say" when faced with the "huge buffet" of "hearty" Pennsylvania Dutch fare; most agree it's "worth the drive", although you may need to "shop to ward off the food coma."

Stoudt's Black Angus *American*   18 | 18 | 18 | $35

Adamstown | 2800 N. Reading Rd. (Pennsylvania Tpke., exit 286) | 717-484-4386 | www.stoudtsbeer.com

"A pint or two" of the craft brews made on premises will bring you to "your knees" at this Traditional American "classic" off the turnpike in Adamstown, known for "fine" fare and "enjoyable" beer festivals; "breweriana" graces the walls of the pub area while the Victorian dining room reminds some of their "grandma's house."

Willow Valley
Family Restaurant   *PA Dutch*

∇ 19 | 16 | 19 | $30

Lancaster | Willow Valley Resort | 2416 Willow Street Pike (Rte. 222 S.) | 717-464-2711 | www.willowvalley.com

"Thundering hordes of tourists" feast on "massive amounts of food" at this 500-seat Pennsylvania Dutch smorgasbord in Lancaster; given the "tremendous variety" of "delicious", "good-value" vittles at breakfast, lunch and dinner, it's generally "jam-packed."

New Jersey Suburbs

TOP FOOD

27| Mélange
    Little Café
    Sagami
26| Giumarello's
    Ritz Seafood

TOP DECOR

25| Food for Thought
23| Chophouse
    Giumarello's
    Catelli
22| Word of Mouth

TOP SERVICE

25| Bàcio Italian
24| Giumarello's
    Sapori
23| Hamilton's
    Manon*

BEST BUYS

1. Five Guys
2. Nifty Fifty's
3. Pop Shop
4. Tacconelli's
5. Kibitz Room

Alisa Cafe ☒ *French/Thai*   22 | 18 | 20 | $36

Cherry Hill | Barclay Farms Shopping Ctr. | 112 Rte. 70 E. (Kings Hwy.) | 856-354-8807 | www.alisacafe.com

Devotees declare Tony Kanjanakorn's "elegant but comfy" French-Thai BYO bistro in a Cherry Hill strip mall an "underappreciated jewel", pointing to its "right-on-target" "creative" dinners (e.g. Thai seafood bouillabaisse); complaints about cost are assuaged by the $30 (three-course) and $35 (four-course) prix fixe specials, and if some have found the room "understaffed", at least service is "friendly."

NEW Aloe Fusion ☒ *Thai*   - | - | - | M
(fka Champa Laos)

Cherry Hill | 219 Haddonfield-Berlin Rd. (Brace Rd.) | 856-795-0188 | www.aloefusion.net

This cheery new Cherry Hill Thai BYO strip-maller (formerly Champa Laos) is distinguished by its reasonably priced, veggie-friendly fare (e.g. tofu supreme) that supplements the usual edibles like chicken satay; N.B. the three-course lunch special (Mondays–Fridays, $8.95) makes it a popular midday stop.

Anthony's ☒ *Italian*   22 | 17 | 20 | $34

Haddon Heights | 512 Station Ave. (White Horse Pike) | 856-310-7766 | www.anthonyscuisine.com

"Homemade" Italian "comfort food" served in a "lovely, intimate" BYO is the draw at Anthony Iannone's "upscale-casual" storefront in Haddon Heights; "it's a good place to take the grandchildren", so "get there early or beware of the crowds."

Anton's at the Swan ☒ *American*   20 | 20 | 18 | $50

Lambertville | Swan Hotel | 43 S. Main St. (Swan St.) | 609-397-1960 | www.antons-at-the-swan.com

Advocates attest this "rustic" New American in a "delightful old hotel" in Lambertville is still "worth the drive – and cost" for an "expertly prepared meal"; while some quibble that the menu is

---

* Indicates a tie with restaurant above

"limited" and the service "slow", for most it "remains a reliable" and "memorable" experience.

☑ Bàcio Italian Cuisine Ⓜ *Italian*
25 | 22 | 25 | $40

Cinnaminson | 2806 Rte. 130 N. (Chestnut Hill Dr.) | 856-303-9100 | www.baciorestaurant.com

"Sumptuous Italian feasts" are what you can expect at this "quiet, romantic" Cinnaminson BYO run by chef Robert Minniti and wife Pam, who make you feel "you're at their home for dinner"; if "a little pricey" for the area, it's "first-class" all the way and "worth the trip over the bridge."

Bahama Breeze *Caribbean*
17 | 19 | 17 | $27

Cherry Hill | Cherry Hill Mall | 2000 Rte. 38 (Haddonfield Rd.) | 856-317-8317 | www.bahamabreeze.com

See review in the Philadelphia Directory.

Barnacle Ben's *Seafood*
20 | 17 | 19 | $31

Moorestown | Acme Shopping Ctr. | 300 Young Ave. (bet. Marne Hwy. & Marter Ave.) | 856-235-5808 | www.barnaclebens.com

"Generously" doled out portions of "fresh", "reliable" seafood help explain why this Moorestown BYO has stayed in business for over a quarter century; the "friendly" service can be "uneven", but "reasonable" tabs mean you'll pay far less than a Franklin.

Barone's *Italian*
21 | 19 | 20 | $29

Moorestown | 280 Young Ave. (Main St.) | 856-234-7900

Villa Barone *Italian*

Collingswood | 753 Haddon Ave. (bet. Frazer & Washington Aves.) | 856-858-2999
www.baronerestaurants.com

"You can't go wrong" at these "traditional" South Jersey BYO trattorias considered by most "better than your average neighborhood Italian joint" for "enormous" portions of "hearty" red-sauce fare worthy of "your best Chianti"; factor in the "family-friendly" atmosphere and "efficient" service and it's clear why many choose to return "again and again."

Benihana *Japanese*
20 | 18 | 20 | $35

Pennsauken | 5255 Marlton Pike (Lexington Ave.) | 856-665-6320 | www.benihana.com

"It's always entertaining" – "even if you know what to expect" – at this "typical" Japanese steakhouse in Pennsauken with "fantastic" teppanyaki shows and "fresh", "straightforward" food; N.B. a recent renovation may not be reflected by the above Decor score.

Bistro di Marino *Italian*
25 | 17 | 20 | $36

Collingswood | 492 Haddon Ave. (Crestmont Terr.) | 856-858-1700

"Italian lovers" tout the "amazing" red-sauce meals at this "friendly", rustic BYO "gem" with a "young vibe" in up-and-coming Collingswood; if you lack leftovers, head to the adjacent market for *ciao* to-go; N.B. there's live jazz on Wednesdays.

	FOOD	DECOR	SERVICE	COST

Blackbird Dining Establishment 🅜 *American* — 26 | 18 | 23 | $45

Collingswood | 619 Collings Ave. (White Horse Pike) | 856-854-3444 | www.blackbirdnj.com

"Philadelphia foodies" wing their way over the Ben Franklin to the "quieter side" of Collingswood for Alex Capasso's "exciting" New American BYO that "never falls short of fab"; "imaginative" dishes (e.g. braised suckling pig, goat cheese tart), "excellent" service and a "contemporary" ambiance also have fans "singing" praises.

Blue Eyes *Steak* — 21 | 22 | 20 | $42

Sewell | 139 Egg Harbor Rd. (County House Rd.) | 856-227-5656 | www.blueeyesrestaurant.com

"The Rat Pack lives" at this "early-'60s"-style Sewell surf 'n' turfer, an homage to you-know-who; so "don your fedora" and "step back in time" for a "great" steak Sinatra, "martinis galore", "lounge-style" singers (Fridays–Sundays) and - what else? - a *Goodfellas* vibe; P.S. an "unbelievable" three-course Sunset Dinner menu ($16) is offered Monday–Thursday evenings and all day Sunday.

Bobby Chez 🅜 *Seafood* — 25 | 11 | 16 | $21

Cherry Hill | Village Walk Shopping Ctr. | 1990 Rte. 70 E. (Old Orchard Rd.) | 856-751-7575 🅢

Collingswood | 33 W. Collings Ave. (bet. Cove Rd. & Norwood Ave.) | 856-869-8000 🅢

Mount Laurel | Centerton Sq. | Marter Ave. & Rte. 38 (bet. Centeron Rd. & New Jersey Tpke. N.) | 856-234-4146

Sewell | 100 Hurffville Cross Keys Rd. (Tuckahoe Rd.) | 856-262-1001

Voorhees | Southgate Plaza | 1225 Haddonfield-Berlin Rd. (South Gate Dr.) | 856-768-6660 🅢

www.bobbychezcrabcakes.com

See review in the Philadelphia Directory.

Bonefish Grill *Seafood* — 21 | 19 | 20 | $34

Deptford | 1709 Deptford Center Rd. (Almonessen Rd.) | 856-848-6261 | www.bonefishgrill.com

See review in the Philadelphia Directory.

Braddock's *American* (fka Braddock's Tavern) — - | - | - | M

Medford | 39 S. Main St. (Coates St.) | 609-654-1604 | www.braddocks.com

Fans of this Traditional American Medford institution with a "warm, Colonial style" look forward to an overall "improvement" with the post-Survey arrival of new owners and chef; an updated menu (with less expensive tabs) and refurbished decor are already in the works.

🆕 Brio Tuscan Grille *Italian* — 19 | 22 | 19 | $33

Cherry Hill | Town Place at Garden State | 901 Haddonfield Rd. (Chapel Ave.) | 856-910-8166 | www.brioitalian.com

Though it's a chain, it's "one of the best around" according to fans of this upscale Italian, an "inviting" "new guy on the block" at the former Garden State Park in Cherry Hill; the "straightforward"

	FOOD	DECOR	SERVICE	COST

Tuscan fare is "surprisingly tasty" and the service, though "slow", is "pleasant"; P.S. "great meals for the kids" too.

Buca di Beppo *Italian*
15 | 17 | 17 | $27

Cherry Hill | 2301 Rte. 38 (Haddonfield Rd.) | 856-779-3288 | www.bucadibeppo.com
See review in the Philadelphia Directory.

Café Gallery *Continental*
21 | 21 | 21 | $39

Burlington | 219 High St. (Pearl St.) | 609-386-6150 | www.cafegalleryburlington.com
For a "great date", try the "lovely" warm weather patio at this "romantic", art-filled bi-level Continental in historic Burlington and watch the Delaware River roll by over a lunch or dinner of "well-done" traditional fare; N.B. there's a "very good" $19.95 Sunday brunch buffet.

Caffe Aldo Lamberti *Italian*
23 | 21 | 22 | $44

Cherry Hill | 2011 Rte. 70 W. (Haddonfield Rd.) | 856-663-1747 | www.lambertis.com
It's a "posh fine dining" experience at "trendy", "super-popular" Cherry Hill Italian (the flagship of a family-owned restaurant group with outposts in Delaware and Pennsylvania) with an "expansive", "expensive" menu, "extensive wine list" and "great" service; N.B. a new indoor/outdoor pool should add to the festivities.

Casona Ⓜ *Cuban*
22 | 21 | 19 | $36

Collingswood | 563 Haddon Ave. (Knight Ave.) | 856-854-5555 | www.mycasona.com
You're "transported" from Collingswood to Havana at this "charming" Cuban–Nuevo Latin BYO in a "converted Victorian", where the "exciting" eats are "authentic enough for New Jersey gringos"; "bring your own tequila" (or rum) for "mix-your-own" margaritas (or mojitos) on the year-round "wraparound porch."

Catelli *Italian*
24 | 23 | 23 | $48

Voorhees | The Plaza | 1000 Main St. (bet. Evesham & Kresson Rds.) | 856-751-6069 | www.catellirestaurant.com
"Impress someone" at this "pricey" "delight for gourmands" in Voorhees proffering "imaginative", "upscale" Italian cuisine (e.g. lobster-stuffed veal chop), "elegant" environs and "no-pressure" servers; N.B. keep tabs on your tab with the $25 three-course early-bird or $40 four-course prixe fixe dinner options.

ⓩ Cheesecake Factory *American*
20 | 18 | 18 | $28

Cherry Hill | Marketplace at Garden State Park | 931 Haddonfield Rd. (bet. Graham & Severn Aves.) | 856-665-7550 | www.thecheesecakefactory.com
See review in the Philadelphia Directory.

Chez Elena Wu *Asian/French*
23 | 18 | 22 | $33

Voorhees | Ritz Shopping Ctr. | 910 Haddonfield-Berlin Rd. (Voorhees Dr.) | 856-566-3222 | www.chezelenawu.com
Even folks who claim they "don't do Chinese" "clean their plates" at this "refined" French-Asian fusion in Voorhees where "everything is

	FOOD	DECOR	SERVICE	COST

done right" – even the sushi; hosts who "aim to please" help ensure a "quiet, relaxed dining experience", making it a "nice alternative" when you want "won ton and ambiance."

Z Chickie's & Pete's Cafe ● *Pub Food* | 18 | 17 | 17 | $24 |

NEW Bordentown | 183 Hwy. 130 (Hwy. 206) | 609-298-9182 | www.chickiesandpetes.com

See review in the Philadelphia Directory.

Z Chophouse, The *Seafood/Steak* | 25 | 23 | 23 | $54 |

Gibbsboro | 4 Lakeview Dr. S./Rte. 561 (E. Clementon Rd.) | 856-566-7300 | www.thechophouse.us

South Jersey meat mavens save the "bridge" tolls and spend it on "solid" steaks and seafood at this "clubby" beefery in "remote" Gibbsboro that befits both "romantic" dinners and "special occasions"; a "great" wine list, "laid-back" ambiance and "professional" service suit its "eclectic" clientele.

Coconut Bay Asian Cuisine Ⓜ *Asian* | 22 | 16 | 21 | $29 |

Voorhees | Echelon Village Plaza | 1120 White Horse Rd. (Berlin Rd.) | 856-783-8878 | www.coconutbayasiancuisine.com

Red hues and low lighting set an "exotic" mood at this Voorhees BYO whose Asian menu incorporates Chinese, Japanese and Thai influences and yields "dependably good" dishes; fans forget the strip-mall location once they notice "attentive" service and "inexpensive" tabs.

Cork *American* | 20 | 17 | 19 | $39 |

Westmont | 90 Haddon Ave. (bet. Cooper St. & Cuthbert Blvd.) | 856-833-9800 | www.corknj.com

This "grown-up" New American in "Speedline-accessible" Westmont works for "tasty" dinners, "late-night drinks and snacks" and "wine tastings"; "crisp" service and "live" weekend jazz are also "worth coming back for."

Creole Cafe Ⓜ *Cajun/Creole* | 22 | 14 | 19 | $32 |

Sewell | Harbor Pl. | 288 Egg Harbor Rd. (Huffville Grenloch Rd.) | 856-582-7222 | www.creole-cafe.com

Supporters of this N'Awlins-style Cajun-Creole report that a relocation to a Sewell strip-mall BYO hasn't "detracted" from the "delicious" "taste sensations" that deliver "a little kick" with "every bite" ("Emeril who?"); still, a few contend the food and decor were "better before the move."

El Azteca *Mexican* | 18 | 10 | 17 | $20 |

Mount Laurel | Ramblewood Shopping Ctr. | 1155 Rte. 73 N. (Church Rd.) | 856-914-9302

See review in the Philadelphia Directory.

Elements Café Ⓩ Ⓜ *American* | 24 | 15 | 21 | $33 |

Haddon Heights | 517 Station Ave. (White Horse Pike) | 856-546-8840 | www.elementscafe.com

It's elemental for fans of this "cute" BYO in Haddon Heights, where the kitchen "conjures amazing little bites" of "innovative" New American fare that offers "fabulous variety"; adding to the "wow" factor is a "knowledgeable" staff and – for some – the realization you'll have "no leftovers."

Elephant & Castle ● *Pub Food* | 11 | 12 | 15 | $24 |

Cherry Hill | Clarion Hotel | 1450 Rte. 70 E. (I-295) | 856-427-0427 | www.elephantcastle.com

See review in the Philadelphia Directory.

Emerald Fish ☒ *Seafood* | 23 | 15 | 22 | $34 |

Cherry Hill | Barclay Farms Shopping Ctr. | 65 Rte. 70 E. (Kings Hwy.) | 856-616-9192 | www.emeraldfish.com

Afishionados in Cherry Hill have caught on to the "imaginative" surf specials at this "comfortable" seafood-centric BYO (now under new management); the quarters are "cozy" (you might "rub elbows with the next table") but service is "friendly", and for most, the owners have kept the place up to "par."

Filomena Cucina Italiana *Italian* | 24 | 22 | 22 | $35 |

Clementon | 1380 Blackwood-Clementon Rd. (Millbridge Rd.) | 856-784-6166 | www.filomenascucina.com

Filomena Cucina Rustica *Italian*

Berlin | 13 Milford Cross Keys Rd. (White Horse Pike) | 856-753-3540 | www.filomenasberlin.com

Filomena Lakeview *Italian*

Deptford | 1738 Cooper St. (Almonesson Rd.) | 856-228-4235 | www.filomenalakeview.com

"That's Italian – oops – that's *excellent* Italian" assert admirers of these separately owned South Jersey trattorias (whose Food scores jumped four points in this Survey); given "comfortable" surroundings, service with "flair" and live entertainment, it's no wonder they're ranked among the "go-to" destinations.

Five Guys Famous | 22 | 9 | 15 | $10 |
Burgers & Fries *Burgers*

Cherry Hill | 1650 Kings Hwy. N. (Hwy. 70) | 856-795-1455
Mount Ephraim | 130 Black Horse Pike (White Horse Pike) | 856-672-0442
www.fiveguys.com

See review in the Philadelphia Directory.

☑ Food for Thought *American* | 24 | 25 | 22 | $43 |

Marlton | Marlton Crossing Shopping Ctr. | 129 Marlton Crossing (Rte. 70) | 856-797-1126

For New American food that "lifts the spirit" in a "magical supper-club" atmosphere replete with weekend piano music, this "romantic little getaway" in a Marlton strip mall comes to mind; it's also favored for an "elegant" lunch, and is BYO to boot.

Fuji Ⓜ *Japanese* | 26 | 20 | 21 | $43 |

Haddonfield | Shops at 116 | 116 Kings Hwy. E. (Tanner St.) | 856-354-8200 | www.fujirestaurant.com

"One of the great pleasures in life" for fishophiles is when sushi master Matt Ito sets you up with "sublime" nibbles in his "lovely" "new digs" in Haddonfield, replete with "kimono ladies"; yes, it's still BYO but worlds away from his former quarters in a run-down Cinnaminson strip mall; P.S. the eight-course tasting menu ($80) is "first-rate."

GG's 🅂 *American*   ▽ 21 | 18 | 20 | $44

Mount Laurel | DoubleTree Guest Suites Mount Laurel | 515 Fellowship Rd. (Rte. 73) | 856-222-0335 | www.ggsrestaurant.com

You're in for a "real surprise" in hotel dining at this "relaxed" New American in the DoubleTree Guest Suites in Mount Laurel, featuring an "exciting choice" of "consistent" cooking and "generous" wine pours by "friendly" bartenders; a nightly "piano player" adds a "nice touch."

ⓩ Giumarello's 🅂 *Italian*   26 | 23 | 24 | $49

Westmont | 329 Haddon Ave. (bet. Cuthbert Blvd. & Kings Hwy.) | 856-858-9400 | www.giumarellos.com

"First-rate" Northern Italian fare is proffered by a "knowledgeable" staff that "makes you feel right at home" at this "elegant" Westmont spot, also distinguished for its "great bar scene" at "happy hour"; those who "wish" for "cheaper" eats can "check out" the "bargain-priced" early-bird (available Mondays–Fridays).

Hamilton's Grill Room *Mediterranean*   25 | 21 | 23 | $50

Lambertville | 8 Coryell St. (N. Union St.) | 609-397-4343 | www.hamiltonsgrillroom.com

For a "special occasion", this "quaint" BYO Med is "well worth the drive" to Lambertville thanks to "consistently excellent" grilled seafood and meats and "attentive" service; there's plenty of "inter-table conviviality", and "summer means outdoor seating" in the courtyard near the Delaware Canal; P.S. "call well in advance for reservations."

High Street Grill *American*   ▽ 23 | 18 | 21 | $40

Mount Holly | 64 High St. (bet. Brainerd & Garden Sts.) | 609-265-9199 | www.highstreetgrill.net

"Good" New Americana is on offer at this spot brightening up Downtown Mount Holly; the hosts "meet and greet" diners in a space divided by an "intimate" upstairs and a tavernlike downstairs, where lunch is served every day.

NEW Il Fiore *Italian*   - | - | - | M

Collingswood | 693-695 Haddon Ave. (Collings Ave.) | 856-833-0808

Into the Italian fray of Downtown Collingswood comes this quiet, white-tablecloth BYO from two veterans of Center City's Bistro La Viola; the simple, South Philly–style menu is priced right at lunch and dinner, and desserts are made in-house.

Inn of the Hawke *American*   ▽ 19 | 18 | 21 | $27

Lambertville | 74 S. Union St. (Mount Hope St.) | 609-397-9555

An "easygoing" "local spot" with the aura of an old English pub, this "lovely" Lambertville bar/restaurant proffers a "fine selection of beers" and an "eclectic" American menu; it's best enjoyed on the

	FOOD	DECOR	SERVICE	COST

"beautiful flagstone garden patio", although the "cozy indoor dining rooms" are winning in winter too.

NEW Javier 🅑Ⓜ *American* ▽ 21 | 24 | 18 | $53

Haddonfield | 208 Kings Hwy. E. (Haddon Ave.) | 856-428-4220 | www.javiercontinental.com

This "regal" New American BYO "addition" to the Haddonfield dining scene offers "tasteful", high-style surroundings and "creative" cuisine recalling its Collingswood sibling Word of Mouth; if some "expected more for price" given the local "competition", others suggest if it "works out the kinks" it could be "excellent."

NEW Joe Pesce *Italian/Seafood* 18 | 18 | 18 | $40

Collingswood | 833 Haddon Ave. (bet. Collings Ave. & Cuthbert Blvd.) | 856-833-9888

See review in the Philadelphia Directory.

Joe's Peking Duck House Ⓜ⊅ *Chinese* 22 | 8 | 18 | $24

Marlton | Marlton Crossing Shopping Ctr. | 145 Rte. 73 S. (Rte. 70) | 856-985-1551

"Awesome" fare, including the signature "go-nowhere-else-for-duck" (or soups), is the calling of this affordable Marlton Chinese BYO; save for "drab" "take-out decor", most agree this spot is "all it's quacked up to be"; N.B. the presence of new owners (post-Survey) may outdate the above scores.

Kibitz Room *Deli* 23 | 8 | 14 | $17

Cherry Hill | Shoppes at Holly Ravine | 100 Springdale Rd. (Evesham Rd.) | 856-428-7878 | www.thekibitzroom.com

The cholesterol crowd kvells over the "great" Jewish "soul food" found in this Cherry Hill deli issuing "really big" corned beef and pastrami sandwiches, matzo ball soup and whatnot; slightly "surly servers" notwithstanding, it's still "the closest thing to the Carnegie in South Jersey."

Kitchen 233 *American* 20 | 22 | 20 | $46

Westmont | 233 Haddon Ave. (Ardmore Terr.) | 856-833-9233 | www.kitchen233.com

Fans of this upscale New American in Westmont find "reliable" appetizers at the bar, "pleasant" dinners in the "sleek" rear addition and an "expansive" wine list; though some suggest the vittles evoke "more potential than reality", the four-course prix fixe dinners (Sundays–Mondays) are a crowd-pleaser.

La Campagne Ⓜ *French* 24 | 22 | 21 | $52

Cherry Hill | 312 Kresson Rd. (bet. Brace & Marlkress Rds.) | 856-429-7647 | www.lacampagne.com

For French cuisine "done right", this "charming", "country"-style BYO in a little, old farmhouse in "the woods" of Cherry Hill is "worth a try" for "loverly" special occasions; chef (and new owner) Richard Benussi has added an Italian accent to the menu, and word is his prix fixe four-course lasagna nights on Fridays are a way to "experience true bliss."

Laceno Italian Grill *Italian/Seafood*

24 | 15 | 20 | $40

Voorhees | Echelon Village Plaza | 1118 White Horse Rd. (Rte. 561) | 856-627-3700

Fans are abuzz over the "wonderful" Italian seafood at this Voorhees "strip-mall" BYO that's "worthy" of a grander location; count on "large portions" of "quality" selections and big crowds at this South Jersey relative of Old City's Radicchio ("it may be a sibling but it's definitely not a stepchild").

La Esperanza Ⓜ *Mexican*

22 | 16 | 20 | $23

Lindenwold | 40 E. Gibbsboro Rd. (Arthur Ave.) | 856-782-7114 | www.mexicanhope.com

For Mexican "as it should be" in South Jersey, aficionados tout this "family-owned" Lindenwold cantina for "large portions" of "inexpensive", "traditional" *comidas* ("you want authentic – how about cactus and goat?"), an "impressive bar" (with some 100 brands of tequila) and a staff that's "willing to please"; simply put – "it's worth the trip."

Lambertville Station *American*

18 | 21 | 20 | $39

Lambertville | 11 Bridge St. (Delaware River) | 609-397-8300 | www.lambertvillestation.com

"Fun and interesting" decor draws "train lovers", "families" and "ladies who lunch" to this Traditional American housed in a converted Victorian-era railway station in Lambertville; though considered a "tourist trap" by some, fans focus on the "great views" of the Delaware and interesting "wild game" dishes offered in the winter.

Lilly's on the Canal *Eclectic*

20 | 19 | 18 | $37

Lambertville | 2 Canal St. (Bridge St.) | 609-397-6242 | www.lillysonthecanal.com

This industrial-chic Lambertville Eclectic proffers "flavorful" fare within its bi-level digs; whereas some favor the "quiet" upper deck to the "frenetic" but "interesting" first floor and its open kitchen, the "beautiful" waterside patio is an all-around crowd-pleaser; N.B. it's BYO, but they sell a few local wines.

🆉 Little Café, A 🅱Ⓜ *Eclectic*

27 | 19 | 23 | $39

Voorhees | Plaza Shoppes | 118 White Horse Rd. E. (Burnt Mill Rd.) | 856-784-3344 | www.alittlecafenj.com

Foodies "pack in" for "huge food" prepared with "imagination" at Marianne Cuneo Powell's tiny, "top-notch" Eclectic BYO "tucked away" in a Voorhees "strip mall"; it "gets crowded" so reserve a table at this "marvel" and "go early" for the wallet-friendly prix fixe.

Little Tuna, The *Seafood*

21 | 17 | 19 | $34

Haddonfield | 141 Kings Hwy. E. (Haddon Ave.) | 856-795-0888 | www.thelittletuna.com

This Haddonfield BYO offers "interesting" "renditions" of the eponymous fish and other "reliable" seafood in "plentiful" portions; those who land in the "deafening downstairs" can always opt for the calmer upstairs on future visits.

	FOOD	DECOR	SERVICE	COST

Luna Rossa Ⓜ *Italian*
— | — | — | | I

Sicklerville | 3210 Rte. 42 (Cross Keys Ave.) | 856-728-4505 | www.lambertis.com

Locals are "fond" of Giuseppe Lamberti's contemporary Italian BYO in Sicklerville for "wonderfully flavored", generous portions "prepared to perfection" at "reasonable" prices; the attentive management "makes sure all is well."

Manon Ⓜ⊄ *French*
25 | 20 | 23 | $47

Lambertville | 19 N. Union St. (Bridge St.) | 609-397-2596

"Like being transported" to "Provence", this "tiny" BYO "charmer" in Lambertville "remains a favorite" for its "stellar" country French cuisine and "delightful" setting (an "eye-catching" mural of 'Starry Night' blankets the ceiling); although tables are "elbow to elbow" and they don't take credit, most maintain this is "a real gem" whose facets include a "caring" staff; N.B. open for dinner only, Wednesday–Sunday.

Mastoris ⏺ *Diner*
20 | 12 | 19 | $23

Bordentown | 144 Hwy. 130 (Hwy. 206) | 609-298-4650 | www.mastoris.com

"Ya wanna lot of food, hon?" – then head to this "bustling" Bordentown "staple" for Jersey "diner dining at its best", featuring a "mile-long menu", "humongous portions" and "fair prices"; service comes "with a smile", and for many loafers (including "politicos" from Trenton), the "cheese bread" alone is "worth the trip."

McCormick & Schmick's *Seafood*
21 | 20 | 21 | $49

NEW **Cherry Hill** | 941 Haddonfield Rd. (bet. Graham & Severn Aves.) | 856-317-1711 | www.mccormickandschmicks.com

See review in the Philadelphia Directory.

Megu Sushi *Japanese*
24 | 16 | 19 | $33

Cherry Hill | Village Walk Shopping Ctr. | 1990 Rte. 70 E. (Old Orchard Rd.) | 856-489-6228 | www.megusushi.com

"Hibachi (teppanyaki) is a welcome addition" to this cool-looking Japanese BYO in Cherry Hill's Village Walk, but finatics gravitate to the "consistently fresh" sushi and sashimi, while hearty-eating couples go for the "Love Boats" (specials served in a wooden boat); N.B. no relation to NYC's Megu.

Z **NEW** Mélange @ Haddonfield *Creole*
27 | 18 | 23 | $40

Haddonfield | 18 Tanner St. (Kings Hwy.) | 856-354-1333

Z Mélange Cafe Ⓜ *Creole*
Cherry Hill | 1601 Chapel Ave. (Woodland Ave.) | 856-663-7339 www.melangecafe.com

For a "trip to New Orleans" without the airfare, Joe Brown's "affordable" Cherry Hill Creole BYO "will knock your socks off"; "homey" digs and a staff that's "always around to check your opinion" are more reasons why it comes "highly recommended"; N.B. a branch recently opened in Haddonfield.

	FOOD	DECOR	SERVICE	COST

Mexican Food Factory *Mexican*   21 | 18 | 19 | $29

Marlton | 601 Rte. 70 W. (Cropwell Rd.) | 856-983-9222
"Even a fussy eater" will enjoy this "bright", "dependable" cantina in Marlton, where "unusual interpretations" of Mexican classics (e.g. "awesome" green salsa) pair well with works of "Kahlo and Rivera on the walls"; a patio that "makes you forget" you're in South Jersey also appeals – especially after a few margaritas.

Mikado *Japanese*   23 | 16 | 21 | $30

Cherry Hill | 2320 Rte. 70 W. (S. Union Ave.) | 856-665-4411
Maple Shade | 468 S. Lenola Rd. (Kings Hwy.) | 856-638-1801
Marlton | Elmwood Shopping Ctr. | 793 Rte. 70 E. (Troth Rd.) | 856-797-8581
www.mikado-us.com
"Head for the sushi bar" at this simple, "pleasant" Japanese trio for "large, fresh slices of fish" and "awesome" rolls dispensed by "cheerful" chefs; there's "always a line" for the "show" at the Marlton and Maple Shade locales, also offering hibachi; N.B. Cherry Hill and Maple Shade are BYO.

Milano Modo *Italian*   ∇ 25 | 26 | 25 | $44

Mount Holly | 1643 Rte. 38 (bet. Madison Ave. & Pine St.) | 609-261-2345 | www.lambertis.com
There's a slick "Vegas feel" running through this "beautifully decorated" Italian in Mount Holly (little sister of Cherry Hill's Caffe Aldo Lamberti), with "excellently prepared", "quality" cuisine to match; half-price bottles of wine on Sundays and Mondays makes it a great deal.

Mirabella Cafe *Italian*   22 | 17 | 18 | $30

Cherry Hill | 210 Barclay Farms Shopping Ctr. | Rte. 70 E. (Kings Hwy.) | 856-354-1888 | www.mirabellacafe.com
"Homemade pasta" "just the way mama made it" and a "loving" if "slow" staff are two reasons "people stand in line" for Joe Palombo's "cozy", Tuscan-style BYO in Cherry Hill; lunch is a "reasonable" option too, but the steal is on Sundays, when it's $15.95 for all-you-can-eat fusilli with gravy.

Mr. Bill's *Deli*   - | - | - | I

Winslow | 453 Rte. 73 S. (Winslow Williamstown Rd.) | 609-561-5400
The new owners of this honest-to-goodness Jewish deli in a former hot-dog-and-custard stand in Winslow on the way to the shore have added Italian-style deli items to the roster of super-sized sandwiches, including prepared-on-premises pastrami and corned beef; top it off with freshly made ice cream.

Nifty Fifty's ∅ *Diner*   19 | 19 | 19 | $13

Clementon | 1310 Blackwood-Clementon Rd. (Millbridge Rd.) | 856-346-1950
NEW **Turnersville** | 4670 Black Horse Pike/Rte. 42 (Fries Mill Rd.) | 856-875-1950
www.niftyfiftys.com
See review in the Philadelphia Directory.

	FOOD	DECOR	SERVICE	COST

No. 9 Ⓜ *American* ▽ 23 | 15 | 20 | $43

Lambertville | 9 Klines Ct. (Bridge St.) | 609-397-6380
The allure of this Lambertville storefront BYO New American lies quite simply in the "creative" cuisine prepared with "top-notch execution" by chef-owner Matthew Kane; the decor draws mixed marks, despite a recent makeover that added Tuscan tones and a display of paintings by local artists.

Norma's Eastern Mediterranean Restaurant *Mideastern* 21 | 14 | 20 | $23

Cherry Hill | Barclay Farms Shopping Ctr. | 132-145 Rte. 70 E. (Kings Hwy.) | 856-795-1373 | www.normasrestaurant.com
"Even less adventurous family members" go for the Middle Eastern dishes at this Cherry Hill BYO whose occasional belly dancing supplies as much of its "cult following" as the "very good", "feast-fit-for-a-king" offerings; the service "charms", and all agree meals here are "the best deal" going.

Nunzio Ristorante Rustico *Italian* 23 | 22 | 21 | $42

Collingswood | 706 Haddon Ave. (Collings Ave.) | 856-858-9840 | www.nunzios.net
At his Collingswood "diamond in the rough", Nunzio Patruno turns out "authentic", "high-end" Italian meals "night after night" in a "charming" "faux piazza" setting; service is "professional" and the BYO policy means "you won't get killed" on wine, and while some critics complain "you can't hear a thing" when it's "packed on weekends", to others it's a "sure bet for a special night out."

Oasis Grill *Mediterranean/Moroccan* ▽ 26 | 20 | 23 | $25

Cherry Hill | 2431 Church Rd. (Kaighn Ave.) | 856-667-8287 | www.oasisgrillnj.com
Locals find this "easy-to-miss" Moroccan BYO in a Cherry Hill strip mall "a real gem" for "excellent" couscous and "honest" tagines at reasonable prices; on weekends, "sit on couches" in the "atmospheric" tented room and "enjoy the belly dancers."

Ota-Ya Ⓜ *Japanese* 24 | 14 | 20 | $35

Lambertville | 21 Ferry St. (S. Union St.) | 609-397-9228 | www.ota-ya.com
See review in the Philadelphia Directory.

ⓩ P.F. Chang's China Bistro *Chinese* 21 | 21 | 19 | $31

Marlton | Promenade at Sagemore | 500 Rte. 73 S. (Rte. 70) | 856-396-0818 | www.pfchangs.com
See review in the Philadelphia Directory.

Pietro's Coal Oven Pizzeria *Pizza* 19 | 15 | 16 | $23

Marlton | 140 Rte. 70 W. (Rte. 73) | 856-596-5500 | www.pietrospizza.com
See review in the Philadelphia Directory.

Pizzicato *Italian* 20 | 16 | 19 | $30

Marlton | Promenade at Sagemore | 500 Rte. 73 S. (Rte. 70) | 856-396-0880
See review in the Philadelphia Directory.

	FOOD	DECOR	SERVICE	COST

P.J. Whelihan's ● *Pub Food* — 15 | 14 | 15 | $21

Cherry Hill | 1854 E. Marlton Pike (Greentree Rd.) | 856-424-8844
Haddonfield | 700 Haddon Ave. (Ardmore Ave.) | 856-427-7888
Maple Shade | 396 S. Lenola Rd. (Kings Hwy.) | 856-234-2345
Medford Lakes | 61 Stokes Rd. (Hampshire Rd.) | 609-714-7900
Sewell | 425 Hurffville-Cross Keys Rd. (Regulus Dr.) | 856-582-7774
www.pjspub.com
See review in the Philadelphia Directory.

Ponzio's ● *Diner* — 17 | 11 | 16 | $21

Cherry Hill | 7 Rte. 70 W. (Kings Hwy.) | 856-428-4808 | www.ponzios.com
Cherry Hill's unofficial "town hall" and South Jersey's "ultimate" diner keeps on dispensing "consistent" coffee-shop chow and "freshly" made sweets from the on-site bakery in "large" digs, and whose staff "keeps things moving"; if it is "not the Ponzio's of yore", many, many more still make it their "landmark."

Pop Shop *American* — 20 | 17 | 18 | $17

Collingswood | 729 Haddon Ave. (Collings Ave.) | 856-869-0111 | www.thepopshopusa.com
"Kids" have so much "fun" wearing "PJs" and noshing on "tasty" treats from the "enormous" American menu at this "old-timey" Collingswood soda shop from "yesteryear", where shakes, burgers and grilled cheese sandwiches rule; the "retro" spot is ultra-"friendly", and the only thing missing is "The Fonz."

Pub, The *Steak* — 21 | 14 | 19 | $30

Pennsauken | Airport Circle | 7600 Kaighns Ave. (S. Crescent Blvd.) | 856-665-6440
"What's not to love?" at this "nostalgic" carnivorium in Pennsauken, where charbroiled "steaks as big as your head" come with "the best salad bar around"; most find the "kitschy", "cavernous" 500-seat medieval-motif dining room (reminiscent of a "'50s college cafeteria" – well, it *has* been around since 1951) and "quick" servers ("you want me to wrap that for you, hon?") a "guilty pleasure."

Red Hot & Blue *BBQ* — 17 | 14 | 16 | $23

Cherry Hill | Holiday Inn | 2175 Old Marlton Pike (Conestoga St.) | 856-665-7427 | www.redhotanblue.com
"Better than you'd expect" ribs, a "party atmosphere" and "great bands" on live-music nights equal "fun" times for fans of this Cherry Hill BBQ chain link; "service can vary, but they try hard", yet the overall package strikes a few as "ordinary."

Redstone American Grill *American* — 21 | 22 | 20 | $36

Marlton | Promenade at Sagemore | 500 Rte. 73 S. (Brick Rd.) | 856-396-0332 | www.redstonegrill.com
This "upscale" Marlton Traditional American "hot spot" knows how to "please" with "crazy-big" portions for "hungry beef eaters", "great" fish and other "sublime" standards; though part of a chain it maintains a "local feeling", so "expect a wait" as "businesspeople" "meet and greet" at the bar and around the "fire pit" on the patio; N.B. another outpost recently debuted in Plymouth Meeting.

	FOOD	DECOR	SERVICE	COST

☑ Ritz Seafood 🅼 *Pan-Asian/Seafood*   26 | 16 | 21 | $37

Voorhees | Ritz Shopping Ctr. | 910 Haddonfield-Berlin Rd. (Voorhees Dr.) | 856-566-6650 | www.ritzseafood.com

"Incredible" Pan-Asian dishes enjoyed amid "pretty" waterfalls keep customers "wanting more" at this "convenient" Voorhees BYO seafooder near the Ritz movie complex; all things considered, "warm" service and "wonderful" food "easily overcome" the "inconvenience" of "cramped" quarters.

Robin's Nest *American*   25 | 22 | 23 | $33

Mount Holly | 2 Washington St. (White St.) | 609-261-6149 | www.robinsnestmountholly.com

Fans of this "quaint", "informal" Traditional American in Mount Holly want to "nest often" thanks to its "beautiful" stream-side deck, "friendly service" and "food so good it blows you away"; it's "hard to get by the dessert case without drooling" so "save room" for sweet endings.

☑ Sagami 🅼 *Japanese*   27 | 14 | 20 | $36

Collingswood | 37 Crescent Blvd. (bet. Haddon & Park Aves.) | 856-854-9773

Aficionados insist this "immensely popular" Japanese BYO in Collingswood is in a "class by itself", serving "fresh", "fabulous" sushi and sashimi for "more than 30 years"; while the setting makes some feel like they're "dining in a crowded basement", with ceilings so "low" those "who are short feel really tall", it's "still one of the tops" for many.

Sakura Spring *Chinese/Japanese*   23 | 20 | 22 | $29

Cherry Hill | 1871 Marlton Pike E. (Greentree Rd.) | 856-489-8018 | www.sakuraspring.com

A "wide", unusual mix of "tasty" Chinese and Japanese specialties greets diners at this Cherry Hill BYO that's good "when you want more than just a take-out" experience; if dinner's out of the picture, lunch is a perfect time to drop by, thanks to modest pricing.

Sapori *Italian*   25 | 20 | 24 | $41

Collingswood | 601 Haddon Ave. (Harvard Ave.) | 856-858-2288 | www.sapori.info

The name translates as 'flavors' ("surprise, it's not Japanese") at Franco Lombardo's "excellent, upscale" BYO Italian on Collingswood's "Restaurant Row", where the "fabulous" fare "always shines" and the specials are "reasonably priced"; the "friendly" Sicilian-born chef-owner table-hops to "greet guests" in the "rustic", "romantic" space that's modeled after a medieval castle.

Siam 🅼🖘 *Thai*   ▽ 22 | 9 | 16 | $29

Lambertville | 61 N. Main St. (bet. Coryell & York Sts.) | 609-397-8128

"If you're looking for authentic, delicious, reasonably priced Thai food", this "casual" storefront BYO in Lambertville will "leave you tongue-Thai-ed"; despite "extremely slow" service and "bland", "unappealing" decor, it's "very popular and deservedly so", making reservations "a must"; P.S. "it's cash-only."

Siri's Thai French Cuisine *French/Thai*   25 | 19 | 23 | $38

Cherry Hill | 2117 Rte. 70 W. (Haddonfield Rd.) | 856-663-6781 | www.siris-nj.com

Though it's "disguised as a strip-mall joint" in Cherry Hill, aficionados take this BYO French-Thai "Siri-ously" thanks to its "always top-notch", "sublime" fare and "attentive" service; while some caution it's "not kid-friendly", it is a good bet for a "business lunch."

Somsak *Thai*   ∇ 25 | 16 | 23 | $25

Voorhees | Echo Shops | 200 White Horse Rd. (bet. 4th & 5th Sts.) | 856-782-1771

Those in-the-know say "wow" to the "excellent" Thai fare at this Voorhees BYO, including "divine" spring rolls and pad Thai that some deem "best on the planet"; service is "polite" and the portions "large", leading fans to insist "you can't get a better meal for the price."

Swanky Bubbles *Pan-Asian*   20 | 19 | 19 | $38

Cherry Hill | Short Hills Towne Ctr. | 482 Evesham Rd. (Short Hills Dr.) | 856-428-4999 | www.swankybubbles.com

See review in the Philadelphia Directory.

Tacconelli's Pizzeria Ⓜ⇗ *Pizza*   25 | 9 | 14 | $18

Maple Shade | 450 S. Lenola Rd. (Rte. 38) | 856-638-0338 | www.tacconellispizzerianj.com

See review in the Philadelphia Directory.

Ted's on Main ⊠Ⓜ *American*   ∇ 26 | 20 | 21 | $39

Medford | 20 S. Main St. (Bank St.) | 609-654-7011 | www.tedsonmain.net

Ted Iwachiw is the main man of many Medfordites who praise his New American BYO "gem" that turns out "first-rate", "innovative" dishes with "subtle influences of contemporary New Orleans" in a white-tablecloth setting full of "charm"; his last name is pronounced 'I-watch-you', and it's apparent the locals are returning the favor.

Tokyo Bleu *Japanese*   ∇ 21 | 19 | 24 | $32

Cinnaminson | 602 Rte. 130 N. (Westfield Lees Dr.) | 856-829-8889 | www.tokyobleusushi.com

"If you can't be in Toyko, go to Cinnaminson" advise aficionados of this Japanese BYO housed in a "quaint" "farmhouse" on Route 130; "top-notch" service (complete with a "hot towel to wash your hands") and a "romantic" atmosphere complement the "light", "tasty" fare and "creative sushi menu."

Tortilla Press *Mexican*   23 | 18 | 21 | $29

Collingswood | 703 Haddon Ave. (Collings Ave.) | 856-869-3345 | www.thetortillapress.com

"Creative but authentic" Mexican eats and "friendly" service have amigos shouting *"olé"* at this "popular" Collingswood BYO; "no reservations" can sometimes mean "long waits" for a table in the "brightly colored" digs, but the "moderately priced" *comida* makes it "very worthwhile", especially on Tuesday night date nights ($38 a couple).

	FOOD	DECOR	SERVICE	COST

NEW Tortilla Press Cantina *Mexican* | 19 | 17 | 20 | $29

Pennsauken | 7716 Maple Ave. (Haddonfield Rd.) | 856-488-0005 | www.tortillapresscantina.com

A "true" and "imaginative" south of the border menu, "good tequila list" and "right-on" service are a source of "joy" for many at Tortilla Press' "festive", "upscale", liquor-serving Mexican *hermano* in Pennsauken; still, to some detractors it's "not outstanding" enough to merit a "special trip."

Tutti Toscani *Italian* | - | - | - | I

Cherry Hill | ShopRite Shopping Ctr. | 1491 Brace Rd. (Berlin Rd.) | 856-354-1157 | www.lambertis.com

"Consistently good" brick-oven pizzas, panini and antipasti, a "casual", "family-friendly" environment and "lower prices" than its siblings' are the hallmarks of this "homey" Lamberti-owned Tuscan BYO in Cherry Hill; it's fresh off a renovation that included the addition of an outdoor patio complete with wishing well.

Water Lily M *Asian/French* | 22 | 19 | 21 | $36

Collingswood | 653 Haddon Ave. (Collings Ave.) | 856-833-0998 | www.waterlilybistro.com

"Reservations are a must" at this Collingswood Asian-French BYO, where "wonderful" "fusion" fare is served by "charming servers" who are "dedicated to your happiness"; the atmosphere is "calming" in the "small" space, but for really "quiet dining", regulars recommend going "during the week"; P.S. the $9.50 "business luncheon" "can't be beat."

NEW William Douglas Steakhouse *Steak* | - | - | - | E

Cherry Hill | Garden State Pk. | 941 Haddonfield Rd. (Rte. 70) | 856-665-6100 | www.williamdouglassteakhouse.com

Horse-theme photos lining the walls of this comfortably manly Cherry Hill steakhouse give a whinny to the site's past as Garden State Park race track; though it's a project of McCormick & Schmick's and shares a kitchen with M&S, there's no duplication of seafood dishes on its menu of pricey chophouse classics.

Word of Mouth M *American* | 24 | 22 | 21 | $41

Collingswood | 729 Haddon Ave. (bet. Collings & Washington Aves.) | 856-858-2228

The word on this "romantic" New American BYO in Collingswood is "classy", with "beautifully done", "creative" dishes proffered by "attentive" servers in an "elegant" environment; while some say it's "pricey" and others opine the "price is right", most concur "you'll want to go back"; N.B. it hasn't lost a step under new ownership.

Wilmington/Nearby Delaware

TOP FOOD		TOP SERVICE	
26	Krazy Kat's	26	Green Room
25	Culinaria	25	Domaine Hudson
	Moro		Eclipse Bistro
	Green Room	23	Krazy Kat's
24	Domaine Hudson		Culinaria
	Mikimotos*		

TOP DECOR

28	Green Room
25	Krazy Kat's
23	Domaine Hudson
22	Harry's Seafood
	Deep Blue

BEST BUYS

1. Brew HaHa!
2. Five Guys
3. Jake's Hamburgers
4. Charcoal Pit
5. Lucky's Coffee Shop

NEW Ameritage *American*　　　　　- | - | - | M

Wilmington | 900 Orange St. (9th St.) | 302-427-2300 |
www.ameritagebistro.com

Vintage iron-and-glass chandeliers and burgundy-and-gold walls create a warm ambiance at this bi-level New American bistro in Downtown Wilmington offering a menu of small, large and shared plates complemented by a reasonably priced wine list; it's twinned with an NYC deli-style prêt-a-manger market for the grab-and-go set.

Back Burner ⑤ *American*　　　20 | 18 | 18 | $37

Hockessin | 425 Hockessin Corner (Old Lancaster Pike) | 302-239-2314 |
www.backburner.com

This country-rustic New American in a Hockessin strip mall has been a front-burner favorite since 1981 for "reliable, tasty" vittles (e.g. "outstanding" pumpkin soup); though some find the setting "posh", others judge it generic, and if dinner seems "pricey", the $25 three-course prix fixe (Mondays–Wednesdays) makes it a "viable option."

Blue Parrot Bar & Grille ● *Cajun*　　18 | 17 | 19 | $25

Wilmington | 1934 W. Sixth St. (Union St.) | 302-655-8990 |
www.blueparrotgrille.com

"Get in a N'Awlins mood" at this "festive" Cajun in Downtown Wilmington, where the "welcome touch of Bourbon Street" ("minus the travel time") means "authentic-tasting" grub done with "zest" and "superb" live blues and jazz; N.B. a warm-weather patio adds to the good times.

Bottom of the Sea ⊅ *Seafood*　　∇ 22 | 11 | 21 | $27

NEW Wilmington | 810 Maryland Ave. (Oak St.) | 302-654-9505
See review in the Philadelphia Directory.

Brew HaHa! *Coffeehouse*　　　18 | 17 | 21 | $9

Greenville | Powder Mill Sq. | 3842 Kennett Pike (Buck Rd.) |
302-658-6336

---

* Indicates a tie with restaurant above

FOOD DECOR SERVICE COST

(continued)

Brew HaHa!

Wilmington | Hotel du Pont | 1007 N. Market St. (10th St.) | 302-656-1171 🗷

Wilmington | Rockford Shops | 1420 N. du Pont St. (Delaware Ave.) | 302-778-2656

Wilmington | Branmar Plaza | 1812 Marsh Rd. (Silverside Rd.) | 302-529-1125

Wilmington | Concord Plaza | 3503 Silverside Rd. (Brookfield Ave.) | 302-472-2001 🗷

Wilmington | Concord Gallery | 3636 Concord Pike (Silverside Rd.) | 302-478-7227

Wilmington | Shops of Limestone Hills | 5329 Limestone Rd. (west of Stoney Batter Rd.) | 302-234-9600

Wilmington | 835 N. Market St. (bet. 8th & 9th Sts.) | 302-777-4499 🗷 www.brew-haha.com

See review in the Philadelphia Directory.

Buckley's Tavern *American*

17 | 16 | 18 | $30

Centerville | 5812 Kennett Pike (4 mi. south of Rte. 1) | 302-656-9776

"Pickups" park "next to Rolls-Royces" at this "clubby" New American Centerville institution (since 1936) in a "somewhat bucolic" setting down the road from Winterthur, where "sensible" "Wasp soul food" pleases palates both indoors or on the deck; insiders advise to "come in your jammies" for Sunday brunch and shave "half off" your tab.

Charcoal Pit *Burgers*

20 | 13 | 16 | $13

Bear | 240 Fox Hunt Dr. (Rte. 40) | 302-834-8000

Wilmington | 2600 Concord Pike (Woodrow Ave.) | 302-478-2165 ◗

Wilmington | 5200 Pike Creek Center Blvd. (Limestone Rd.) | 302-999-7483

Wilmington | 714 Greenbank Rd. (Kirkwood Hwy.) | 302-998-8853

"Being in The Pits" is a good thing at this Delaware-based mini-chain where "1950s" "nostalgia" is served with "old-school" burgers, "mm-mm-good" malts and "fabulous" ice cream sundaes made the way they were "before they knew what cholesterol was"; N.B. Greenbank Road is licensed for alcohol.

China Royal 🅼 *Chinese*

24 | 14 | 19 | $23

Wilmington | 1845 Marsh Rd. (Silverside Rd.) | 302-475-3686

Solid food scores confirm "well-executed" offerings at this Mandarin-style Northern Wilmington Chinese, but "be prepared to eat quickly" or "hold onto your plate" because the "attentive" waiters are in a "rush" to clear.

Conley Ward's *Steak*

17 | 20 | 17 | $56

Wilmington | 110 S. West St. (Martin Luther King Jr. Blvd.) | 302-658-6626 | www.conleywards.com

Most head for the "outstanding" patio "overlooking the river" at this "posh" steakhouse in Wilmington, also distinguished for its 1,800-bottle exposed wine room; if critics find the "typical", "high-end" victuals "not up to the prices" and the "parking situation" an "Achilles heel", others take solace in the "value" lunch and happy hour.

Corner Bistro *Eclectic*   21 | 19 | 21 | $31

Wilmington | Talleyville Towne Shoppes | 3604 Silverside Rd. (Concord Pike) | 302-477-1778 | www.mybistro.com

"Solid", "innovative" fare comes with a "touch of adventure" at this "city"-style Eclectic "gleaming" in a Talleyville strip mall, where "you feel a world away from Route 202"; add "flattering" lighting, a "nice" wine list and a "knowledgeable" staff for a welcome "break" from the routine.

☑ Culinaria ⑤Ⓜ *American*   25 | 21 | 23 | $35

Wilmington | Branmar Plaza | 1812 Marsh Rd. (Silverside Rd.) | 302-475-4860 | www.culinariarestaurant.com

"So what if it's in a strip mall and doesn't take reservations?" ask admirers of this "urban-chic" New American in northern Wilmington, who affirm it's all about the "properly priced", "creative" food, "lovely" wine list and "efficient" staff; P.S. "go early" or "late" – or be prepared "to wait."

Deep Blue ⑤ *Seafood*   22 | 22 | 22 | $44

Wilmington | 111 W. 11th St. (bet. Orange & Tatnall Sts.) | 302-777-2040 | www.deepbluebarandgrill.com

When in Wilmington, "don't deep six" this "New York–slick" seafooder near the Dupont Theater, where there's nothing fishy about the "creative", "well-prepared" fin fare served by "professionals" amid "trendy" decor ("cool" colors and "relaxed" lighting); while some carp it can "get loud", at least there's a "good bar crowd."

☑ Domaine Hudson ⑤ *American*   24 | 23 | 25 | $44

Wilmington | 1314 N. Washington St. (bet. 13th & 14th Sts.) | 302-655-9463 | www.domainehudson.com

Oenophiles seeking a "sophisticated" "change of pace" take "flight" to Downtown Wilmington to "experiment" with "eclectic" wine choices, "magnificent" cheese courses and "innovative" New American small plates served by a "knowledgeable" staff "invested" in your meal; for most, this "NY-worthy" spot "surpasses" expectations.

Eclipse Bistro *American*   23 | 20 | 25 | $40

Wilmington | 1020 N. Union St. (10th St.) | 302-658-1588 | www.eclipsebistro.com

A good bet for a "nice evening out", this "casual" bistro in Downtown Wilmington "delivers big time" with "inventive" Traditional American fare from an "open kitchen" and a "dependable" list of "affordable" wines; not to be eclipsed by the aforementioned is the "consistently strong", "professional" service.

Feby's Fishery *Seafood*   18 | 11 | 16 | $31

Wilmington | 3701 Lancaster Pike (bet. Centre & du Pont Rds.) | 302-998-9501 | www.febysfishery.com

The variety of "fresh" and "simply prepared" seafood offerings reel 'em in to this Wilmington fishery attached to a market; despite relatively recent renovations, the nautical look is still "plain", so the word is "go for the food, not the decor."

Five Guys Famous Burgers & Fries *Burgers*   22 | 9 | 15 | $10
Wilmington | 2217 Concord Pike (Falk Rd.) | 302-654-5489 |
www.fiveguys.com
See review in the Philadelphia Directory.

Z Green Room *French*   25 | 28 | 26 | $59
Wilmington | Hotel du Pont | 11th & Market Sts. | 302-594-3154 |
www.hoteldupont.com
"Dine like royalty" amid "luxurious" splendor at this "breathtaking" French classic inside Downtown Wilmington's Hotel du Pont, noted for its "outstanding" service and "wonderful" food; most maintain "nobody should miss this experience" but "go with deep pockets", though the Sunday brunch buffet ($45 per person) "might be the best deal around"; N.B. jacket required Friday–Saturday evenings.

Harry's Savoy Grill *American*   23 | 20 | 22 | $45
Wilmington | 2020 Naamans Rd. (Foulk Rd.) | 302-475-3000 |
www.harrys-savoy.com
Fans attest "you can always count on" this Wilmington New American, a local "standby" for "power dining" proffering "awesome" prime rib and other "consistent" selections, complemented by an "excellent" wine list; an "attentive" staff waits on an "older crowd" in the "comfortable" dining room, while a "young and hip" clientele gathers in the bar.

Harry's Seafood Grill *Seafood*   22 | 22 | 21 | $46
Wilmington | 101 S. Market St. (Shipley St.) | 302-777-1500 |
www.harrysseafoodgrill.com
"Startlingly fresh" seafood, "great raw-bar" offerings and a "top-notch" wine list are served in a "cool", "trendy" (and "loud") setting at this nautical sibling of Harry's Savoy Grill in Wilmington, where the waterside deck is "always a great draw"; critics, though, find the service "hit-or-miss" and expect "more consistency" "at these prices."

Hibachi *Japanese*   18 | 17 | 19 | $28
Wilmington | 5607 Concord Pike (Naamans Rd.) | 302-477-0194
See review in the Philadelphia Directory.

Iron Hill Brewery & Restaurant *American*   18 | 18 | 18 | $27
Newark | Traders Alley | 147 E. Main St. (bet. Chapel & Haines Sts.) |
302-266-9000
Wilmington | 710 S. Madison St. (Beech St.) | 302-658-8200
www.ironhillbrewery.com
See review in the Philadelphia Directory.

Jake's Hamburgers *Burgers*   21 | 8 | 16 | $10
Bear | 1643 Pulaski Hwy. (Porter Rd.) | 302-832-2230
New Castle | 150 S. du Pont Hwy./Rte. 113 (off Rte. 273) | 302-322-0200
Wilmington | Roselle Ctr. | 2401 Kirkwood Hwy. (Rte. 141) | 302-994-6800
www.jakeshamburgers.com
These "bare-bones", "quick-serve" "joints" continue to delight Delawareans with "fresh, tasty" burgers, "homemade" fries and

"killer", "old-time" shakes "for the price of fast food"; it's become "somewhat of a cult favorite" – "every town needs one."

Jasmine *Pan-Asian*

| 22 | 19 | 17 | $33 |

Wilmington | Concord Gallery | 3618 Concord Pike (Mt. Lebanon Rd.) | 302-479-5618

"Outstanding" sushi jazzes a "well-priced" menu teeming with "variety" at this "always busy", "hip-for-Wilmington" Pan-Asian in a strip mall; most talk up "friendly", "knowledgeable" service, while others say "slow" pacing is the "only downer."

⚡ Krazy Kat's *French*

| 26 | 25 | 23 | $57 |

Montchanin | Inn at Montchanin Vill. | 504 Montchanin Rd. (Kirk Rd.) | 302-888-4200 | www.montchanin.com

Seekers of gourmet Gallic in northern Delaware lick their lips at this "whimsical" yet "classy" country inn proffering "excellent" New French fare ideal for "a special night out"; "you don't need to be krazy" to enjoy it, although it would help if you were "a fat cat to afford it."

Lamberti's Cucina *Italian*

| 19 | 18 | 19 | $31 |

Wilmington | Prices Corner Shopping Ctr. | 1300 Centerville Rd. (Kirkwood Hwy.) | 302-995-6955
Wilmington | 514 Philadelphia Pike (Marsh Rd.) | 302-762-9094
www.lambertis.com

"Bring an appetite" and "go easy" on the bread at this Lamberti family duo in Wilmington offering "well-executed" Italian basics at "affordable" prices; "welcoming" service is a "cut above", and generous portions make for good "follow-up" meals at home.

La Tolteca *Mexican*

| 20 | 13 | 18 | $19 |

Wilmington | Fairfax Shopping Ctr. | 2209 Concord Pike (Rte. 141) | 302-778-4646
Wilmington | Talleyville Shopping Ctr. | 4015 Concord Pike (bet. Brandywine Blvd. & Silverside Rd.) | 302-478-9477
www.lastoltecas.com

The "prices can't be beat" at these "lively" "local favorite" Wilmington shopping-mall *hermanos* where the Mexican *comidas* come "fast" and "hot" "almost before you close your menu" and the margaritas are "amazing"; you could just eat the "fresh" salsa and chips and "be very happy."

NEW Lucky's Coffee Shop *American*

| 17 | 17 | 16 | $15 |

Wilmington | 4003 Concord Pike (Silverside Rd.) | 302-477-0240

"Omelets do not disappoint" at this "close to being cool" New American on Concord Pike, which Wilmingtonians describe as a "perfect diner combo" of "mod and classic" complete with attempts at "gourmet" grub; still, a few would prefer a staff that gets "orders right."

Mexican Post *Mexican*

| 17 | 14 | 16 | $22 |

Wilmington | 3100 Naamans Rd. (Shipley Rd.) | 302-478-3939 | www.mexicanpost.com
See review in the Philadelphia Directory.

	FOOD	DECOR	SERVICE	COST

Mikimotos Asian Grill &
Sushi Bar *Japanese/Pan-Asian*   24 | 20 | 19 | $34

Wilmington | 1212 N. Washington St. (12th St.) | 302-656-8638 |
www.mikimotos.com

Two-for-one happy-hour roll specials "at the bar" and in an enclosed
patio plus "efficiently" served, "unexpected" Japanese–Pan-Asian
"treats" get Wilmingtonians' motors running over this "modern",
"trendy" Downtown spot; a "loud and lively" atmosphere attracts a
"see-and-be-seen" crowd.

☑ Moro ⑤Ⓜ *American*   25 | 21 | 23 | $53

Wilmington | 1307 N. Scott St. (bet. 13th & 14th Sts.) | 302-777-1800 |
www.mororestaurant.net

Michael DiBianca's "cutting-edge" cuisine and "excellent" wine list
make this "attractive" New American in Downtown Wilmington one
of the "First State's first-class" experiences for a "romantic" dinner,
"business" meal or evening with "out-of-town guests"; if the staff
draws mixed marks ("pleasant" vs. "pretentious"), for most it's all-
around "marvelous"; N.B. look for "over-the-top" monthly wine dinners and a choice of four tasting dinners.

Mrs. Robino's *Italian*   20 | 10 | 17 | $19

Wilmington | 520 N. Union St. (bet. 5th & 6th Sts.) | 302-652-9223 |
www.mrsrobinos.com

Locals line up for "gravy at its finest" at this "easy-on-the-
pocketbook", "hole-in-the-wall" Italian, a circa-1940s mainstay in
Downtown Wilmington's Little Italy; it's like "grandma's in the
kitchen", which means "you'll never leave hungry."

NEW Pomodoro *Italian*   ▽ 20 | 14 | 15 | $34

Wilmington | 729 N. Union St. (8th St.) | 302-574-9800 |
www.pomodorowilmington.com

"These guys want to cook for you" say fans of the chefs' kitchen
skills at this "relatively new" Wilmington Italian; though the brick-
walled space can be "loud" at times and the service "slow", some
find the "best tiramisu on the planet" makes things *buono.*

Sugarfoot Fine Foods ⑤ *American*   ▽ 27 | 21 | 23 | $17

Wilmington | Nemours Bldg. | 1007 N. Orange St. (10th St.) |
302-654-1600
Wilmington | 1014 Lincoln St. (bet. 10th & 11th Sts.) | 302-655-4800 Ⓜ
www.sugarfootfinefood.com

"Fresh", "inventive" New American lunch fare makes these
Wilmington sandwich shops popular "workday" options even
among "food snobs" who marvel that the "sides" "keep things interesting"; "you will feel welcome, comfortable and nourished" in the
casual, counter-service settings; P.S. they also offer some of the
"best catering in the area."

Sullivan's Steakhouse *Steak*   23 | 21 | 21 | $54

Wilmington | Brandywine Town Ctr. | 5525 Concord Pike (Naamans Rd.) |
302-479-7970 | www.sullivanssteakhouse.com
See review in the Philadelphia Directory.

Toscana Kitchen & Bar *Italian*
24 | 19 | 21 | $39

Wilmington | Rockford Shops | 1412 N. du Pont St. (Delaware Ave.) | 302-654-8001 | www.toscanakitchen.com

Amici would stack up the "interesting, fresh" *mangiare* (including "superior" daily specials) at Dan Butler's Wilmington Italian "against any grandmother's in Italy"; an "affordable" wine list, "solid" service and a "sleek, comfy" interior with a "great lounge area" help make it a "reasonable alternative to the corporate chains."

Utage *Japanese*
24 | 14 | 21 | $33

Wilmington | Independence Mall | 1601 Concord Pike (Powder Mill Rd.) | 302-652-1230 | www.oka-utage.com

Many find the "best sushi in town" at this "peaceful", "unpretentious" Japanese in Independence Mall where "you can always count on" a "friendly" staff to deliver; calls for interior "updating" have been answered post-Survey.

Walter's Steakhouse *Steak*
∇ 27 | 19 | 21 | $52

Wilmington | 802 N. Union St. (8th St.) | 302-652-6780 | www.waltersteakhouse.com

At this "homey" Wilmington steakhouse run by "some of the nicest people in Delaware", "families" "enjoy themselves" in the clubby environs over "plentiful" steaks and a "complimentary raw bar" offered Sundays, Mondays and Thursdays; it's "highly recommended" by locals who "wonder why there are chains."

Washington St. Ale House ● *Pub Food*
17 | 17 | 20 | $25

Wilmington | 1206 Washington St. (12th St.) | 302-658-2537 | www.wsalehouse.com

"Exactly what's needed in Wilmington" is how fans assess this Downtown pub that underwent a renovation in 2007; some "unexpected twists" liven up the "dependable" American "standards", and while the "casual" setting is "comfy", it gets "wickedly loud", so you might have to show up "grandma-early" to have a "conversation."

INDEXES

LOCATION MAPS

All restaurants are in the Philadelphia area unless otherwise
noted (LB=Lancaster/Berks Counties; NJ=New Jersey Suburbs;
DE=Wilmington/Nearby Delaware).

Cuisines

Includes restaurant names, locations and Food ratings. ☑ indicates places with the highest ratings, popularity and importance.

AFGHAN

Ariana	**Old City**	20
Kabul	**Old City**	22
NEW Yalda Grill	**Horsham**	20

AMERICAN (NEW)

Alfa	**Ctr City W**	16
☑ Alison/Blue Bell	**Blue Bell**	26
America B&G	**multi.**	17
NEW Ameritage	**Wilming/DE**	–
Anton's/Swan	**Lambertville/NJ**	20
NEW Apothecary	**Ctr City E**	–
Avalon	**W Chester**	21
Back Burner	**Hockessin/DE**	20
Basil Bistro	**Paoli**	18
Big Fork	**Chadds Ford**	21
Bistro 7	**Old City**	24
Blackbird	**Collingswood/NJ**	26
☑ Blackfish	**Consho**	26
Bliss	**Ave of Arts**	22
Blue Horse	**Blue Bell**	17
NEW Blue Pear	**W Chester**	22
Brick Hotel	**Newtown**	18
Bridget Foy's	**South St.**	19
☑ Bridgetown Mill	**Langhorne**	25
Bridgets	**Ambler**	22
Buckley's	**Centerville/DE**	17
Butterfish	**W Chester**	25
Cameron Estate	**Mt Joy/LB**	–
Carambola	**Dresher**	23
Carr's	**Lancaster/LB**	25
Catherine's	**Unionville**	24
Cedar Hollow	**Malvern**	20
Centre Bridge	**New Hope**	19
Chlöe	**Old City**	25
Christopher's	**Wayne**	17
Coleman	**Blue Bell**	20
Copper Bistro	**N Liberties**	22
Cork	**Westmont/NJ**	20
Cosimo	**Malvern**	22
NEW Cravings	**Lansdale**	21
Cresheim Cottage	**Mt Airy**	18
☑ Culinaria	**Wilming/DE**	25
Dark Horse	**Society Hill**	17

Derek's	**Manayunk**	19
Devil's Alley	**Ctr City W**	19
NEW Devil's Den	**S Philly**	–
Dilworth. Inn	**W Chester**	25
☑ Dom. Hudson	**Wilming/DE**	24
Drafting Rm.	**multi.**	18
Elements	**Haddon Hts/NJ**	24
Epicurean	**Phoenixville**	21
Fayette St.	**Consho**	23
☑ Food/Thought	**Marlton/NJ**	24
☑ Fork	**Old City**	24
Four Dogs	**W Chester**	18
Freight House	**Doylestown**	19
Funky Lil' Kitchen	**Pottstown**	23
Gables	**Chadds Ford**	20
Gayle	**South St.**	25
GG's	**Mt Laurel/NJ**	21
Grace Tavern	**Ctr City W**	19
Half Moon	**Kennett Sq**	20
Happy Rooster	**Ctr City W**	17
Harry's Savoy	**Wilming/DE**	23
Havana	**New Hope**	15
High St. Grill	**Mt Holly/NJ**	23
Honey	**Doylestown**	25
Iron Hill	**multi.**	18
Isaac Newton's	**Newtown**	16
Jake's	**Manayunk**	25
James	**S Philly**	25
Jasper	**Downingtown**	25
NEW Javier	**Haddonfield/NJ**	21
J.B. Dawson's/Austin's	**Lancaster/LB**	18
NEW J.L. Sullivan's	**Ave of Arts**	–
Joseph Ambler	**N Wales**	23
Kitchen 233	**Westmont/NJ**	20
Knight House	**Doylestown**	21
NEW Knock	**Ctr City E**	19
Landing	**New Hope**	16
La Terrasse	**Univ City**	18
Latest Dish	**South St.**	24
☑ Lily's on Main	**Ephrata/LB**	24
Loie	**Ctr City W**	17
London Grill	**Fairmount**	18

NEW Lucky's Coffee | Wilming/DE	17
Mainland Inn | Mainland	26
Majolica | Phoenixville	26
Marathon Grill | multi.	18
Marathon/Sq. | Ctr City W	19
Margot | Narberth	20
Marigold Kitchen | Univ City	24
Z Matyson | Ctr City W	26
Brandywine | Chadds Ford	20
Mendenhall Inn | Mendenhall	21
Meritage | Ctr City W	23
Z Moro | Wilming/DE	25
Moshulu | DE River	22
Museum Rest. | Fairmount	19
New Wave | Queen Vill	18
NEW Nicholas | S Philly	-
Z Nineteen | Ave of Arts	23
No. 9 | Lambertville/NJ	23
N. 3rd | N Liberties	22
Orchard | Kennett Sq	-
Pace One | Thornton	21
Parc Bistro | Skippack	25
NEW Peppercorns | S Philly	-
Pistachio Grille | Maple Glen	19
Pumpkin | Ctr City W	24
Rae | Univ City	22
Z Rest. Alba | Malvern	27
Rest./Doneckers | Ephrata/LB	19
Rose Tattoo | Fairmount	22
Rouge | Ctr City W	22
Rouget | Newtown	-
Roux 3 | Newtown Sq	21
Royal Tavern | S Philly	23
Rylei | NE Philly	24
Salt & Pepper | S Philly	23
Shula's 347 | W Consho	21
Silk City | N Liberties	20
Simon Pearce | W Chester	20
Snackbar | Ctr City W	18
Z Sola | Bryn Mawr	27
Solaris Grille | Ches Hill	16
Southwark | South St.	22
NEW Station Bistro | Kimberton	-
Stella Blu | W Consho	-
Sugarfoot | Wilming/DE	27
NEW Supper | South St.	23
Z Swann Lounge | Ctr City W	27

Tango | Bryn Mawr	20
Tavern 17 | Ctr City W	18
Ted's on Main | Medford/NJ	26
NEW 10 Arts | Ave of Arts	-
333 Belrose | Radnor	23
Twenty Manning | Ctr City W	22
211 York | Jenkintown	22
NEW Ugly American | S Philly	19
NEW Union Gourmet | Ctr City E	-
Winnie's Le Bus | Manayunk	21
Word of Mouth | Collingswood/NJ	24
Yardley Inn | Yardley	21
yello'bar | S Philly	16
NEW Zacharias | Lansdale	21
Zakes Cafe | Ft Wash	23

AMERICAN (TRADITIONAL)

Bay Pony Inn | Lederach	19
Blue Bell Inn | Blue Bell	21
Braddock's | Medford/NJ	-
NEW Café Estelle | N Liberties	-
Cheeseburger/Paradise | Langhorne	15
Z Cheesecake Fact. | multi.	20
Chestnut Grill | Ches Hill	17
Z Chickie's/Pete's | multi.	18
City Tavern | Old City	19
Cock 'n Bull | Lahaska	17
Copabanana | multi.	16
Cuttalossa Inn | Lumberville	16
Dave & Buster's | multi.	13
Day by Day | Ctr City W	21
NEW Dock Street | Univ City	18
Eclipse Bistro | Wilming/DE	23
NEW Field House | Ctr City E	13
Fountain Side | Horsham	19
Fox & Hound | multi.	12
Friday Sat. Sun. | Ctr City W	23
Gen. Lafayette | Lafayette Hill	15
Gen. Warren | Malvern	25
Good Dog | Ctr City W	22
Z Green Hills Inn | Reading/LB	26
Gullifty's | Rosemont	15
Gypsy Saloon | Consho	22
Hank's Place | Chadds Ford	19
Hard Rock | Ctr City E	14
Haydn Zug's | E Petersburg/LB	18

Ida Mae's | **Fishtown**	22
Inn/Hawke | **Lambertville/NJ**	19
J.B. Dawson's/Austin's | **multi.**	18
Johnny Brenda's | **Fishtown**	21
Jonathan's | **Jenkintown**	17
Jones | **Ctr City E**	20
K.C.'s Alley | **Ambler**	17
☑ Kimberton Inn | **Kimberton**	25
King George II | **Bristol**	21
Lambertville Station | **Lambertville/NJ**	18
Liberties | **multi.**	14
L2 | **Ctr City W**	17
Manayunk Brew. | **Manayunk**	18
Mastoris | **Bordentown/NJ**	20
Max & Erma's | **multi.**	15
McFadden's | **multi.**	13
☑ Mercato | **Ctr City E**	26
Mercer Café | **Port Richmond**	26
Misconduct Tav. | **Ctr City W**	17
More Than Ice Crm. | **Ctr City E**	20
Mother's | **New Hope**	18
New Tavern | **Bala Cynwyd**	16
Nodding Head | **Ctr City W**	18
North by NW | **Mt Airy**	16
Old Guard Hse. | **Gladwyne**	23
Ortlieb's Jazz | **N Liberties**	-
Paradigm | **Old City**	18
P.J. Whelihan's | **multi.**	15
Plate | **Ardmore**	16
Plumsteadville Inn | **Plumsteadville**	19
Ponzio's | **Cherry Hill/NJ**	17
Pop Shop | **Collingswood/NJ**	20
Public Hse./Logan | **Ctr City W**	15
Redstone | **multi.**	21
Rembrandt's | **Fairmount**	20
Robin's Nest | **Mt Holly/NJ**	25
Rose Tree Inn | **Media**	22
Society Hill Hotel | **Old City**	18
Spotted Hog | **Lahaska**	17
☑ Standard Tap | **N Liberties**	24
Stoudt's | **Adamstown/LB**	18
Ted's Montana | **multi.**	16
Ten Stone | **Ctr City W**	18
10th St. Pour House | **Ctr City E**	21
Trax Café | **Ambler**	23
Triumph Brewing | **multi.**	19
Trolley Car | **Mt Airy**	14

NEW Urban Saloon | **Fairmount**	16
Wash. Cross. | **Wash Cross**	17
William Penn | **Gwynedd**	22
Winberie's | **Wayne**	16
Wooden Iron | **Wayne**	18
World Café | **Univ City**	14

ASIAN

Anjou | **Old City**	19
Bunha Faun | **Malvern**	25
Chez Elena Wu | **Voorhees/NJ**	23
Coconut Bay | **Voorhees/NJ**	22
Twenty Manning | **Ctr City W**	22
Water Lily | **Collingswood/NJ**	22

ASIAN FUSION

Anjou | **Old City**	19
☑ NEW Azie | **Media**	24
Duck Sauce | **Newtown**	25
FuziOn | **Worcester**	23
Ly Michael's | **Chinatown**	21
Roy's | **Ctr City W**	23
Shangrila | **Devon**	20
Umai Umai | **Fairmount**	24

BAKERIES

NEW Cake | **Ches Hill**	21
Mastoris | **Bordentown/NJ**	20
More Than Ice Crm. | **Ctr City E**	20
Pink Rose | **South St.**	21
Ponzio's | **Cherry Hill/NJ**	17

BARBECUE

Abner's BBQ | **Jenkintown**	20
☑ Bomb Bomb BBQ | **S Philly**	23
Devil's Alley | **Ctr City W**	19
Red Hot & Blue | **Cherry Hill/NJ**	17
Rib Crib | **Germantown**	22
Sweet Lucy's | **NE Philly**	21
NEW Tennessee's BBQ | **Levittown**	-

BELGIAN

Abbaye | **N Liberties**	22
NEW Belgian Café | **Fairmount**	15
NEW Beneluxx | **Old City**	20
Eulogy Belgian | **Old City**	18
Monk's Cafe | **Ctr City W**	22
Teresa's Next Dr. | **Wayne**	20
ZoT | **Society Hill**	20

BRAZILIAN

NEW Chima	Ctr City W	-
🅩 Fogo de Chão	Ave of Arts	23

BRITISH

Dark Horse	Society Hill	17
Elephant & Castle	multi.	11
Whip Tavern	Coatesville	20

BURGERS

Charcoal Pit	multi.	20
Charlie's Hamburgers	Folsom	24
Cheeseburger/Paradise	Langhorne	15
Chestnut Grill	Ches Hill	17
Five Guys	multi.	22
NEW goodburger	Ctr City W	-
Jake's Hamburgers	multi.	21
Manayunk Brew.	Manayunk	18
McFadden's	multi.	13
Nifty Fifty's	multi.	19
Pop Shop	Collingswood/NJ	20
Rembrandt's	Fairmount	20
Rouge	Ctr City W	22
Ruby's	multi.	16
Sassafras Int'l	Old City	-

BURMESE

Rangoon	Chinatown	24

CAJUN

Blue Parrot	Wilming/DE	18
Bourbon Blue	Manayunk	19
Carmine's Creole	Bryn Mawr	22
Creole Cafe	Sewell/NJ	22
High St. Caffé	W Chester	24
NEW Les Bons Temps	Ctr City E	-
Ortlieb's Jazz	N Liberties	-

CALIFORNIAN

California Cafe	King of Prussia	20
Sovalo	N Liberties	25

CARIBBEAN

Bahama Breeze	multi.	17

CHEESE STEAKS

Campo's Deli	Old City	22
Dalessandro's	Roxborough	24
Geno's Steaks	S Philly	19
Jim's Steaks	multi.	22
Pat's Steaks	S Philly	20
Steve's Prince/Stks.	multi.	24
🅩 Tony Luke's	S Philly	25

CHINESE

(* dim sum specialist)

Abacus	Lansdale	24
NEW Auspicious	Ardmore	19
Beijing	Univ City	16
Charles Plaza	Chinatown	23
China Royal	Wilming/DE	24
Chun Hing	Wynnefield	22
CinCin	Ches Hill	24
Duck Sauce	Newtown	25
Four Rivers	Chinatown	24
Harmony Veg.*	Chinatown	20
H.K. Gold. Phoenix*	Chinatown	20
Hunan	Ardmore	21
Imperial Inn*	Chinatown	20
Joe's Peking	Marlton/NJ	22
Joy Tsin Lau*	Chinatown	20
Kingdom of Veg.*	Chinatown	19
Lee How Fook	Chinatown	24
Mandarin Gdn.	Willow Grove	20
Marg. Kuo	Wayne	23
Marg. Kuo Mandarin	Frazer	23
Marg. Kuo Media	Media	22
Marg. Kuo Peking	Media	22
Mustard Greens	Queen Vill	21
Ocean Harbor*	Chinatown	20
🅩 P.F. Chang's	multi.	21
Ray's Cafe	Chinatown	25
Sakura Spring	Cherry Hill/NJ	23
Sang Kee Asian	Wynnewood	24
🅩 Sang Kee Duck	multi.	25
Shiao Lan Kung	Chinatown	25
Singapore Kosher	Chinatown	19
🅩 Susanna Foo	Ctr City W	24
Tai Lake	Chinatown	24
🅩 Yangming	Bryn Mawr	25
NEW Zhi Wei Guan*	Chinatown	-

COFFEEHOUSES

Almaz Café	Ctr City W	22
Bonté Wafflerie	multi.	19
Brew HaHa!	multi.	18
La Colombe	multi.	23

COFFEE SHOPS/DINERS

Ardmore Station	**Ardmore**	19
Hank's Place	**Chadds Ford**	19
Little Pete's	**multi.**	16
Mastoris	**Bordentown/NJ**	20
Mayfair Diner	**NE Philly**	15
Melrose Diner	**S Philly**	16
Morning Glory	**S Philly**	24
Nifty Fifty's	**multi.**	19
Ponzio's	**Cherry Hill/NJ**	17
Ruby's	**multi.**	16
Silk City	**N Liberties**	20
Trolley Car	**Mt Airy**	14

COLOMBIAN

Tierra Colombiana	**N Philly**	22

CONTINENTAL

⚡ Bridgetown Mill	**Langhorne**	25
Café Gallery	**Burlington/NJ**	21
Chef Charin	**Bala Cynwyd**	20
⚡ Duling-Kurtz	**Exton**	25
Farmicia	**Old City**	20
Fioravanti	**Downingtown**	26
⚡ Fountain	**Ctr City W**	29
Seven Stars Inn	**Phoenixville**	23
NEW Time	**Ctr City E**	–
Vincent's	**W Chester**	16
William Penn	**Gwynedd**	22
⚡ Yangming	**Bryn Mawr**	25

CREOLE

Bourbon Blue	**Manayunk**	19
Carmine's Creole	**Bryn Mawr**	22
Creole Cafe	**Sewell/NJ**	22
High St. Caffé	**W Chester**	24
NEW Les Bons Temps	**Ctr City E**	–
Marsha Brown	**New Hope**	20
⚡ Mélange	**multi.**	27

CUBAN

Casona	**Collingswood/NJ**	22
⚡ Cuba Libre	**Old City**	21
Tierra Colombiana	**N Philly**	22

DELIS

Ben & Irv Deli	**Hunt Vly**	19
Campo's Deli	**Old City**	22
Famous 4th St. Deli	**South St.**	22
Hymie's Deli	**Merion Sta**	17
Isaac's	**multi.**	17
Izzy & Zoe's	**Univ City**	15
Kibitz in City	**Ctr City E**	21
Kibitz Room	**Cherry Hill/NJ**	23
Mr. Bill's	**Winslow/NJ**	–
Murray's Deli	**Bala Cynwyd**	19
NEW Murray's Deli/bistro M	**Berwyn**	19

DESSERT

Beau Monde	**South St.**	23
Melting Pot	**multi.**	20
More Than Ice Crm.	**Ctr City E**	20
Naked Choco.	**Ave of Arts**	25
Pink Rose	**South St.**	21
Roselena's	**S Philly**	21

EASTERN EUROPEAN

NEW Max & David's	**Elkins Pk**	23

ECLECTIC

AllWays Café	**Hunt Vly**	22
Ansill	**South St.**	24
Beige & Beige	**Hunt Vly**	20
Blush	**Bryn Mawr**	20
Bridgid's	**Fairmount**	21
Cafe Preeya	**Hunt Vly**	21
Cafette	**Ches Hill**	20
Carman's Country	**S Philly**	25
Cebu	**Old City**	–
Chick's	**South St.**	23
⚡ Citrus	**Ches Hill**	25
⚡ Continental, The	**Old City**	22
⚡ Continental Mid-town	**Ctr City W**	21
Corner Bistro	**Wilming/DE**	21
Day by Day	**Ctr City W**	21
Full Plate	**N Liberties**	21
Georges'	**Wayne**	20
⚡ Gracie's	**Pine Forge/LB**	26
Havana	**New Hope**	15
Johnny Brenda's	**Fishtown**	21
Lilly's/Canal	**Lambertville/NJ**	20
⚡ Little Café	**Voorhees/NJ**	27
Margot	**Narberth**	20
Meridith's	**Berwyn**	22
Mimosa	**W Chester**	24
Mirna's Café	**multi.**	22
NEW Murray's Deli/bistro M	**Berwyn**	19

Pub/Penn Valley | **Narberth**	19
🔻 Reading Term. Mkt. | **Ctr City E**	23
Roller's/Flying Fish | **Ches Hill**	21
Rx | **Univ City**	23
Sabrina's Café | **multi.**	25
Sassafras Int'l | **Old City**	–
Serrano | **Old City**	20
Sidecar | **S Philly**	19
Spamps | **Consho**	17
Spence Cafe | **W Chester**	23
Summer Kitchen | **Penns Park**	23
Thomas' | **Manayunk**	–
Totaro's | **Consho**	24
Tria | **multi.**	23
Twin Bays | **Phoenixville**	24
Umbria | **Mt Airy**	24
🔻 White Dog | **Univ City**	21

EGYPTIAN

Aya's Café | **Ctr City W**	20

ERITREAN

Dahlak | **multi.**	22

ETHIOPIAN

Abyssinia | **Univ City**	24
Almaz Café | **Ctr City W**	22
Dahlak | **multi.**	22

EUROPEAN

Bonté Wafflerie | **multi.**	19
Django | **South St.**	25
La Pergola | **Jenkintown**	19
NEW Maia | **Villanova**	–
NEW Swallow | **N Liberties**	–
🔻 Talula's Table | **Kennett Sq**	26

FONDUE

NEW Beneluxx | **Old City**	20
Melting Pot | **multi.**	20

FRENCH

Alisa Cafe | **Cherry Hill/NJ**	22
Beau Monde | **South St.**	23
🔻 Birchrunville Store | **Birchrunville**	28
Bistro Cassis | **Radnor**	20
Bunha Faun | **Malvern**	25
Chez Colette | **Ctr City W**	20

Chez Elena Wu | **Voorhees/NJ**	23
NEW Cochon | **Queen Vill**	24
🔻 Fountain | **Ctr City W**	29
FuziOn | **Worcester**	23
🔻 Gilmore's | **W Chester**	28
Golden Pheasant | **Erwinna**	23
🔻 Green Hills Inn | **Reading/LB**	26
🔻 Green Room | **Wilming/DE**	25
Happy Rooster | **Ctr City W**	17
Hotel du Village | **New Hope**	22
Inn/Phillips Mill | **New Hope**	24
Inn/St. Peter's | **St Peters**	–
🔻 Krazy Kat's | **Montchanin/DE**	26
🔻 La Bonne Auberge | **New Hope**	27
La Campagne | **Cherry Hill/NJ**	24
🔻 Lacroix | **Ctr City W**	28
La Na | **Media**	21
La Terrasse | **Univ City**	18
La Vang | **Willow Grove**	22
🔻 Le Bec-Fin | **Ctr City W**	27
Loie | **Ctr City W**	17
Manon | **Lambertville/NJ**	25
Nan | **Univ City**	25
🔻 Paloma | **NE Philly**	27
Patou | **Old City**	18
Rest. Taquet | **Wayne**	24
Savona | **Gulph Mills**	25
Siam Cuisine/Black | **Doylestown**	23
Siri's | **Cherry Hill/NJ**	25
🔻 Susanna Foo | **Ctr City W**	24
🔻 Swann Lounge | **Ctr City W**	27
Water Lily | **Collingswood/NJ**	22
Zinc | **Ctr City E**	22

FRENCH (BISTRO)

Bistro St. Tropez | **Ctr City W**	20
Brasserie 73 | **Skippack**	22
Caribou Cafe | **Ctr City E**	19
Coquette | **South St.**	18
La Belle Epoque | **Media**	19
🔻 Le Bar Lyonnais | **Ctr City W**	28
NEW Parc | **Ctr City W**	–
Pond | **Radnor**	21
Slate Bleu | **Doylestown**	22
🔻 Sovana Bistro | **Kennett Sq**	26
Spring Mill | **Consho**	23
NEW Supper | **South St.**	23
Vintage | **Ctr City E**	19

FRENCH (BRASSERIE)

🅉 Brasserie Perrier | Ctr City W   24

GASTROPUB

NEW Devil's Den | Amer. | S Philly   -

NEW Ugly American | Amer. | 19
S Philly

GERMAN

Otto's Brauhaus | Horsham   20

GREEK

Athena | Glenside   21
🅉 Dmitri's | multi.   25
Effie's | Ctr City E   21
Estia | Ave of Arts   23
NEW Kanella | Ctr City E   -
Lourdas Greek | Bryn Mawr   21
Olive Tree | Downingtown   23
South St. Souvlaki | South St.   21
Zesty's | Manayunk   20
Zorba's Taverna | Fairmount   20

HAWAIIAN

Roy's | Ctr City W   23

INDIAN

NEW Ashoka Palace | -
Ctr City W
NEW Bindi | Ctr City E   22
Cafe Spice | multi.   20
Karma | Old City   23
Khajuraho | Ardmore   21
NEW Minar Palace | Ctr City E   -
New Delhi | Univ City   20
New Samosa | Ctr City E   16
Palace/Ben | Ctr City E   21
Palace of Asia | Ft Wash   24
Passage/India | Ave of Arts   19
Sitar India | Univ City   20
Tandoor India | Univ City   20
🅉 Tiffin Store | multi.   26

IRISH

Black Sheep | Ctr City W   16
Fadó Irish | Ctr City W   15
Fergie's Pub | Ctr City E   17
Ida Mae's | Fishtown   22
Kildare's | multi.   16
Plough & Stars | Old City   18

Shanachie | Ambler   17
St. Stephens Green | Fairmount   19
Tír na nÓg | Ctr City W   14

ISRAELI

Maccabeam | Ctr City E   18
NEW Zahav | Society Hill   -

ITALIAN

(N=Northern; S=Southern)
Abbraccio | Univ City   13
Anthony's | Haddon Hts/NJ   22
Arpeggio | Spring House   23
August | S Philly   26
Ava | South St.   24
Avalon | N | W Chester   21
🅉 Bàcio | Cinnaminson/NJ   25
Barone's | multi.   21
🅉 Bella Tori | N | Langhorne   19
Bella Tratt. | Manayunk   22
Bellini Grill | Ctr City W   19
Bensí | multi.   18
Bertolini's | King of Prussia   18
🅉 Birchrunville Store | 28
Birchrunville
Bistro di Marino | 25
Collingswood/NJ
Bistro Juliana | Fishtown   23
Bistro La Baia | Ctr City W   20
Bistro La Viola | Ctr City W   24
Bistro Romano | Society Hill   21
Bocelli | multi.   -
🅉 Bomb Bomb BBQ | S Philly   23
Bona Cucina | N | Upper Darby   25
Branzino | Ctr City W   23
NEW Brio | Cherry Hill/NJ   19
Buca di Beppo | multi.   15
NEW Buona Via | Horsham   19
Caffe Aldo | Cherry Hill/NJ   23
Caffe Casta Diva | Ctr City W   24
Caffe Valentino | multi.   19
Catelli | Voorhees/NJ   24
Chiarella's | S Philly   19
Core De Roma | S | South St.   23
Criniti | S | S Philly   19
Cucina Forte | N | S Philly   24
D'Angelo's | Ctr City W   18
Dante & Luigi's | S Philly   23
Davio's | N | Ctr City W   23

Dolce | **Old City**	21
Ecco Qui | **Univ City**	17
Ernesto's 1521 | **Ctr City W**	21
Fellini Cafe | **multi.**	21
Filomena | S | **multi.**	24
Fountain Side | **Horsham**	19
Franco's HighNote | S | **S Philly**	23
Franco's Tratt. | **East Falls**	20
Z Giumarello's | N | **Westmont/NJ**	26
Gnocchi | N | **South St.**	22
Gypsy Saloon | **Consho**	22
Hostaria Da Elio | **South St.**	20
Il Cantuccio | N | **N Liberties**	23
NEW Il Fiore | **Collingswood/NJ**	-
Illuminare | **Fairmount**	18
Il Portico | N | **Ctr City W**	20
Il Tartufo | N | **Manayunk**	23
Italian Bistro | **multi.**	16
NEW Joe Pesce | **multi.**	18
Kristian's | **S Philly**	25
Laceno Italian | **Voorhees/NJ**	24
La Collina | N | **Bala Cynwyd**	23
La Famiglia | **Old City**	24
La Fontana | **Ctr City W**	20
La Locanda | **Old City**	23
Lamberti's | **Wilming/DE**	19
Z L'Angolo † S | **S Philly**	26
LaScala's | **Ctr City E**	20
La Veranda | **DE River**	23
La Viola Ovest | **Ctr City W**	23
Le Castagne | N | **Ctr City W**	22
NEW Le Virtù | S | **S Philly**	26
L'Oca | N | **Fairmount**	23
Luna Rossa | **Sicklerville/NJ**	-
Z Maggiano's | **multi.**	20
Maggio's | **Southampton**	17
Mama Palma's | S | **Ctr City W**	23
Mamma Maria | **S Philly**	22
Marco Polo | **Elkins Pk**	19
Maria's/Summit | **Roxborough**	21
Marra's | S | **S Philly**	22
Mazzi | **Leola/LB**	-
Z Mercato | N | **Ctr City E**	26
Mercer Café | **Port Richmond**	26
Mezza Luna | **S Philly**	21
Milano Modo | **Mt Holly/NJ**	25
Mio Sogno | **S Philly**	23
Mirabella | **Cherry Hill/NJ**	22
Modo Mio | **N Liberties**	26
Moonstruck | **NE Philly**	21
Mr. Martino's | **S Philly**	22
Mrs. Robino's | **Wilming/DE**	20
Newtown Grill | N | **Newtown Sq**	21
Nunzio | **Collingswood/NJ**	23
Z Osteria | N | **N Philly**	26
Paradiso | **S Philly**	23
Penne | **Univ City**	18
Pepper's | **Ardmore**	23
Picasso | **Media**	17
Piccolo Tratt. | **Newtown**	21
Pietro's Pizzeria | **multi.**	19
Pizzicato | **multi.**	20
NEW Pomodoro | **Wilming/DE**	20
Porcini | **Ctr City W**	22
Portofino | **Ctr City E**	20
Positano Coast | **Society Hill**	21
Primavera Pizza | **multi.**	18
PTG | **Roxborough**	20
Radicchio | N | **Old City**	24
Ralph's | **S Philly**	22
Rist. Il Melograno | **Doylestown**	24
Rist. La Buca | **Ctr City E**	22
Rist. Panorama | N | **Old City**	24
Rist. Pesto | **S Philly**	22
Rist. Primavera | **Wayne**	17
Z Rist. San Marco | **Ambler**	26
Roselena's | **S Philly**	21
Salento | S | **Ctr City W**	21
Saloon | **S Philly**	24
Sapori | **Collingswood/NJ**	25
Savona | **Gulph Mills**	25
Scannicchio's | **S Philly**	25
Scoogi's | **Flourtown**	19
Shank's & Evelyn's | **S Philly**	24
Sovalo | **N Liberties**	25
Spasso | **Old City**	23
Stefano's | **Hunt Vly**	19
Teca | **W Chester**	21
Teresa's Cafe | **Wayne**	22
NEW Toscana 52 | N | **Feasterville**	-
Toscana Kitchen | N | **Wilming/DE**	24
Tratt. Alberto | N | **W Chester**	21
Tratt. Primadonna | **Ctr City W**	17

Tratt. San Nicola | **multi.**	22
Tre Scalini | **S Philly**	24
Trinacria | **S | Blue Bell**	25
Tutti Toscani | **Cherry Hill/NJ**	–
Upstares/Varalli | **N | Ave of Arts**	21
Vesuvio | **S Philly**	17
☑ Vetri | **Ave of Arts**	27
Victor Café | **S Philly**	20
Viggiano's | **S | Consho**	19
Villa di Roma | **S Philly**	21
Vinny T's | **Wynnewood**	15
Zesty's | **S | Manayunk**	20

JAMAICAN

Jamaican Jerk Hut | **Ave of Arts**	20

JAPANESE

(* sushi specialist)

Aoi* | **Ctr City E**	16
NEW Asuka | **Blue Bell**	–
August Moon* | **Norristown**	23
Benihana | **Pennsauken/NJ**	20
☑ Bluefin* | **Plymouth Meeting**	26
Blue Pacific* | **King of Prussia**	21
Fuji | **Haddonfield/NJ**	26
Fuji Mtn.* | **Ctr City W**	22
Genji* | **Ctr City W**	21
Haru* | **Old City**	21
NEW Harusame | **Ardmore**	–
Hibachi* | **multi.**	18
Hikaru* | **multi.**	21
Hokka Hokka* | **Ches Hill**	20
Jasmine* | **Wilming/DE**	22
Kisso Sushi* | **Old City**	22
Koi* | **N Liberties**	23
Kotatsu | **Ardmore**	22
Lai Lai Garden* | **Blue Bell**	22
Madame Butterfly* | **Doylestown**	22
Manayunk Brew.* | **Manayunk**	18
Marg. Kuo* | **Wayne**	23
Marg. Kuo Mandarin* | **Frazer**	23
Marg. Kuo Media* | **Media**	22
Marg. Kuo Peking* | **Media**	22
Megu Sushi* | **Cherry Hill/NJ**	24
Mikado* | **Ardmore**	22
Mikado* | **multi.**	23
Mikimotos* | **Wilming/DE**	24
NEW Misso | **Ave of Arts**	–
Mizu* | **multi.**	19

☑ Morimoto | **Ctr City E**	26
Ooka* | **multi.**	25
Osaka* | **multi.**	23
Ota-Ya* | **multi.**	24
Raw Sushi* | **Ctr City E**	24
☑ Sagami* | **Collingswood/NJ**	27
Sakura Spring | **Cherry Hill/NJ**	23
Shinju Sushi* | **Ctr City E**	28
Shiroi Hana* | **Ctr City W**	23
Sushikazu* | **Blue Bell**	24
Swanky Bubbles* | **multi.**	20
Tampopo | **multi.**	22
Teikoku | **Newtown Sq**	24
Tokyo Bleu | **Cinnaminson/NJ**	21
Tokyo Hibachi | **Ctr City W**	17
Umai Umai | **Fairmount**	24
Utage* | **Wilming/DE**	24
Uzu Sushi* | **Old City**	26
NEW Yakitori Boy | **Chinatown**	22
☑ Zento* | **Old City**	26

JEWISH

Ben & Irv Deli | **Hunt Vly**	19
Famous 4th St. Deli | **South St.**	22
☑ Honey's Sit 'n Eat | **N Liberties**	25
Hymie's Deli | **Merion Sta**	17
Izzy & Zoe's | **Univ City**	15
Kibitz in City | **Ctr City E**	21
Kibitz Room | **Cherry Hill/NJ**	23

KOREAN

(* barbecue specialist)

August Moon* | **Norristown**	23
NEW Gaya* | **Blue Bell**	–
Giwa | **Ctr City W**	25
Jong Ka Jib | **E Oak Ln**	–
Koi | **N Liberties**	23
Tampopo | **multi.**	22

KOSHER

Harmony Veg. | **Chinatown**	20
Maccabeam | **Ctr City E**	18
NEW Max & David's | **Elkins Pk**	23
Singapore Kosher | **Chinatown**	19

LAOTIAN

Cafe de Laos | **S Philly**	24
Vientiane Café | **Univ City**	23

LEBANESE

Cedars | **South St.**   19

MALAYSIAN

Aqua | **Ctr City E**   19
Banana Leaf | **Chinatown**   22
Penang | **Chinatown**   22

MEDITERRANEAN

Al Dar Bistro | **Bala Cynwyd**   17
Arpeggio | **Spring House**   23
Audrey Claire | **Ctr City W**   22
Bistro Cassis | **Radnor**   20
Byblos | **Ctr City W**   16
Cafe Fresko | **Bryn Mawr**   22
Figs | **Fairmount**   23
🄴 Gibraltar | **Lancaster/LB**   27
Hamilton's | **Lambertville/NJ**   25
Little Marakesh | **Dresher**   21
NEW Max & David's | **Elkins Pk**   23
Meredith's | **Berwyn**   22
Mirna's Café | **multi.**   22
Oasis Grill | **Cherry Hill/NJ**   26
Patou | **Old City**   18
Pistachio Grille | **Maple Glen**   19
Pond | **Radnor**   21
Rest. Taquet | **Wayne**   24
🄴 Sovana Bistro | **Kennett Sq**   26
🄴 Tangerine | **Old City**   24
Valanni | **Ctr City E**   23
🄴 Water Works | **Fairmount**   21

MEXICAN

NEW Azul Cantina | **Ctr City E**   –
Baja Fresh Mex. | **multi.**   17
Cantina Caballitos/Segundos | **multi.**   21
Copabanana | **multi.**   16
Coyote Cross. | **multi.**   20
NEW Distrito | **Univ City**   –
El Azteca | **multi.**   18
NEW El Portal | **W Chester**   –
NEW El Ranchito | **N Philly**   –
El Sarape | **multi.**   23
🄴 El Vez | **Ctr City E**   21
Johnny Mañana's | **East Falls**   15
NEW José Pistola's | **Ctr City W**   16
La Cava | **Ambler**   21
La Esperanza | **Lindenwold/NJ**   22
La Lupe | **S Philly**   22

NEW Las Bugambilias | **South St.**   26
Las Cazuelas | **N Liberties**   24
La Tolteca | **Wilming/DE**   20
🄴 Lolita | **Ctr City E**   25
Los Catrines | **Ctr City W**   24
Mexican Food | **Marlton/NJ**   21
Mexican Post | **multi.**   17
🄴 Paloma | **NE Philly**   27
Qdoba | **multi.**   17
Tamarindo's | **Broad Axe**   23
Taq. La Michoacana | **Norristown**   23
Taq. La Veracruz. | **S Philly**   22
Taq. Moroleon | **Kennett Sq**   24
Taq. Puerto Veracruz. | **S Philly**   –
Tortilla Press | **Collingswood/NJ**   23
NEW Tortilla Press Cantina | **Pennsauken/NJ**   19
Xochitl | **Society Hill**   23
Zocalo | **Univ City**   20

MIDDLE EASTERN

Alyan's | **South St.**   21
Bitar's | **multi.**   23
La Pergola | **Jenkintown**   19
Maoz Veg. | **multi.**   22
Norma's | **Cherry Hill/NJ**   21

MOROCCAN

Casablanca | **multi.**   21
Fez Moroccan | **South St.**   21
Little Marakesh | **Dresher**   21
Marrakesh | **South St.**   23
Oasis Grill | **Cherry Hill/NJ**   26

NOODLE SHOPS

Nan Zhou | **Chinatown**   22
Pho 75 | **multi.**   22
🄴 Sang Kee Duck | **multi.**   25

NUEVO LATINO

🄴 Alma de Cuba | **Ctr City W**   25
Casona | **Collingswood/NJ**   22
El Serrano | **Lancaster/LB**   19

PAKISTANI

Kabobeesh | **Univ City**   23

PAN-ASIAN

Blue Pacific | **King of Prussia**   21
🄴 Buddakan | **Old City**   26

CUISINES

Jasmine | **Wilming/DE**	22
Lai Lai Garden | **Blue Bell**	22
Mantra | **Ctr City W**	19
NEW Masamoto | **Glen Mills**	27
Mikimotos | **Wilming/DE**	24
Z Nectar | **Berwyn**	26
Z Oishi | **Newtown**	26
NEW Pearl | **Ctr City W**	-
Pod | **Univ City**	23
Z Ritz Seafood | **Voorhees/NJ**	26
Susanna Foo's Kitchen | **Wayne**	21
Swanky Bubbles | **multi.**	20
Trio | **Fairmount**	22
NEW Vango | **Ctr City W**	16
Yazmin | **Warminster**	21

PAN-LATIN

Mixto | **Ctr City E**	21
Pura Vida | **N Liberties**	24

PENNSYLVANIA DUTCH

Bird-in-Hand | **Bird-in-Hand/LB**	18
Good 'N Plenty | **Smoketown/LB**	19
Miller's Smorgas. | **Ronks/LB**	18
Plain/Fancy Farm | **Bird-in-Hand/LB**	19
Shady Maple | **East Earl/LB**	19
Willow Valley | **Lancaster/LB**	19

PERSIAN

Persian Grill | **Lafayette Hill**	20

PERUVIAN

El Serrano | **Lancaster/LB**	19

PIZZA

Arpeggio | **Spring House**	23
Bella Tratt. | **Manayunk**	22
Bertolini's | **King of Prussia**	18
Calif. Pizza | **multi.**	19
Celebre's | **S Philly**	24
Gullifty's | **Rosemont**	15
Illuminare | **Fairmount**	18
Maggio's | **Southampton**	17
Mama Palma's | **Ctr City W**	23
Manayunk Brew. | **Manayunk**	18
Marra's | **S Philly**	22
Z Osteria | **N Philly**	26
Pietro's Pizzeria | **multi.**	19

Pizzicato | **Marlton/NJ**	20
Primavera Pizza | **multi.**	18
Tacconelli's | **multi.**	25

POLISH

Warsaw Cafe | **Ctr City W**	18

POLYNESIAN

Moshulu | **DE River**	22

PUB FOOD

Abbaye | **N Liberties**	22
America B&G | **multi.**	17
Black Sheep | **Ctr City W**	16
Z Chickie's/Pete's | **multi.**	18
Dark Horse | **Society Hill**	17
NEW Dock Street | **Univ City**	18
Drafting Rm. | **multi.**	18
Elephant & Castle | **multi.**	11
Fadó Irish | **Ctr City W**	15
Fergie's Pub | **Ctr City E**	17
NEW Field House | **Ctr City E**	13
Fox & Hound | **multi.**	12
Good Dog | **Ctr City W**	22
Grey Lodge | **NE Philly**	18
Gullifty's | **Rosemont**	15
Happy Rooster | **Ctr City W**	17
Inn/Hawke | **Lambertville/NJ**	19
NEW J.L. Sullivan's | **Ave of Arts**	-
K.C.'s Alley | **Ambler**	17
Kildare's | **multi.**	16
Liberties | **multi.**	14
Manayunk Brew. | **Manayunk**	18
McFadden's | **multi.**	13
McGillin's | **Ctr City E**	16
NEW Memphis Taproom | **Port Richmond**	-
Misconduct Tav. | **Ctr City W**	17
Monk's Cafe | **Ctr City W**	22
Moriarty's | **Ctr City E**	19
National Mech. | **Old City**	17
Nodding Head | **Ctr City W**	18
N. 3rd | **N Liberties**	22
P.J. Whelihan's | **multi.**	15
Plough & Stars | **Old City**	18
Pub/Penn Valley | **Narberth**	19
Rock Bottom | **King of Prussia**	16
NEW Sláinte | **Univ City**	18
Sly Fox | **multi.**	15

Z Standard Tap | N Liberties — 24
St. Stephens Green | Fairmount — 19
Teresa's Next Dr. | Wayne — 20
NEW Urban Saloon | Fairmount — 16
Victory Brewing | Downingtown — 15
Wash. St. Ale | Wilming/DE — 17
yello'bar | S Philly — 16

PUERTO RICAN

NEW Cafe Coláo | N Liberties — -

SANDWICHES

Ben & Irv Deli | Hunt Vly — 19
Campo's Deli | Old City — 22
Dalessandro's | Roxborough — 24
Geno's Steaks | S Philly — 19
Hymie's Deli | Merion Sta — 17
Isaac's | multi. — 17
Izzy & Zoe's | Univ City — 15
Jim's Steaks | multi. — 22
Z John's Roast Pork | S Philly — 27
Kibitz in City | Ctr City E — 21
Pat's Steaks | S Philly — 20
Pepper's | Ardmore — 23
Shank's & Evelyn's | S Philly — 24
Sugarfoot | Wilming/DE — 27
Teca | W Chester — 21
Z Tony Luke's | S Philly — 25

SEAFOOD

Anastasi | S Philly — 22
Athena | Glenside — 21
Barnacle Ben's | Moorestown/NJ — 20
Z Blackfish | Consho — 26
Bobby Chez | multi. — 25
Bonefish Grill | multi. — 21
Bottom of Sea | multi. — 22
Branzino | Ctr City W — 23
Bridgets | Ambler — 22
Chart House | DE River — 18
Z Chophouse | Gibbsboro/NJ — 25
Clam Tavern | Clifton Hts — 21
Creed's | King of Prussia — 23
Deep Blue | Wilming/DE — 22
Devon Seafood | Ctr City W — 23
DiNardo's | Old City — 19
Z Dmitri's | multi. — 25
Doc Magrogan | W Chester — 16
Earl's Prime | Lahaska — 24

Emerald Fish | Cherry Hill/NJ — 23
Feby's Fish. | Wilming/DE — 18
Gables | Chadds Ford — 20
Z Gibraltar | Lancaster/LB — 27
Hamilton's | Lambertville/NJ — 25
Harry's Seafood | Wilming/DE — 22
NEW Joe Pesce | multi. — 18
Laceno Italian | Voorhees/NJ — 24
Legal Sea | King of Prussia — 20
Z Little Fish | S Philly — 28
Little Tuna | Haddonfield/NJ — 21
NEW Maia | Villanova — -
Manny's | multi. — 22
Marco Polo | Elkins Pk — 19
McCormick/Schmick | multi. — 21
Z Nineteen | Ave of Arts — 23
Oceanaire | Ctr City E — 22
Old Orig. Bookbinder | Old City — 19
Palm | Ave of Arts — 23
Phila. Fish | Old City — 21
Phillips Sea. | Ctr City W — 19
Radicchio | Old City — 24
Rist. La Buca | Ctr City E — 22
Z Ritz Seafood | Voorhees/NJ — 26
Seafood Unltd. | Ctr City W — 20
Snockey's Oyster | S Philly — 18
SoleFood | Ctr City E — 21
Sotto Varalli | Ave of Arts — 21
Tai Lake | Chinatown — 24
Zinc | Ctr City E — 22

SMALL PLATES

(See also Spanish tapas specialist)
NEW Ameritage | Amer. | — -
  Wilming/DE
Ansill | Eclectic | South St. — 24
Chick's | Eclectic | South St. — 23
Z Continental, The | Eclectic | — 22
  Old City
Z Continental Mid-town | — 21
  Eclectic | Ctr City W
Derek's | Amer. | Manayunk — 19
Z Dom. Hudson | Amer. | — 24
  Wilming/DE
Elements | Amer. | — 24
  Haddon Hts/NJ
Havana | Eclectic | New Hope — 15
Honey | Amer. | Doylestown — 25
NEW J.L. Sullivan's | Amer. | — -
  Ave of Arts

Z Lacroix | French | **Ctr City W** — 28

NEW Les Bons Temps | — ⏄
Cajun/Creole | **Ctr City E**

Modo Mio | Italian | **N Liberties** — 26

Snackbar | Amer. | **Ctr City W** — 18

Stella Blu | Amer. | **W Consho** — ⏄

Teca | Italian | **W Chester** — 21

Tria | Eclectic | **multi.** — 23

Valanni | Med. | **Ctr City E** — 23

Z Water Works | Med. | — 21
Fairmount

NEW Yakitori Boy | Japanese | — 22
Chinatown

SOUL FOOD

Fatou & Fama | **Univ City** — 16

Geechee Girl | **Germantown** — 23

Ms. Tootsie's | **South St.** — 21

Warmdaddy's | **S Philly** — 20

SOUTHERN

Abner's BBQ | **Jenkintown** — 20

Carversville Inn | **Carversville** — 22

Down Home | **Ctr City E** — 18

Geechee Girl | **Germantown** — 23

Z Honey's Sit 'n Eat | **N Liberties** — 25

Jack's Firehse. | **Fairmount** — 19

Marsha Brown | **New Hope** — 20

Ms. Tootsie's | **South St.** — 21

Warmdaddy's | **S Philly** — 20

SOUTHWESTERN

Adobe Cafe | **Roxborough** — 18

Agave Grille | **Ambler** — 16

Mission Grill | **Ctr City W** — 21

SPANISH

(* tapas specialist)

Z Amada* | **Old City** — 28

Apamate* | **Ctr City W** — 23

Bar Ferdinand* | **N Liberties** — 23

Picasso | **Media** — 17

Z Tinto* | **Ctr City W** — 27

STEAKHOUSES

Z Barclay Prime | **Ctr City W** — 26

Blue Eyes | **Sewell/NJ** — 21

Bonefish Grill | **multi.** — 21

Bridgets | **Ambler** — 22

Z Capital Grille | **Ave of Arts** — 26

NEW Chima | **Ctr City W** — ⏄

Z Chophouse | **Gibbsboro/NJ** — 25

Chops | **Bala Cynwyd** — 19

Conley Ward's | **Wilming/DE** — 17

Creed's | **King of Prussia** — 23

Davio's | **Ctr City W** — 23

Delmonico's | **Wynnefield** — 20

Earl's Prime | **Lahaska** — 24

Fleming's Prime | **Wayne** — 25

Z Fogo de Chão | **Ave of Arts** — 23

Hibachi | **multi.** — 18
Brandywine | **Chadds Ford** — 20

Z Morton's | **multi.** — 25

Newtown Grill | **Newtown Sq** — 21

Palm | **Ave of Arts** — 23

NEW Pietro's Prime | **W Chester** — 24

Prime Rib | **Ctr City W** — 25

Pub | **Pennsauken/NJ** — 21

Ruth's Chris | **multi.** — 23

Saloon | **S Philly** — 24

Seven Stars Inn | **Phoenixville** — 23

Smith/Wollensky | **Ctr City W** — 22

Spamps | **Consho** — 17

Sullivan's Steak | **multi.** — 23

NEW Table 31 | **Ctr City W** — ⏄

Ted's Montana | **multi.** — 16

Walter's Steak. | **Wilming/DE** — 27

NEW William Douglas | — ⏄
Cherry Hill/NJ

TAIWANESE

Ray's Cafe | **Chinatown** — 25

TEAROOMS

Cassatt Tea Rm. | **Ctr City W** — 23

Ray's Cafe | **Chinatown** — 25

TEX-MEX

Tex Mex Connect. | **N Wales** — 20

THAI

Alisa Cafe | **Cherry Hill/NJ** — 22

NEW Aloe Fusion | **Cherry Hill/NJ** — ⏄

Aqua | **Ctr City E** — 19

Cafe de Laos | **S Philly** — 24

Chabaa Thai | **Manayunk** — 25

Chiangmai | **Consho** — 25

La Na | **Media** — 21

Lemon Grass | **multi.** — 22

My Thai | **Ctr City W** — 18

Nan | **Univ City** 25
Pattaya | **Univ City** 19
Penang | **Chinatown** 22
Pho Thai Nam | **Blue Bell** 21
Siam | **Lambertville/NJ** 22
Siam Cuisine | **multi.** 22
Siam Cuisine/Black | **Doylestown** 23
Silk Cuisine | **Bryn Mawr** 23
Siri's | **Cherry Hill/NJ** 25
Somsak/Taan | **Voorhees/NJ** 25
NEW Sweet Basil | **Chadds Ford** 21
Teikoku | **Newtown Sq** 24
Thai L'Elephant | **Phoenixville** 23
Thai Orchid | **Blue Bell** 25
Thai Pepper | **Ardmore** 19
Thai Singha | **Univ City** 19
Vientiane Café | **Univ City** 23
White Elephant | **Hunt Vly** 22

TURKISH

Divan | **S Philly** 21
Konak | **Old City** 20

VEGETARIAN

(* vegan)
AllWays Café | **Hunt Vly** 22
Z Blue Sage | **Southampton** 27

Full Plate* | **N Liberties** 21
Harmony Veg.* | **Chinatown** 20
Horizons* | **South St.** 26
Kingdom of Veg.* | **Chinatown** 19
Maoz Veg. | **multi.** 22
New Samosa | **Ctr City E** 16
Singapore Kosher | **Chinatown** 19
Winnie's Le Bus | **Manayunk** 21

VENEZUELAN

Sazon | **N Philly** 21

VIETNAMESE

Ha Long Bay | **Bryn Mawr** 22
La Vang | **Willow Grove** 22
Nam Phuong | **S Philly** 24
Pho 75 | **multi.** 22
Pho Thai Nam | **Blue Bell** 21
Pho Xe Lua | **Chinatown** 24
NEW Savor Saigon | **Levittown** 21
Z Vietnam | **Chinatown** 25
NEW Vietnam Café | **W Philly** 23
Vietnam Palace | **Chinatown** 23

WEST AFRICAN

Fatou & Fama | **Univ City** 16

Locations

Includes restaurant names, cuisines, Food ratings and, for locations that are mapped, top list and map coordinates. ⚡ indicates places with the highest ratings, popularity and importance.

Philadelphia

AVENUE OF THE ARTS

(See map on page 206)

TOP FOOD

Vetri	*Italian*	**G7**	27
Capital Grille	*Steak*	**E7**	26
Naked Choco.	*Dessert*	**F7**	25
Morton's	*Steak*	**F7**	25
Bobby Chez	*Seafood*	**I7**	25
Estia	*Greek*	**F7**	23
Palm	*Steak*	**F7**	23
Ruth's Chris	*Steak*	**G7**	23
Nineteen	*Amer./Seafood*	**F7**	23
Fogo de Chão	*Brazilian*	**E7**	23

LISTING

Bliss	*Amer.*	22
Bonté Wafflerie	*Coffee*	19
Italian Bistro	*Italian*	16
Jamaican Jerk Hut	*Jamaican*	20
NEW J.L. Sullivan's	*Pub*	–
Marathon Grill	*Amer.*	18
McCormick/Schmick	*Seafood*	21
NEW Misso	*Japanese*	–
Passage/India	*Indian*	19
Sotto Varalli	*Seafood*	21
Ted's Montana	*Steak*	16
NEW 10 Arts	*Amer.*	–
Upstares/Varalli	*Italian*	21

CENTER CITY EAST
(EAST OF BROAD ST.)

(See map on page 206)

TOP FOOD

Morimoto	*Japanese*	**E11**	26
Mercato	*Amer./Italian*	**G8**	26
Lolita	*Mex.*	**E7**	25
Raw Sushi	*Japanese*	**F8**	24
Reading Term. Mkt.	*Eclectic*	**D8**	23
Tria	*Eclectic*	**G8**	23
Valanni	*Med.*	**G8**	23
Maoz Veg.	*Mideast.*	**F8**	22
Rist. La Buca	*Italian*	**F11**	22
Tampopo	*Japanese/Korean*	**F11**	22

LISTING

Aoi	*Japanese*	16
NEW Apothecary	*Amer.*	–
Aqua	*Malaysian/Thai*	19
NEW Azul Cantina	*Mex.*	–
NEW Bindi	*Indian*	22
Bonté Wafflerie	*Coffee*	19
Brew HaHa!	*Coffee*	18
Caffe Valentino	*Italian*	19
Caribou Cafe	*French*	19
Down Home	*Southern*	18
Effie's	*Greek*	21
El Azteca	*Mex.*	18
⚡ El Vez	*Mex.*	21
Fergie's Pub	*Pub*	17
NEW Field House	*Amer.*	13
Hard Rock	*Amer.*	14
NEW Joe Pesce	*Italian/Seafood*	18
Jones	*Amer.*	20
NEW Kanella	*Greek*	–
Kibitz in City	*Deli*	21
NEW Knock	*Amer.*	19
LaScala's	*Italian*	20
NEW Les Bons Temps	*Cajun/Creole*	–
Maccabeam	*Indian*	18
⚡ Maggiano's	*Italian*	20
Marathon Grill	*Amer.*	18
McGillin's	*Pub*	16
Melting Pot	*Fondue*	20
NEW Minar Palace	*Indian*	–
Mixto	*Pan-Latin*	21
More Than Ice Crm.	*Dessert*	20
Moriarty's	*Pub*	19
New Samosa	*Indian*	16
Oceanaire	*Seafood*	22
Palace/Ben	*Indian*	21
Portofino	*Italian*	20
⚡ Sang Kee Duck	*Chinese*	25
Shinju Sushi	*Japanese*	28
SoleFood	*Seafood*	21
10th St. Pour House	*Amer.*	21
NEW Time	*Continental*	–

subscribe to ZAGAT.com

LOCATIONS

Ⓩ Susanna Foo | *Chinese/French*	24
NEW Table 31 | *Steak*	-
Tampopo | *Japanese/Korean*	22
Tavern 17 | *Amer.*	18
Ten Stone | *Amer.*	18
Tír na nÓg | *Pub*	14
Tokyo Hibachi | *Japanese*	17
Tratt. Primadonna | *Italian*	17
Tria | *Eclectic*	23
Twenty Manning | *Amer.*	22
NEW Vango | *Pan-Asian*	16
Warsaw Cafe | *Polish*	18

CHINATOWN

(See map on page 206)

TOP FOOD

Sang Kee Duck | *Chinese* | **B10**	25
Shiao Lan Kung | *Chinese* | **C9**	25
Vietnam | *Viet.* | **B9**	25
Lee How Fook | *Chinese* | **B9**	24
Pho Xe Lua | *Viet.* | **C10**	24
Rangoon | *Burmese* | **C10**	24
Charles Plaza | *Chinese* | **B9**	23
Vietnam Palace | *Viet.* | **B9**	23
Penang | *Malaysian* | **C9**	22
Nan Zhou | *Noodles* | **B9**	22

LISTING

Banana Leaf | *Malaysian*	22
Four Rivers | *Chinese*	24
Harmony Veg. | *Chinese*	20
H.K. Gold. Phoenix | *Chinese*	20
Imperial Inn | *Chinese*	20
Joy Tsin Lau | *Chinese*	20
Kingdom of Veg. | *Chinese*	19
Ly Michael's | *Asian Fusion*	21
Ocean Harbor | *Chinese*	20
Pho 75 | *Viet.*	22
Ray's Cafe | *Chinese*	25
Siam Cuisine | *Thai*	22
Singapore Kosher | *Chinese*	19
Tai Lake | *Chinese*	24
NEW Yakitori Boy | *Japanese*	22
NEW Zhi Wei Guan | *Chinese*	-

DELAWARE RIVERFRONT

Chart House | *Seafood*	18
Dave & Buster's | *Amer.*	13
Hibachi | *Japanese*	18
La Veranda | *Italian*	23
Moshulu | *Amer.*	22

EAST FALLS/ MANAYUNK/ ROXBOROUGH

Adobe Cafe | *SW*	18
Bella Tratt. | *Italian*	22
Bourbon Blue | *Cajun/Creole*	19
Chabaa Thai | *Thai*	25
Dalessandro's | *Cheese Stks.*	24
Derek's | *Amer.*	19
Franco's Tratt. | *Italian*	20
Hikaru | *Japanese*	21
Il Tartufo | *Italian*	23
Jake's | *Amer.*	25
Johnny Mañana's | *Mex.*	15
Kildare's | *Pub*	16
La Colombe | *Coffee*	23
Liberties | *Pub*	14
Manayunk Brew. | *Pub*	18
Maria's/Summit | *Italian*	21
PTG | *Italian*	20
Thomas' | *Eclectic*	-
Winnie's Le Bus | *Amer.*	21
Zesty's | *Greek/Italian*	20

FAIRMOUNT

NEW Belgian Café | *Belgian*	15
Bridgid's | *Eclectic*	21
Figs | *Med.*	23
Illuminare | *Italian*	18
Jack's Firehse. | *Southern*	19
Little Pete's | *Diner*	16
L'Oca | *Italian*	23
London Grill | *Amer.*	18
Museum Rest. | *Amer.*	19
Rembrandt's | *Amer.*	20
Rose Tattoo | *Amer.*	22
Sabrina's Café | *Eclectic*	25
St. Stephens Green | *Irish*	19
Trio | *Pan-Asian*	22
Umai Umai | *Asian Fusion*	24
NEW Urban Saloon | *Pub*	16
Ⓩ Water Works | *Med.*	21
Zorba's Taverna | *Greek*	20

FISHTOWN

Bistro Juliana | *Italian*	23
Ida Mae's | *Amer./Irish*	22
Johnny Brenda's | *Amer./Eclectic*	21

NORTHEAST PHILLY

Z Chickie's/Pete's | *Pub*	18
Copabanana | *Amer./Mex.*	16
Dave & Buster's | *Amer.*	13
El Azteca | *Mex.*	18
Grey Lodge | *Pub*	18
Italian Bistro | *Italian*	16
Jim's Steaks | *Cheese Stks.*	22
Mayfair Diner | *Diner*	15
Moonstruck | *Italian*	21
Nifty Fifty's | *Diner*	19
Z Paloma | *French/Mex.*	27
Pho 75 | *Viet.*	22
Rylei | *Amer.*	24
Steve's Prince/Stks. | *Cheese Stks.*	24
Sweet Lucy's | *BBQ*	21

NORTHERN LIBERTIES

(See map on page 205)

TOP FOOD

Tiffin Store | *Indian* | **A1**	26
Modo Mio | *Italian* | **A3**	26
Honey's Sit 'n Eat | *Jewish/Southern* | **D1**	25
Sovalo | *Calif./Italian* | **D2**	25
Standard Tap | *Amer.* | **C2**	24
Las Cazuelas | *Mex.* | **A1**	24
Il Cantuccio | *Italian* | **D2**	23
Bar Ferdinand | *Spanish* | **B2**	23
N. 3rd | *Amer.* | **D2**	22
Abbaye | *Belgian* | **D2**	22

LISTING

NEW Cafe Coláo | *Puerto Rican*	–
NEW Café Estelle | *Amer.*	–
Cantina Caballitos/Segundos | *Mex.*	21
Copper Bistro | *Amer.*	22
Full Plate | *Eclectic*	21
Koi | *Japanese/Korean*	23
Liberties | *Pub*	14
McFadden's | *Pub*	13
Ortlieb's Jazz | *Cajun*	–
Pura Vida | *Pan-Latin*	24
Silk City | *Amer.*	20
NEW Swallow | *Euro.*	–

NORTH PHILLY

NEW El Ranchito | *Mex.*	–
Jong Ka Jib | *Korean*	–
Z Osteria | *Italian*	26

Qdoba | *Mex.*	17
Sazon | *Venez.*	21
Tierra Colombiana | *Colombian/Cuban*	22

NORTHWEST PHILLY

(Chestnut Hill/
Germantown/Mt. Airy)

Bitar's | *Mideast.*	23
Bocelli | *Italian*	–
Cafette | *Eclectic*	20
NEW Cake | *Bakery*	21
Chestnut Grill | *Amer.*	17
CinCin | *Chinese*	24
Z Citrus | *Eclectic*	25
Cresheim Cottage | *Amer.*	18
Dahlak | *Eritrean*	22
Geechee Girl | *Southern*	23
Hokka Hokka | *Japanese*	20
Manny's | *Seafood*	22
Melting Pot | *Fondue*	20
North by NW | *Amer.*	16
Osaka | *Japanese*	23
Rib Crib | *BBQ*	22
Roller's/Flying Fish | *Eclectic*	21
Solaris Grille | *Amer.*	16
Z Tiffin Store | *Indian*	26
Trolley Car | *Diner*	14
Umbria | *Eclectic*	24

OLD CITY

(See map on page 205)

TOP FOOD

Amada | *Spanish* | **J2**	28
Buddakan | *Pan-Asian* | **J1**	26
Zento | *Japanese* | **J3**	26
Chlöe | *Amer.* | **I2**	25
Radicchio | *Italian* | **G1**	24
Tangerine | *Med.* | **J2**	24
Bistro 7 | *Amer.* | **J2**	24
La Famiglia | *Italian* | **J3**	24
Fork | *Amer.* | **J2**	24
Rist. Panorama | *Italian* | **I3**	24

LISTING

Anjou | *Asian Fusion*	19
Ariana | *Afghan*	20
NEW Beneluxx | *Belgian*	20
Cafe Spice | *Indian*	20
Campo's Deli | *Cheese Stks.*	22
Cebu | *Eclectic*	–

City Tavern | *Amer.* 19
☑ Continental, The | *Eclectic* 22
☑ Cuba Libre | *Cuban* 21
DiNardo's | *Seafood* 19
Dolce | *Italian* 21
Eulogy Belgian | *Belgian* 18
Farmicia | *Continental* 20
Haru | *Japanese* 21
Kabul | *Afghan* 22
Karma | *Indian* 23
Kisso Sushi | *Japanese* 22
Konak | *Turkish* 20
La Locanda | *Italian* 23
Mexican Post | *Mex.* 17
Mizu | *Japanese* 19
National Mech. | *Pub* 17
Old Orig. Bookbinder | 19
  Seafood
Paradigm | *Amer.* 18
Patou | *French/Med.* 18
Phila. Fish | *Seafood* 21
Pizzicato | *Italian* 20
Plough & Stars | *Pub* 18
Sassafras Int'l | *Eclectic* –
Serrano | *Eclectic* 20
Society Hill Hotel | *Amer.* 18
Spasso | *Italian* 23
Swanky Bubbles | *Pan-Asian* 20
Triumph Brewing | *Amer.* 19
Uzu Sushi | *Japanese* 26

PORT RICHMOND

🆕 Memphis Taproom | *Pub* –
Mercer Café | *Amer./Italian* 26
Tacconelli's | *Pizza* 25

QUEEN VILLAGE/ SOCIETY HILL/ SOUTH ST.

(See map on page 208)

TOP FOOD

Horizons | *Vegan* | **F1** 26
Gayle | *Amer.* | **F5** 25
Dmitri's | *Greek* | **I5** 25
Django | *Euro.* | **F4** 25
Cochon | *French* | **I2** 24
Ansill | *Eclectic* | **G5** 24
Ava | *Italian* | **F5** 24
Latest Dish | *Amer.* | **F4** 24
Beau Monde | *French* | **G2** 23

Xochitl | *Mex.* | **D6** 23
Supper | *Amer.* | **F1** 23
Chick's | *Eclectic* | **F1** 23
Marrakesh | *Moroccan* | **F4** 23
Mustard Greens | *Chinese* | **F6** 21
Bistro Romano | *Italian* | **E7** 21
Positano Coast | *Italian* | **A6** 21
ZoT | *Belgian* | **E7** 20
New Wave | *Amer.* | **I5** 18

LISTING

Alyan's | *Mideast.* 21
Bottom of Sea | *Seafood* 22
Bridget Foy's | *Amer.* 19
Cedars | *Lebanese* 19
Copabanana | *Amer./Mex.* 16
Coquette | *French* 18
Core De Roma | *Italian* 23
Dark Horse | *Pub* 17
Famous 4th St. Deli | *Deli* 22
Fez Moroccan | *Moroccan* 21
Gnocchi | *Italian* 22
Hikaru | *Japanese* 21
Hostaria Da Elio | *Italian* 20
Jim's Steaks | *Cheese Stks.* 22
Kildare's | *Pub* 16
🆕 Las Bugambilias | *Mex.* 26
Maoz Veg. | *Mideast.* 22
Ms. Tootsie's | *Soul Food* 21
Pietro's Pizzeria | *Pizza* 19
Pink Rose | *Bakery* 21
South St. Souvlaki | *Greek* 21
Southwark | *Amer.* 22
🆕 Zahav | *Israeli* –

SOUTH PHILLY

Anastasi | *Seafood* 22
August | *Italian* 26
Bitar's | *Mideast.* 23
☑ Bomb Bomb BBQ | *BBQ* 23
Cafe de Laos | *Laotian/Thai* 24
Caffe Valentino | *Italian* 19
Cantina Caballitos/Segundos | 21
  Mex.
Carman's Country | *Eclectic* 25
Celebre's | *Pizza* 24
Chiarella's | *Italian* 19
☑ Chickie's/Pete's | *Pub* 18
Criniti | *Italian* 19
Cucina Forte | *Italian* 24

Dante & Luigi's	*Italian*	23
NEW Devil's Den	*Amer.*	-
Divan	*Turkish*	21
Franco's HighNote	*Italian*	23
Geno's Steaks	*Cheese Stks.*	19
James	*Amer.*	25
Z John's Roast Pork	*Sandwiches*	27
Kristian's	*Italian*	25
La Lupe	*Mex.*	22
Z L'Angolo	*Italian*	26
NEW Le Virtù	*Italian*	26
Z Little Fish	*Seafood*	28
Mamma Maria	*Italian*	22
Marra's	*Italian*	22
McFadden's	*Pub*	13
Melrose Diner	*Diner*	16
Mezza Luna	*Italian*	21
Mio Sogno	*Italian*	23
Morning Glory	*Diner*	24
Mr. Martino's	*Italian*	22
Nam Phuong	*Viet.*	24
NEW Nicholas	*Amer.*	-
Paradiso	*Italian*	23
Pat's Steaks	*Cheese Stks.*	20
NEW Peppercorns	*Amer.*	-
Pho 75	*Viet.*	22
Ralph's	*Italian*	22
Rist. Pesto	*Italian*	22
Roselena's	*Italian*	21
Royal Tavern	*Amer.*	23
Sabrina's Café	*Eclectic*	25
Saloon	*Italian/Steak*	24
Salt & Pepper	*Amer.*	23
Scannicchio's	*Italian*	25
Shank's & Evelyn's	*Italian*	24
Sidecar	*Eclectic*	19
Snockey's Oyster	*Seafood*	18
Taq. La Veracruz.	*Mex.*	22
Taq. Puerto Veracruz.	*Mex.*	-
Z Tony Luke's	*Cheese Stks.*	25
Tre Scalini	*Italian*	24
NEW Ugly American	*Amer.*	19
Vesuvio	*Italian*	17
Victor Café	*Italian*	20
Villa di Roma	*Italian*	21
Warmdaddy's	*Soul Food*	20
yello'bar	*Amer.*	16

UNIVERSITY CITY

Abbraccio	*Italian*	13
Abyssinia	*Ethiopian*	24
Beijing	*Chinese*	16
Copabanana	*Amer./Mex.*	16
Dahlak	*Eritrean*	22
NEW Distrito	*Mex.*	-
NEW Dock Street	*Pub*	18
Ecco Qui	*Italian*	17
Fatou & Fama	*African/Soul Food*	16
Izzy & Zoe's	*Deli*	15
Kabobeesh	*Pakistani*	23
La Terrasse	*Amer./French*	18
Lemon Grass	*Thai*	22
Marathon Grill	*Amer.*	18
Marigold Kitchen	*Amer.*	24
Mizu	*Japanese*	19
Nan	*French/Thai*	25
New Delhi	*Indian*	20
Pattaya	*Thai*	19
Penne	*Italian*	18
Pod	*Pan-Asian*	23
Qdoba	*Mex.*	17
Rae	*Amer.*	22
Rx	*Eclectic*	23
Sitar India	*Indian*	20
NEW Sláinte	*Pub*	18
Tandoor India	*Indian*	20
Thai Singha	*Thai*	19
Vientiane Café	*Laotian/Thai*	23
Z White Dog	*Eclectic*	21
World Café	*Amer.*	14
Zocalo	*Mex.*	20

WEST PHILLY

Bottom of Sea	*Seafood*	22
Jim's Steaks	*Cheese Stks.*	22
NEW Vietnam Café	*Viet.*	23

WYNNEFIELD

Calif. Pizza	*Pizza*	19
Casablanca	*Moroccan*	21
Chun Hing	*Chinese*	22
Delmonico's	*Steak*	20

Philadelphia Suburbs

BUCKS COUNTY

Z Bella Tori	*Italian*	19
Z Blue Sage	*Veg.*	27

LOCATIONS

Brick Hotel | *Amer.*	18
🅩 Bridgetown Mill | *Amer.*	25
Carversville Inn | *Southern*	22
Casablanca | *Moroccan*	21
Centre Bridge | *Amer.*	19
Cheeseburger/Paradise | *Burgers*	15
Cock 'n Bull | *Amer.*	17
Cuttalossa Inn | *Amer.*	16
Duck Sauce | *Chinese*	25
Earl's Prime | *Seafood/Steak*	24
El Sarape | *Mex.*	23
Five Guys | *Burgers*	22
Freight House | *Amer.*	19
Golden Pheasant | *French*	23
Havana | *Amer./Eclectic*	15
Honey | *Amer.*	25
Hotel du Village | *French*	22
Inn/Phillips Mill | *French*	24
Isaac Newton's | *Amer.*	16
J.B. Dawson's/Austin's | *Amer.*	18
King George II | *Amer.*	21
Knight House | *Amer.*	21
🅩 La Bonne Auberge | *French*	27
Landing | *Amer.*	16
Liberties | *Pub*	14
Madame Butterfly | *Japanese*	22
Maggio's | *Italian/Pizza*	17
Marsha Brown | *Creole/Southern*	20
Mother's | *Amer.*	18
Nifty Fifty's | *Diner*	19
🅩 Oishi | *Pan-Asian*	26
Ooka | *Japanese*	25
Ota-Ya | *Japanese*	24
🅩 P.F. Chang's | *Chinese*	21
Piccolo Tratt. | *Italian*	21
Plumsteadville Inn | *Amer.*	19
Rist. Il Melograno | *Italian*	24
Rouget | *Amer.*	-
NEW Savor Saigon | *Viet.*	21
Siam Cuisine | *Thai*	22
Siam Cuisine/Black | *French/Thai*	23
Slate Bleu | *French*	22
Spotted Hog | *Amer.*	17
Steve's Prince/Stks. | *Cheese Stks.*	24
Summer Kitchen | *Eclectic*	23
Ted's Montana | *Steak*	16
NEW Tennessee's BBQ | *BBQ*	-
NEW Toscana 52 | *Italian*	-

Triumph Brewing | *Amer.*	19
Wash. Cross. | *Amer.*	17
Yardley Inn | *Amer.*	21
Yazmin | *Pan-Asian*	21

CHESTER COUNTY

America B&G | *Amer.*	17
Avalon | *Italian*	21
🅩 Birchrunville Store | *French/Italian*	28
NEW Blue Pear | *Amer.*	22
Bonefish Grill | *Seafood*	21
Buca di Beppo | *Italian*	15
Butterfish | *Amer.*	25
Catherine's | *Amer.*	24
Coyote Cross. | *Mex.*	20
Dilworth. Inn | *Amer.*	25
Doc Magrogan | *Seafood*	16
Drafting Rm. | *Amer.*	18
🅩 Duling-Kurtz | *Continental*	25
NEW El Portal | *Mex.*	-
Epicurean | *Amer.*	21
Four Dogs | *Amer.*	18
🅩 Gilmore's | *French*	28
Half Moon | *Amer.*	20
High St. Caffé | *Cajun/Creole*	24
Inn/St. Peter's | *French*	-
Iron Hill | *Amer.*	18
Isaac's | *Deli*	17
Kildare's | *Pub*	16
🅩 Kimberton Inn | *Amer.*	25
Majolica | *Amer.*	26
Marg. Kuo Mandarin | *Chinese/Japanese*	23
Mendenhall Inn | *Amer.*	21
Mimosa | *Eclectic*	24
Orchard | *Amer.*	-
NEW Pietro's Prime | *Steak*	24
Seven Stars Inn | *Continental*	23
Simon Pearce | *Amer.*	20
Sly Fox | *Pub*	15
🅩 Sovana Bistro | *French/Med.*	26
Spence Cafe | *Eclectic*	23
NEW Station Bistro | *Amer.*	-
🅩 Talula's Table | *Euro.*	26
Taq. Moroleon | *Mex.*	24
Teca | *Italian*	21
Thai L'Elephant | *Thai*	23
Tratt. Alberto | *Italian*	21

Twin Bays	*Eclectic*	24
Vincent's	*Continental*	16
Whip Tavern	*Pub*	20

DELAWARE COUNTY

America B&G	*Amer.*	17
Z NEW Azie	*Asian Fusion*	24
Baja Fresh Mex.	*Mex.*	17
Big Fork	*Amer.*	21
Bobby Chez	*Seafood*	25
Bona Cucina	*Italian*	25
Bonefish Grill	*Seafood*	21
Charlie's Hamburgers	*Burgers*	24
Clam Tavern	*Seafood*	21
Fellini Cafe	*Italian*	21
Five Guys	*Burgers*	22
Gables	*Amer.*	20
Hank's Place	*Diner*	19
Hibachi	*Japanese*	18
Iron Hill	*Amer.*	18
J.B. Dawson's/Austin's	*Amer.*	18
Jim's Steaks	*Cheese Stks.*	22
La Belle Epoque	*French*	19
La Na	*French/Thai*	21
Marg. Kuo Media	*Chinese/Japanese*	22
Marg. Kuo Peking	*Chinese/Japanese*	22
NEW Masamoto	*Pan-Asian*	27
Brandywine	*Steak*	20
Newtown Grill	*Italian/Steak*	21
Nifty Fifty's	*Diner*	19
Pace One	*Amer.*	21
Z P.F. Chang's	*Chinese*	21
Picasso	*Italian/Spanish*	17
Qdoba	*Mex.*	17
Rose Tree Inn	*Amer.*	22
Roux 3	*Amer.*	21
Ruby's	*Diner*	16
NEW Sweet Basil	*Thai*	21
Teikoku	*Japanese/Thai*	24

KING OF PRUSSIA

Bahama Breeze	*Carib.*	17
Baja Fresh Mex.	*Mex.*	17
Bertolini's	*Italian*	18
Blue Pacific	*Pan-Asian*	21
California Cafe	*Calif.*	20
Calif. Pizza	*Pizza*	19

Z Cheesecake Fact.	*Amer.*	20
Creed's	*Seafood/Steak*	23
Fox & Hound	*Pub*	12
Kildare's	*Pub*	16
Legal Sea	*Seafood*	20
Lemon Grass	*Thai*	22
Z Maggiano's	*Italian*	20
Melting Pot	*Fondue*	20
Z Morton's	*Steak*	25
Rock Bottom	*Pub*	16
Ruby's	*Diner*	16
Ruth's Chris	*Steak*	23
Sullivan's Steak	*Steak*	23

MAIN LINE

Al Dar Bistro	*Med.*	17
Ardmore Station	*Diner*	19
August Moon	*Japanese/Korean*	23
NEW Auspicious	*Chinese*	19
Basil Bistro	*Amer.*	18
Bistro Cassis	*French/Med.*	20
Blush	*Eclectic*	20
Bunha Faun	*Asian/French*	25
Cafe Fresko	*Med.*	22
Carmine's Creole	*Cajun/Creole*	22
Cedar Hollow	*Amer.*	20
Chef Charin	*Continental*	20
Chops	*Steak*	19
Christopher's	*Amer.*	17
Cosimo	*Amer.*	22
Fellini Cafe	*Italian*	21
Fioravanti	*Continental*	26
Five Guys	*Burgers*	22
Fleming's Prime	*Steak*	25
Gen. Warren	*Amer.*	25
Georges'	*Eclectic*	20
Gullifty's	*Amer.*	15
Ha Long Bay	*Viet.*	22
NEW Harusame	*Japanese*	-
Hibachi	*Japanese*	18
Hunan	*Chinese*	21
Hymie's Deli	*Deli*	17
Jasper	*Amer.*	25
Khajuraho	*Indian*	21
Kotatsu	*Japanese*	22
La Collina	*Italian*	23
Lourdas Greek	*Greek*	21
NEW Maia	*Euro.*	-
Manny's	*Seafood*	22

LOCATIONS

Marg. Kuo | *Chinese/Japanese*	23
Margot | *Amer./Eclectic*	20
Max & Erma's | *Amer.*	15
Meridith's | *Eclectic/Med.*	22
Mikado | *Japanese*	22
Murray's Deli | *Deli*	19
NEW Murray's Deli/bistro M | *Deli*	19
Z Nectar | *Pan-Asian*	26
New Tavern | *Amer.*	16
Old Guard Hse. | *Amer.*	23
Olive Tree | *Greek*	23
Osaka | *Japanese*	23
Pepper's | *Italian*	23
Plate | *Amer.*	16
Pond | *French/Med.*	21
Primavera Pizza | *Pizza*	18
Pub/Penn Valley | *Eclectic*	19
Qdoba | *Mex.*	17
Z Rest. Alba | *Amer.*	27
Rest. Taquet | *French/Med.*	24
Rist. Primavera | *Italian*	17
Ruby's | *Diner*	16
Sang Kee Asian | *Chinese*	24
Savona | *French/Italian*	25
Shangrila | *Asian Fusion*	20
Silk Cuisine | *Thai*	23
Z Sola | *Amer.*	27
Susanna Foo's Kitchen | *Pan-Asian*	21
Tango | *Amer.*	20
Taq. La Michoacana | *Mex.*	23
Teresa's Cafe | *Italian*	22
Teresa's Next Dr. | *Belgian*	20
Thai Pepper | *Thai*	19
333 Belrose | *Amer.*	23
Tratt. San Nicola | *Italian*	22
Victory Brewing | *Pub*	15
Vinny T's | *Italian*	15
Winberie's | *Amer.*	16
Wooden Iron | *Amer.*	18
Z Yangming | *Chinese/Continental*	25

MONTGOMERY COUNTY

Abacus | *Chinese*	24
Abner's BBQ | *BBQ*	20
Agave Grille | *SW*	16
Z Alison/Blue Bell | *Amer.*	26
AllWays Café | *Eclectic*	22
Arpeggio | *Italian/Med.*	23

NEW Asuka | *Japanese*	-
Athena | *Greek/Seafood*	21
Baja Fresh Mex. | *Mex.*	17
Bay Pony Inn | *Amer.*	19
Beige & Beige | *Eclectic*	20
Ben & Irv Deli | *Deli*	19
Bensí | *Italian*	18
Z Blackfish | *Seafood*	26
Blue Bell Inn | *Amer.*	21
Z Bluefin | *Japanese*	26
Blue Horse | *Amer.*	17
Bocelli | *Italian*	-
Bonefish Grill | *Seafood*	21
Brasserie 73 | *French*	22
Bridgets | *Amer./Steak*	22
Buca di Beppo | *Italian*	15
NEW Buona Via | *Italian*	19
Cafe Preeya | *Eclectic*	21
Calif. Pizza | *Pizza*	19
Carambola | *Amer.*	23
Z Cheesecake Fact. | *Amer.*	20
Chiangmai | *Thai*	25
Coleman | *Amer.*	20
Coyote Cross. | *Mex.*	20
NEW Cravings | *Amer.*	21
Drafting Rm. | *Amer.*	18
El Sarape | *Mex.*	23
Fayette St. | *Amer.*	23
Fountain Side | *Amer./Italian*	19
Funky Lil' Kitchen | *Amer.*	23
FuziOn | *Asian Fusion*	23
NEW Gaya | *Korean*	-
Gen. Lafayette | *Amer.*	15
Gypsy Saloon | *Amer./Italian*	22
Hibachi | *Japanese*	18
Iron Hill | *Amer.*	18
J.B. Dawson's/Austin's | *Amer.*	18
Jonathan's | *Amer.*	17
Joseph Ambler | *Amer.*	23
K.C.'s Alley | *Pub*	17
La Cava | *Mex.*	21
Lai Lai Garden | *Pan-Asian*	22
La Pergola | *Mideast.*	19
La Vang | *French/Viet.*	22
Little Marakesh | *Moroccan*	21
Mainland Inn | *Amer.*	26
Mandarin Gdn. | *Chinese*	20
Marco Polo | *Italian*	19

NEW Max & David's | *Med.*	23
Max & Erma's | *Amer.*	15
Mirna's Café | *Eclectic/Med.*	22
Ooka | *Japanese*	25
Otto's Brauhaus | *German*	20
Palace of Asia | *Indian*	24
Parc Bistro | *Amer.*	25
Persian Grill | *Persian*	20
Z P.F. Chang's | *Chinese*	21
Pho Thai Nam | *Thai/Viet.*	21
Pistachio Grille | *Amer./Med.*	19
P.J. Whelihan's | *Pub*	15
Redstone | *Amer.*	21
Z Rist. San Marco | *Italian*	26
Scoogi's | *Italian*	19
Shanachie | *Indian*	17
Shula's 347 | *Amer.*	21
Sly Fox | *Pub*	15
Spamps | *Eclectic/Steak*	17
Spring Mill | *French*	23
Stefano's | *Italian*	19
Stella Blu | *Amer.*	-
Sushikazu | *Japanese*	24
Tamarindo's | *Mex.*	23
Tex Mex Connect. | *Tex-Mex*	20
Thai Orchid | *Thai*	25
Totaro's | *Eclectic*	24
Trax Café | *Amer.*	23
Trinacria | *Italian*	25
211 York | *Amer.*	22
Viggiano's | *Italian*	19
White Elephant | *Thai*	22
William Penn | *Amer./Continental*	22
NEW Yalda Grill | *Afghan*	20
NEW Zacharias | *Amer.*	21
Zakes Cafe | *Amer.*	23

Lancaster/ Berks Counties

ADAMSTOWN

Stoudt's | *Amer.*	18

BIRD-IN-HAND

Bird-in-Hand | *PA Dutch*	18
Plain/Fancy Farm | *PA Dutch*	19

EAST EARL

Shady Maple | *PA Dutch*	19

EAST PETERSBURG

Haydn Zug's | *Amer.*	18

EPHRATA

Isaac's | *Deli*	17
Z Lily's on Main | *Amer.*	24
Rest./Doneckers | *Amer.*	19

LANCASTER

Carr's | *Amer.*	25
El Serrano | *Nuevo Latino*	19
Five Guys | *Burgers*	22
Z Gibraltar | *Med./Seafood*	27
Iron Hill | *Amer.*	18
Isaac's | *Deli*	17
J.B. Dawson's/Austin's | *Amer.*	18
Lemon Grass | *Thai*	22
Qdoba | *Mex.*	17
Willow Valley | *PA Dutch*	19

LEOLA

Mazzi | *Italian*	-

LITITZ

Isaac's | *Deli*	17

MT. JOY

Cameron Estate | *Amer.*	-

PINE FORGE

Z Gracie's | *Eclectic*	26

READING

Z Green Hills Inn | *Amer./French*	26
J.B. Dawson's/Austin's | *Amer.*	18

RONKS

Miller's Smorgas. | *PA Dutch*	18

SMOKETOWN

Good 'N Plenty | *PA Dutch*	19

STRASBURG

Isaac's | *Deli*	17

WYOMISSING

Bensí | *Italian*	18
Isaac's | *Deli*	17

New Jersey

BERLIN

Filomena | *Italian*	24

LOCATIONS

BORDENTOWN

Z Chickie's/Pete's | *Pub*	18
Mastoris | *Diner*	20

BURLINGTON

Café Gallery | *Continental*	21

CHERRY HILL

Alisa Cafe | *French/Thai*	22
NEW Aloe Fusion | *Thai*	-
Bahama Breeze | *Carib.*	17
Bobby Chez | *Seafood*	25
NEW Brio | *Italian*	19
Buca di Beppo | *Italian*	15
Caffe Aldo | *Italian*	23
Z Cheesecake Fact. | *Amer.*	20
Elephant & Castle | *Pub*	11
Emerald Fish | *Seafood*	23
Five Guys | *Burgers*	22
Kibitz Room | *Deli*	23
La Campagne | *French*	24
McCormick/Schmick | *Seafood*	21
Megu Sushi | *Japanese*	24
Z Mélange | *Creole*	27
Mikado | *Japanese*	23
Mirabella | *Italian*	22
Norma's | *Mideast.*	21
Oasis Grill | *Med./Moroccan*	26
P.J. Whelihan's | *Pub*	15
Ponzio's | *Diner*	17
Red Hot & Blue | *BBQ*	17
Sakura Spring | *Chinese/Japanese*	23
Siri's | *French/Thai*	25
Swanky Bubbles | *Pan-Asian*	20
Tutti Toscani | *Italian*	-
NEW William Douglas | *Steak*	-

CINNAMINSON

Z Bàcio | *Italian*	25
Tokyo Bleu | *Japanese*	21

CLEMENTON

Filomena | *Italian*	24
Nifty Fifty's | *Diner*	19

COLLINGSWOOD

Barone's | *Italian*	21
Bistro di Marino | *Italian*	25
Blackbird | *Amer.*	26
Bobby Chez | *Seafood*	25
Casona | *Cuban*	22
NEW Il Fiore | *Italian*	-
NEW Joe Pesce | *Italian/Seafood*	18
Nunzio | *Italian*	23
Pop Shop | *Amer.*	20
Z Sagami | *Japanese*	27
Sapori | *Italian*	25
Tortilla Press | *Mex.*	23
Water Lily | *Asian/French*	22
Word of Mouth | *Amer.*	24

DEPTFORD

Bonefish Grill | *Seafood*	21
Filomena | *Italian*	24

GIBBSBORO

Z Chophouse | *Seafood/Steak*	25

HADDONFIELD

Fuji | *Japanese*	26
NEW Javier | *Amer.*	21
Little Tuna | *Seafood*	21
Z Mélange | *Creole*	27
P.J. Whelihan's | *Pub*	15

HADDON HEIGHTS

Anthony's | *Italian*	22
Elements | *Amer.*	24

LAMBERTVILLE

Anton's/Swan | *Amer.*	20
Hamilton's | *Med.*	25
Inn/Hawke | *Amer.*	19
Lambertville Station | *Amer.*	18
Lilly's/Canal | *Eclectic*	20
Manon | *French*	25
No. 9 | *Amer.*	23
Ota-Ya | *Japanese*	24
Siam | *Thai*	22

LINDENWOLD

La Esperanza | *Mex.*	22

MAPLE SHADE

Mikado | *Japanese*	23
P.J. Whelihan's | *Pub*	15
Tacconelli's | *Pizza*	25

MARLTON

Z Food/Thought | *Amer.*	24
Joe's Peking | *Chinese*	22

Mexican Food | *Mex.* 21
Mikado | *Japanese* 23
Ⓩ P.F. Chang's | *Chinese* 21
Pietro's Pizzeria | *Pizza* 19
Pizzicato | *Italian* 20
Redstone | *Amer.* 21

MEDFORD
Braddock's | *Amer.* -
Ted's on Main | *Amer.* 26

MEDFORD LAKES
P.J. Whelihan's | *Pub* 15

MOORESTOWN
Barnacle Ben's | *Seafood* 20
Barone's | *Italian* 21

MOUNT EPHRAIM
Five Guys | *Burgers* 22

MOUNT HOLLY
High St. Grill | *Amer.* 23
Milano Modo | *Italian* 25
Robin's Nest | *Amer.* 25

MOUNT LAUREL
Bobby Chez | *Seafood* 25
El Azteca | *Mex.* 18
GG's | *Amer.* 21

PENNSAUKEN
Benihana | *Japanese* 20
Pub | *Steak* 21
NEW Tortilla Press Cantina | *Mex.* 19

SEWELL
Blue Eyes | *Steak* 21
Bobby Chez | *Seafood* 25
Creole Cafe | *Cajun/Creole* 22
P.J. Whelihan's | *Pub* 15

SICKLERVILLE
Luna Rossa | *Italian* -

TURNERSVILLE
Nifty Fifty's | *Diner* 19

VOORHEES
Bobby Chez | *Seafood* 25
Catelli | *Italian* 24

Chez Elena Wu | *Asian/French* 23
Coconut Bay | *Asian* 22
Laceno Italian | *Italian/Seafood* 24
Ⓩ Little Café | *Eclectic* 27
Ⓩ Ritz Seafood |
    Pan-Asian/Seafood 26
Somsak/Taan | *Thai* 25

WESTMONT
Cork | *Amer.* 20
Ⓩ Giumarello's | *Italian* 26
Kitchen 233 | *Amer.* 20

WINSLOW
Mr. Bill's | *Deli* -

Delaware

BEAR
Charcoal Pit | *Burgers* 20
Jake's Hamburgers | *Burgers* 21

CENTERVILLE
Buckley's | *Amer.* 17

GREENVILLE
Brew HaHa! | *Coffee* 18

HOCKESSIN
Back Burner | *Amer.* 20

MONTCHANIN
Ⓩ Krazy Kat's | *French* 26

NEWARK
Iron Hill | *Amer.* 18

NEW CASTLE
Jake's Hamburgers | *Burgers* 21

WILMINGTON
NEW Ameritage | *Amer.* -
Blue Parrot | *Cajun* 18
Bottom of Sea | *Seafood* 22
Brew HaHa! | *Coffee* 18
Charcoal Pit | *Burgers* 20
China Royal | *Chinese* 24
Conley Ward's | *Steak* 17
Corner Bistro | *Eclectic* 21
Ⓩ Culinaria | *Amer.* 25
Deep Blue | *Seafood* 22

Z Dom. Hudson	*Amer.*	24
Eclipse Bistro	*Amer.*	23
Feby's Fish.	*Seafood*	18
Five Guys	*Burgers*	22
Z Green Room	*French*	25
Harry's Savoy	*Amer.*	23
Harry's Seafood	*Seafood*	22
Hibachi	*Japanese*	18
Iron Hill	*Amer.*	18
Jake's Hamburgers	*Burgers*	21
Jasmine	*Pan-Asian*	22
Lamberti's	*Italian*	19
La Tolteca	*Mex.*	20

NEW Lucky's Coffee	*Amer.*	17
Mexican Post	*Mex.*	17
Mikimotos	*Japanese/Pan-Asian*	24
Z Moro	*Amer.*	25
Mrs. Robino's	*Italian*	20
NEW Pomodoro	*Italian*	20
Sugarfoot	*Amer.*	27
Sullivan's Steak	*Steak*	23
Toscana Kitchen	*Italian*	24
Utage	*Japanese*	24
Walter's Steak.	*Steak*	27
Wash. St. Ale	*Pub*	17

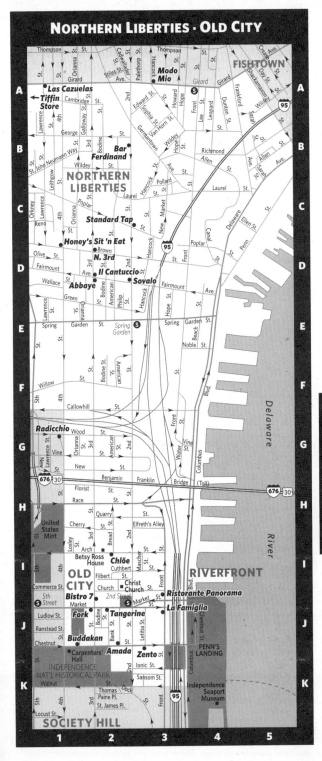

FISHTOWN

Thompson St.
Thompson St.
Creek Ave.

Modo Mio

Girard

Girard

95

Las Cazuelas
Tiffin Store

Cambridge

Edward St.
Sophia St.
Van Horn
Hope
Howard
Front
Lee
Leopard
Sarah St.
Dunton
Frankford
Wilder
Day St.
Shackamaxon

Bar Ferdinand

John Neumann Way
Wildey
Germantown
Hope
Ave.
Richmond
Allen
Allen St.
Sarah St.
Ave.

NORTHERN LIBERTIES

Leithgow
Lawrence
Oranna
Poplar
Hancock
Pollard
Laurel
Laurel
Delaware

Orkney
Lawrence
Reno

Standard Tap
New Market
Canal
Penn
Ellen St.

Honey's Sit 'n Eat
Brown
95
Poplar

N. 3rd
Il Cantuccio
Sovalo
Hancock
Front
Fairmount
Ave.

Olive
Fairmount
Wallace
Abbaye
Bodine
American
Philip
Hancock

Green
Oranna St.
Spring
Garden
Spring
Garden
Beach
Garden St.

Spring Garden
Noble St.

Willow
Bodine St.
American St.

Delaware

5th
4th
Callowhill
Front St.
Blvd.

Radicchio
Wood
Oranna
3rd
American
2nd
Vine St.
Water St.
Columbus

676 30
Vine
New
Benjamin
Franklin
Bridge (Toll)
676 30

Florist
Race
Quarry

United States Mint
Cherry
Loxley
3rd
Bread
Arch
Elfreth's Alley

River

RIVERFRONT

Betsy Ross House
Chlöe
Cuthbert
Mascher
Front St.

OLD CITY
Bistro 7
Filbert
Church
Christ Church
2nd Street
Market St.
Ristorante Panorama

5th Street
Market
La Famiglia

Fork
Tangerine
Bodine
Bank St.
Letitia St.
Chestnut St.

Ludlow St.
Ranstead St.
Chestnut
Buddakan
Amada
Zento
Ionic St.
Columbus
PENN'S LANDING

Carpenters' Hall
INDEPENDENCE NAT'L HISTORICAL PARK
Sansom St.
Independence Seaport Museum

Walnut
Dock
95

5th
4th
Thomas Paine Pl.
St. James Pl.
Front St.

Locust St.

SOCIETY HILL

A B C D E F G H I J K
1 2 3 4 5

MAPS

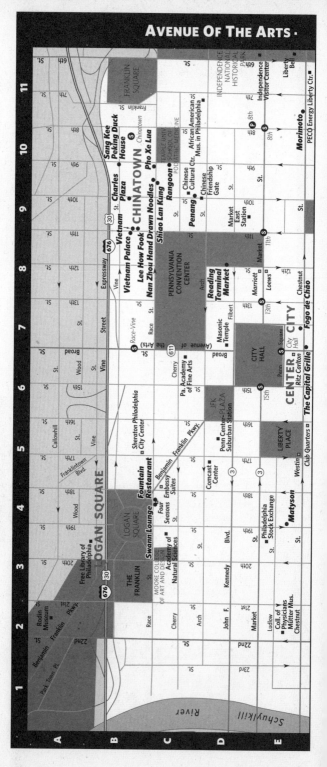

· CENTER CITY · CHINATOWN

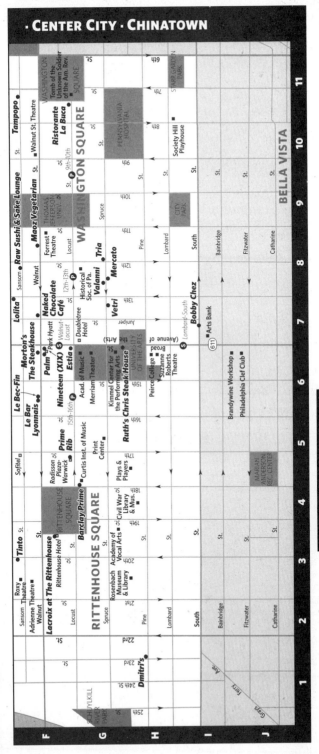

WASHINGTON SQUARE

RITTENHOUSE SQUARE

BELLA VISTA

MAPS

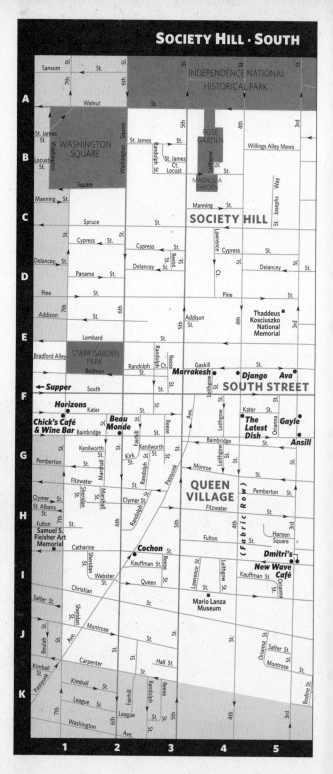

Sansom St.

7th St.

6th St.

St.

INDEPENDENCE NATIONAL HISTORICAL PARK

St.

A

Walnut St.

5th St.

4th St.

3rd St.

St. James St.

WASHINGTON SQUARE

Washington

St. James St.

Randolph St.

ROSE GARDEN

Willings Alley Mews

B

Locust St.

Square

Washington

St. James Ct. Locust

St. James St.

Leithgow

MAGNOLIA GARDEN

St.

Josephs Way

Manning St.

Square

Manning St.

SOCIETY HILL

St.

Josephs

C

Spruce St.

Cypress St.

Cypress St. Reese

Cypress St.

Lawrence Ct.

Delancey St.

Delancey St.

7th

St.

6th

Panama St.

Delancey St. Reese

Delancey St.

D

Pine St.

St.

Pine St.

Addison St.

7th St.

5th

Addison St.

4th

Thaddeus Kosciuszko National Memorial

3rd

E

Lombard St.

Bradford Alley

STARR GARDEN PARK

Randolph St.

Reese Ct.

Gaskill St.

Marrakesh

Leithgow

Django Ava

Rodman

Randolph St.

SOUTH STREET

F

← Supper

South St.

Leithgow

Orianna

Gayle

Horizons

Kater St.

St.

Ave.

Kater St.

The Latest Dish

Chick's Café & Wine Bar

Bainbridge St.

Beau Monde

Fairhill

Kenilworth St.

Reese

Leithgow

Bainbridge

Ansill

G

Kenilworth St.

Kirk St.

Randolph St.

Passyunk

Monroe

St.

Pemberton St.

Pemberton St.

Marshall

Fitzwater St.

QUEEN VILLAGE

Clymer St.

Sheridan

Marshall

Clymer St.

5th

Fitzwater

4th

(Fabric Row)

St.

H

St. Albans St.

Randolph

Hansen Square

Fulton St.

7th

6th

Fulton

3rd

Samuel S. Fleisher Art Memorial

Catharine

Sheridan

Cochon

Kauffman St.

Reese

Lawrence St.

Leithgow

Dmitri's

New Wave Café

I

Webster St.

Queen

Kauffman St.

Orianna

Christian

St.

Mario Lanza Museum

Salter St.

Sheridan Ave.

Montrose

St.

St.

Orianna St.

Salter St.

J

Beulah St.

St.

St.

Montrose St.

Carpenter St.

Kimball St.

Passyunk

Kimball St.

Fairhill

Randolph

Reese

5th

Bodine St.

K

7th

League St.

League St.

6th

4th

3rd

Washington Ave.

1 2 3 4 5

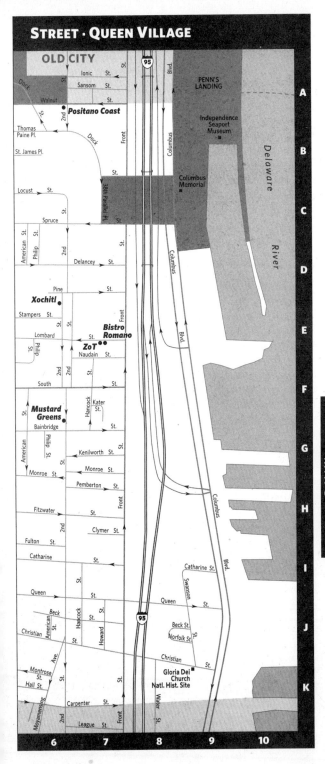

STREET · QUEEN VILLAGE

OLD CITY

PENN'S LANDING

Ionic St.

Sansom St.

Walnut St.

Positano Coast

Thomas Paine Pl.

St. James Pl.

Independence Seaport Museum

Dock

Front St.

Columbus

Delaware

River

Columbus Memorial

Locust St.

Spruce St.

38th Parallel Pl.

American St.

Philip St.

2nd St.

Delancey St.

Pine St.

Xochitl

Columbus Blvd.

Stampers St.

Front St.

Lombard St.

Bistro Romano

Philip St.

ZoT

2nd St.

Naudain St.

South St.

Mustard Greens

American St.

Philip St.

Hancock St.

Kater St.

Bainbridge St.

Kenilworth St.

2nd St.

Monroe St.

Monroe St.

Pemberton St.

Fitzwater St.

Front St.

Columbus Blvd.

2nd St.

Clymer St.

Fulton St.

Catharine St.

Catharine St.

Queen St.

Swanson

Queen St.

Beck St.

Hancock St.

Howard St.

American St.

Christian St.

Beck St.

Norfolk St.

Montrose Ave.

Christian St.

Hall St.

Gloria Dei Church Natl. Hist. Site

Moyamensing

Carpenter St.

2nd St.

Front St.

Water St.

Columbus Blvd.

League St.

MAPS

A B C D E F G H I J K

6 7 8 9 10

Special Features

Listings cover the best in each category and include names, locations and Food ratings. Multi-location restaurants' features may vary by branch. ☒ indicates places with the highest ratings, popularity and importance.

BREAKFAST

(See also Hotel Dining)

Ardmore Station | **Ardmore**	19
Ben & Irv Deli | **Hunt Vly**	19
Bird-in-Hand | **Bird-in-Hand/LB**	18
Carman's Country | **S Philly**	25
Down Home | **Ctr City E**	18
Famous 4th St. Deli | **South St.**	22
Hank's Place | **Chadds Ford**	19
☒ Honey's Sit 'n Eat | **N Liberties**	25
Hymie's Deli | **Merion Sta**	17
Izzy & Zoe's | **Univ City**	15
La Colombe | **multi.**	23
La Lupe | **S Philly**	22
Little Pete's | **Ctr City W**	16
Marathon Grill | **multi.**	18
Mayfair Diner | **NE Philly**	15
Melrose Diner | **S Philly**	16
Morning Glory | **S Philly**	24
Mother's | **New Hope**	18
Murray's Deli | **Bala Cynwyd**	19
Nifty Fifty's | **multi.**	19
Pink Rose | **South St.**	21
Ponzio's | **Cherry Hill/NJ**	17
☒ Reading Term. Mkt. | **Ctr City E**	23
Ruby's | **multi.**	16
Sabrina's Café | **S Philly**	25
Shank's & Evelyn's | **S Philly**	24
Spotted Hog | **Lahaska**	17
10th St. Pour House | **Ctr City E**	21
Tierra Colombiana | **N Philly**	22
Trolley Car | **Mt Airy**	14

BRUNCH

Abbraccio | **Univ City**	13
Bay Pony Inn | **Lederach**	19
Beau Monde | **South St.**	23
Black Sheep | **Ctr City W**	16
Braddock's | **Medford/NJ**	-
Brick Hotel | **Newtown**	18
Buckley's | **Centerville/DE**	17
Café Gallery | **Burlington/NJ**	21
Cafette | **Ches Hill**	20

Caribou Cafe | **Ctr City E**	19
Carman's Country | **S Philly**	25
Chart House | **DE River**	18
Cock 'n Bull | **Lahaska**	17
Coleman | **Blue Bell**	20
☒ Continental, The | **Old City**	22
☒ Cuba Libre | **Old City**	21
Dark Horse | **Society Hill**	17
Epicurean | **Phoenixville**	21
Fadó Irish | **Ctr City W**	15
Figs | **Fairmount**	23
☒ Fork | **Old City**	24
☒ Fountain | **Ctr City W**	29
Four Dogs | **W Chester**	18
Golden Pheasant | **Erwinna**	23
☒ Green Room | **Wilming/DE**	25
Gullifty's | **Rosemont**	15
Hibachi | **DE River**	18
Illuminare | **Fairmount**	18
Iron Hill | **multi.**	18
Jack's Firehse. | **Fairmount**	19
Jake's | **Manayunk**	25
Jones | **Ctr City E**	20
Khajuraho | **Ardmore**	21
Kildare's | **multi.**	16
☒ Kimberton Inn | **Kimberton**	25
La Campagne | **Cherry Hill/NJ**	24
☒ Lacroix | **Ctr City W**	28
Lambertville Station | **Lambertville/NJ**	18
Las Cazuelas | **N Liberties**	24
Little Pete's | **Fairmount**	16
Loie | **Ctr City W**	17
Mainland Inn | **Mainland**	26
Marathon Grill | **multi.**	18
Marathon/Sq. | **Ctr City W**	19
Mixto | **Ctr City E**	21
Monk's Cafe | **Ctr City W**	22
More Than Ice Crm. | **Ctr City E**	20
Morning Glory | **S Philly**	24
Moshulu | **DE River**	22
Mother's | **New Hope**	18
Newtown Grill | **Newtown Sq**	21

New Wave | **Queen Vill**	18
Nodding Head | **Ctr City W**	18
Pace One | **Thornton**	21
Palace of Asia | **Ft Wash**	24
Plough & Stars | **Old City**	18
Plumsteadville Inn | **Plumsteadville**	19
Rembrandt's | **Fairmount**	20
Roselena's | **S Philly**	21
Rx | **Univ City**	23
Shangrila | **Devon**	20
Solaris Grille | **Ches Hill**	16
Spring Mill | **Consho**	23
⚡ Standard Tap | **N Liberties**	24
Summer Kitchen | **Penns Park**	23
⚡ Swann Lounge | **Ctr City W**	27
Tango | **Bryn Mawr**	20
10th St. Pour House | **Ctr City E**	21
Thomas' | **Manayunk**	-
Tortilla Press | **Collingswood/NJ**	23
Valanni | **Ctr City E**	23
Vietnam Palace | **Chinatown**	23
Wash. Cross. | **Wash Cross**	17
⚡ White Dog | **Univ City**	21
William Penn | **Gwynedd**	22
Yardley Inn | **Yardley**	21
Zesty's | **Manayunk**	20

BUFFET

(Check availability)

America B&G | **multi.**	17
Aoi | **Ctr City E**	16
Bay Pony Inn | **Lederach**	19
Beige & Beige | **Hunt Vly**	20
⚡ Bella Tori | **Langhorne**	19
Bird-in-Hand | **Bird-in-Hand/LB**	18
Bistro Cassis | **Radnor**	20
Brick Hotel | **Newtown**	18
Café Gallery | **Burlington/NJ**	21
Cafe Spice | **Old City**	20
Cock 'n Bull | **Lahaska**	17
Coleman | **Blue Bell**	20
Dahlak | **Germantown**	22
Drafting Rm. | **multi.**	18
Fatou & Fama | **Univ City**	16
Gen. Lafayette | **Lafayette Hill**	15
Georges' | **Wayne**	20
⚡ Green Room | **Wilming/DE**	25
Hibachi | **multi.**	18

Karma | **Old City**	23
Khajuraho | **Ardmore**	21
Kingdom of Veg. | **Chinatown**	19
⚡ Lacroix | **Ctr City W**	28
Lambertville Station | **Lambertville/NJ**	18
Manayunk Brew. | **Manayunk**	18
Marg. Kuo Mandarin | **Frazer**	23
Brandywine | **Chadds Ford**	20
Miller's Smorgas. | **Ronks/LB**	18
Moshulu | **DE River**	22
Museum Rest. | **Fairmount**	19
New Delhi | **Univ City**	20
New Samosa | **Ctr City E**	16
⚡ Nineteen | **Ave of Arts**	23
Otto's Brauhaus | **Horsham**	20
Palace of Asia | **Ft Wash**	24
Passage/India | **Ave of Arts**	19
Plumsteadville Inn | **Plumsteadville**	19
Rouget | **Newtown**	-
Sitar India | **Univ City**	20
⚡ Swann Lounge | **Ctr City W**	27
Tandoor India | **Univ City**	20
Wash. Cross. | **Wash Cross**	17
William Penn | **Gwynedd**	22
Willow Valley | **Lancaster/LB**	19
Winberie's | **Wayne**	16

BUSINESS DINING

⚡ Amada | **Old City**	28
NEW Ameritage | **Wilming/DE**	-
⚡NEW Azie | **Media**	24
⚡ Barclay Prime | **Ctr City W**	26
⚡ Bella Tori | **Langhorne**	19
Benihana | **Pennsauken/NJ**	20
Big Fork | **Chadds Ford**	21
Bistro Cassis | **Radnor**	20
⚡ Blackfish | **Consho**	26
Blue Bell Inn | **Blue Bell**	21
NEW Blue Pear | **W Chester**	22
Blush | **Bryn Mawr**	20
Bonefish Grill | **multi.**	21
⚡ Brasserie Perrier | **Ctr City W**	24
NEW Buona Via | **Horsham**	19
⚡ Capital Grille | **Ave of Arts**	26
NEW Chima | **Ctr City W**	-
Chops | **Bala Cynwyd**	19
Conley Ward's | **Wilming/DE**	17

Dilworth. Inn | **W Chester**	25
Doc Magrogan | **W Chester**	16
Z Dom. Hudson | **Wilming/DE**	24
Earl's Prime | **Lahaska**	24
Estia | **Ave of Arts**	23
Fleming's Prime | **Wayne**	25
Z Fogo de Chão | **Ave of Arts**	23
Z Fountain | **Ctr City W**	29
Fuji | **Haddonfield/NJ**	26
Gen. Warren | **Malvern**	25
Georges' | **Wayne**	20
Z Green Room | **Wilming/DE**	25
NEW Il Fiore | **Collingswood/NJ**	-
Il Portico | **Ctr City W**	20
Inn/St. Peter's | **St Peters**	-
J.B. Dawson's/Austin's | **multi.**	18
NEW J.L. Sullivan's | **Ave of Arts**	-
NEW Joe Pesce | **Ctr City E**	18
Jonathan's | **Jenkintown**	17
Kitchen 233 | **Westmont/NJ**	20
La Veranda | **DE River**	23
Z Le Bec-Fin | **Ctr City W**	27
Le Castagne | **Ctr City W**	22
Legal Sea | **King of Prussia**	20
NEW Les Bons Temps | **Ctr City E**	-
NEW Maia | **Villanova**	-
Marg. Kuo | **Wayne**	23
McCormick/Schmick | **multi.**	21
Brandywine | **Chadds Ford**	20
NEW Misso | **Ave of Arts**	-
Z Morton's | **Ave of Arts**	25
Newtown Grill | **Newtown Sq**	21
Z Nineteen | **Ave of Arts**	23
Oceanaire | **Ctr City E**	22
Old Orig. Bookbinder | **Old City**	19
Z Osteria | **N Philly**	26
Palm | **Ave of Arts**	23
Parc Bistro | **Skippack**	25
Z P.F. Chang's | **multi.**	21
Phillips Sea. | **Ctr City W**	19
NEW Pietro's Prime | **W Chester**	24
Pond | **Radnor**	21
Prime Rib | **Ctr City W**	25
Rae | **Univ City**	22
Rest. Taquet | **Wayne**	24
Rist. Panorama | **Old City**	24
Rouget | **Newtown**	-
Roy's | **Ctr City W**	23
Ruth's Chris | **multi.**	23
Saloon | **S Philly**	24
Savona | **Gulph Mills**	25
Shula's 347 | **W Consho**	21
Smith/Wollensky | **Ctr City W**	22
Spamps | **Consho**	17
Sullivan's Steak | **multi.**	23
Z Susanna Foo | **Ctr City W**	24
Susanna Foo's Kitchen | **Wayne**	21
NEW Table 31 | **Ctr City W**	-
Z Tangerine | **Old City**	24
Tavern 17 | **Ctr City W**	18
Ted's Montana | **Warrington**	16
NEW 10 Arts | **Ave of Arts**	-
NEW Time | **Ctr City E**	-
NEW Toscana 52 | **Feasterville**	-
Z Water Works | **Fairmount**	21
NEW William Douglas | **Cherry Hill/NJ**	-
NEW Zahav | **Society Hill**	-

BYO

Abacus | **Lansdale**	24
Abner's BBQ | **Jenkintown**	20
Alisa Cafe | **Cherry Hill/NJ**	22
NEW Aloe Fusion | **Cherry Hill/NJ**	-
Alyan's | **South St.**	21
Anthony's | **Haddon Hts/NJ**	22
Apamate | **Ctr City W**	23
Aqua | **Ctr City E**	19
Ariana | **Old City**	20
Arpeggio | **Spring House**	23
NEW Ashoka Palace | **Ctr City W**	-
Athena | **Glenside**	21
Audrey Claire | **Ctr City W**	22
August | **S Philly**	26
NEW Auspicious | **Ardmore**	19
Ava | **South St.**	24
Avalon | **W Chester**	21
Aya's Café | **Ctr City W**	20
Z Bàcio | **Cinnaminson/NJ**	25
Banana Leaf | **Chinatown**	22
Barnacle Ben's | **Moorestown/NJ**	20
Barone's | **multi.**	21
Beige & Beige | **Hunt Vly**	20
Beijing | **Univ City**	16
Bellini Grill | **Ctr City W**	19
Big Fork | **Chadds Ford**	21
NEW Bindi | **Ctr City E**	22

Z Birchrunville Store | **Birchrunville**	28
Bistro di Marino | **Collingswood/NJ**	25
Bistro Juliana | **Fishtown**	23
Bistro La Baia | **Ctr City W**	20
Bistro La Viola | **Ctr City W**	24
Bistro 7 | **Old City**	24
Blackbird | **Collingswood/NJ**	26
Z Blackfish | **Consho**	26
Z Bluefin | **Plymouth Meeting**	26
Z Blue Sage | **Southampton**	27
Bobby Chez | **multi.**	25
Bocelli | **multi.**	-
Bona Cucina | **Upper Darby**	25
Branzino | **Ctr City W**	23
Bunha Faun | **Malvern**	25
Butterfish | **W Chester**	25
NEW Cafe Coláo | **N Liberties**	-
Cafe de Laos | **S Philly**	24
Cafe Fresko | **Bryn Mawr**	22
Cafe Preeya | **Hunt Vly**	21
Cafette | **Ches Hill**	20
Caffe Casta Diva | **Ctr City W**	24
Caffe Valentino | **multi.**	19
NEW Cake | **Ches Hill**	21
Carambola | **Dresher**	23
Carman's Country | **S Philly**	25
Casablanca | **Warrington**	21
Casona | **Collingswood/NJ**	22
Catherine's | **Unionville**	24
Chabaa Thai | **Manayunk**	25
Charles Plaza | **Chinatown**	23
Chef Charin | **Bala Cynwyd**	20
Chez Elena Wu | **Voorhees/NJ**	23
Chiangmai | **Consho**	25
Chiarella's | **S Philly**	19
Chlöe | **Old City**	25
Chun Hing | **Wynnefield**	22
Z Citrus | **Ches Hill**	25
NEW Cochon | **Queen Vill**	24
Coconut Bay | **Voorhees/NJ**	22
Copabanana | **Univ City**	16
Copper Bistro | **N Liberties**	22
Creole Cafe | **Sewell/NJ**	22
Cucina Forte | **S Philly**	24
Day by Day | **Ctr City W**	21
Divan | **S Philly**	21
Django | **South St.**	25

Z Dmitri's | **Queen Vill**	25
Duck Sauce | **Newtown**	25
Effie's | **Ctr City E**	21
El Azteca | **multi.**	18
Elements | **Haddon Hts/NJ**	24
NEW El Portal | **W Chester**	-
NEW El Ranchito | **N Philly**	-
Emerald Fish | **Cherry Hill/NJ**	23
Famous 4th St. Deli | **South St.**	22
Fatou & Fama | **Univ City**	16
Fayette St. | **Consho**	23
Fellini Cafe | **multi.**	21
Figs | **Fairmount**	23
Fioravanti | **Downingtown**	26
Z Food/Thought | **Marlton/NJ**	24
Fountain Side | **Horsham**	19
Four Rivers | **Chinatown**	24
Franco's HighNote | **S Philly**	23
Fuji | **Haddonfield/NJ**	26
Full Plate | **N Liberties**	21
Funky Lil' Kitchen | **Pottstown**	23
FuziOn | **Worcester**	23
Geechee Girl | **Germantown**	23
Z Gilmore's | **W Chester**	28
Gnocchi | **South St.**	22
Ha Long Bay | **Bryn Mawr**	22
Hamilton's | **Lambertville/NJ**	25
Hank's Place | **Chadds Ford**	19
Harmony Veg. | **Chinatown**	20
Z Honey's Sit 'n Eat | **N Liberties**	25
Hostaria Da Elio | **South St.**	20
Hunan | **Ardmore**	21
Ida Mae's | **Fishtown**	22
Il Cantuccio | **N Liberties**	23
NEW Il Fiore | **Collingswood/NJ**	-
Inn/Phillips Mill | **New Hope**	24
Isaac's | **multi.**	17
Jamaican Jerk Hut | **Ave of Arts**	20
Jasper | **Downingtown**	25
NEW Javier | **Haddonfield/NJ**	21
NEW Joe Pesce | **Collingswood/NJ**	18
Joe's Peking | **Marlton/NJ**	22
Jong Ka Jib | **E Oak Ln**	-
Kabobeesh | **Univ City**	23
Kabul | **Old City**	22
NEW Kanella | **Ctr City E**	-
Khajuraho | **Ardmore**	21

Kibitz in City	**Ctr City E**	21	Mizu	**multi.**	19
Kibitz Room	**Cherry Hill/NJ**	23	Modo Mio	**N Liberties**	26
Kingdom of Veg.	**Chinatown**	19	More Than Ice Crm.	**Ctr City E**	20
Kisso Sushi	**Old City**	22	Mr. Martino's	**S Philly**	22
Kotatsu	**Ardmore**	22	Ms. Tootsie's	**South St.**	21
La Campagne	**Cherry Hill/NJ**	24	**NEW** Murray's Deli/bistro M	**Berwyn**	19
La Cava	**Ambler**	21	
Laceno Italian	**Voorhees/NJ**	24	Nan	**Univ City**	25
La Fontana	**Ctr City W**	20	Nan Zhou	**Chinatown**	22
La Locanda	**Old City**	23	New Samosa	**Ctr City E**	16
La Lupe	**S Philly**	22	**NEW** Nicholas	**S Philly**	-
La Na	**Media**	21	No. 9	**Lambertville/NJ**	23
Z L'Angolo	**S Philly**	26	Norma's	**Cherry Hill/NJ**	21
La Pergola	**Jenkintown**	19	Nunzio	**Collingswood/NJ**	23
Las Cazuelas	**N Liberties**	24	Oasis Grill	**Cherry Hill/NJ**	26
La Vang	**Willow Grove**	22	**Z** Oishi	**Newtown**	26
La Viola Ovest	**Ctr City W**	23	Olive Tree	**Downingtown**	23
Lee How Fook	**Chinatown**	24	Ooka	**Willow Grove**	25
Lemon Grass	**multi.**	22	Orchard	**Kennett Sq**	-
Lilly's/Canal	**Lambertville/NJ**	20	Ota-Ya	**multi.**	24
Z Little Café	**Voorhees/NJ**	27	Pepper's	**Ardmore**	23
Z Little Fish	**S Philly**	28	Pho Thai Nam	**Blue Bell**	21
Little Marakesh	**Dresher**	21	Piccolo Tratt.	**Newtown**	21
Little Tuna	**Haddonfield/NJ**	21	Pistachio Grille	**Maple Glen**	19
L'Oca	**Fairmount**	23	Pizzicato	**Marlton/NJ**	20
Z Lolita	**Ctr City E**	25	Pop Shop	**Collingswood/NJ**	20
Lourdas Greek	**Bryn Mawr**	21	PTG	**Roxborough**	20
Mama Palma's	**Ctr City W**	23	Pumpkin	**Ctr City W**	24
Mamma Maria	**S Philly**	22	Pura Vida	**N Liberties**	24
Manny's	**multi.**	22	Radicchio	**Old City**	24
Manon	**Lambertville/NJ**	25	Ray's Cafe	**Chinatown**	25
Marathon Grill	**Ave of Arts**	18	**Z** Rest. Alba	**Malvern**	27
Marg. Kuo Mandarin	**Frazer**	23	Rist. Pesto	**S Philly**	22
Margot	**Narberth**	20	**Z** Ritz Seafood	**Voorhees/NJ**	26
Marigold Kitchen	**Univ City**	24	Roselena's	**S Philly**	21
NEW Masamoto	**Glen Mills**	27	Rouget	**Newtown**	-
Z Matyson	**Ctr City W**	26	Rx	**Univ City**	23
NEW Max & David's	**Elkins Pk**	23	Rylei	**NE Philly**	24
Megu Sushi	**Cherry Hill/NJ**	24	Sabrina's Café	**S Philly**	25
Z Mélange	**multi.**	27	**Z** Sagami	**Collingswood/NJ**	27
Z Mercato	**Ctr City E**	26	Sakura Spring	**Cherry Hill/NJ**	23
Mercer Café	**Port Richmond**	26	Salento	**Ctr City W**	21
Meridith's	**Berwyn**	22	Salt & Pepper	**S Philly**	23
Mikado	**multi.**	23	Sapori	**Collingswood/NJ**	25
Mimosa	**W Chester**	24	**NEW** Savor Saigon	**Levittown**	21
Mirabella	**Cherry Hill/NJ**	22	Sazon	**N Philly**	21
Mirna's Café	**multi.**	22	Scannicchio's	**S Philly**	25
NEW Misso	**Ave of Arts**	-	Shank's & Evelyn's	**S Philly**	24

Shiao Lan Kung | **Chinatown**	25
Shinju Sushi | **Ctr City E**	28
Siam | **Lambertville/NJ**	22
Siam Cuisine | **multi.**	22
Siam Cuisine/Black | **Doylestown**	23
Silk Cuisine | **Bryn Mawr**	23
Singapore Kosher | **Chinatown**	19
Siri's | **Cherry Hill/NJ**	25
☑ Sola | **Bryn Mawr**	27
Somsak/Taan | **Voorhees/NJ**	25
☑ Sovana Bistro | **Kennett Sq**	26
Spring Mill | **Consho**	23
NEW Station Bistro | **Kimberton**	–
Stefano's | **Hunt Vly**	19
Summer Kitchen | **Penns Park**	23
Sushikazu | **Blue Bell**	24
NEW Swallow | **N Liberties**	–
NEW Sweet Basil | **Chadds Ford**	21
Sweet Lucy's | **NE Philly**	21
Tacconelli's | **multi.**	25
☑ Talula's Table | **Kennett Sq**	26
Tamarindo's | **Broad Axe**	23
Tampopo | **multi.**	22
Tandoor India | **Univ City**	20
Taq. La Veracruz. | **S Philly**	22
Taq. Moroleon | **Kennett Sq**	24
Taq. Puerto Veracruz. | **S Philly**	–
Ted's on Main | **Medford/NJ**	26
Thai L'Elephant | **Phoenixville**	23
Thai Orchid | **Blue Bell**	25
☑ Tiffin Store | **multi.**	26
Tokyo Bleu | **Cinnaminson/NJ**	21
Tortilla Press | **Collingswood/NJ**	23
Trax Café | **Ambler**	23
Tre Scalini | **S Philly**	24
Trio | **Fairmount**	22
Tutti Toscani | **Cherry Hill/NJ**	–
Twin Bays | **Phoenixville**	24
Umai Umai | **Fairmount**	24
Umbria | **Mt Airy**	24
NEW Union Gourmet | **Ctr City E**	–
Uzu Sushi | **Old City**	26
Vientiane Café | **Univ City**	23
NEW Vietnam Café | **W Philly**	23
Viggiano's | **Consho**	19
Water Lily | **Collingswood/NJ**	22
White Elephant | **Hunt Vly**	22

Word of Mouth | **Collingswood/NJ**	24
NEW Yalda Grill | **Horsham**	20
Yazmin | **Warminster**	21
NEW Zacharias | **Lansdale**	21
Zakes Cafe | **Ft Wash**	23
NEW Zhi Wei Guan | **Chinatown**	–
Zorba's Taverna | **Fairmount**	20

CATERING

Abacus | **Lansdale**	24
Abbaye | **N Liberties**	22
Abbraccio | **Univ City**	13
Abner's BBQ | **Jenkintown**	20
Abyssinia | **Univ City**	24
Adobe Cafe | **Roxborough**	18
Al Dar Bistro | **Bala Cynwyd**	17
Alyan's | **South St.**	21
Aoi | **Ctr City E**	16
Ardmore Station | **Ardmore**	19
Athena | **Glenside**	21
August Moon | **Norristown**	23
Ava | **South St.**	24
Barone's | **multi.**	21
Basil Bistro | **Paoli**	18
Beijing | **Univ City**	16
Bellini Grill | **Ctr City W**	19
Ben & Irv Deli | **Hunt Vly**	19
Bistro St. Tropez | **Ctr City W**	20
Bitar's | **S Philly**	23
☑ Blue Sage | **Southampton**	27
☑ Bomb Bomb BBQ | **S Philly**	23
Brick Hotel | **Newtown**	18
Buca di Beppo | **Exton**	15
Cafette | **Ches Hill**	20
Caffe Aldo | **Cherry Hill/NJ**	23
Campo's Deli | **Old City**	22
Caribou Cafe | **Ctr City E**	19
Carmine's Creole | **Bryn Mawr**	22
Carr's | **Lancaster/LB**	25
Catelli | **Voorhees/NJ**	24
Cedars | **South St.**	19
Copabanana | **Univ City**	16
☑ Cuba Libre | **Old City**	21
Dahlak | **Univ City**	22
Day by Day | **Ctr City W**	21
El Azteca | **multi.**	18
Famous 4th St. Deli | **South St.**	22
Fatou & Fama | **Univ City**	16

SPECIAL FEATURES

Fayette St. | **Consho**	23
Feby's Fish. | **Wilming/DE**	18
Figs | **Fairmount**	23
Filomena | **Berlin/NJ**	24
FuziOn | **Worcester**	23
Hamilton's | **Lambertville/NJ**	25
Havana | **New Hope**	15
Hibachi | **Jenkintown**	18
Hunan | **Ardmore**	21
Hymie's Deli | **Merion Sta**	17
Isaac's | **Lititz/LB**	17
Izzy & Zoe's | **Univ City**	15
Jack's Firehse. | **Fairmount**	19
Jamaican Jerk Hut | **Ave of Arts**	20
Joe's Peking | **Marlton/NJ**	22
Joy Tsin Lau | **Chinatown**	20
Kabul | **Old City**	22
Karma | **Old City**	23
Khajuraho | **Ardmore**	21
Kibitz in City | **Ctr City E**	21
Kibitz Room | **Cherry Hill/NJ**	23
Kildare's | **King of Prussia**	16
Kisso Sushi | **Old City**	22
Knight House | **Doylestown**	21
Koi | **N Liberties**	23
Konak | **Old City**	20
La Campagne | **Cherry Hill/NJ**	24
La Lupe | **S Philly**	22
Lamberti's | **Wilming/DE**	19
La Pergola | **Jenkintown**	19
Las Cazuelas | **N Liberties**	24
☑ Le Bar Lyonnais | **Ctr City W**	28
☑ Le Bec-Fin | **Ctr City W**	27
Lemon Grass | **Lancaster/LB**	22
Liberties | **N Liberties**	14
☑ Little Café | **Voorhees/NJ**	27
Little Marakesh | **Dresher**	21
Little Tuna | **Haddonfield/NJ**	21
Lourdas Greek | **Bryn Mawr**	21
L2 | **Ctr City W**	17
Mamma Maria | **S Philly**	22
Marathon Grill | **multi.**	18
Marathon/Sq. | **Ctr City W**	19
Marg. Kuo Mandarin | **Frazer**	23
Maria's/Summit | **Roxborough**	21
Mendenhall Inn | **Mendenhall**	21
Moonstruck | **NE Philly**	21
Moriarty's | **Ctr City E**	19

☑ Moro | **Wilming/DE**	25
Mrs. Robino's | **Wilming/DE**	20
Murray's Deli | **Bala Cynwyd**	19
No. 9 | **Lambertville/NJ**	23
Norma's | **Cherry Hill/NJ**	21
Old Guard Hse. | **Gladwyne**	23
Ortlieb's Jazz | **N Liberties**	-
Otto's Brauhaus | **Horsham**	20
Pace One | **Thornton**	21
Passage/India | **Ave of Arts**	19
Pat's Steaks | **S Philly**	20
Pepper's | **Ardmore**	23
Persian Grill | **Lafayette Hill**	20
Phila. Fish | **Old City**	21
Pho Xe Lua | **Chinatown**	24
Pizzicato | **Old City**	20
Red Hot & Blue | **Cherry Hill/NJ**	17
Roselena's | **S Philly**	21
Rx | **Univ City**	23
Sabrina's Café | **S Philly**	25
☑ Sang Kee Duck | **Chinatown**	25
Seafood Unltd. | **Ctr City W**	20
Shiroi Hana | **Ctr City W**	23
Siam Cuisine/Black | **Doylestown**	23
Silk Cuisine | **Bryn Mawr**	23
Siri's | **Cherry Hill/NJ**	25
Sitar India | **Univ City**	20
Sugarfoot | **Wilming/DE**	27
Sushikazu | **Blue Bell**	24
Tamarindo's | **Broad Axe**	23
Tandoor India | **Univ City**	20
Tango | **Bryn Mawr**	20
Taq. Moroleon | **Kennett Sq**	24
Tex Mex Connect. | **N Wales**	20
Thai Singha | **Univ City**	19
333 Belrose | **Radnor**	23
Tierra Colombiana | **N Philly**	22
Trax Café | **Ambler**	23
Twin Bays | **Phoenixville**	24
Upstares/Varalli | **Ave of Arts**	21
Utage | **Wilming/DE**	24
Vesuvio | **S Philly**	17
Victor Café | **S Philly**	20
Vientiane Café | **Univ City**	23
Wash. Cross. | **Wash Cross**	17
White Elephant | **Hunt Vly**	22
Yardley Inn | **Yardley**	21
Zesty's | **Manayunk**	20

CELEBRITY CHEFS

🏆 Alma de Cuba | *Douglas Rodriguez* | **Ctr City W** — 25

🏆 Amada | *Jose Garces* | **Old City** — 28

Ansill | *David Ansill* | **South St.** — 24

🏆 Birchrunville Store | *Francis Trzeciak* | **Birchrunville** — 28

Bistro Cassis | *Abde Dahrouch* | **Radnor** — 20

Blush | *Nicholas Farina* | **Bryn Mawr** — 20

🏆 Brasserie Perrier | *Georges Perrier/Chris Scarduzio* | **Ctr City W** — 24

🏆 Buddakan | *Scott Swiderski* | **Old City** — 26

Coleman | *Jim Coleman* | **Blue Bell** — 20

🏆 Cuba Libre | *Guillermo Pernot* | **Old City** — 21

NEW Distrito | *Jose Garces* | **Univ City** — -

🏆 Fountain | *Martin Hamann* | **Ctr City W** — 29

Fuji | *Matt Ito* | **Haddonfield/NJ** — 26

Gayle | *Daniel Stern* | **South St.** — 25

Georges' | *Georges Perrier* | **Wayne** — 20

🏆 Gilmore's | *Peter Gilmore* | **W Chester** — 28

Horizons | *Rich Landau* | **South St.** — 26

James | *Jim Burke* | **S Philly** — 25

🏆 Lacroix | *Matthew Levin* | **Ctr City W** — 28

La Famiglia | *Gino Sena* | **Old City** — 24

🏆 Le Bec-Fin | *Georges Perrier* | **Ctr City W** — 27

London Grill | *Michael McNally* | **Fairmount** — 18

NEW Maia | *Terence Feury & Patrick Feury* | **Villanova** — -

Mantra | *Albert Paris* | **Ctr City W** — 19

🏆 Mélange | *Joe Brown* | **Cherry Hill/NJ** — 27

🏆 Morimoto | *Masaharu Morimoto* | **Ctr City E** — 26

Moshulu | *Ralph Fernandez* | **DE River** — 22

🏆 Nectar | *Patrick Feury* | **Berwyn** — 26

Nunzio | *Nunzio Patruno* | **Collingswood/NJ** — 23

🏆 Osteria | *Marc Vetri/Jeff Michaud* | **N Philly** — 26

Pond | *Abde Dahrouch* | **Radnor** — 21

Rae | *Daniel Stern* | **Univ City** — 22

🏆 Susanna Foo | *Susanna Foo* | **Ctr City W** — 24

Susanna Foo's Kitchen | *Susanna Foo* | **Wayne** — 21

NEW Table 31 | *Georges Perrier/Chris Scarduzio* | **Ctr City W** — -

🏆 Talula's Table | *Bryan Sikora* | **Kennett Sq** — 26

NEW 10 Arts | *Eric Ripert/Jennifer Carroll* | **Ave of Arts** — -

🏆 Tinto | *Jose Garces* | **Ctr City W** — 27

Twenty Manning | *Kiong Banh* | **Ctr City W** — 22

🏆 Vetri | *Marc Vetri* | **Ave of Arts** — 27

CHILD-FRIENDLY

(Alternatives to the usual fast-food places; * children's menu available)

Abbraccio* | **Univ City** — 13

Adobe Cafe* | **Roxborough** — 18

Alisa Cafe | **Cherry Hill/NJ** — 22

America B&G* | **multi.** — 17

Ardmore Station* | **Ardmore** — 19

Ariana | **Old City** — 20

Arpeggio* | **Spring House** — 23

Athena | **Glenside** — 21

Bahama Breeze* | **multi.** — 17

Barone's* | **multi.** — 21

Basil Bistro* | **Paoli** — 18

Bella Tratt.* | **Manayunk** — 22

Ben & Irv Deli* | **Hunt Vly** — 19

Bertolini's | **King of Prussia** — 18

Bird-in-Hand* | **Bird-in-Hand/LB** — 18

Bistro Romano* | **Society Hill** — 21

Bitar's | **S Philly** — 23

Blue Bell Inn* | **Blue Bell** — 21

Bobby Chez | **multi.** — 25

🏆 Bomb Bomb BBQ* | **S Philly** — 23

Braddock's* | **Medford/NJ** — -

Brick Hotel* | **Newtown** — 18

Bridget Foy's* | **South St.** — 19

Buckley's* | **Centerville/DE** — 17

Cafette* | **Ches Hill** — 20

California Cafe* | **King of Prussia** — 20

Calif. Pizza* | **King of Prussia** — 19

Campo's Deli* | **Old City** — 22

Casablanca* | **Wynnefield** — 21

Charcoal Pit* | **multi.** — 20

SPECIAL FEATURES

Chart House* | **DE River**	_18_
Z Cheesecake Fact.* | **King of Prussia**	_20_
Chestnut Grill* | **Ches Hill**	_17_
Z Chickie's/Pete's | **multi.**	_18_
Christopher's* | **Wayne**	_17_
City Tavern* | **Old City**	_19_
Cock 'n Bull* | **Lahaska**	_17_
Corner Bistro | **Wilming/DE**	_21_
Cresheim Cottage* | **Mt Airy**	_18_
Dave & Buster's* | **DE River**	_13_
Day by Day* | **Ctr City W**	_21_
Delmonico's* | **Wynnefield**	_20_
Devon Seafood* | **Ctr City W**	_23_
DiNardo's* | **Old City**	_19_
Down Home* | **Ctr City E**	_18_
Drafting Rm.* | **multi.**	_18_
Z Duling-Kurtz* | **Exton**	_25_
El Azteca* | **multi.**	_18_
Elephant & Castle* | **multi.**	_11_
Epicurean* | **Phoenixville**	_21_
Famous 4th St. Deli | **South St.**	_22_
Fatou & Fama | **Univ City**	_16_
Feby's Fish.* | **Wilming/DE**	_18_
Fellini Cafe | **multi.**	_21_
Filomena* | **multi.**	_24_
Z Food/Thought* | **Marlton/NJ**	_24_
Four Dogs* | **W Chester**	_18_
Fuji Mtn. | **Ctr City W**	_22_
FuziOn | **Worcester**	_23_
Geechee Girl | **Germantown**	_23_
Gen. Lafayette* | **Lafayette Hill**	_15_
Geno's Steaks | **S Philly**	_19_
Z Gibraltar* | **Lancaster/LB**	_27_
Good 'N Plenty | **Smoketown/LB**	_19_
Z Gracie's* | **Pine Forge/LB**	_26_
Z Green Room* | **Wilming/DE**	_25_
Gullifty's* | **Rosemont**	_15_
Hank's Place* | **Chadds Ford**	_19_
Hard Rock* | **Ctr City E**	_14_
Harry's Savoy* | **Wilming/DE**	_23_
Harry's Seafood* | **Wilming/DE**	_22_
Havana* | **New Hope**	_15_
Haydn Zug's* | **E Petersburg/LB**	_18_
Hibachi* | **multi.**	_18_
Z Honey's Sit 'n Eat* | **N Liberties**	_25_
Hymie's Deli* | **Merion Sta**	_17_
Il Portico | **Ctr City W**	_20_
Inn/Hawke* | **Lambertville/NJ**	_19_
Iron Hill* | **multi.**	_18_
Isaac Newton's* | **Newtown**	_16_
Isaac's* | **multi.**	_17_
Italian Bistro* | **multi.**	_16_
Izzy & Zoe's* | **Univ City**	_15_
Jack's Firehse.* | **Fairmount**	_19_
Jake's Hamburgers | **Wilming/DE**	_21_
J.B. Dawson's/Austin's* | **multi.**	_18_
Jim's Steaks* | **multi.**	_22_
Johnny Mañana's* | **East Falls**	_15_
Jones | **Ctr City E**	_20_
Kabobeesh* | **Univ City**	_23_
Kibitz Room* | **Cherry Hill/NJ**	_23_
Kildare's* | **multi.**	_16_
Z Kimberton Inn | **Kimberton**	_25_
Konak | **Old City**	_20_
La Campagne* | **Cherry Hill/NJ**	_24_
La Esperanza* | **Lindenwold/NJ**	_22_
La Lupe | **S Philly**	_22_
Landing* | **New Hope**	_16_
La Pergola* | **Jenkintown**	_19_
Las Cazuelas | **N Liberties**	_24_
La Tolteca* | **Wilming/DE**	_20_
Little Pete's* | **multi.**	_16_
Little Tuna | **Haddonfield/NJ**	_21_
Z Maggiano's* | **multi.**	_20_
Mama Palma's | **Ctr City W**	_23_
Mamma Maria | **S Philly**	_22_
Manayunk Brew.* | **Manayunk**	_18_
Mandarin Gdn. | **Willow Grove**	_20_
Marathon Grill* | **multi.**	_18_
Marathon/Sq.* | **Ctr City W**	_19_
Maria's/Summit* | **Roxborough**	_21_
Marra's | **S Philly**	_22_
Max & Erma's* | **multi.**	_15_
Mayfair Diner* | **NE Philly**	_15_
McGillin's* | **Ctr City E**	_16_
Melrose Diner* | **S Philly**	_16_
Mexican Food* | **Marlton/NJ**	_21_
Mexican Post* | **Wilming/DE**	_17_
Mikado | **Ardmore**	_22_
Mikado | **Cherry Hill/NJ**	_23_
Miller's Smorgas.* | **Ronks/LB**	_18_
Mirna's Café* | **multi.**	_22_
Moonstruck* | **NE Philly**	_21_
Moriarty's* | **Ctr City E**	_19_

Moshulu* | **DE River**	22
Mrs. Robino's* | **Wilming/DE**	20
New Tavern* | **Bala Cynwyd**	16
Nifty Fifty's | **multi.**	19
No. 9 | **Lambertville/NJ**	23
Norma's* | **Cherry Hill/NJ**	21
North by NW* | **Mt Airy**	16
Old Guard Hse.* | **Gladwyne**	23
Ooka* | **multi.**	25
Ota-Ya | **Lambertville/NJ**	24
Otto's Brauhaus* | **Horsham**	20
Pace One* | **Thornton**	21
Penne* | **Univ City**	18
Persian Grill* | **Lafayette Hill**	20
☑ P.F. Chang's | **multi.**	21
Phila. Fish* | **Old City**	21
Pietro's Pizzeria* | **multi.**	19
Pizzicato* | **multi.**	20
Plate* | **Ardmore**	16
Plough & Stars* | **Old City**	18
Plumsteadville Inn* | **Plumsteadville**	19
Ponzio's* | **Cherry Hill/NJ**	17
Pop Shop* | **Collingswood/NJ**	20
Primavera Pizza* | **multi.**	18
Pub* | **Pennsauken/NJ**	21
Qdoba* | **multi.**	17
Ralph's | **S Philly**	22
Rangoon | **Chinatown**	24
Red Hot & Blue* | **Cherry Hill/NJ**	17
Rist. Primavera* | **Wayne**	17
☑ Ritz Seafood | **Voorhees/NJ**	26
Rock Bottom* | **King of Prussia**	16
Rose Tattoo | **Fairmount**	22
Ruby's* | **multi.**	16
Sabrina's Café | **S Philly**	25
☑ Sagami | **Collingswood/NJ**	27
Sassafras Int'l | **Old City**	–
Scannicchio's | **S Philly**	25
Serrano | **Old City**	20
Seven Stars Inn* | **Phoenixville**	23
Shank's & Evelyn's | **S Philly**	24
Shiao Lan Kung | **Chinatown**	25
Shiroi Hana | **Ctr City W**	23
Siam Cuisine | **multi.**	22
Silk City | **N Liberties**	20
Siri's | **Cherry Hill/NJ**	25
Sitar India | **Univ City**	20

Snockey's Oyster* | **S Philly**	18
Solaris Grille* | **Ches Hill**	16
Somsak/Taan | **Voorhees/NJ**	25
South St. Souvlaki | **South St.**	21
Spasso | **Old City**	23
Spotted Hog* | **Lahaska**	17
Stoudt's* | **Adamstown/LB**	18
Sushikazu | **Blue Bell**	24
Sweet Lucy's* | **NE Philly**	21
Tamarindo's | **Broad Axe**	23
Tango* | **Bryn Mawr**	20
Taq. Moroleon* | **Kennett Sq**	24
Teca | **W Chester**	21
Tex Mex Connect.* | **N Wales**	20
Tierra Colombiana* | **N Philly**	22
Tortilla Press* | **Collingswood/NJ**	23
Toscana Kitchen | **Wilming/DE**	24
Totaro's* | **Consho**	24
Tre Scalini | **S Philly**	24
Trinacria | **Blue Bell**	25
Trolley Car* | **Mt Airy**	14
Vesuvio* | **S Philly**	17
Victory Brewing* | **Downingtown**	15
☑ Vietnam | **Chinatown**	25
Vietnam Palace* | **Chinatown**	23
Viggiano's* | **Consho**	19
Villa di Roma | **S Philly**	21
Vincent's | **W Chester**	16
Vinny T's* | **Wynnewood**	15
Wash. Cross.* | **Wash Cross**	17
Wash. St. Ale* | **Wilming/DE**	17
☑ White Dog* | **Univ City**	21
White Elephant | **Hunt Vly**	22
William Penn* | **Gwynedd**	22
Willow Valley* | **Lancaster/LB**	19
Winberie's* | **Wayne**	16
Winnie's Le Bus* | **Manayunk**	21
Word of Mouth | **Collingswood/NJ**	24
☑ Yangming | **Bryn Mawr**	25
Zesty's* | **Manayunk**	20
Zocalo* | **Univ City**	20

DELIVERY/TAKEOUT

(D=delivery, T=takeout)

Abacus | D | **Lansdale**	24
Alisa Cafe | T | **Cherry Hill/NJ**	22
America B&G | D | **Chester Springs**	17

Anjou | D | **Old City** 19

Ardmore Station | D | **Ardmore** 19

August Moon | D | **Norristown** 23

Bahama Breeze | T | 17
  Cherry Hill/NJ

Beijing | D | **Univ City** 16

Ben & Irv Deli | D | **Hunt Vly** 19

Bobby Chez | T | **multi.** 25

Buca di Beppo | D | **Ctr City W** 15

Byblos | D | **Ctr City W** 16

Cafe Spice | D | **Old City** 20

Campo's Deli | D | **Old City** 22

Carr's | D | **Lancaster/LB** 25

Cedars | D | **South St.** 19

Celebre's | D | **S Philly** 24

Charcoal Pit | D | **multi.** 20

Charles Plaza | D | **Chinatown** 23

CinCin | D | **Ches Hill** 24

Copabanana | D | **Univ City** 16

Davio's | D | **Ctr City W** 23

Day by Day | D | **Ctr City W** 21

Effie's | D | **Ctr City E** 21

Fez Moroccan | D | **South St.** 21

Filomena | T | **multi.** 24

Franco's HighNote | D | **S Philly** 23

Fuji Mtn. | D | **Ctr City W** 22

Harmony Veg. | D | **Chinatown** 20

Hymie's Deli | D | **Merion Sta** 17

Italian Bistro | D | **Ave of Arts** 16

Izzy & Zoe's | D | **Univ City** 15

Joe's Peking | T | **Marlton/NJ** 22

Kingdom of Veg. | D | **Chinatown** 19

La Lupe | D | **S Philly** 22

Little Pete's | D | **multi.** 16

Maccabeam | D | **Ctr City E** 18

Marathon Grill | D | **multi.** 18

Marathon/Sq. | D | **Ctr City W** 19

Marra's | D | **S Philly** 22

Mastoris | T | **Bordentown/NJ** 20

Mikado | D | **Ardmore** 22

Mikado | T | **Cherry Hill/NJ** 23

Murray's Deli | D | **Bala Cynwyd** 19

New Delhi | D | **Univ City** 20

Norma's | T | **Cherry Hill/NJ** 21

Ota-Ya | T | **Lambertville/NJ** 24

Passage/India | D | **Ave of Arts** 19

☑ P.F. Chang's | T | **Marlton/NJ** 21

Pink Rose | D | **South St.** 21

Seafood Unltd. | D | **Ctr City W** 20

Shiroi Hana | D | **Ctr City W** 23

Siam | T | **Lambertville/NJ** 22

Singapore Kosher | D | **Chinatown** 19

Sitar India | D | **Univ City** 20

Stella Blu | D | **W Consho** -

Tandoor India | D | **Univ City** 20

Taq. La Veracruz. | D | **S Philly** 22

10th St. Pour House | D | 21
  Ctr City E

Thai Pepper | D | **Ardmore** 19

Vesuvio | D | **S Philly** 17

DINING ALONE

(Other than hotels and places with
counter service)

AllWays Café | **Hunt Vly** 22

Aoi | **Ctr City E** 16

Ardmore Station | **Ardmore** 19

Beau Monde | **South St.** 23

Ben & Irv Deli | **Hunt Vly** 19

Bitar's | **S Philly** 23

Black Sheep | **Ctr City W** 16

Bobby Chez | **multi.** 25

Bonté Wafflerie | **multi.** 19

Brew HaHa! | **multi.** 18

Cafette | **Ches Hill** 20

Caribou Cafe | **Ctr City E** 19

Charlie's Hamburgers | **Folsom** 24

Cheeseburger/Paradise | 15
  Langhorne

☑ Chickie's/Pete's | 18
  Bordentown/NJ

Copabanana | **South St.** 16

Criniti | **S Philly** 19

Dalessandro's | **Roxborough** 24

Devon Seafood | **Ctr City W** 23

Down Home | **Ctr City E** 18

Effie's | **Ctr City E** 21

Famous 4th St. Deli | **South St.** 22

Farmicia | **Old City** 20

Five Guys | **multi.** 22

☑ Honey's Sit 'n Eat | **N Liberties** 25

Horizons | **South St.** 26

Iron Hill | **Lancaster/LB** 18

Izzy & Zoe's | **Univ City** 15

Jake's Hamburgers |
  New Castle/DE

Jim's Steaks | **multi.** 22

☑ John's Roast Pork | **S Philly** 27

Jonathan's | **Jenkintown** _17_
K.C.'s Alley | **Ambler** _17_
Kibitz Room | **Cherry Hill/NJ** _23_
Kildare's | **South St.** _16_
La Pergola | **Jenkintown** _19_
Liberties | **Hulmeville** _14_
Ly Michael's | **Chinatown** _21_
Maccabeam | **Ctr City E** _18_
Marathon Grill | **multi.** _18_
Mayfair Diner | **NE Philly** _15_
Mexican Post | **Old City** _17_
Mizu | **Old City** _19_
Monk's Cafe | **Ctr City W** _22_
Morning Glory | **S Philly** _24_
New Samosa | **Ctr City E** _16_
Nifty Fifty's | **multi.** _19_
Pat's Steaks | **S Philly** _20_
Pho 75 | **Chinatown** _22_
P.J. Whelihan's | **Blue Bell** _15_
Pop Shop | **Collingswood/NJ** _20_
Positano Coast | **Society Hill** _21_
Raw Sushi | **Ctr City E** _24_
🔡 Reading Term. Mkt. | _23_
  Ctr City E
🔡 Sang Kee Duck | **multi.** _25_
Seafood Unltd. | **Ctr City W** _20_
Shank's & Evelyn's | **S Philly** _24_
NEW Sláinte | **Univ City** _18_
Steve's Prince/Stks. | **NE Philly** _24_
Tango | **Bryn Mawr** _20_
Ted's Montana | **Ave of Arts** _16_
🔡 Tony Luke's | **S Philly** _25_
Trolley Car | **Mt Airy** _14_
Zorba's Taverna | **Fairmount** _20_

ENTERTAINMENT

(Call for days and times of
performances)
Abbraccio | varies | **Univ City** _13_
America B&G | bands | _17_
  Glen Mills
Anjou | DJ | **Old City** _19_
Bahama Breeze | Caribbean | _17_
  multi.
Bay Pony Inn | varies | **Lederach** _19_
Beau Monde | cabaret/DJ | _23_
  South St.
Bistro Romano | piano | _21_
  Society Hill
Blue Bell Inn | bands | **Blue Bell** _21_

Blue Eyes | singer | **Sewell/NJ** _21_
Blue Horse | bands | **Blue Bell** _17_
Bourbon Blue | bands | _19_
  Manayunk
Brick Hotel | varies | **Newtown** _18_
Buckley's | vocals | **Centerville/DE** _17_
Cafe Spice | DJ/Indian | **Old City** _20_
Casablanca | belly dancing | _21_
  multi.
Catelli | bands | **Voorhees/NJ** _24_
🔡 Chickie's/Pete's | varies | _18_
  multi.
Christopher's | DJ | **Wayne** _17_
City Tavern | harpsichord | _19_
  Old City
Cock 'n Bull | dinner theater | _17_
  Lahaska
Coleman | jazz/piano | **Blue Bell** _20_
Creed's | varies | **King of Prussia** _23_
🔡 Cuba Libre | varies | **Old City** _21_
Cuttalossa Inn | varies | _16_
  Lumberville
D'Angelo's | DJ | **Ctr City W** _18_
Deep Blue | jazz/rock | _22_
  Wilming/DE
Epicurean | varies | **Phoenixville** _21_
Eulogy Belgian | bands | **Old City** _18_
Fadó Irish | DJ | **Ctr City W** _15_
Fergie's Pub | bands | **Ctr City E** _17_
Fez Moroccan | belly dancing | _21_
  South St.
Filomena | varies | **multi.** _24_
🔡 Food/Thought | piano | _24_
  Marlton/NJ
🔡 Fountain | bands | **Ctr City W** _29_
Four Dogs | acoustic | **W Chester** _18_
Franco's HighNote | open mic | _23_
  S Philly
Freight House | varies | _19_
  Doylestown
Gables | jazz | **Chadds Ford** _20_
Gen. Lafayette | folk/rock | _15_
  Lafayette Hill
🔡 Green Room | jazz | _25_
  Wilming/DE
Gullifty's | varies | **Rosemont** _15_
Half Moon | varies | **Kennett Sq** _20_
Happy Rooster | karaoke | _17_
  Ctr City W
Harry's Savoy | varies | _23_
  Wilming/DE

Havana | varies | **New Hope**	15
High St. Caffé | jazz | **W Chester**	24
Jamaican Jerk Hut | varies | **Ave of Arts**	20
Johnny Mañana's | varies | **East Falls**	15
Joseph Ambler | piano | **N Wales**	23
Kildare's | bands/DJ | **multi.**	16
🔒 Kimberton Inn | jazz | **Kimberton**	25
King George II | piano | **Bristol**	21
Konak | Turkish | **Old City**	20
La Collina | jazz/piano | **Bala Cynwyd**	23
La Locanda | guitar | **Old City**	23
La Tolteca | mariachi | **Wilming/DE**	20
Little Marakesh | belly dancing | **Dresher**	21
Loie | DJ | **Ctr City W**	17
L2 | jazz | **Ctr City W**	17
🔒 Maggiano's | jazz/piano | **King of Prussia**	20
Mamma Maria | accordion | **S Philly**	22
Manayunk Brew. | varies | **Manayunk**	18
Marrakesh | belly dancing | **South St.**	23
McFadden's | bands/DJ | **N Liberties**	13
Mendenhall Inn | varies | **Mendenhall**	21
Norma's | belly dancing | **Cherry Hill/NJ**	21
North by NW | salsa | **Mt Airy**	16
Ortlieb's Jazz | jazz | **N Liberties**	-
Plough & Stars | Irish bands | **Old City**	18
Plumsteadville Inn | piano | **Plumsteadville**	19
Prime Rib | bass/piano | **Ctr City W**	25
Pub | jazz | **Pennsauken/NJ**	21
🔒 Reading Term. Mkt. | jazz | **Ctr City E**	23
Red Hot & Blue | blues | **Cherry Hill/NJ**	17
Rembrandt's | jazz | **Fairmount**	20
Rest./Doneckers | piano | **Ephrata/LB**	19
🔒 Rist. San Marco | piano | **Ambler**	26
Rose Tree Inn | piano | **Media**	22
Serrano | varies | **Old City**	20
Silk City | DJ | **N Liberties**	20
Singapore Kosher | karaoke | **Chinatown**	19
Sotto Varalli | jazz | **Ave of Arts**	21
Spence Cafe | jazz/rock | **W Chester**	23
Sullivan's Steak | jazz | **multi.**	23
Swanky Bubbles | DJ | **Old City**	20
🔒 Swann Lounge | jazz | **Ctr City W**	27
Tai Lake | karaoke | **Chinatown**	24
Taq. La Veracruz. | varies | **S Philly**	22
Tex Mex Connect. | varies | **N Wales**	20
Tierra Colombiana | salsa | **N Philly**	22
Tír na nÓg | Irish/trivia | **Ctr City W**	14
Tortilla Press | guitar | **Collingswood/NJ**	23
Toscana Kitchen | jazz | **Wilming/DE**	24
Tratt. Alberto | varies | **W Chester**	21
Tratt. Primadonna | guitar | **Ctr City W**	17
Trinacria | guitar | **Blue Bell**	25
Victor Café | opera | **S Philly**	20
Vincent's | varies | **W Chester**	16
🔒 White Dog | piano | **Univ City**	21
William Penn | jazz | **Gwynedd**	22
World Café | varies | **Univ City**	14

FAMILY-STYLE

Bellini Grill | **Ctr City W**	19
Bird-in-Hand | **Bird-in-Hand/LB**	18
Buca di Beppo | **multi.**	15
Fez Moroccan | **South St.**	21
Gnocchi | **South St.**	22
Good 'N Plenty | **Smoketown/LB**	19
Il Tartufo | **Manayunk**	23
Joe's Peking | **Marlton/NJ**	22
Joy Tsin Lau | **Chinatown**	20
La Vang | **Willow Grove**	22
La Veranda | **DE River**	23
🔒 Maggiano's | **multi.**	20

Mandarin Gdn. | **Willow Grove** 20
Marg. Kuo | **Wayne** 23
Miller's Smorgas. | **Ronks/LB** 18
Pho Xe Lua | **Chinatown** 24
Plain/Fancy Farm |
    Bird-in-Hand/LB 19
🔼 Sang Kee Duck | **Chinatown** 25
Scoogi's | **Flourtown** 19
Swanky Bubbles | **Old City** 20
Viggiano's | **Consho** 19
Vinny T's | **Wynnewood** 15

FIREPLACES

Abbraccio | **Univ City** 13
America B&G | **Glen Mills** 17
Anton's/Swan | **Lambertville/NJ** 20
Arpeggio | **Spring House** 23
Avalon | **W Chester** 21
Back Burner | **Hockessin/DE** 20
Bay Pony Inn | **Lederach** 19
Beau Monde | **South St.** 23
🔼 Bella Tori | **Langhorne** 19
Black Sheep | **Ctr City W** 16
Blue Bell Inn | **Blue Bell** 21
Blush | **Bryn Mawr** 20
Braddock's | **Medford/NJ** –
🔼 Bridgetown Mill | **Langhorne** 25
Bridgid's | **Fairmount** 21
Buckley's | **Centerville/DE** 17
Cameron Estate | **Mt Joy/LB** –
Carversville Inn | **Carversville** 22
Casona | **Collingswood/NJ** 22
Cebu | **Old City** –
Centre Bridge | **New Hope** 19
🔼 Chophouse | **Gibbsboro/NJ** 25
NEW Cochon | **Queen Vill** 24
Cock 'n Bull | **Lahaska** 17
Cork | **Westmont/NJ** 20
Cosimo | **Malvern** 22
Coyote Cross. | **Consho** 20
Creed's | **King of Prussia** 23
Cresheim Cottage | **Mt Airy** 18
Cuttalossa Inn | **Lumberville** 16
Delmonico's | **Wynnefield** 20
NEW Devil's Den | **S Philly** –
Dilworth. Inn | **W Chester** 25
🔼 Duling-Kurtz | **Exton** 25
Elephant & Castle | **multi.** 11
El Serrano | **Lancaster/LB** 19

Epicurean | **Phoenixville** 21
Fadó Irish | **Ctr City W** 15
Filomena | **multi.** 24
🔼 Fogo de Chão | **Ave of Arts** 23
Four Dogs | **W Chester** 18
Gables | **Chadds Ford** 20
Gen. Lafayette | **Lafayette Hill** 15
Gen. Warren | **Malvern** 25
Georges' | **Wayne** 20
🔼 Giumarello's | **Westmont/NJ** 26
Golden Pheasant | **Erwinna** 23
Grace Tavern | **Ctr City W** 19
🔼 Gracie's | **Pine Forge/LB** 26
🔼 Green Hills Inn | **Reading/LB** 26
Harry's Savoy | **Wilming/DE** 23
Harry's Seafood | **Wilming/DE** 22
Havana | **New Hope** 15
Hibachi | **Berwyn** 18
High St. Grill | **Mt Holly/NJ** 23
Hokka Hokka | **Ches Hill** 20
Horizons | **South St.** 26
Hotel du Village | **New Hope** 22
Illuminare | **Fairmount** 18
Inn/Phillips Mill | **New Hope** 24
Inn/St. Peter's | **St Peters** –
Inn/Hawke | **Lambertville/NJ** 19
James | **S Philly** 25
Jones | **Ctr City E** 20
Kildare's | **multi.** 16
🔼 Kimberton Inn | **Kimberton** 25
King George II | **Bristol** 21
Kitchen 233 | **Westmont/NJ** 20
🔼 Krazy Kat's |
    Montchanin/DE 26
🔼 La Bonne Auberge |
    New Hope 27
La Campagne | **Cherry Hill/NJ** 24
La Collina | **Bala Cynwyd** 23
Landing | **New Hope** 16
Las Cazuelas | **N Liberties** 24
Mantra | **Ctr City W** 19
Marathon Grill | **Ctr City E** 18
Marigold Kitchen | **Univ City** 24
Mastoris | **Bordentown/NJ** 20
Mazzi | **Leola/LB** –
McGillin's | **Ctr City E** 16
Mendenhall Inn | **Mendenhall** 21
Mexican Post | **Wilming/DE** 17
Moriarty's | **Ctr City E** 19

Mother's | **New Hope**	18
Naked Choco. | **Ave of Arts**	25
Newtown Grill | **Newtown Sq**	21
Old Guard Hse. | **Gladwyne**	23
P.J. Whelihan's | **Medford Lakes/NJ**	15
Plough & Stars | **Old City**	18
Plumsteadville Inn | **Plumsteadville**	19
Pond | **Radnor**	21
Pub | **Pennsauken/NJ**	21
Redstone | **Plymouth Meeting**	21
Rest./Doneckers | **Ephrata/LB**	19
Rose Tree Inn | **Media**	22
Saloon | **S Philly**	24
Sassafras Int'l | **Old City**	–
Scoogi's | **Flourtown**	19
Serrano | **Old City**	20
Shanachie | **Ambler**	17
Sly Fox | **Royersford**	15
Snackbar | **Ctr City W**	18
Spamps | **Consho**	17
☑ Standard Tap | **N Liberties**	24
NEW Station Bistro | **Kimberton**	–
Swanky Bubbles | **Cherry Hill/NJ**	20
☑ Swann Lounge | **Ctr City W**	27
Twin Bays | **Phoenixville**	24
NEW Vango | **Ctr City W**	16
Vesuvio | **S Philly**	17
Viggiano's | **Consho**	19
Vincent's | **W Chester**	16
Wash. Cross. | **Wash Cross**	17
Wash. St. Ale | **Wilming/DE**	17
Whip Tavern | **Coatesville**	20
William Penn | **Gwynedd**	22
Yardley Inn | **Yardley**	21
Zesty's | **Manayunk**	20

HISTORIC PLACES

(Year opened; * building)

1681 | King George II | **Bristol**	21
1700 | Cresheim Cottage* | **Mt Airy**	18
1714 | William Penn* | **Gwynedd**	22
1726 | La Famiglia* | **Old City**	24
1734 | Joseph Ambler* | **N Wales**	23
1736 | Seven Stars Inn | **Phoenixville**	23
1740 | La Bonne Auberge* | **New Hope**	27
1740 | Pace One* | **Thornton**	21
1743 | Blue Bell Inn* | **Blue Bell**	21
1745 | Gen. Warren* | **Malvern**	25
1750 | Brandywine* | **Chadds Ford**	20
1751 | Plumsteadville Inn | **Plumsteadville**	19
1756 | Inn/Phillips Mill* | **New Hope**	24
1758 | Cuttalossa Inn* | **Lumberville**	16
1758 | Dilworth. Inn* | **W Chester**	25
1760 | Wash. Cross.* | **Wash Cross**	17
1764 | Brick Hotel* | **Newtown**	18
1765 | Yangming* | **Bryn Mawr**	25
1773 | City Tavern* | **Old City**	19
1776 | DiNardo's* | **Old City**	19
1776 | Twin Bays* | **Phoenixville**	24
1790 | Mainland Inn* | **Mainland**	26
1791 | Bridgetown Mill* | **Langhorne**	25
1796 | Kimberton Inn* | **Kimberton**	25
1800 | Bistro Romano* | **Society Hill**	21
1800 | Bourbon Blue* | **Manayunk**	19
1800 | Old Guard Hse.* | **Gladwyne**	23
1800 | Robin's Nest* | **Mt Holly/NJ**	25
1801 | London Grill* | **Fairmount**	18
1805 | Cameron Estate* | **Mt Joy/LB**	–
1806 | Snockey's Oyster* | **S Philly**	18
1813 | Carversville Inn* | **Carversville**	22
1823 | Braddock's* | **Medford/NJ**	–
1830 | Bay Pony Inn* | **Lederach**	19
1830 | Duling-Kurtz | **Exton**	25
1830 | Rist. San Marco* | **Ambler**	26
1832 | Yardley Inn* | **Yardley**	21
1833 | New Tavern* | **Bala Cynwyd**	16

subscribe to ZAGAT.com

1837 | National Mech.* | **Old City**	17
1846 | Knight House* | **Doylestown**	21
1849 | Dante & Luigi's* | **S Philly**	23
1850 | Roselena's* | **S Philly**	21
1850 | Siam Cuisine/Black* | **Doylestown**	23
1851 | Catherine's* | **Unionville**	24
1852 | Haydn Zug's* | **E Petersburg/LB**	18
1854 | Los Catrines* | **Ctr City W**	24
1855 | Mendenhall Inn* | **Mendenhall**	21
1856 | High St. Grill* | **Mt Holly/NJ**	23
1857 | Golden Pheasant* | **Erwinna**	23
1860 | Inn/Hawke* | **Lambertville/NJ**	19
1860 | Little Fish* | **S Philly**	28
1860 | McGillin's | **Ctr City E**	16
1861 | Palace/Ben* | **Ctr City E**	21
1863 | Lambertville Station* | **Lambertville/NJ**	18
1864 | Slate Bleu* | **Doylestown**	22
1865 | Old Orig. Bookbinder* | **Old City**	19
1867 | Ida Mae's* | **Fishtown**	22
1870 | Ernesto's 1521* | **Ctr City W**	21
1870 | Marsha Brown* | **New Hope**	20
1878 | Coleman* | **Blue Bell**	20
1890 | Jack's Firehse.* | **Fairmount**	19
1890 | Spamps* | **Consho**	17
1892 | Birchrunville Store* | **Birchrunville**	28
1892 | Reading Term. Mkt.* | **Ctr City E**	23
1896 | Bella Tori* | **Langhorne**	19
1896 | Rx* | **Univ City**	23
1897 | Gables* | **Chadds Ford**	20
1900 | Cucina Forte* | **S Philly**	24
1900 | Jasper* | **Downingtown**	25
1900 | Ralph's | **S Philly**	22
1900 | Winnie's Le Bus* | **Manayunk**	21
1905 | Casona* | **Collingswood/NJ**	22

1907 | Hotel du Village* | **New Hope**	22
1907 | Marigold Kitchen* | **Univ City**	24
1908 | Anastasi | **S Philly**	22
1910 | Victor Café | **S Philly**	20
1913 | Green Room | **Wilming/DE**	25
1920 | Susanna Foo* | **Ctr City W**	24
1923 | Famous 4th St. Deli | **South St.**	22
1927 | Marra's | **S Philly**	22
1929 | Miller's Smorgas. | **Ronks/LB**	18
1930 | Anthony's* | **Haddon Hts/NJ**	22
1930 | John's Roast Pork | **S Philly**	27
1930 | Otto's Brauhaus | **Horsham**	20
1930 | Pat's Steaks | **S Philly**	20
1932 | Mayfair Diner | **NE Philly**	15
1935 | Charlie's Hamburgers | **Folsom**	24
1935 | Melrose Diner | **S Philly**	16
1936 | Buckley's | **Centerville/DE**	17
1939 | Jim's Steaks | **W Philly**	22
1940 | Mrs. Robino's | **Wilming/DE**	20
1940 | Pub/Penn Valley* | **Narberth**	19
1945 | Murray's Deli | **Bala Cynwyd**	19
1948 | Tacconelli's | **Port Richmond**	25
1950 | Ben & Irv Deli | **Hunt Vly**	19
1950 | Rose Tree Inn | **Media**	22
1951 | Pub | **Pennsauken/NJ**	21
1955 | Hank's Place | **Chadds Ford**	19
1955 | Hymie's Deli | **Merion Sta**	17
1956 | Charcoal Pit | **Wilming/DE**	20

HOTEL DINING

Best Western Inn	
Palace of Asia | **Ft Wash**	24
Brick Hotel	
Brick Hotel | **Newtown**	18
Centre Bridge Inn	
Centre Bridge | **New Hope**	19

Chestnut Hill Hotel
Chestnut Grill | **Ches Hill** _17_

Clarion Hotel
Elephant & Castle |
Cherry Hill/NJ _11_

Clarion Inn at Mendenhall
Mendenhall Inn | **Mendenhall** _21_

Crowne Plaza Center City
Elephant & Castle |
Ctr City W _11_

DoubleTree Guest Suites
GG's | **Mt Laurel/NJ** _21_

Duling-Kurtz House
🛂 Duling-Kurtz | **Exton** _25_

Four Seasons Hotel
🛂 Fountain | **Ctr City W** _29_
🛂 Swann Lounge | **Ctr City W** _27_

General Lafayette Inn
Gen. Lafayette | **Lafayette Hill** _15_

General Warren Inne
Gen. Warren | **Malvern** _25_

Golden Pheasant Inn
Golden Pheasant | **Erwinna** _23_

Hilton Philadelphia City Ave.
Delmonico's | **Wynnefield** _20_

Holiday Inn
Red Hot & Blue | **Cherry Hill/NJ** _17_

Hotel du Pont
Brew HaHa! | **Wilming/DE** _18_
🛂 Green Room | **Wilming/DE** _25_

Hotel du Village
Hotel du Village | **New Hope** _22_

Inn at Leola Village
Mazzi | **Leola/LB** _–_

Inn at Montchanin Village
🛂 Krazy Kat's |
Montchanin/DE _26_

Inn at Penn
Penne | **Univ City** _18_

Inn at Phillips Mill
Inn/Phillips Mill | **New Hope** _24_

Joseph Ambler Inn
Joseph Ambler | **N Wales** _23_

Loews Philadelphia Hotel
SoleFood | **Ctr City E** _21_

Parc Rittenhouse
🆕 Parc | **Ctr City W** _–_

Park Hyatt at the Bellevue
🛂 Nineteen | **Ave of Arts** _23_

Penn's View Hotel
Rist. Panorama | **Old City** _24_

Philadelphia Marriott West
Shula's 347 | **W Consho** _21_

Plumsteadville Inn
Plumsteadville Inn |
Plumsteadville _19_

Radisson Plaza-Warwick Hotel
Prime Rib | **Ctr City W** _25_
Tavern 17 | **Ctr City W** _18_

Rittenhouse Hotel
Cassatt Tea Rm. | **Ctr City W** _23_
🛂 Lacroix | **Ctr City W** _28_
Smith/Wollensky |
Ctr City W _22_

Ritz-Carlton Hotel
🆕 10 Arts | **Ave of Arts** _–_

Sheraton City Center Hotel
Phillips Sea. | **Ctr City W** _19_

Society Hill Hotel
Society Hill Hotel | **Old City** _18_

Sofitel Philadelphia
Chez Colette | **Ctr City W** _20_

Swan Hotel
Anton's/Swan |
Lambertville/NJ _20_

Wayne Hotel
Rest. Taquet | **Wayne** _24_

William Penn Inn
William Penn | **Gwynedd** _22_

Willow Valley Resort
Willow Valley | **Lancaster/LB** _19_

JACKET REQUIRED

🛂 Fountain | **Ctr City W** _29_
Prime Rib | **Ctr City W** _25_

LATE DINING

(Weekday closing hour)
Abyssinia | 1 AM | **Univ City** _24_
Alfa | 1 AM | **Ctr City W** _16_
Anjou | 12 AM | **Old City** _19_
🆕 Apothecary | 2 AM |
Ctr City E _–_
🆕 Azul Cantina | 2 AM |
Ctr City E _–_
Bahama Breeze | varies |
King of Prussia _17_
Banana Leaf | 2 AM | **Chinatown** _22_
Bar Ferdinand | 12 AM |
N Liberties _23_

Name	Rating
NEW Belgian Café	12 AM	**Fairmount**	15
NEW Beneluxx	12 AM	**Old City**	20
Black Sheep	12 AM	**Ctr City W**	16
Bottom of Sea	1 AM	**W Philly**	22
Bridget Foy's	12 AM	**South St.**	19
Byblos	2 AM	**Ctr City W**	16
Cantina Caballitos/Segundos	1 AM	**S Philly**	21
Charcoal Pit	varies	**Wilming/DE**	20
Z Chickie's/Pete's	varies	**multi.**	18
Christopher's	1 AM	**Wayne**	17
Copabanana	varies	**multi.**	16
Dalessandro's	12 AM	**Roxborough**	24
D'Angelo's	12 AM	**Ctr City W**	18
Dark Horse	12 AM	**Society Hill**	17
NEW Devil's Den	2 AM	**S Philly**	-
Elephant & Castle	varies	**multi.**	11
Eulogy Belgian	1:30 AM	**Old City**	18
Fadó Irish	12 AM	**Ctr City W**	15
Fergie's Pub	12 AM	**Ctr City E**	17
Fox & Hound	varies	**multi.**	12
Fuji Mtn.	1:30 AM	**Ctr City W**	22
Geno's Steaks	24 hrs.	**S Philly**	19
Good Dog	1 AM	**Ctr City W**	22
Grace Tavern	2 AM	**Ctr City W**	19
Grey Lodge	2 AM	**NE Philly**	18
NEW Harusame	12 AM	**Ardmore**	-
H.K. Gold. Phoenix	12 AM	**Chinatown**	20
Imperial Inn	12 AM	**Chinatown**	20
Iron Hill	varies	**W Chester**	18
Jim's Steaks	varies	**multi.**	22
Johnny Brenda's	1 AM	**Fishtown**	21
Jones	12 AM	**Ctr City E**	20
NEW José Pistola's	1 AM	**Ctr City W**	16
Joy Tsin Lau	11:30 PM	**Chinatown**	20
Kildare's	12 AM	**multi.**	16
La Lupe	12 AM	**S Philly**	22
Liberties	2 AM	**Hulmeville**	14
Little Pete's	varies	**Ctr City W**	16
Manayunk Brew.	1 AM	**Manayunk**	18
Maoz Veg.	1 AM	**South St.**	22
Marathon Grill	12 AM	**Ctr City E**	18
Mastoris	1 AM	**Bordentown/NJ**	20
Mayfair Diner	24 hrs.	**NE Philly**	15
McFadden's	2 AM	**S Philly**	13
McGillin's	1 AM	**Ctr City E**	16
Melrose Diner	24 hrs.	**S Philly**	16
NEW Memphis Taproom	12 AM	**Port Richmond**	-
Mexican Post	varies	**Old City**	17
Misconduct Tav.	1:30 AM	**Ctr City W**	17
Monk's Cafe	1 AM	**Ctr City W**	22
Moriarty's	1 AM	**Ctr City E**	19
National Mech.	1 AM	**Old City**	17
New Wave	1 AM	**Queen Vill**	18
Nodding Head	12 AM	**Ctr City W**	18
N. 3rd	1 AM	**N Liberties**	22
Ortlieb's Jazz	12 AM	**N Liberties**	-
Pat's Steaks	24 hrs.	**S Philly**	20
Penang	1 AM	**Chinatown**	22
P.J. Whelihan's	varies	**multi.**	15
Ponzio's	1 AM	**Cherry Hill/NJ**	17
Redstone	varies	**Plymouth Meeting**	21
Royal Tavern	1 AM	**S Philly**	23
Sassafras Int'l	12 AM	**Old City**	-
Shiao Lan Kung	12:30 AM	**Chinatown**	25
Silk City	12 AM	**N Liberties**	20
Smith/Wollensky	1:30 AM	**Ctr City W**	22
Snackbar	1 AM	**Ctr City W**	18
Society Hill Hotel	12 AM	**Old City**	18
Z Standard Tap	1 AM	**N Liberties**	24
Steve's Prince/Stks.	12 AM	**NE Philly**	24
St. Stephens Green	12 AM	**Fairmount**	19

Swanky Bubbles | 1 AM | Old City | 20

☑ Swann Lounge | 12 AM | Ctr City W | 27

Tai Lake | 3 AM | Chinatown | 24

Taq. La Veracruz. | 12 AM | S Philly | 22

Taq. Puerto Veracruz. | 12 AM | S Philly | -

Tavern 17 | 1 AM | Ctr City W | 18

Teca | 2 AM | W Chester | 21

Teresa's Next Dr. | 1 AM | Wayne | 20

NEW Time | 1 AM | Ctr City E | -

☑ Tinto | 12 AM | Ctr City W | 27

☑ Tony Luke's | varies | S Philly | 25

Tria | varies | multi. | 23

Triumph Brewing | varies | multi. | 19

NEW Urban Saloon | 2 AM | Fairmount | 16

Valanni | 1 AM | Ctr City E | 23

NEW Vango | 2 AM | Ctr City W | 16

Vesuvio | 12 AM | S Philly | 17

Victory Brewing | 12 AM | Downingtown | 15

Vintage | 2 AM | Ctr City E | 19

Warmdaddy's | 2 AM | S Philly | 20

Wash. St. Ale | 1 AM | Wilming/DE | 17

NEW Yakitori Boy | 2 AM | Chinatown | 22

yello'bar | 1 AM | S Philly | 16

MEET FOR A DRINK

Abbaye | N Liberties | 22

Al Dar Bistro | Bala Cynwyd | 17

Alfa | Ctr City W | 16

☑ Alma de Cuba | Ctr City W | 25

NEW Ameritage | Wilming/DE | -

NEW Apothecary | Ctr City E | -

☑NEW Azie | Media | 24

NEW Azul Cantina | Ctr City E | -

Bar Ferdinand | N Liberties | 23

Beau Monde | South St. | 23

NEW Belgian Café | Fairmount | 15

NEW Beneluxx | Old City | 20

Bensí | N Wales | 18

Bistro Cassis | Radnor | 20

Black Sheep | Ctr City W | 16

NEW Blue Pear | W Chester | 22

Blush | Bryn Mawr | 20

Bonefish Grill | multi. | 21

☑ Brasserie Perrier | Ctr City W | 24

Calif. Pizza | Plymouth Meeting | 19

Cantina Caballitos/Segundos | S Philly | 21

☑ Capital Grille | Ave of Arts | 26

Caribou Cafe | Ctr City E | 19

Carmine's Creole | Bryn Mawr | 22

Cebu | Old City | -

Cheeseburger/Paradise | Langhorne | 15

☑ Chickie's/Pete's | Bordentown/NJ | 18

Chick's | South St. | 23

Chops | Bala Cynwyd | 19

☑ Continental, The | Old City | 22

☑ Continental Mid-town | Ctr City W | 21

Coquette | South St. | 18

Cosimo | Malvern | 22

Coyote Cross. | Consho | 20

☑ Cuba Libre | Old City | 21

Dark Horse | Society Hill | 17

Davio's | Ctr City W | 23

Delmonico's | Wynnefield | 20

Derek's | Manayunk | 19

Devil's Alley | Ctr City W | 19

NEW Devil's Den | S Philly | -

Doc Magrogan | W Chester | 16

Earl's Prime | Lahaska | 24

Ecco Qui | Univ City | 17

Eulogy Belgian | Old City | 18

Fadó Irish | Ctr City W | 15

Fergie's Pub | Ctr City E | 17

NEW Field House | Ctr City E | 13

Georges' | Wayne | 20

Good Dog | Ctr City W | 22

Grey Lodge | NE Philly | 18

Happy Rooster | Ctr City W | 17

Horizons | South St. | 26

Inn/Hawke | Lambertville/NJ | 19

Iron Hill | multi. | 18

J.B. Dawson's/Austin's | multi. | 18

NEW J.L. Sullivan's | Ave of Arts | -

Jonathan's | Jenkintown | 17

Jones | Ctr City E | 20

NEW José Pistola's | Ctr City W | 16

Kildare's | South St. | 16

Kitchen 233 | **Westmont/NJ**	20	
NEW Knock | **Ctr City E**	19	
NEW Les Bons Temps | **Ctr City E**	-	
Liberties | **Manayunk**	14	
Loie | **Ctr City W**	17	
London Grill | **Fairmount**	18	
Los Catrines | **Ctr City W**	24	
L2 | **Ctr City W**	17	
Maggio's | **Southampton**	17	
NEW Maia | **Villanova**	-	
Manayunk Brew. | **Manayunk**	18	
Mantra | **Ctr City W**	19	
McCormick/Schmick | **multi.**	21	
McFadden's | **multi.**	13	
Brandywine | **Chadds Ford**	20	
NEW Memphis Taproom | **Port Richmond**	-	
Mexican Post | **Ctr City W**	17	
Misconduct Tav. | **Ctr City W**	17	
Mission Grill | **Ctr City W**	21	
Mixto | **Ctr City E**	21	
Monk's Cafe | **Ctr City W**	22	
Moriarty's | **Ctr City E**	19	
National Mech. | **Old City**	17	
Newtown Grill | **Newtown Sq**	21	
New Wave | **Queen Vill**	18	
Z Nineteen | **Ave of Arts**	23	
Oceanaire | **Ctr City E**	22	
Z Osteria | **N Philly**	26	
NEW Pearl | **Ctr City W**	-	
Penne | **Univ City**	18	
NEW Peppercorns | **S Philly**	-	
Z P.F. Chang's | **multi.**	21	
NEW Pietro's Prime | **W Chester**	24	
P.J. Whelihan's | **multi.**	15	
Plough & Stars | **Old City**	18	
Prime Rib | **Ctr City W**	25	
Rae | **Univ City**	22	
Redstone | **Marlton/NJ**	21	
Rist. Panorama | **Old City**	24	
Royal Tavern | **S Philly**	23	
Sassafras Int'l | **Old City**	-	
Shanachie | **Ambler**	17	
Sidecar | **S Philly**	19	
Silk City | **N Liberties**	20	
NEW Sláinte | **Univ City**	18	
Sly Fox | **multi.**	15	

Snackbar | **Ctr City W**	18	
Society Hill Hotel | **Old City**	18	
Spamps | **Consho**	17	
Z Standard Tap | **N Liberties**	24	
St. Stephens Green | **Fairmount**	19	
NEW Supper | **South St.**	23	
Swanky Bubbles | **Cherry Hill/NJ**	20	
Z Swann Lounge | **Ctr City W**	27	
NEW Table 31 | **Ctr City W**	-	
Tango | **Bryn Mawr**	20	
Tavern 17 | **Ctr City W**	18	
Ted's Montana | **multi.**	16	
NEW 10 Arts | **Ave of Arts**	-	
Teresa's Next Dr. | **Wayne**	20	
NEW Time | **Ctr City E**	-	
Z Tinto | **Ctr City W**	27	
Tír na nÓg | **Ctr City W**	14	
Tokyo Bleu | **Cinnaminson/NJ**	21	
NEW Tortilla Press Cantina | **Pennsauken/NJ**	19	
NEW Toscana 52 | **Feasterville**	-	
Tria | **Ctr City E**	23	
Triumph Brewing | **multi.**	19	
Twenty Manning | **Ctr City W**	22	
NEW Ugly American | **S Philly**	19	
NEW Urban Saloon | **Fairmount**	16	
Valanni | **Ctr City E**	23	
NEW Vango | **Ctr City W**	16	
Vintage | **Ctr City E**	19	
Warmdaddy's | **S Philly**	20	
Z Water Works | **Fairmount**	21	
Wooden Iron | **Wayne**	18	
Xochitl | **Society Hill**	23	
NEW Yakitori Boy | **Chinatown**	22	
yello'bar | **S Philly**	16	
ZoT | **Society Hill**	20	

MICROBREWERIES

NEW Dock Street | **Univ City**	18	
Gen. Lafayette | **Lafayette Hill**	15	
Iron Hill | **multi.**	18	
Manayunk Brew. | **Manayunk**	18	
Nodding Head | **Ctr City W**	18	
Rock Bottom | **King of Prussia**	16	
Sly Fox | **Phoenixville**	15	
Stoudt's | **Adamstown/LB**	18	
Triumph Brewing | **multi.**	19	
Victory Brewing | **Downingtown**	15	

NATURAL/ORGANIC

(These restaurants often or always use organic, local ingredients)

Alisa Cafe | **Cherry Hill/NJ**	22
Apamate | **Ctr City W**	23
NEW Auspicious | **Ardmore**	19
Baja Fresh Mex. | **multi.**	17
Barnacle Ben's | **Moorestown/NJ**	20
Bensí | **N Wales**	18
Bistro La Baia | **Ctr City W**	20
Bistro La Viola | **Ctr City W**	24
Bistro 7 | **Old City**	24
Bliss | **Ave of Arts**	22
Brick Hotel | **Newtown**	18
California Cafe | **King of Prussia**	20
Carr's | **Lancaster/LB**	25
Catelli | **Voorhees/NJ**	24
Charles Plaza | **Chinatown**	23
Chiangmai | **Consho**	25
Chlöe | **Old City**	25
☑ Citrus | **Ches Hill**	25
Coleman | **Blue Bell**	20
☑ Continental, The | **Old City**	22
Copper Bistro | **N Liberties**	22
Corner Bistro | **Wilming/DE**	21
Cresheim Cottage | **Mt Airy**	18
D'Angelo's | **Ctr City W**	18
Farmicia | **Old City**	20
Good Dog | **Ctr City W**	22
Half Moon | **Kennett Sq**	20
Hamilton's | **Lambertville/NJ**	25
Harry's Savoy | **Wilming/DE**	23
High St. Grill | **Mt Holly/NJ**	23
Il Tartufo | **Manayunk**	23
Inn/St. Peter's | **St Peters**	-
Jack's Firehse. | **Fairmount**	19
Jake's | **Manayunk**	25
James | **S Philly**	25
NEW Javier | **Haddonfield/NJ**	21
Jonathan's | **Jenkintown**	17
☑ Kimberton Inn | **Kimberton**	25
Kitchen 233 | **Westmont/NJ**	20
NEW Knock | **Ctr City E**	19
☑ La Bonne Auberge | **New Hope**	27
☑ Lacroix | **Ctr City W**	28
La Vang | **Willow Grove**	22
☑ Le Bec-Fin | **Ctr City W**	27
Le Castagne | **Ctr City W**	22

☑ Little Fish | **S Philly**	28
Loie | **Ctr City W**	17
NEW Maia | **Villanova**	-
Majolica | **Phoenixville**	26
Marathon Grill | **Ctr City W**	18
Marco Polo | **Elkins Pk**	19
Marigold Kitchen | **Univ City**	24
Meritage | **Ctr City W**	23
Mission Grill | **Ctr City W**	21
NEW Murray's Deli/bistro M | **Berwyn**	19
NEW Nicholas | **S Philly**	-
Oceanaire | **Ctr City E**	22
Phila. Fish | **Old City**	21
Portofino | **Ctr City E**	20
PTG | **Roxborough**	20
Pumpkin | **Ctr City W**	24
☑ Rest. Alba | **Malvern**	27
Roller's/Flying Fish | **Ches Hill**	21
Rouge | **Ctr City W**	22
Royal Tavern | **S Philly**	23
Rx | **Univ City**	23
Salt & Pepper | **S Philly**	23
Sazon | **N Philly**	21
Simon Pearce | **W Chester**	20
Sovalo | **N Liberties**	25
NEW Supper | **South St.**	23
☑ Susanna Foo | **Ctr City W**	24
NEW Swallow | **N Liberties**	-
☑ Talula's Table | **Kennett Sq**	26
Tavern 17 | **Ctr City W**	18
Ted's Montana | **multi.**	16
NEW 10 Arts | **Ave of Arts**	-
Vesuvio | **S Philly**	17
Wash. Cross. | **Wash Cross**	17
☑ Water Works | **Fairmount**	21
Whip Tavern | **Coatesville**	20
☑ White Dog | **Univ City**	21
Winberie's | **Wayne**	16

NOTEWORTHY NEWCOMERS

Aloe Fusion | **Cherry Hill/NJ**	-
Ameritage | **Wilming/DE**	-
Apothecary | **Ctr City E**	-
Ashoka Palace | **Ctr City W**	-
Asuka | **Blue Bell**	-
Auspicious | **Ardmore**	19
☑ Azie | **Media**	24

Azul Cantina | **Ctr City E**	⌐
Belgian Café | **Fairmount**	15
Beneluxx | **Old City**	20
Bindi | **Ctr City E**	22
Blue Pear | **W Chester**	22
Brio | **Cherry Hill/NJ**	19
Buona Via | **Horsham**	19
Cafe Coláo | **N Liberties**	⌐
Café Estelle | **N Liberties**	⌐
Cake | **Ches Hill**	21
Cantina Dos Segundos | **N Liberties**	21
Chima | **Ctr City W**	⌐
Cochon | **Queen Vill**	24
Cravings | **Lansdale**	21
Devil's Den | **S Philly**	⌐
Distrito | **Univ City**	⌐
Dock Street | **Univ City**	18
El Portal | **W Chester**	⌐
El Ranchito | **N Philly**	⌐
Field House | **Ctr City E**	13
Gaya | **Blue Bell**	⌐
goodburger | **Ctr City W**	⌐
Harusame | **Ardmore**	⌐
Il Fiore | **Collingswood/NJ**	⌐
Javier | **Haddonfield/NJ**	21
J.L. Sullivan's | **Ave of Arts**	⌐
Joe Pesce | **multi.**	18
José Pistola's | **Ctr City W**	16
Kanella | **Ctr City E**	⌐
Knock | **Ctr City E**	19
Las Bugambilias | **South St.**	26
Les Bons Temps | **Ctr City E**	⌐
Le Virtù | **S Philly**	26
Lucky's Coffee | **Wilming/DE**	17
Maia | **Villanova**	⌐
Masamoto | **Glen Mills**	27
Max & David's | **Elkins Pk**	23
Memphis Taproom | **Port Richmond**	⌐
Minar Palace | **Ctr City E**	⌐
Misso | **Ave of Arts**	⌐
Murray's Deli/bistro M | **Berwyn**	19
Nicholas | **S Philly**	⌐
Parc | **Ctr City W**	⌐
Pearl | **Ctr City W**	⌐
Peppercorns | **S Philly**	⌐
Pietro's Prime | **W Chester**	24
Pomodoro | **Wilming/DE**	20
Savor Saigon | **Levittown**	21
Sláinte | **Univ City**	18
Station Bistro | **Kimberton**	⌐
Supper | **South St.**	23
Swallow | **N Liberties**	⌐
Sweet Basil | **Chadds Ford**	21
Table 31 | **Ctr City W**	⌐
10 Arts | **Ave of Arts**	⌐
Tennessee's BBQ | **Levittown**	⌐
Time | **Ctr City E**	⌐
Tortilla Press Cantina | **Pennsauken/NJ**	19
Toscana 52 | **Feasterville**	⌐
Ugly American | **S Philly**	19
Union Gourmet | **Ctr City E**	⌐
Urban Saloon | **Fairmount**	16
Vango | **Ctr City W**	16
Vietnam Café | **W Philly**	23
William Douglas | **Cherry Hill/NJ**	⌐
Yakitori Boy | **Chinatown**	22
Yalda Grill | **Horsham**	20
Zacharias | **Lansdale**	21
Zahav | **Society Hill**	⌐
Zhi Wei Guan | **Chinatown**	⌐

OFFBEAT

AllWays Café | **Hunt Vly**	22
Ansill | **South St.**	24
Bitar's | **S Philly**	23
Bonté Wafflerie | **multi.**	19
Buca di Beppo | **multi.**	15
Carman's Country | **S Philly**	25
Charlie's Hamburgers | **Folsom**	24
☒ Continental Mid-town | **Ctr City W**	21
☒ El Vez | **Ctr City E**	21
Farmicia | **Old City**	20
☒ Gracie's | **Pine Forge/LB**	26
☒ Honey's Sit 'n Eat | **N Liberties**	25
Jake's Hamburgers | **New Castle/DE**	21
Jones | **Ctr City E**	20
La Esperanza | **Lindenwold/NJ**	22
La Lupe | **S Philly**	22
☒ Little Café | **Voorhees/NJ**	27
Little Pete's | **Ctr City W**	16
☒ Maggiano's | **Ctr City E**	20
Manon | **Lambertville/NJ**	25
Melrose Diner | **S Philly**	16

☑ Morimoto | **Ctr City E**	26	Estia | **Ave of Arts**	23
Morning Glory | **S Philly**	24	Fayette St. | **Consho**	23
Moshulu | **DE River**	22	Fellini Cafe | **Ardmore**	21
Nifty Fifty's | **Turnersville/NJ**	19	Figs | **Fairmount**	23
Norma's | **Cherry Hill/NJ**	21	Filomena | **Berlin/NJ**	24
Ota-Ya | **multi.**	24	Fioravanti | **Downingtown**	26
Penang | **Chinatown**	22	Fleming's Prime | **Wayne**	25
Pod | **Univ City**	23	☑ Fork | **Old City**	24
Pop Shop | **Collingswood/NJ**	20	Funky Lil' Kitchen | **Pottstown**	23
Pub | **Pennsauken/NJ**	21	Gables | **Chadds Ford**	20
Shanachie | **Ambler**	17	GG's | **Mt Laurel/NJ**	21
Shank's & Evelyn's | **S Philly**	24	☑ Gibraltar | **Lancaster/LB**	27
Siam | **Lambertville/NJ**	22	Gnocchi | **South St.**	22
Silk City | **N Liberties**	20	Harry's Seafood | **Wilming/DE**	22
Simon Pearce | **W Chester**	20	High St. Grill | **Mt Holly/NJ**	23
Siri's | **Cherry Hill/NJ**	25	Ida Mae's | **Fishtown**	22
Somsak/Taan | **Voorhees/NJ**	25	Il Cantuccio | **N Liberties**	23
Tacconelli's | **Port Richmond**	25	Illuminare | **Fairmount**	18
Trolley Car | **Mt Airy**	14	Jasper | **Downingtown**	25
Water Lily | **Collingswood/NJ**	22	🆕 Joe Pesce | **Collingswood/NJ**	18
		Joe's Peking | **Marlton/NJ**	22
OPEN KITCHEN		Johnny Mañana's | **East Falls**	15
Alisa Cafe | **Cherry Hill/NJ**	22	Jonathan's | **Jenkintown**	17
☑ Alison/Blue Bell | **Blue Bell**	26	Jones | **Ctr City E**	20
☑ Amada | **Old City**	28	Kabobeesh | **Univ City**	23
Apamate | **Ctr City W**	23	Karma | **Old City**	23
Audrey Claire | **Ctr City W**	22	Kibitz Room | **Cherry Hill/NJ**	23
☑ Bàcio | **Cinnaminson/NJ**	25	La Esperanza | **Lindenwold/NJ**	22
Barone's | **Moorestown/NJ**	21	La Lupe | **S Philly**	22
Basil Bistro | **Paoli**	18	☑ L'Angolo | **S Philly**	26
🆕 Beneluxx | **Old City**	20	Las Cazuelas | **N Liberties**	24
Bistro Juliana | **Fishtown**	23	Latest Dish | **South St.**	24
Bistro 7 | **Old City**	24	La Vang | **Willow Grove**	22
Bocelli | **Ambler**	–	🆕 Le Virtù | **S Philly**	26
Bonefish Grill | **multi.**	21	Lilly's/Canal | **Lambertville/NJ**	20
🆕 Café Estelle | **N Liberties**	–	☑ Little Fish | **S Philly**	28
California Cafe | **King of Prussia**	20	L'Oca | **Fairmount**	23
Carambola | **Dresher**	23	☑ Lolita | **Ctr City E**	25
Cebu | **Old City**	–	Maccabeam | **Ctr City E**	18
☑ Chophouse | **Gibbsboro/NJ**	25	Maggio's | **Southampton**	17
🆕 Cochon | **Queen Vill**	24	Majolica | **Phoenixville**	26
Coconut Bay | **Voorhees/NJ**	22	Margot | **Narberth**	20
Copper Bistro | **N Liberties**	22	🆕 Masamoto | **Glen Mills**	27
Dilworth. Inn | **W Chester**	25	🆕 Max & David's | **Elkins Pk**	23
☑ Dmitri's | **multi.**	25	☑ Mercato | **Ctr City E**	26
🆕 Dock Street | **Univ City**	18	Mirabella | **Cherry Hill/NJ**	22
Ecco Qui | **Univ City**	17	More Than Ice Crm. | **Ctr City E**	20
Eclipse Bistro | **Wilming/DE**	23		
Emerald Fish | **Cherry Hill/NJ**	23		

Morning Glory | **S Philly**	24	Athena | P | **Glenside**	21
🄩 Moro | **Wilming/DE**	25	Audrey Claire | S | **Ctr City W**	22
🄩 Morton's | **multi.**	25	Bay Pony Inn | T | **Lederach**	19
Mr. Bill's | **Winslow/NJ**	-	Beau Monde | T | **South St.**	23
Ms. Tootsie's | **South St.**	21	Bistro La Baia | S | **Ctr City W**	20
Murray's Deli | **Bala Cynwyd**	19	Bistro La Viola | S | **Ctr City W**	24
🄽🄴🅆 Murray's Deli/bistro M |	19	Bliss | S | **Ave of Arts**	22
Berwyn		Blue Parrot | P | **Wilming/DE**	18
Old Orig. Bookbinder | **Old City**	19	Branzino | P | **Ctr City W**	23
🄩 Osteria | **N Philly**	26	🄩 Brasserie Perrier | S |	24
Paradiso | **S Philly**	23	**Ctr City W**	
Pho Thai Nam | **Blue Bell**	21	Brasserie 73 | P | **Skippack**	22
Pizzicato | **Marlton/NJ**	20	Brick Hotel | G | **Newtown**	18
🄽🄴🅆 Pomodoro | **Wilming/DE**	20	Bridget Foy's | S | **South St.**	19
Pumpkin | **Ctr City W**	24	🄩 Bridgetown Mill | P | **Langhorne**	25
Pura Vida | **N Liberties**	24	Buckley's | T | **Centerville/DE**	17
Radicchio | **Old City**	24	Café Gallery | T | **Burlington/NJ**	21
Rae | **Univ City**	22	Cafette | G | **Ches Hill**	20
🄩 Rest. Alba | **Malvern**	27	Caffe Aldo | P | **Cherry Hill/NJ**	23
Roy's | **Ctr City W**	23	Caribou Cafe | T | **Ctr City E**	19
Sabrina's Café | **Fairmount**	25	Catherine's | P | **Unionville**	24
Salt & Pepper | **S Philly**	23	Centre Bridge | T | **New Hope**	19
Sidecar | **S Philly**	19	Chart House | T | **DE River**	18
Sullivan's Steak | **multi.**	23	Chestnut Grill | P, S | **Ches Hill**	17
🄽🄴🅆 Supper | **South St.**	23	City Tavern | G | **Old City**	19
Susanna Foo's Kitchen | **Wayne**	21	🄩 Continental, The | S | **Old City**	22
🄽🄴🅆 Swallow | **N Liberties**	-	🄩 Continental Mid-town | P, S |	21
Swanky Bubbles | **Cherry Hill/NJ**	20	**Ctr City W**	
🄩 Talula's Table | **Kennett Sq**	26	Coyote Cross. | P | **Consho**	20
Taq. Moroleon | **Kennett Sq**	24	Cresheim Cottage | P | **Mt Airy**	18
Ted's Montana | **Warrington**	16	🄩 Cuba Libre | S | **Old City**	21
Teresa's Next Dr. | **Wayne**	20	Cuttalossa Inn | T | **Lumberville**	16
Thai L'Elephant | **Phoenixville**	23	Derek's | P, S | **Manayunk**	19
Thai Pepper | **Ardmore**	19	Devon Seafood | P | **Ctr City W**	23
🄩 Tinto | **Ctr City W**	27	Dilworth. Inn | P | **W Chester**	25
Toscana Kitchen | **Wilming/DE**	24	El Serrano | P | **Lancaster/LB**	19
Tratt. Primadonna | **Ctr City W**	17	Figs | S | **Fairmount**	23
🄽🄴🅆 Urban Saloon | **Fairmount**	16	🄩 Fork | S | **Old City**	24
		Four Dogs | P | **W Chester**	18
OUTDOOR DINING		Freight House | T | **Doylestown**	19
(G=garden; P=patio; S=sidewalk; T=terrace)		FuziOn | P | **Worcester**	23
		Gables | P | **Chadds Ford**	20
Abbaye | S | **N Liberties**	22	Gen. Warren | P | **Malvern**	25
Adobe Cafe | P | **Roxborough**	18	🄩 Giumarello's | P |	26
🄩 Alma de Cuba | S | **Ctr City W**	25	**Westmont/NJ**	
Anjou | S | **Old City**	19	Golden Pheasant | G, T | **Erwinna**	23
Anton's/Swan | P |	20	🄩 Gracie's | G, P | **Pine Forge/LB**	26
Lambertville/NJ		Hamilton's | P | **Lambertville/NJ**	25
Arpeggio | S | **Spring House**	23	Harry's Savoy | P, T | **Wilming/DE**	23

Havana | P | **New Hope** | _15_
Hostaria Da Elio | P | **South St.** | _20_
Illuminare | G, T | **Fairmount** | _18_
Inn/Phillips Mill | G | **New Hope** | _24_
Inn/Hawke | P | **Lambertville/NJ** | _19_
Isaac Newton's | G | **Newtown** | _16_
Izzy & Zoe's | S | **Univ City** | _15_
Jack's Firehse. | P, S | **Fairmount** | _19_
Jamaican Jerk Hut | G |
   Ave of Arts | _20_
Joseph Ambler | P | **N Wales** | _23_
La Campagne | G, T |
   Cherry Hill/NJ | _24_
La Colombe | S | **Manayunk** | _23_
Landing | G, T | **New Hope** | _16_
La Veranda | T | **DE River** | _23_
Lilly's/Canal | P | **Lambertville/NJ** | _20_
🄕 Lolita | S | **Ctr City E** | _25_
🄕 Maggiano's | P | **multi.** | _20_
Manayunk Brew. | T | **Manayunk** | _18_
🄕 Mélange | P | **Cherry Hill/NJ** | _27_
Mexican Food | P | **Marlton/NJ** | _21_
Mimosa | P | **W Chester** | _24_
Morning Glory | G, P | **S Philly** | _24_
Moshulu | T | **DE River** | _22_
Mother's | S | **New Hope** | _18_
Newtown Grill | P | **Newtown Sq** | _21_
New Wave | S | **Queen Vill** | _18_
🄕 Nineteen | T | **Ave of Arts** | _23_
North by NW | P | **Mt Airy** | _16_
Oceanaire | P | **Ctr City E** | _22_
Otto's Brauhaus | G | **Horsham** | _20_
Pace One | G | **Thornton** | _21_
Pattaya | P, S | **Univ City** | _19_
Pepper's | P | **Ardmore** | _23_
Phila. Fish | P | **Old City** | _21_
Pietro's Pizzeria | P, S, T | **multi.** | _19_
Pizzicato | S | **Old City** | _20_
Plate | P | **Ardmore** | _16_
Plough & Stars | S | **Old City** | _18_
Pond | G | **Radnor** | _21_
Positano Coast | P | **Society Hill** | _21_
Primavera Pizza | P | **Downingtown** | _18_
Rembrandt's | S | **Fairmount** | _20_
Rest. Taquet | P | **Wayne** | _24_
Robin's Nest | T | **Mt Holly/NJ** | _25_
Rouge | P | **Ctr City W** | _22_
Roux 3 | P | **Newtown Sq** | _21_
Rx | S | **Univ City** | _23_

Savona | T | **Gulph Mills** | _25_
Serrano | S | **Old City** | _20_
Society Hill Hotel | S | **Old City** | _18_
Solaris Grille | G, P | **Ches Hill** | _16_
Spasso | P | **Old City** | _23_
Spring Mill | P | **Consho** | _23_
Summer Kitchen | P |
   Penns Park | _23_
Tango | P | **Bryn Mawr** | _20_
Taq. La Veracruz. | S | **S Philly** | _22_
Teca | P, S | **W Chester** | _21_
Thomas' | S | **Manayunk** | _–_
333 Belrose | P | **Radnor** | _23_
Tír na nÓg | P | **Ctr City W** | _14_
Toscana Kitchen | P | **Wilming/DE** | _24_
Tratt. Alberto | G, S | **W Chester** | _21_
Tratt. Primadonna | S | **Ctr City W** | _17_
Tria | S | **Ctr City W** | _23_
Twenty Manning | S | **Ctr City W** | _22_
Vesuvio | S | **S Philly** | _17_
Vincent's | P | **W Chester** | _16_
Wash. Cross. | G, P | **Wash Cross** | _17_
Wash. St. Ale | P | **Wilming/DE** | _17_
🄕 Water Works | T | **Fairmount** | _21_
Winberie's | P | **Wayne** | _16_
Zesty's | S | **Manayunk** | _20_
Zocalo | P | **Univ City** | _20_

PARKING

(V=valet, *=validated)
🄕 Alma de Cuba | V |
   Ctr City W | _25_
🄕 Amada | V | **Old City** | _28_
Ariana | V | **Old City** | _20_
🄕 Barclay Prime | V |
   Ctr City W | _26_
Bliss* | **Ave of Arts** | _22_
Bourbon Blue | V | **Manayunk** | _19_
🄕 Brasserie Perrier | V |
   Ctr City W | _24_
Bridgets | V | **Ambler** | _22_
Buca di Beppo* | **Ctr City W** | _15_
🄕 Buddakan | V | **Old City** | _26_
Caffe Aldo | V | **Cherry Hill/NJ** | _23_
Caffe Valentino | V | **Ctr City W** | _19_
🄕 Capital Grille | V |
   Ave of Arts | _26_
Cassatt Tea Rm. | V | **Ctr City W** | _23_
Cebu | V | **Old City** | _–_
Centre Bridge | V | **New Hope** | _19_

Chart House | V | **DE River**	18
Chez Colette | V | **Ctr City W**	20
NEW Chima | V | **Ctr City W**	-
Z Chophouse | V | **Gibbsboro/NJ**	25
Chops | V | **Bala Cynwyd**	19
Conley Ward's | V | **Wilming/DE**	17
Z Cuba Libre | V | **Old City**	21
D'Angelo's* | **Ctr City W**	18
Dave & Buster's* | **DE River**	13
Davio's | V | **Ctr City W**	23
Delmonico's | V | **Wynnefield**	20
Derek's* | **Manayunk**	19
DiNardo's* | **Old City**	19
Dolce | V | **Old City**	21
Z El Vez* | **Ctr City E**	21
Estia | V* | **Ave of Arts**	23
Fleming's Prime | V | **Wayne**	25
Z Fogo de Chão | V | **Ave of Arts**	23
Z Fountain | V | **Ctr City W**	29
Fox & Hound* | **Ctr City W**	12
Freight House | V | **Doylestown**	19
Z Giumarello's | V | **Westmont/NJ**	26
Z Green Room | V | **Wilming/DE**	25
H.K. Gold. Phoenix* | **Chinatown**	20
Il Portico | V | **Ctr City W**	20
Il Tartufo | V | **Manayunk**	23
Iron Hill* | **W Chester**	18
Jake's* | **Manayunk**	25
NEW Joe Pesce* | **Ctr City E**	18
Jones | V | **Ctr City E**	20
Joy Tsin Lau* | **Chinatown**	20
Kildare's | V | **King of Prussia**	16
King George II | V | **Bristol**	21
Kristian's | V | **S Philly**	25
La Collina | V | **Bala Cynwyd**	23
Z Lacroix | V | **Ctr City W**	28
La Famiglia | V | **Old City**	24
LaScala's* | **Ctr City E**	20
La Veranda | V | **DE River**	23
Z Le Bar Lyonnais | V | **Ctr City W**	28
Z Le Bec-Fin | V | **Ctr City W**	27
Z Maggiano's | V* | **multi.**	20
Manayunk Brew. | V | **Manayunk**	18
Marsha Brown | V | **New Hope**	20
Z Matyson* | **Ctr City W**	26
Mazzi | V | **Leola/LB**	-

McCormick/Schmick | V | **Ave of Arts**	21
Melting Pot* | **Ctr City E**	20
Meritage* | **Ctr City W**	23
Z Morimoto | V | **Ctr City E**	26
Z Morton's | V | **multi.**	25
Moshulu | V | **DE River**	22
Ms. Tootsie's | V | **South St.**	21
Z Nectar | V | **Berwyn**	26
Newtown Grill | V | **Newtown Sq**	21
Z Nineteen | V* | **Ave of Arts**	23
Oceanaire | V | **Ctr City E**	22
Palm | V | **Ave of Arts**	23
Paradigm | V | **Old City**	18
Patou | V | **Old City**	18
Penne | V | **Univ City**	18
Pho Xe Lua* | **Chinatown**	24
Pod | V | **Univ City**	23
NEW Pomodoro | V | **Wilming/DE**	20
Portofino* | **Ctr City E**	20
Positano Coast | V | **Society Hill**	21
Prime Rib | V | **Ctr City W**	25
Pumpkin* | **Ctr City W**	24
Rae | V | **Univ City**	22
Rist. La Buca* | **Ctr City E**	22
Rist. Panorama | V* | **Old City**	24
Rist. Primavera | V | **Wayne**	17
Roy's | V | **Ctr City W**	23
Ruth's Chris | V | **Ave of Arts**	23
Savona | V | **Gulph Mills**	25
Shiroi Hana* | **Ctr City W**	23
Smith/Wollensky | V | **Ctr City W**	22
Solaris Grille* | **Ches Hill**	16
SoleFood | V | **Ctr City E**	21
Spamps | V | **Consho**	17
Sullivan's Steak | V | **King of Prussia**	23
Z Susanna Foo | V | **Ctr City W**	24
Susanna Foo's Kitchen | V | **Wayne**	21
Swanky Bubbles | V | **Old City**	20
Z Swann Lounge | V | **Ctr City W**	27
Tai Lake* | **Chinatown**	24
Z Tangerine | V | **Old City**	24
Tavern 17* | **Ctr City W**	18
Ted's Montana | V | **Ave of Arts**	16

NEW Time* | Ctr City E — | _

Tír na nÓg | V | Ctr City W — 14

Tratt. Alberto | V | W Chester — 21

Tratt. Primadonna* | Ctr City W — 17

Triumph Brewing | V | Old City — 19

Upstares/Varalli* | Ave of Arts — 21

Vesuvio | V | S Philly — 17

Victor Café | V | S Philly — 20

Z Water Works | V | Fairmount — 21

William Penn | V | Gwynedd — 22

Winnie's Le Bus* | Manayunk — 21

Zesty's | V | Manayunk — 20

PEOPLE-WATCHING

Alfa | Ctr City W — 16

Z Alma de Cuba | Ctr City W — 25

Almaz Café | Ctr City W — 22

Z Amada | Old City — 28

NEW Ameritage | Wilming/DE — _

NEW Apothecary | Ctr City E — _

Audrey Claire | Ctr City W — 22

Z NEW Azie | Media — 24

NEW Azul Cantina | Ctr City E — _

Z Bàcio | Cinnaminson/NJ — 25

Z Barclay Prime | Ctr City W — 26

Bar Ferdinand | N Liberties — 23

NEW Belgian Café | Fairmount — 15

NEW Bindi | Ctr City E — 22

Bistro Cassis | Radnor — 20

Bistro di Marino | Collingswood/NJ — 25

NEW Blue Pear | W Chester — 22

Blush | Bryn Mawr — 20

Bourbon Blue | Manayunk — 19

Z Brasserie Perrier | Ctr City W — 24

Bridget Foy's | South St. — 19

NEW Brio | Cherry Hill/NJ — 19

Z Buddakan | Old City — 26

Caffe Aldo | Cherry Hill/NJ — 23

Calif. Pizza | Plymouth Meeting — 19

Cantina Caballitos/Segundos | S Philly — 21

Z Capital Grille | Ave of Arts — 26

Carmine's Creole | Bryn Mawr — 22

Catelli | Voorhees/NJ — 24

Cebu | Old City — _

Z Chickie's/Pete's | multi. — 18

NEW Chima | Ctr City W — _

Chops | Bala Cynwyd — 19

Z Continental, The | Old City — 22

Z Continental Mid-town | Ctr City W — 21

Copabanana | South St. — 16

Coquette | South St. — 18

Cosimo | Malvern — 22

Creed's | King of Prussia — 23

Z Cuba Libre | Old City — 21

Dalessandro's | Roxborough — 24

Derek's | Manayunk — 19

Devil's Alley | Ctr City W — 19

Z Dmitri's | Ctr City W — 25

NEW Dock Street | Univ City — 18

Doc Magrogan | W Chester — 16

NEW El Portal | W Chester — _

Eulogy Belgian | Old City — 18

Fadó Irish | Ctr City W — 15

Famous 4th St. Deli | South St. — 22

Z Fogo de Chão | Ave of Arts — 23

Z Fork | Old City — 24

Geno's Steaks | S Philly — 19

Georges' | Wayne — 20

Hokka Hokka | Ches Hill — 20

Honey | Doylestown — 25

Hymie's Deli | Merion Sta — 17

Inn/St. Peter's | St Peters — _

Iron Hill | Lancaster/LB — 18

Jake's | Manayunk — 25

James | S Philly — 25

NEW J.L. Sullivan's | Ave of Arts — _

NEW Joe Pesce | Ctr City E — 18

Jones | Ctr City E — 20

NEW José Pistola's | Ctr City W — 16

Kildare's | South St. — 16

Kitchen 233 | Westmont/NJ — 20

NEW Knock | Ctr City E — 19

Z Lacroix | Ctr City W — 28

Latest Dish | South St. — 24

Le Castagne | Ctr City W — 22

Legal Sea | King of Prussia — 20

NEW Les Bons Temps | Ctr City E — _

Loie | Ctr City W — 17

London Grill | Fairmount — 18

Los Catrines | Ctr City W — 24

Maggio's | Southampton — 17

NEW Maia | Villanova — _

Mantra | Ctr City W — 19

McCormick/Schmick | multi. — 21

McFadden's	**S Philly**	13
🅉 Mélange	**Haddonfield/NJ**	27
Melrose Diner	**S Philly**	16
Brandywine	**Chadds Ford**	20
NEW Memphis Taproom	**Port Richmond**	-
Mexican Post	**Ctr City W**	17
Mirna's Café	**multi.**	22
Misconduct Tav.	**Ctr City W**	17
Mission Grill	**Ctr City W**	21
Mixto	**Ctr City E**	21
🅉 Morimoto	**Ctr City E**	26
🅉 Moro	**Wilming/DE**	25
Moshulu	**DE River**	22
NEW Murray's Deli/bistro M	**Berwyn**	19
Oceanaire	**Ctr City E**	22
🅉 Osteria	**N Philly**	26
Palm	**Ave of Arts**	23
Pat's Steaks	**S Philly**	20
NEW Pearl	**Ctr City W**	-
NEW Pietro's Prime	**W Chester**	24
P.J. Whelihan's	**Blue Bell**	15
Plate	**Ardmore**	16
Pod	**Univ City**	23
Pond	**Radnor**	21
Ponzio's	**Cherry Hill/NJ**	17
Pop Shop	**Collingswood/NJ**	20
Prime Rib	**Ctr City W**	25
Pub	**Pennsauken/NJ**	21
Public Hse./Logan	**Ctr City W**	15
Raw Sushi	**Ctr City E**	24
Rist. Panorama	**Old City**	24
Rouge	**Ctr City W**	22
Roux 3	**Newtown Sq**	21
Royal Tavern	**S Philly**	23
Shiao Lan Kung	**Chinatown**	25
Sidecar	**S Philly**	19
Silk City	**N Liberties**	20
Smith/Wollensky	**Ctr City W**	22
Snackbar	**Ctr City W**	18
St. Stephens Green	**Fairmount**	19
Sullivan's Steak	**multi.**	23
Susanna Foo's Kitchen	**Wayne**	21
Swanky Bubbles	**Cherry Hill/NJ**	20
🅉 Swann Lounge	**Ctr City W**	27
NEW Table 31	**Ctr City W**	-
🅉 Tangerine	**Old City**	24
Tango	**Bryn Mawr**	20

Tavern 17	**Ctr City W**	18
Ted's Montana	**Warrington**	16
Teikoku	**Newtown Sq**	24
NEW 10 Arts	**Ave of Arts**	-
NEW Tennessee's BBQ	**Levittown**	-
Teresa's Next Dr.	**Wayne**	20
NEW Time	**Ctr City E**	-
🅉 Tinto	**Ctr City W**	27
Tír na nÓg	**Ctr City W**	14
🅉 Tony Luke's	**S Philly**	25
Tria	**Ctr City E**	23
Triumph Brewing	**Old City**	19
Twenty Manning	**Ctr City W**	22
NEW Ugly American	**S Philly**	19
Upstares/Varalli	**Ave of Arts**	21
NEW Urban Saloon	**Fairmount**	16
Uzu Sushi	**Old City**	26
Valanni	**Ctr City E**	23
NEW Vango	**Ctr City W**	16
Vesuvio	**S Philly**	17
Vintage	**Ctr City E**	19
🅉 Water Works	**Fairmount**	21
Xochitl	**Society Hill**	23
NEW Yakitori Boy	**Chinatown**	22
yello'bar	**S Philly**	16
NEW Zacharias	**Lansdale**	21
ZoT	**Society Hill**	20

POWER SCENES

🅉 Alma de Cuba	**Ctr City W**	25
🅉 Amada	**Old City**	28
🅉 NEW Azie	**Media**	24
🅉 Barclay Prime	**Ctr City W**	26
🅉 Bella Tori	**Langhorne**	19
Bistro Cassis	**Radnor**	20
🅉 Blackfish	**Consho**	26
NEW Blue Pear	**W Chester**	22
Blush	**Bryn Mawr**	20
🅉 Brasserie Perrier	**Ctr City W**	24
🅉 Buddakan	**Old City**	26
Caffe Aldo	**Cherry Hill/NJ**	23
🅉 Capital Grille	**Ave of Arts**	26
Catelli	**Voorhees/NJ**	24
NEW Chima	**Ctr City W**	-
Chops	**Bala Cynwyd**	19
🅉 Continental Mid-town	**Ctr City W**	21
Doc Magrogan	**W Chester**	16

SPECIAL FEATURES

Earl's Prime | **Lahaska** 24

Estia | **Ave of Arts** 23

Famous 4th St. Deli | **South St.** 22

Fleming's Prime | **Wayne** 25

Z Fogo de Chão | **Ave of Arts** 23

Z Fountain | **Ctr City W** 29

Georges' | **Wayne** 20

Z Green Room | **Wilming/DE** 25

Z Lacroix | **Ctr City W** 28

La Veranda | **DE River** 23

Z Le Bec-Fin | **Ctr City W** 27

Le Castagne | **Ctr City W** 22

McCormick/Schmick | **multi.** 21

Brandywine | **Chadds Ford** 20

Z Morimoto | **Ctr City E** 26

Z Morton's | **multi.** 25

Ms. Tootsie's | **South St.** 21

Oceanaire | **Ctr City E** 22

Z Osteria | **N Philly** 26

Palm | **Ave of Arts** 23

Phillips Sea. | **Ctr City W** 19

NEW Pietro's Prime | **W Chester** 24

Pond | **Radnor** 21

Ponzio's | **Cherry Hill/NJ** 17

Prime Rib | **Ctr City W** 25

Rae | **Univ City** 22

Redstone | **Marlton/NJ** 21

Rouge | **Ctr City W** 22

Roy's | **Ctr City W** 23

Ruth's Chris | **multi.** 23

Saloon | **S Philly** 24

Smith/Wollensky | **Ctr City W** 22

Sullivan's Steak | **multi.** 23

Z Susanna Foo | **Ctr City W** 24

NEW Table 31 | **Ctr City W** -

NEW 10 Arts | **Ave of Arts** -

NEW Time | **Ctr City E** -

NEW Toscana 52 | **Feasterville** -

Z Water Works | **Fairmount** 21

NEW William Douglas | **Cherry Hill/NJ** -

Wooden Iron | **Wayne** 18

NEW Zahav | **Society Hill** -

PRE-THEATER DINING

(Call for prices and times)

Bay Pony Inn | **Lederach** 19

Deep Blue | **Wilming/DE** 22

Toscana Kitchen | **Wilming/DE** 24

PRIVATE ROOMS

(Restaurants charge less at off times; call for capacity)

Abbraccio | **Univ City** 13

Adobe Cafe | **Roxborough** 18

Z Alma de Cuba | **Ctr City W** 25

Alyan's | **South St.** 21

America B&G | **Chester Springs** 17

August Moon | **Norristown** 23

Avalon | **W Chester** 21

Back Burner | **Hockessin/DE** 20

Barone's | **Moorestown/NJ** 21

Basil Bistro | **Paoli** 18

Bay Pony Inn | **Lederach** 19

Bistro Romano | **Society Hill** 21

Bistro St. Tropez | **Ctr City W** 20

Black Sheep | **Ctr City W** 16

Blue Bell Inn | **Blue Bell** 21

Blue Horse | **Blue Bell** 17

Bourbon Blue | **Manayunk** 19

Z Brasserie Perrier | **Ctr City W** 24

Brick Hotel | **Newtown** 18

Z Bridgetown Mill | **Langhorne** 25

Buca di Beppo | **multi.** 15

Byblos | **Ctr City W** 16

Caffe Aldo | **Cherry Hill/NJ** 23

California Cafe | **King of Prussia** 20

Z Capital Grille | **Ave of Arts** 26

Casablanca | **Wynnefield** 21

Catelli | **Voorhees/NJ** 24

Centre Bridge | **New Hope** 19

Chart House | **DE River** 18

Chez Elena Wu | **Voorhees/NJ** 23

Z Chickie's/Pete's | **NE Philly** 18

Chops | **Bala Cynwyd** 19

CinCin | **Ches Hill** 24

City Tavern | **Old City** 19

Coleman | **Blue Bell** 20

Copabanana | **South St.** 16

Coyote Cross. | **W Chester** 20

Creed's | **King of Prussia** 23

Cresheim Cottage | **Mt Airy** 18

Z Cuba Libre | **Old City** 21

Dark Horse | **Society Hill** 17

Dave & Buster's | **DE River** 13

Davio's | **Ctr City W** 23

Derek's | **Manayunk** 19

Devon Seafood | **Ctr City W** 23

Dilworth. Inn | **W Chester** 25

Restaurant	Score
DiNardo's | **Old City**	19
Drafting Rm. | **Spring House**	18
☑ Duling-Kurtz | **Exton**	25
Epicurean | **Phoenixville**	21
Feby's Fish. | **Wilming/DE**	18
Fez Moroccan | **South St.**	21
☑ Food/Thought | **Marlton/NJ**	24
Fountain Side | **Horsham**	19
Freight House | **Doylestown**	19
Gen. Lafayette | **Lafayette Hill**	15
Gen. Warren | **Malvern**	25
☑ Giumarello's | **Westmont/NJ**	26
☑ Gracie's | **Pine Forge/LB**	26
☑ Green Hills Inn | **Reading/LB**	26
Hamilton's | **Lambertville/NJ**	25
Hard Rock | **Ctr City E**	14
Harry's Savoy | **Wilming/DE**	23
H.K. Gold. Phoenix | **Chinatown**	20
Il Portico | **Ctr City W**	20
Iron Hill | **Newark/DE**	18
Italian Bistro | **NE Philly**	16
Jack's Firehse. | **Fairmount**	19
Joseph Ambler | **N Wales**	23
King George II | **Bristol**	21
☑ La Bonne Auberge | **New Hope**	27
La Collina | **Bala Cynwyd**	23
☑ Lacroix | **Ctr City W**	28
Lai Lai Garden | **Blue Bell**	22
Lamberti's | **Wilming/DE**	19
La Veranda | **DE River**	23
☑ Le Bec-Fin | **Ctr City W**	27
Liberties | **N Liberties**	14
☑ Lily's on Main | **Ephrata/LB**	24
Los Catrines | **Ctr City W**	24
☑ Maggiano's | **multi.**	20
Mainland Inn | **Mainland**	26
Mamma Maria | **S Philly**	22
Marg. Kuo Peking | **Media**	22
McCormick/Schmick | **Ave of Arts**	21
McGillin's | **Ctr City E**	16
Meritage | **Ctr City W**	23
Mio Sogno | **S Philly**	23
☑ Morton's | **multi.**	25
Moshulu | **DE River**	22
Mrs. Robino's | **Wilming/DE**	20
☑ Nectar | **Berwyn**	26
New Tavern | **Bala Cynwyd**	16
Newtown Grill | **Newtown Sq**	21
Old Orig. Bookbinder | **Old City**	19
Osaka | **Wayne**	23
Pace One | **Thornton**	21
Palace of Asia | **Ft Wash**	24
Patou | **Old City**	18
Pho Xe Lua | **Chinatown**	24
Pietro's Pizzeria | **South St.**	19
Plate | **Ardmore**	16
Plumsteadville Inn | **Plumsteadville**	19
Pod | **Univ City**	23
Portofino | **Ctr City E**	20
Primavera Pizza | **Ardmore**	18
Prime Rib | **Ctr City W**	25
Pub | **Pennsauken/NJ**	21
Ralph's | **S Philly**	22
Rest. Taquet | **Wayne**	24
☑ Rist. San Marco | **Ambler**	26
Roselena's | **S Philly**	21
Rose Tree Inn | **Media**	22
Roux 3 | **Newtown Sq**	21
Roy's | **Ctr City W**	23
Ruth's Chris | **multi.**	23
Saloon | **S Philly**	24
Savona | **Gulph Mills**	25
Serrano | **Old City**	20
Seven Stars Inn | **Phoenixville**	23
Shangrila | **Devon**	20
Shiroi Hana | **Ctr City W**	23
Simon Pearce | **W Chester**	20
Smith/Wollensky | **Ctr City W**	22
Solaris Grille | **Ches Hill**	16
Spasso | **Old City**	23
Spring Mill | **Consho**	23
Stefano's | **Hunt Vly**	19
Sullivan's Steak | **Wilming/DE**	23
☑ Susanna Foo | **Ctr City W**	24
Tai Lake | **Chinatown**	24
☑ Tangerine | **Old City**	24
Tango | **Bryn Mawr**	20
Teikoku | **Newtown Sq**	24
Ten Stone | **Ctr City W**	18
Thomas' | **Manayunk**	-
333 Belrose | **Radnor**	23
Tierra Colombiana | **N Philly**	22
Totaro's | **Consho**	24
Tratt. Alberto | **W Chester**	21

Tratt. Primadonna | **Ctr City W** 17
Trinacria | **Blue Bell** 25
Twin Bays | **Phoenixville** 24
Upstares/Varalli | **Ave of Arts** 21
Utage | **Wilming/DE** 24
Vesuvio | **S Philly** 17
☒ Vietnam | **Chinatown** 25
Viggiano's | **Consho** 19
Vincent's | **W Chester** 16
Wash. Cross. | **Wash Cross** 17
☒ White Dog | **Univ City** 21
World Café | **Univ City** 14
Yardley Inn | **Yardley** 21

PRIX FIXE MENUS

(Call for prices and times)
Aoi | **Ctr City E** 16
Bay Pony Inn | **Lederach** 19
☒ Birchrunville Store | **Birchrunville** 28
☒ Bridgetown Mill | **Langhorne** 25
Caribou Cafe | **Ctr City E** 19
Carmine's Creole | **Bryn Mawr** 22
Casablanca | **multi.** 21
Chez Colette | **Ctr City W** 20
☒ Cuba Libre | **Old City** 21
Devon Seafood | **Ctr City W** 23
Drafting Rm. | **multi.** 18
Fayette St. | **Consho** 23
Fez Moroccan | **South St.** 21
☒ Fountain | **Ctr City W** 29
Gen. Lafayette | **Lafayette Hill** 15
Gnocchi | **South St.** 22
Golden Pheasant | **Erwinna** 23
Good 'N Plenty | **Smoketown/LB** 19
☒ Green Hills Inn | **Reading/LB** 26
Haydn Zug's | **E Petersburg/LB** 18
☒ Kimberton Inn | **Kimberton** 25
Koi | **N Liberties** 23
☒ Lacroix | **Ctr City W** 28
La Locanda | **Old City** 23
☒ Le Bec-Fin | **Ctr City W** 27
Lemon Grass | **Lancaster/LB** 22
Little Marakesh | **Dresher** 21
Mainland Inn | **Mainland** 26
Mamma Maria | **S Philly** 22
Manon | **Lambertville/NJ** 25
Marrakesh | **South St.** 23
Mendenhall Inn | **Mendenhall** 21

Meritage | **Ctr City W** 23
Miller's Smorgas. | **Ronks/LB** 18
☒ Morimoto | **Ctr City E** 26
☒ Moro | **Wilming/DE** 25
My Thai | **Ctr City W** 18
Norma's | **Cherry Hill/NJ** 21
Nunzio | **Collingswood/NJ** 23
Pace One | **Thornton** 21
Paradigm | **Old City** 18
Pattaya | **Univ City** 19
Rest. Taquet | **Wayne** 24
Roy's | **Ctr City W** 23
Savona | **Gulph Mills** 25
Summer Kitchen | **Penns Park** 23
☒ Susanna Foo | **Ctr City W** 24
Thai Orchid | **Blue Bell** 25
Thai Singha | **Univ City** 19
☒ Vetri | **Ave of Arts** 27
Zocalo | **Univ City** 20

QUICK BITES

Alfa | **Ctr City W** 16
AllWays Café | **Hunt Vly** 22
Almaz Café | **Ctr City W** 22
Alyan's | **South St.** 21
Apamate | **Ctr City W** 23
Aqua | **Ctr City E** 19
Ardmore Station | **Ardmore** 19
NEW Ashoka Palace | **Ctr City W** –
NEW Auspicious | **Ardmore** 19
Banana Leaf | **Chinatown** 22
Bar Ferdinand | **N Liberties** 23
Bensí | **N Wales** 18
Bitar's | **S Philly** 23
Bobby Chez | **multi.** 25
Bonté Wafflerie | **multi.** 19
Bottom of Sea | **multi.** 22
Brew HaHa! | **multi.** 18
NEW Cafe Coláo | **N Liberties** –
NEW Café Estelle | **N Liberties** –
NEW Cake | **Ches Hill** 21
Campo's Deli | **Old City** 22
Cantina Caballitos/Segundos | **S Philly** 21
Charlie's Hamburgers | **Folsom** 24
Cheeseburger/Paradise | **Langhorne** 15
☒ Chickie's/Pete's | **Bordentown/NJ** 18

Cosimo | **Malvern**	22
Devil's Alley | **Ctr City W**	19
NEW Dock Street | **Univ City**	18
Ecco Qui | **Univ City**	17
NEW El Portal | **W Chester**	-
Five Guys | **multi.**	22
Franco's Tratt. | **East Falls**	20
Full Plate | **N Liberties**	21
Giwa | **Ctr City W**	25
NEW goodburger | **Ctr City W**	-
Good Dog | **Ctr City W**	22
Grey Lodge | **NE Philly**	18
Ha Long Bay | **Bryn Mawr**	22
NEW Harusame | **Ardmore**	-
Ida Mae's | **Fishtown**	22
Iron Hill | **Lancaster/LB**	18
Isaac's | **multi.**	17
Jake's Hamburgers | **New Castle/DE**	21
Jim's Steaks | **multi.**	22
☑ John's Roast Pork | **S Philly**	27
NEW José Pistola's | **Ctr City W**	16
Kibitz Room | **Cherry Hill/NJ**	23
Kildare's | **South St.**	16
Kotatsu | **Ardmore**	22
La Lupe | **S Philly**	22
LaScala's | **Ctr City E**	20
Liberties | **Manayunk**	14
Little Pete's | **Ctr City W**	16
Maggio's | **Southampton**	17
NEW Maia | **Villanova**	-
Manny's | **multi.**	22
Maoz Veg. | **multi.**	22
Mastoris | **Bordentown/NJ**	20
NEW Max & David's | **Elkins Pk**	23
Mayfair Diner | **NE Philly**	15
McFadden's | **S Philly**	13
Melrose Diner | **S Philly**	16
NEW Memphis Taproom | **Port Richmond**	-
Mexican Food | **Marlton/NJ**	21
Mexican Post | **Ctr City W**	17
Mizu | **multi.**	19
Monk's Cafe | **Ctr City W**	22
Mr. Bill's | **Winslow/NJ**	-
Naked Choco. | **Ave of Arts**	25
National Mech. | **Old City**	17
Nifty Fifty's | **Turnersville/NJ**	19
Pat's Steaks | **S Philly**	20

P.J. Whelihan's | **Blue Bell**	15
Ponzio's | **Cherry Hill/NJ**	17
Pop Shop | **Collingswood/NJ**	20
Pura Vida | **N Liberties**	24
☑ Reading Term. Mkt. | **Ctr City E**	23
Royal Tavern | **S Philly**	23
Sabrina's Café | **Fairmount**	25
Scoogi's | **Flourtown**	19
Shanachie | **Ambler**	17
Sidecar | **S Philly**	19
Silk City | **N Liberties**	20
NEW Sláinte | **Univ City**	18
Snackbar | **Ctr City W**	18
South St. Souvlaki | **South St.**	21
NEW Station Bistro | **Kimberton**	-
Steve's Prince/Stks. | **NE Philly**	24
St. Stephens Green | **Fairmount**	19
Taq. Puerto Veracruz. | **S Philly**	-
Tavern 17 | **Ctr City W**	18
NEW Tennessee's BBQ | **Levittown**	-
Tierra Colombiana | **N Philly**	22
☑ Tiffin Store | **N Liberties**	26
☑ Tony Luke's | **S Philly**	25
NEW Tortilla Press Cantina | **Pennsauken/NJ**	19
Triumph Brewing | **Old City**	19
Trolley Car | **Mt Airy**	14
NEW Union Gourmet | **Ctr City E**	-
NEW Urban Saloon | **Fairmount**	16
yello'bar | **S Philly**	16
☑ Zento | **Old City**	26
Zorba's Taverna | **Fairmount**	20

QUIET CONVERSATION

☑ Bella Tori | **Langhorne**	19
☑ Birchrunville Store | **Birchrunville**	28
Bistro Juliana | **Fishtown**	23
Bistro 7 | **Old City**	24
NEW Blue Pear | **W Chester**	22
Bocelli | **multi.**	-
Braddock's | **Medford/NJ**	-
NEW Buona Via | **Horsham**	19
Butterfish | **W Chester**	25
Caffe Casta Diva | **Ctr City W**	24
NEW Cake | **Ches Hill**	21
Chiarella's | **S Philly**	19
NEW Cochon | **Queen Vill**	24

SPECIAL FEATURES

Dilworth. Inn | **W Chester**	25
Estia | **Ave of Arts**	23
☑ Food/Thought | **Marlton/NJ**	24
☑ Fountain | **Ctr City W**	29
Full Plate | **N Liberties**	21
NEW Gaya | **Blue Bell**	-
☑ Gilmore's | **W Chester**	28
Gypsy Saloon | **Consho**	22
Honey | **Doylestown**	25
NEW Il Fiore | **Collingswood/NJ**	-
Inn/Phillips Mill | **New Hope**	24
Inn/St. Peter's | **St Peters**	-
☑ La Bonne Auberge | **New Hope**	27
☑ Lacroix | **Ctr City W**	28
La Famiglia | **Old City**	24
NEW Las Bugambilias | **South St.**	26
La Vang | **Willow Grove**	22
La Viola Ovest | **Ctr City W**	23
Le Castagne | **Ctr City W**	22
NEW Le Virtù | **S Philly**	26
Margot | **Narberth**	20
NEW Masamoto | **Glen Mills**	27
NEW Misso | **Ave of Arts**	-
Modo Mio | **N Liberties**	26
NEW Nicholas | **S Philly**	-
☑ Nineteen | **Ave of Arts**	23
Parc Bistro | **Skippack**	25
NEW Peppercorns | **S Philly**	-
Pistachio Grille | **Maple Glen**	19
PTG | **Roxborough**	20
Roselena's | **S Philly**	21
Rouget | **Newtown**	-
Rylei | **NE Philly**	24
Sassafras Int'l | **Old City**	-
Simon Pearce | **W Chester**	20
Singapore Kosher | **Chinatown**	19
Slate Bleu | **Doylestown**	22
Spamps | **Consho**	17
☑ Susanna Foo | **Ctr City W**	24
NEW Swallow | **N Liberties**	-
☑ Swann Lounge | **Ctr City W**	27
☑ Talula's Table | **Kennett Sq**	26
Ted's on Main | **Medford/NJ**	26
Thai L'Elephant | **Phoenixville**	23
Tokyo Hibachi | **Ctr City W**	17
NEW Toscana 52 | **Feasterville**	-
Trio | **Fairmount**	22
Umbria | **Mt Airy**	24

☑ Water Works | **Fairmount**	21
NEW William Douglas | **Cherry Hill/NJ**	-
NEW Yalda Grill | **Horsham**	20
Yardley Inn | **Yardley**	21
Yazmin | **Warminster**	21
NEW Zahav | **Society Hill**	-
☑ Zento | **Old City**	26

RAW BARS

Blue Eyes | **Sewell/NJ**	21
Caffe Aldo | **Cherry Hill/NJ**	23
Catelli | **Voorhees/NJ**	24
Coquette | **South St.**	18
Creed's | **King of Prussia**	23
Doc Magrogan | **W Chester**	16
Earl's Prime | **Lahaska**	24
Feby's Fish. | **Wilming/DE**	18
Freight House | **Doylestown**	19
Harry's Seafood | **Wilming/DE**	22
Johnny Brenda's | **Fishtown**	21
Koi | **N Liberties**	23
Legal Sea | **King of Prussia**	20
Little Tuna | **Haddonfield/NJ**	21
Marsha Brown | **New Hope**	20
Brandywine | **Chadds Ford**	20
☑ Nineteen | **Ave of Arts**	23
Oceanaire | **Ctr City E**	22
Old Orig. Bookbinder | **Old City**	19
Osaka | **Wayne**	23
Pace One | **Thornton**	21
Snockey's Oyster | **S Philly**	18
SoleFood | **Ctr City E**	21
Sotto Varalli | **Ave of Arts**	21
Stoudt's | **Adamstown/LB**	18
Walter's Steak. | **Wilming/DE**	27

ROMANTIC PLACES

Alfa | **Ctr City W**	16
Anton's/Swan | **Lambertville/NJ**	20
Apamate | **Ctr City W**	23
☑ Bàcio | **Cinnaminson/NJ**	25
☑ Barclay Prime | **Ctr City W**	26
Beau Monde | **South St.**	23
☑ Bella Tori | **Langhorne**	19
☑ Birchrunville Store | **Birchrunville**	28
Bistro Romano | **Society Hill**	21
Bistro 7 | **Old City**	24
Blackbird | **Collingswood/NJ**	26

Ⓩ Blackfish	**Consho**	26	Mendenhall Inn	**Mendenhall**	21
Blush	**Bryn Mawr**	20	Modo Mio	**N Liberties**	26
NEW Buona Via	**Horsham**	19	Mr. Martino's	**S Philly**	22
Caffe Casta Diva	**Ctr City W**	24	Ms. Tootsie's	**South St.**	21
Caffe Valentino	**multi.**	19	Ⓩ Nineteen	**Ave of Arts**	23
Carversville Inn	**Carversville**	22	Oceanaire	**Ctr City E**	22
Catelli	**Voorhees/NJ**	24	Ⓩ Osteria	**N Philly**	26
Chlöe	**Old City**	25	Paradiso	**S Philly**	23
NEW Cochon	**Queen Vill**	24	Parc Bistro	**Skippack**	25
Copper Bistro	**N Liberties**	22	NEW Pietro's Prime	**W Chester**	24
Coquette	**South St.**	18	Pistachio Grille	**Maple Glen**	19
Cosimo	**Malvern**	22	Pond	**Radnor**	21
Creole Cafe	**Sewell/NJ**	22	PTG	**Roxborough**	20
Dilworth. Inn	**W Chester**	25	Roselena's	**S Philly**	21
Divan	**S Philly**	21	Rose Tattoo	**Fairmount**	22
Ⓩ Duling-Kurtz	**Exton**	25	Rylei	**NE Philly**	24
Earl's Prime	**Lahaska**	24	Salento	**Ctr City W**	21
Estia	**Ave of Arts**	23	Simon Pearce	**W Chester**	20
Ⓩ Fountain	**Ctr City W**	29	Slate Bleu	**Doylestown**	22
Franco's Tratt.	**East Falls**	20	Southwark	**South St.**	22
Fuji	**Haddonfield/NJ**	26	Spring Mill	**Consho**	23
NEW Gaya	**Blue Bell**	–	NEW Station Bistro	**Kimberton**	–
Gayle	**South St.**	25	Summer Kitchen	**Penns Park**	23
Ⓩ Gilmore's	**W Chester**	28	Ⓩ Susanna Foo	**Ctr City W**	24
Ⓩ Giumarello's	**Westmont/NJ**	26	NEW Swallow	**N Liberties**	–
Golden Pheasant	**Erwinna**	23	Ⓩ Tangerine	**Old City**	24
Honey	**Doylestown**	25	Ted's on Main	**Medford/NJ**	26
Horizons	**South St.**	26	NEW 10 Arts	**Ave of Arts**	–
Hotel du Village	**New Hope**	22	NEW Time	**Ctr City E**	–
Il Portico	**Ctr City W**	20	NEW Toscana 52	**Feasterville**	–
Inn/Phillips Mill	**New Hope**	24	Tria	**Ctr City E**	23
Inn/St. Peter's	**St Peters**	–	Trio	**Fairmount**	22
James	**S Philly**	25	Twenty Manning	**Ctr City W**	22
Jasper	**Downingtown**	25	NEW Ugly American	**S Philly**	19
Ⓩ La Bonne Auberge	**New Hope**	27	Umai Umai	**Fairmount**	24
Ⓩ Lacroix	**Ctr City W**	28	Umbria	**Mt Airy**	24
NEW Las Bugambilias	**South St.**	26	Valanni	**Ctr City E**	23
La Viola Ovest	**Ctr City W**	23	Ⓩ Vetri	**Ave of Arts**	27
Ⓩ Le Bar Lyonnais	**Ctr City W**	28	Water Lily	**Collingswood/NJ**	22
Ⓩ Le Bec-Fin	**Ctr City W**	27	Ⓩ Water Works	**Fairmount**	21
NEW Les Bons Temps	**Ctr City E**	–	NEW Yalda Grill	**Horsham**	20
Ⓩ Le Virtù	**S Philly**	26	Yardley Inn	**Yardley**	21
Lilly's/Canal	**Lambertville/NJ**	20	Yazmin	**Warminster**	21
L'Oca	**Fairmount**	23	NEW Zahav	**Society Hill**	–
Majolica	**Phoenixville**	26		
Margot	**Narberth**	20	**SENIOR APPEAL**	
Marigold Kitchen	**Univ City**	24	Abacus	**Lansdale**	24
			AllWays Café	**Hunt Vly**	22
			Aqua	**Ctr City E**	19

Aya's Café | **Ctr City W**	20	Inn/St. Peter's | **St Peters**	-
Bay Pony Inn | **Lederach**	19	Isaac's | **multi.**	17
☑ Bella Tori | **Langhorne**	19	Italian Bistro | **Ave of Arts**	16
Ben & Irv Deli | **Hunt Vly**	19	Jasper | **Downingtown**	25
Bird-in-Hand | **Bird-in-Hand/LB**	18	J.B. Dawson's/Austin's | **multi.**	18
Bistro Cassis | **Radnor**	20	NEW Joe Pesce |	18
Bistro di Marino |	25	**Collingswood/NJ**	
Collingswood/NJ		Jonathan's | **Jenkintown**	17
Blackbird | **Collingswood/NJ**	26	Kibitz Room | **Cherry Hill/NJ**	23
☑ Blackfish | **Consho**	26	Kitchen 233 | **Westmont/NJ**	20
NEW Blue Pear | **W Chester**	22	La Fontana | **Ctr City W**	20
Blush | **Bryn Mawr**	20	La Pergola | **Jenkintown**	19
Bocelli | **Ambler**	-	NEW Las Bugambilias | **South St.**	26
Bonefish Grill | **multi.**	21	Legal Sea | **King of Prussia**	20
NEW Brio | **Cherry Hill/NJ**	19	NEW Les Bons Temps |	-
Buca di Beppo | **Cherry Hill/NJ**	15	**Ctr City E**	
NEW Buona Via | **Horsham**	19	NEW Le Virtù | **S Philly**	26
Butterfish | **W Chester**	25	Little Pete's | **Ctr City W**	16
Cafe Preeya | **Hunt Vly**	21	Little Tuna | **Haddonfield/NJ**	21
Caffe Casta Diva | **Ctr City W**	24	Maggio's | **Southampton**	17
Caffe Valentino | **multi.**	19	Majolica | **Phoenixville**	26
NEW Cake | **Ches Hill**	21	Manny's | **Wayne**	22
Calif. Pizza | **Plymouth Meeting**	19	Marg. Kuo | **Wayne**	23
Cedar Hollow | **Malvern**	20	Margot | **Narberth**	20
☑ Cheesecake Fact. |	20	Marigold Kitchen | **Univ City**	24
Willow Grove		NEW Max & David's | **Elkins Pk**	23
☑ Chophouse | **Gibbsboro/NJ**	25	Mayfair Diner | **NE Philly**	15
Copper Bistro | **N Liberties**	22	McCormick/Schmick |	21
NEW Cravings | **Lansdale**	21	**Cherry Hill/NJ**	
Divan | **S Philly**	21	Melrose Diner | **S Philly**	16
Doc Magrogan | **W Chester**	16	Brandywine | **Chadds Ford**	20
Earl's Prime | **Lahaska**	24	Miller's Smorgas. | **Ronks/LB**	18
Ernesto's 1521 | **Ctr City W**	21	Moonstruck | **NE Philly**	21
Estia | **Ave of Arts**	23	Mr. Bill's | **Winslow/NJ**	-
Fleming's Prime | **Wayne**	25	Murray's Deli | **Bala Cynwyd**	19
Franco's Tratt. | **East Falls**	20	NEW Murray's Deli/bistro M |	19
NEW Gaya | **Blue Bell**	-	**Berwyn**	
Gen. Lafayette | **Lafayette Hill**	15	Nifty Fifty's | **Turnersville/NJ**	19
Georges' | **Wayne**	20	☑ Nineteen | **Ave of Arts**	23
Giwa | **Ctr City W**	25	Oceanaire | **Ctr City E**	22
Good 'N Plenty | **Smoketown/LB**	19	Old Guard Hse. | **Gladwyne**	23
Gypsy Saloon | **Consho**	22	☑ Osteria | **N Philly**	26
Ha Long Bay | **Bryn Mawr**	22	Otto's Brauhaus | **Horsham**	20
Hank's Place | **Chadds Ford**	19	Palace/Ben | **Ctr City E**	21
Hokka Hokka | **Ches Hill**	20	Parc Bistro | **Skippack**	25
☑ Honey's Sit 'n Eat | **N Liberties**	25	☑ P.F. Chang's | **Warrington**	21
Horizons | **South St.**	26	Phillips Sea. | **Ctr City W**	19
NEW Il Fiore | **Collingswood/NJ**	-	NEW Pietro's Prime | **W Chester**	24
		Pistachio Grille | **Maple Glen**	19

Plain/Fancy Farm | Bird-in-Hand/LB	19
Plate | Ardmore	16
Pond | Radnor	21
Pop Shop | Collingswood/NJ	20
PTG | Roxborough	20
Pub | Pennsauken/NJ	21
Radicchio | Old City	24
Rae | Univ City	22
Rist. Il Melograno | Doylestown	24
Roller's/Flying Fish | Ches Hill	21
Rouget | Newtown	-
Rylei | NE Philly	24
Scoogi's | Flourtown	19
Simon Pearce | W Chester	20
Spamps | Consho	17
St. Stephens Green | Fairmount	19
Susanna Foo's Kitchen | Wayne	21
NEW Table 31 | Ctr City W	-
Ted's Montana | Warrington	16
Ted's on Main | Medford/NJ	26
Thai L'Elephant | Phoenixville	23
NEW Toscana 52 | Feasterville	-
Vesuvio | S Philly	17
Viggiano's | Consho	19
Vinny T's | Wynnewood	15
Water Lily | Collingswood/NJ	22
Z Water Works | Fairmount	21
White Elephant | Hunt Vly	22
NEW William Douglas | Cherry Hill/NJ	-
William Penn | Gwynedd	22
Willow Valley | Lancaster/LB	19
NEW Yalda Grill | Horsham	20
Yardley Inn | Yardley	21
Yazmin | Warminster	21
NEW Zahav | Society Hill	-

SINGLES SCENES

Alfa | Ctr City W	16
Z Alma de Cuba | Ctr City W	25
Z Amada | Old City	28
NEW Ameritage | Wilming/DE	-
Ansill | South St.	24
NEW Apothecary | Ctr City E	-
NEW Azul Cantina | Ctr City E	-
Bar Ferdinand | N Liberties	23
NEW Belgian Café | Fairmount	15
NEW Beneluxx | Old City	20

Bensí | N Wales	18
Bistro Cassis | Radnor	20
Black Sheep | Ctr City W	16
Bottom of Sea | South St.	22
Bourbon Blue | Manayunk	19
Cantina Caballitos/Segundos | S Philly	21
Carmine's Creole | Bryn Mawr	22
Z Chickie's/Pete's | Bordentown/NJ	18
Chick's | South St.	23
Z Continental Mid-town | Ctr City W	21
Coyote Cross. | Consho	20
Z Cuba Libre | Old City	21
Derek's | Manayunk	19
Devil's Alley | Ctr City W	19
NEW Devil's Den | S Philly	-
NEW Dock Street | Univ City	18
Ecco Qui | Univ City	17
Eulogy Belgian | Old City	18
Fadó Irish | Ctr City W	15
Fergie's Pub | Ctr City E	17
NEW Field House | Ctr City E	13
NEW goodburger | Ctr City W	-
Good Dog | Ctr City W	22
NEW J.L. Sullivan's | Ave of Arts	-
Jones | Ctr City E	20
NEW José Pistola's | Ctr City W	16
Kildare's | South St.	16
Kisso Sushi | Old City	22
NEW Knock | Ctr City E	19
Latest Dish | South St.	24
Loie | Ctr City W	17
Los Catrines | Ctr City W	24
L2 | Ctr City W	17
Manayunk Brew. | Manayunk	18
Mantra | Ctr City W	19
Marathon/Sq. | Ctr City W	19
McFadden's | N Liberties	13
NEW Memphis Taproom | Port Richmond	-
Mexican Post | Ctr City W	17
Misconduct Tav. | Ctr City W	17
Mission Grill | Ctr City W	21
Mixto | Ctr City E	21
Naked Choco. | Ave of Arts	25
National Mech. | Old City	17
North by NW | Mt Airy	16

N. 3rd | **N Liberties**	22
Ortlieb's Jazz | **N Liberties**	-
NEW Pearl | **Ctr City W**	-
P.J. Whelihan's | **multi.**	15
Plough & Stars | **Old City**	18
Pod | **Univ City**	23
Public Hse./Logan | **Ctr City W**	15
Raw Sushi | **Ctr City E**	24
Redstone | **Marlton/NJ**	21
Sidecar | **S Philly**	19
Silk City | **N Liberties**	20
Sly Fox | **Royersford**	15
Snackbar | **Ctr City W**	18
Z Standard Tap | **N Liberties**	24
St. Stephens Green | **Fairmount**	19
Sullivan's Steak | **multi.**	23
Swanky Bubbles | **multi.**	20
Tavern 17 | **Ctr City W**	18
Teresa's Next Dr. | **Wayne**	20
Tír na nÓg | **Ctr City W**	14
Tria | **Ctr City E**	23
Triumph Brewing | **Old City**	19
Twenty Manning | **Ctr City W**	22
NEW Urban Saloon | **Fairmount**	16
Uzu Sushi | **Old City**	26
Valanni | **Ctr City E**	23
NEW Vango | **Ctr City W**	16
Xochitl | **Society Hill**	23
ZoT | **Society Hill**	20

SLEEPERS

(Good to excellent food, but little known)

Almaz Café | **Ctr City W**	22
Bistro Juliana | **Fishtown**	23
NEW Blue Pear | **W Chester**	22
Bona Cucina | **Upper Darby**	25
Bottom of Sea | **multi.**	22
Carr's | **Lancaster/LB**	25
Carversville Inn | **Carversville**	22
Cassatt Tea Rm. | **Ctr City W**	23
Charlie's Hamburgers | **Folsom**	24
Chiangmai | **Consho**	25
China Royal | **Wilming/DE**	24
Coconut Bay | **Voorhees/NJ**	22
Core De Roma | **South St.**	23
Creole Cafe | **Sewell/NJ**	22
Eclipse Bistro | **Wilming/DE**	23
Elements | **Haddon Hts/NJ**	24

Four Rivers | **Chinatown**	24
Franco's HighNote | **S Philly**	23
Funky Lil' Kitchen | **Pottstown**	23
Giwa | **Ctr City W**	25
Golden Pheasant | **Erwinna**	23
Ha Long Bay | **Bryn Mawr**	22
High St. Grill | **Mt Holly/NJ**	23
Hotel du Village | **New Hope**	22
Ida Mae's | **Fishtown**	22
Jasper | **Downingtown**	25
Kabobeesh | **Univ City**	23
Koi | **N Liberties**	23
Kotatsu | **Ardmore**	22
Kristian's | **S Philly**	25
La Esperanza | **Lindenwold/NJ**	22
NEW Las Bugambilias | **South St.**	26
La Vang | **Willow Grove**	22
NEW Le Virtù | **S Philly**	26
Madame Butterfly | **Doylestown**	22
Manny's | **multi.**	22
Manon | **Lambertville/NJ**	25
NEW Masamoto | **Glen Mills**	27
NEW Max & David's | **Elkins Pk**	23
Megu Sushi | **Cherry Hill/NJ**	24
Mercer Café | **Port Richmond**	26
Mikado | **Ardmore**	22
Milano Modo | **Mt Holly/NJ**	25
Mimosa | **W Chester**	24
Mio Sogno | **S Philly**	23
Mirabella | **Cherry Hill/NJ**	22
No. 9 | **Lambertville/NJ**	23
Oasis Grill | **Cherry Hill/NJ**	26
Pepper's | **Ardmore**	23
NEW Pietro's Prime | **W Chester**	24
Pura Vida | **N Liberties**	24
Ray's Cafe | **Chinatown**	25
Rist. Il Melograno | **Doylestown**	24
Rylei | **NE Philly**	24
Sakura Spring | **Cherry Hill/NJ**	23
Salt & Pepper | **S Philly**	23
Shinju Sushi | **Ctr City E**	28
Siam | **Lambertville/NJ**	22
Siam Cuisine/Black | **Doylestown**	23
Silk Cuisine | **Bryn Mawr**	23
Slate Bleu | **Doylestown**	22
Somsak/Taan | **Voorhees/NJ**	25
Spence Cafe | **W Chester**	23

Sugarfoot | **Wilming/DE**	27	Rest. Taquet | **Wayne**	24
Sushikazu | **Blue Bell**	24	Savona | **Gulph Mills**	25
Tai Lake | **Chinatown**	24	Shiroi Hana | **Ctr City W**	23
Taq. Moroleon | **Kennett Sq**	24	Spence Cafe | **W Chester**	23
Ted's on Main | **Medford/NJ**	26	☑ Susanna Foo | **Ctr City W**	24
Thai L'Elephant | **Phoenixville**	23	☑ Talula's Table | **Kennett Sq**	26
Trinacria | **Blue Bell**	25	☑ Tinto | **Ctr City W**	27
Twin Bays | **Phoenixville**	24	Tratt. Alberto | **W Chester**	21
Utage | **Wilming/DE**	24	Twenty Manning | **Ctr City W**	22
Uzu Sushi | **Old City**	26	Upstares/Varalli | **Ave of Arts**	21
Walter's Steak. | **Wilming/DE**	27	☑ Vetri | **Ave of Arts**	27
NEW Yakitori Boy | **Chinatown**	22	☑ Yangming | **Bryn Mawr**	25

TASTING MENUS

☑ Amada | **Old City**	28
☑ Birchrunville Store | **Birchrunville**	28
Bistro 7 | **Old City**	24
Blue Horse | **Blue Bell**	17
☑ Bridgetown Mill | **Langhorne**	25
Carmine's Creole | **Bryn Mawr**	22
☑ Cuba Libre | **Old City**	21
☑ Fountain | **Ctr City W**	29
Fuji | **Haddonfield/NJ**	26
☑ Gibraltar | **Lancaster/LB**	27
☑ Gilmore's | **W Chester**	28
Horizons | **South St.**	26
Jasper | **Downingtown**	25
Koi | **N Liberties**	23
La Campagne | **Cherry Hill/NJ**	24
La Cava | **Ambler**	21
☑ Le Bec-Fin | **Ctr City W**	27
☑ Little Fish | **S Philly**	28
London Grill | **Fairmount**	18
Majolica | **Phoenixville**	26
Marigold Kitchen | **Univ City**	24
☑ Matyson | **Ctr City W**	26
Mazzi | **Leola/LB**	-
☑ Mélange | **Cherry Hill/NJ**	27
☑ Mercato | **Ctr City E**	26
Meritage | **Ctr City W**	23
☑ Morimoto | **Ctr City E**	26
☑ Moro | **Wilming/DE**	25
Norma's | **Cherry Hill/NJ**	21
Nunzio | **Collingswood/NJ**	23
Orchard | **Kennett Sq**	-
Pond | **Radnor**	21
☑ Rest. Alba | **Malvern**	27
Rest./Doneckers | **Ephrata/LB**	19

TEEN APPEAL

Alyan's | **South St.**	21
Brew HaHa! | **multi.**	18
Buca di Beppo | **E Norriton**	15
Calif. Pizza | **King of Prussia**	19
Charcoal Pit | **multi.**	20
☑ Cheesecake Fact. | **King of Prussia**	20
Dave & Buster's | **DE River**	13
El Azteca | **multi.**	18
Fatou & Fama | **Univ City**	16
Geno's Steaks | **S Philly**	19
Hard Rock | **Ctr City E**	14
Hibachi | **multi.**	18
Italian Bistro | **Ave of Arts**	16
Jim's Steaks | **multi.**	22
Jones | **Ctr City E**	20
Laceno Italian | **Voorhees/NJ**	24
La Lupe | **S Philly**	22
Marathon Grill | **multi.**	18
Melting Pot | **Ches Hill**	20
Pat's Steaks | **S Philly**	20
Red Hot & Blue | **Cherry Hill/NJ**	17
South St. Souvlaki | **South St.**	21
Tacconelli's | **Port Richmond**	25
☑ Tony Luke's | **S Philly**	25
Trolley Car | **Mt Airy**	14
Vinny T's | **Wynnewood**	15

TRANSPORTING EXPERIENCES

Anton's/Swan | **Lambertville/NJ**	20
☑ Birchrunville Store | **Birchrunville**	28
Fatou & Fama | **Univ City**	16
☑ Gilmore's | **W Chester**	28
Hamilton's | **Lambertville/NJ**	25

SPECIAL FEATURES

Illuminare | **Fairmount** _18_
Jamaican Jerk Hut | **Ave of Arts** _20_
Kabul | **Old City** _22_
🅩 Krazy Kat's | **Montchanin/DE** _26_
La Campagne | **Cherry Hill/NJ** _24_
🅩 Lacroix | **Ctr City W** _28_
🅩 Le Bec-Fin | **Ctr City W** _27_
Le Castagne | **Ctr City W** _22_
Little Marakesh | **Dresher** _21_
Manon | **Lambertville/NJ** _25_
Marg. Kuo | **Wayne** _23_
Marrakesh | **South St.** _23_
🅩 Morimoto | **Ctr City E** _26_
🅩 Moro | **Wilming/DE** _25_
Moshulu | **DE River** _22_
🅩 Paloma | **NE Philly** _27_
Penang | **Chinatown** _22_
Rest./Doneckers | **Ephrata/LB** _19_
Siri's | **Cherry Hill/NJ** _25_
🅩 Tangerine | **Old City** _24_
Taq. Moroleon | **Kennett Sq** _24_
🅩 Vetri | **Ave of Arts** _27_

TRENDY

🅩 Alma de Cuba | **Ctr City W** _25_
🅩 Amada | **Old City** _28_
🅽🅴🆆 Ameritage | **Wilming/DE** _–_
Ansill | **South St.** _24_
🅽🅴🆆 Apothecary | **Ctr City E** _–_
🅽🅴🆆 Auspicious | **Ardmore** _19_
🅩🅽🅴🆆 Azie | **Media** _24_
🅽🅴🆆 Azul Cantina | **Ctr City E** _–_
🅩 Barclay Prime | **Ctr City W** _26_
Bar Ferdinand | **N Liberties** _23_
🅽🅴🆆 Beneluxx | **Old City** _20_
🅽🅴🆆 Bindi | **Ctr City E** _22_
🅩 Buddakan | **Old City** _26_
Cantina Caballitos/Segundos | _21_
  S Philly
🅩 Capital Grille | **Ave of Arts** _26_
🅩 Continental, The | **Old City** _22_
🅩 Continental Mid-town | _21_
  Ctr City W
Coquette | **South St.** _18_
🅩 Cuba Libre | **Old City** _21_
🅽🅴🆆 Devil's Den | **S Philly** _–_
🅽🅴🆆 Dock Street | **Univ City** _18_
🅩 Dom. Hudson | **Wilming/DE** _24_
Eulogy Belgian | **Old City** _18_

Fleming's Prime | **Wayne** _25_
🅽🅴🆆 goodburger | **Ctr City W** _–_
Good Dog | **Ctr City W** _22_
James | **S Philly** _25_
🅽🅴🆆 J.L. Sullivan's | **Ave of Arts** _–_
🅽🅴🆆 José Pistola's | **Ctr City W** _16_
🅽🅴🆆 Knock | **Ctr City E** _19_
Legal Sea | **King of Prussia** _20_
🅽🅴🆆 Les Bons Temps | **Ctr City E** _–_
🅽🅴🆆 Maia | **Villanova** _–_
Mantra | **Ctr City W** _19_
🅩 Mélange | **multi.** _27_
Brandywine | **Chadds Ford** _20_
🅽🅴🆆 Memphis Taproom | _–_
  Port Richmond
Misconduct Tav. | **Ctr City W** _17_
Mission Grill | **Ctr City W** _21_
Mixto | **Ctr City E** _21_
🅩 Morimoto | **Ctr City E** _26_
Naked Choco. | **Ave of Arts** _25_
Nunzio | **Collingswood/NJ** _23_
Oceanaire | **Ctr City E** _22_
🅩 Osteria | **N Philly** _26_
Palace/Ben | **Ctr City E** _21_
🅽🅴🆆 Pearl | **Ctr City W** _–_
🅽🅴🆆 Pietro's Prime | **W Chester** _24_
Pod | **Univ City** _23_
Rae | **Univ City** _22_
Rouge | **Ctr City W** _22_
Royal Tavern | **S Philly** _23_
Sidecar | **S Philly** _19_
Silk City | **N Liberties** _20_
Snackbar | **Ctr City W** _18_
St. Stephens Green | **Fairmount** _19_
🅽🅴🆆 Supper | **South St.** _23_
Susanna Foo's Kitchen | **Wayne** _21_
Swanky Bubbles | **multi.** _20_
🅽🅴🆆 Table 31 | **Ctr City W** _–_
🅩 Tangerine | **Old City** _24_
🅽🅴🆆 10 Arts | **Ave of Arts** _–_
Teresa's Next Dr. | **Wayne** _20_
🅽🅴🆆 Time | **Ctr City E** _–_
🅩 Tinto | **Ctr City W** _27_
Tír na nÓg | **Ctr City W** _14_
Tokyo Bleu | **Cinnaminson/NJ** _21_
🅽🅴🆆 Toscana 52 | **Feasterville** _–_
Tria | **Ctr City E** _23_
Triumph Brewing | **Old City** _19_

Twenty Manning | **Ctr City W**	22
NEW Ugly American | **S Philly**	19
Uzu Sushi | **Old City**	26
Valanni | **Ctr City E**	23
NEW Vango | **Ctr City W**	16
Z Vetri | **Ave of Arts**	27
NEW Vietnam Café | **W Philly**	23
Z Water Works | **Fairmount**	21
Xochitl | **Society Hill**	23
NEW Yakitori Boy | **Chinatown**	22
NEW Zahav | **Society Hill**	-
ZoT | **Society Hill**	20
Pond | **Radnor**	21
Rae | **Univ City**	22
Rembrandt's | **Fairmount**	20
Robin's Nest | **Mt Holly/NJ**	25
Rouge | **Ctr City W**	22
Simon Pearce | **W Chester**	20
Z Swann Lounge | **Ctr City W**	27
Trax Café | **Ambler**	23
Upstares/Varalli | **Ave of Arts**	21
Wash. Cross. | **Wash Cross**	17
Z Water Works | **Fairmount**	21
Yardley Inn | **Yardley**	21

VIEWS

Ardmore Station | **Ardmore**	19
Bay Pony Inn | **Lederach**	19
Bistro Cassis | **Radnor**	20
Bistro St. Tropez | **Ctr City W**	20
Café Gallery | **Burlington/NJ**	21
Cassatt Tea Rm. | **Ctr City W**	23
Chart House | **DE River**	18
Z Chophouse | **Gibbsboro/NJ**	25
Conley Ward's | **Wilming/DE**	17
Cuttalossa Inn | **Lumberville**	16
Dave & Buster's | **DE River**	13
Devon Seafood | **Ctr City W**	23
DiNardo's | **Old City**	19
Ecco Qui | **Univ City**	17
Z Fountain | **Ctr City W**	29
Hamilton's | **Lambertville/NJ**	25
Harry's Seafood | **Wilming/DE**	22
Hibachi | **DE River**	18
Jake's | **Manayunk**	25
Kildare's | **Manayunk**	16
King George II | **Bristol**	21
Z La Bonne Auberge | **New Hope**	27
Z Lacroix | **Ctr City W**	28
Lambertville Station | **Lambertville/NJ**	18
Landing | **New Hope**	16
La Veranda | **DE River**	23
Lilly's/Canal | **Lambertville/NJ**	20
L'Oca | **Fairmount**	23
Moshulu | **DE River**	22
Mother's | **New Hope**	18
Z Nineteen | **Ave of Arts**	23
Oceanaire | **Ctr City E**	22
P.J. Whelihan's | **Medford Lakes/NJ**	15

VISITORS ON EXPENSE ACCOUNT

Z NEW Azie | **Media**	24
Z Barclay Prime | **Ctr City W**	26
Z Bella Tori | **Langhorne**	19
Blush | **Bryn Mawr**	20
Z Brasserie Perrier | **Ctr City W**	24
Z Capital Grille | **Ave of Arts**	26
NEW Chima | **Ctr City W**	-
Chops | **Bala Cynwyd**	19
Dilworth. Inn | **W Chester**	25
Estia | **Ave of Arts**	23
Fleming's Prime | **Wayne**	25
Z Fogo de Chão | **Ave of Arts**	23
Z Fountain | **Ctr City W**	29
Il Portico | **Ctr City W**	20
Inn/St. Peter's | **St Peters**	-
Z Le Bec-Fin | **Ctr City W**	27
NEW Maia | **Villanova**	-
McCormick/Schmick | **multi.**	21
Z Morimoto | **Ctr City E**	26
Z Morton's | **Ave of Arts**	25
Z Nineteen | **Ave of Arts**	23
Oceanaire | **Ctr City E**	22
Old Orig. Bookbinder | **Old City**	19
NEW Pearl | **Ctr City W**	-
Phillips Sea. | **Ctr City W**	19
Pond | **Radnor**	21
Prime Rib | **Ctr City W**	25
Rae | **Univ City**	22
Roy's | **Ctr City W**	23
Ruth's Chris | **Ave of Arts**	23
Smith/Wollensky | **Ctr City W**	22
Sullivan's Steak | **multi.**	23
Z Susanna Foo | **Ctr City W**	24
NEW Table 31 | **Ctr City W**	-

☑ Tangerine | **Old City**	24
🆕 10 Arts | **Ave of Arts**	-
☑ Water Works | **Fairmount**	21
🆕 Zahav | **Society Hill**	-

WATERSIDE

Bourbon Blue | **Manayunk**	19
Café Gallery | **Burlington/NJ**	21
Centre Bridge | **New Hope**	19
Chart House | **DE River**	18
☑ Chophouse | **Gibbsboro/NJ**	25
Conley Ward's | **Wilming/DE**	17
Cuttalossa Inn | **Lumberville**	16
Dave & Buster's | **DE River**	13
Golden Pheasant | **Erwinna**	23
Hamilton's | **Lambertville/NJ**	25
Harry's Seafood | **Wilming/DE**	22
King George II | **Bristol**	21
Lambertville Station | **Lambertville/NJ**	18
Landing | **New Hope**	16
La Veranda | **DE River**	23
Lilly's/Canal | **Lambertville/NJ**	20
Manayunk Brew. | **Manayunk**	18
Moshulu | **DE River**	22
Robin's Nest | **Mt Holly/NJ**	25
Simon Pearce | **W Chester**	20
☑ Water Works | **Fairmount**	21

WINE BARS

Ansill | **South St.**	24
Bar Ferdinand | **N Liberties**	23
🆕 Beneluxx | **Old City**	20
Chick's | **South St.**	23
Cosimo | **Malvern**	22
☑ Dom. Hudson | **Wilming/DE**	24
Fleming's Prime | **Wayne**	25
Horizons | **South St.**	26
Kitchen 233 | **Westmont/NJ**	20
Penne | **Univ City**	18
Rist. Panorama | **Old City**	24
Teca | **W Chester**	21
☑ Tinto | **Ctr City W**	27
Tria | **multi.**	23
Vintage | **Ctr City E**	19

WINNING WINE LISTS

☑ Amada | **Old City**	28
Ansill | **South St.**	24

Back Burner | **Hockessin/DE**	20
☑ Bella Tori | **Langhorne**	19
🆕 Beneluxx | **Old City**	20
Bistro Cassis | **Radnor**	20
Blue Bell Inn | **Blue Bell**	21
Blush | **Bryn Mawr**	20
Bobby Chez | **Sewell/NJ**	25
☑ Capital Grille | **Ave of Arts**	26
Caribou Cafe | **Ctr City E**	19
Chick's | **South St.**	23
🆕 Chima | **Ctr City W**	-
Chops | **Bala Cynwyd**	19
Coquette | **South St.**	18
Cosimo | **Malvern**	22
Dilworth. Inn | **W Chester**	25
☑ Dom. Hudson | **Wilming/DE**	24
Fleming's Prime | **Wayne**	25
☑ Fogo de Chão | **Ave of Arts**	23
☑ Fountain | **Ctr City W**	29
Georges' | **Wayne**	20
☑ Green Hills Inn | **Reading/LB**	26
Harry's Savoy | **Wilming/DE**	23
Haydn Zug's | **E Petersburg/LB**	18
Inn/St. Peter's | **St Peters**	-
Jake's | **Manayunk**	25
Kitchen 233 | **Westmont/NJ**	20
☑ La Bonne Auberge | **New Hope**	27
☑ Lacroix | **Ctr City W**	28
La Famiglia | **Old City**	24
☑ Le Bar Lyonnais | **Ctr City W**	28
☑ Le Bec-Fin | **Ctr City W**	27
Le Castagne | **Ctr City W**	22
🆕 Le Virtù | **S Philly**	26
🆕 Maia | **Villanova**	-
Mainland Inn | **Mainland**	26
Brandywine | **Chadds Ford**	20
Meritage | **Ctr City W**	23
Mission Grill | **Ctr City W**	21
☑ Morton's | **Ave of Arts**	25
☑ Osteria | **N Philly**	26
Penne | **Univ City**	18
Pond | **Radnor**	21
Prime Rib | **Ctr City W**	25
Rae | **Univ City**	22
Rest. Taquet | **Wayne**	24
Rist. Panorama | **Old City**	24
Roux 3 | **Newtown Sq**	21
Saloon | **S Philly**	24

WORTH A TRIP

SPECIAL FEATU

Wine Vintage Chart

This chart, based on our 0 to 30 scale, is designed to help you select wine. The ratings (by **Howard Stravitz,** a law professor at the University of South Carolina) reflect the vintage quality and the wine's readiness to drink. We exclude the 1991–1993 vintages because they are not that good. A dash indicates the wine is either past its peak or too young to rate. Loire ratings are for dry white wines.

Whites	88	89	90	94	95	96	97	98	99	00	01	02	03	04	05	06
French:																
Alsace	-	25	25	24	23	23	22	25	23	25	27	25	22	24	25	-
Burgundy	-	23	22	-	28	27	24	22	26	25	24	27	23	27	26	24
Loire Valley	-	-	-	-	-	-	-	-	-	24	25	26	23	24	27	24
Champagne	24	26	29	-	26	27	24	23	24	24	22	26	-	-	-	-
Sauternes	29	25	28	-	21	23	25	23	24	24	28	25	26	21	26	23
California:																
Chardonnay	-	-	-	-	-	-	-	-	24	23	26	26	25	27	29	25
Sauvignon Blanc	-	-	-	-	-	-	-	-	-	-	27	28	26	27	26	27
Austrian:																
Grüner Velt./ Riesling	-	-	-	-	25	21	26	26	25	22	23	25	26	25	26	-
German:	25	26	27	24	23	26	25	26	23	21	29	27	24	26	28	-

Reds	88	89	90	94	95	96	97	98	99	00	01	02	03	04	05	06
French:																
Bordeaux	23	25	29	22	26	25	23	25	24	29	26	24	25	24	27	25
Burgundy	-	24	26	-	26	27	25	22	27	22	24	27	25	25	27	25
Rhône	26	28	28	24	26	22	25	27	26	27	26	-	25	24	25	-
Beaujolais	-	-	-	-	-	-	-	-	-	24	-	23	25	22	28	26
California:																
Cab./Merlot	-	-	28	29	27	25	28	23	26	22	27	26	25	24	24	23
Pinot Noir	-	-	-	-	-	-	24	23	24	23	27	28	26	25	24	-
Zinfandel	-	-	-	-	-	-	-	-	-	-	25	23	27	24	23	-
Oregon:																
Pinot Noir	-	-	-	-	-	-	-	-	-	-	-	27	25	26	27	-
Italian:																
Tuscany	-	-	25	22	24	20	29	24	27	24	27	20	25	25	22	24
Piedmont	-	27	27	-	23	26	27	26	25	28	27	20	24	25	26	-
Spanish:																
Rioja	-	-	-	26	26	24	25	22	25	24	27	20	24	25	26	24
Ribera del Duero/Priorat	-	-	-	26	26	27	25	24	25	24	27	20	24	26	26	24
Australian:																
Shiraz/Cab.	-	-	-	24	26	23	26	28	24	24	27	27	25	26	24	-
Chilean:	-	-	-	-	-	-	24	-	25	23	26	24	25	24	26	-

subscribe to ZAGAT.com

ON THE GO.
IN THE KNOW.

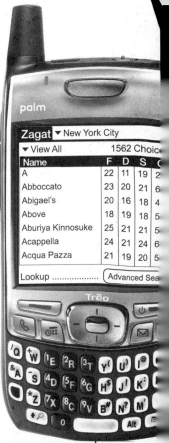

ZAGAT TO GO℠

Unlimited access
to Zagat dining &
travel content
in hundreds of
major cities.

Search by name,
location, ratings,
cuisine, special
features & Top Lists.

For BlackBerry,® Palm,®
Windows Mobile®
and mobile phones.

Get it now at **mobile.zagat.com**
or text* **ZAGAT** to **78247**

Products

TS & MAPS

America's Top Restaurants
Atlanta
Beijing
Boston
Brooklyn
California Wine Country
Cape Cod & The Islands
Chicago
Connecticut
Europe's Top Restaurants
Hamptons (incl. wineries)
Hong Kong
Las Vegas
London
Long Island (incl. wineries)
Los Angeles I So. California
(guide & map)
Miami Beach
Miami I So. Florida
Montréal
New Jersey
New Jersey Shore
New Orleans
New York City (guide & map)
Palm Beach
Paris
Philadelphia
San Diego
San Francisco (guide & map)
Seattle
Shanghai
Texas
Tokyo
Toronto
Vancouver
Washington, DC I Baltimore
Westchester I Hudson Valley
World's Top Restaurants

LIFESTYLE GUIDES

America's Top Golf Courses
Movie Guide
Music Guide
NYC Gourmet Shop./Entertaining
NYC Shopping

NIGHTLIFE GUIDES

Los Angeles
New York City
San Francisco

HOTEL & TRAVEL GUIDES

Beijing
Hong Kong
Las Vegas
London
New Orleans
Montréal
Shanghai
Top U.S. Hotels, Resorts & Spas
Toronto
U.S. Family Travel
Vancouver
Walt Disney World Insider's Guide
World's Top Hotels, Resorts & Spas

WEB & WIRELESS SERVICES

ZAGAT TO GO[SM] for handhelds
ZAGAT.com[SM] • ZAGAT.mobi[SM]

**Available wherever books are sold or at ZAGAT.com. To customize
Zagat guides as gifts or marketing tools, call 800-540-9609.**

0 20613 06994 2